Assessing Mental Capaci

This practical, how-to handbook provides essential resources to help clinicians and other professionals to assess mental capacity in key decisions. The book illustrates the basics of capacity assessments before discussing a variety of complex issues of which professionals will need to be aware. Providing expertise from a multi-disciplinary perspective, the book provides hands-on coverage of mental capacity law (concentrating on England and Wales).

Chapters are written by a variety of different professionals with extensive experience in the assessment of mental capacity. Coverage includes:

- Explanations of mental capacity law and how to put it into practice across a range of settings, services and populations
- A "how to" approach for administering assessments of mental capacity both for professionals who are new to the area and for more experienced professionals
- Information on practical aspects of assessing mental capacity for commonly occurring decisions and for more specialist and complex decisions
- Consideration of the best interests process and Liberty Protection Safeguards (LPS).

With easily accessible information, case studies, examples from case law and internationally relevant discussions on ethical issues, this is the perfect companion to help busy professionals understand complex concepts relating to mental capacity.

Dr. Janice A. Mackenzie is a consultant clinical neuropsychologist who has a specialist interest in mental capacity dating back to 2002. She has published research, presented at conferences and provided training in mental capacity to numerous professionals. She developed a semi-structured interview which has been adapted for various different mental capacity assessments.

Dr. Kate E. Wilkinson is a consultant clinical neuropsychologist who has been carrying out complex capacity assessments since 2010 and has developed a particular interest in the complex ethical and sociopolitical aspects of such work. She routinely provides formal teaching, supervision and consultation on mental capacity to professionals from other disciplines.

Assessing Mental Capacity

A Handbook to Guide Professionals
from Basic to Advanced Practice

Edited by Janice A. Mackenzie
and Kate E. Wilkinson

Routledge
Taylor & Francis Group

LONDON AND NEW YORK

First published 2020
by Routledge
2 Park Square, Milton Park, Abingdon, Oxon OX14 4RN

and by Routledge
52 Vanderbilt Avenue, New York, NY 10017

Routledge is an imprint of the Taylor & Francis Group, an informa business

British Library Cataloguing-in-Publication Data
A catalogue record for this book is available from the British Library

Library of Congress Cataloging-in-Publication Data
A catalog record for this book has been requested

ISBN: 978-1-138-10274-3 (hbk)
ISBN: 978-1-138-10277-4 (pbk)
ISBN: 978-1-315-10344-0 (ebk)

Typeset in Perpetua
by Apex CoVantage, LLC

Contents

APPENDICES 373

About the book

Mental capacity is the ability to make specific decisions at specific time-points. Everyone is assumed to have it until proven otherwise. Unfortunately, when an injury, illness or difficulty with the mind or brain occurs, we can lose the capacity to make certain decisions. Laws have been put in place to ensure that people without mental capacity will be supported and their rights protected. But how do we decide if someone lacks mental capacity?

This book includes:

- Explanations of mental capacity law and how to put it into practice across a range of settings, services and populations
- A "how to" approach for administering assessments of mental capacity both for professionals who are new to the area and for more experienced professionals coming across:

  ○ Situations which are not clear-cut
  ○ Assessments that have been disputed
  ○ Decisions which have been referred to the Court of Protection.

- Information on practical aspects of assessing mental capacity for commonly occurring decisions and for more specialist and complex decisions such as:

  ○ Where to live, and care and support needs
  ○ Managing finances, swallowing and litigation.

- Information on:

  ○ Liberty Protection Safeguards (LPS)
  ○ Overlap with other legislation
  ○ Best interests decisions.

The book aims to help busy professionals understand complex concepts by using straightforward language, easily accessible information, case studies and examples from case law. It provides practical resources to help professionals assess mental capacity for several decisions. Legal aspects are UK-focused; however, the discussions and ethical issues involved are internationally relevant.

Disclaimer

You must obtain specialist or professional advice or exercise your own specialist and professional knowledge before taking, or refraining from, any action based on this publication. The creators shall not be liable in any way whether in tort (including for negligence or breach of statutory duty), contract, misrepresentation, restitution or otherwise for any liability, loss, cost, charges or other damages incurred as a result of reliance on the advice in this book.

Appendices

Acknowledgements

I would like to thank all of my supervisors and mentors who have helped me get to this point in my career: David Johnson, Andy Tyerman, Kerry Young, Tom McMillan, Nadina Lincoln, Gavin Newby and, especially, June Robson for her support and encouragement through various stages of my qualified career. I would also like to thank my managers, David Rees, Alison Marriott and Padraig McDonnell, for supporting my continuing professional development, which sparked the idea of this book, and a flexible way of working, which helped me manage my time over the past few months. I would like to thank all of the clients and patients I have worked with over the years, as they have taught me so much and have made my job enjoyable, and the professionals whom I have trained and supervised who help to keep me on my toes and continue my learning when interesting questions come up. I would like to thank the Manchester Neuropsychology CPD group for encouraging the idea of the book, the BPS Mental Capacity Advisory Group for helping me keep up to date with new developments over the past few years and all of the contributors for putting up with our comments and requests and for producing fantastic work. I would like to acknowledge Kate, my co-editor, for sharing my vision and helping to deliver a high-quality book and for being there during every step of this long and sometimes arduous journey! Finally, I would like to thank my friends who have supported me through this process and my family who have been amazing at putting up with me working so much and for making this possible.

Janice Mackenzie

First, I would like to thank my co-editor, Janice, for inviting me to embark on this long process with her and for her exceptionally hard work in bringing the book to fruition. I would also like to thank all the contributors to this book for producing some excellent work and for bearing with us through the editing process.

I would like to thank all my previous supervisors, but in particular Janice Mackenzie and Jacqueline Woods for their longstanding support during my qualified career. I would also like to thank all the clients and professionals I have worked with over the years, who have all taught me so much. Finally, I would like to thank my family for all their support and making this book possible.

Kate Wilkinson

Contributors

Catherine Blakemore, Senior Specialist Speech and Language Therapist, Manchester University NHS Foundation Trust

Helen Claridge, Solicitor, Hempsons

Karen Dean, Solicitor, Hempsons

Kate Dimmock, Clinical Neuropsychologist, Pennine Care NHS Foundation Trust

David Fowler, Independent Social Worker and Best Interests Assessor

Emma Fowler, Trainee Clinical Psychologist, Lancaster University, and Specialist Safeguarding Trainer

Adam Hartrick, Solicitor, Hempsons

Jane Jolliffe, Professional Lead Speech and Language Therapy and Health Service Manager (retired), Manchester Local Care Organisation (Manchester University NHS Foundation Trust)

Sam Jones, Senior Specialist Occupational Therapist, Manchester University NHS Foundation Trust

Ian Leonard, Consultant Psychiatrist, Lancashire

Janice Mackenzie, Consultant Clinical Neuropsychologist, Greater Manchester Mental Health NHS Foundation Trust

Chris Martin, Clinical Neuropsychologist, Greater Manchester Mental Health NHS Foundation Trust and Consultant Clinical Neuropsychologist, Salford Royal NHS Foundation Trust

Reg Morris, Programme Director, South Wales Clinical Psychology Training Programme

Stephen Mullin, Consultant Clinical Neuropsychologist, North West Boroughs Healthcare NHS Foundation Trust

Dan Ratcliff, Clinical Psychologist, Manchester University NHS Foundation Trust

Deborah Slater, Neuro Rehabilitation Case Manager, NHS England and NHS Improvement

Victoria Teggart, Clinical Neuropsychologist, Greater Manchester Mental Health NHS Foundation Trust

Kate Wilkinson, Consultant Clinical Neuropsychologist, Bradford Teaching Hospitals NHS Foundation Trust

Introduction

Janice Mackenzie and Kate Wilkinson

In our clinical practice, we have noticed that the number of mental capacity assessments that professionals are being asked to carry out has increased in recent years. Mental capacity is a complex subject that can take away someone's independence and ability to make their own decisions. Notwithstanding this, professionals often receive very little training on the topic and rarely any that helps them to understand how to practically assess someone's mental capacity confidently. Complex capacity assessments can raise more questions than answers at times, and this book should help to answer some of them. It is important to remember that capacity assessments are only one part of the decision-making process, and supported decision-making is what we should be aiming for in order to maximise the number of people able to make decisions about their own lives (NICE, 2018). However, even with support, some people do not have the capacity to make a decision about a specific area of their life at the time the decision is required. In these circumstances, different countries apply different procedures to how the decision is finally made, but all of them attempt to keep the person at the centre of the decision-making process. It is important to remember why we follow mental capacity processes: to empower and enable people who may not have been allowed to make decisions for themselves previously, as well as protecting those who are vulnerable. The aim is also to avoid restricting people's rights and freedom wherever possible and to limit them in the least restrictive way when it is not.

How to use the book

This book is aimed at the kind of people from different professions whom we have taught and trained throughout the years and who always have thoughtful and considered questions and discussion points to raise. It is also for those who are more experienced in assessing mental capacity but who would like guidance in more complex cases, legal aspects or training other professionals, or even just reassurance that they are doing the right thing. We have tried to make the majority of the book practical, rather than academic, to help you apply the mental capacity law in your country to the people you see for mental capacity assessments. It is important to read the book in conjunction with the Code of Practice that accompanies the specific mental capacity law you are applying. Naturally, as we are based in England, the Mental Capacity Act (MCA, 2005) is discussed in depth, but we have tried to include legislation from other UK countries, and the issues raised in several chapters will transcend the minor legal differences between these laws. There is no need to read the book from cover to cover, as you can dip into the section you need and you may find other useful chapters referenced. We have chosen to intersperse *he* and *she* throughout the book rather than use *he/she* or *them*.

We have been lucky to work with some excellent occupational therapists, speech and language therapists, physiotherapists, social workers, nurses, doctors and clinical psychologists/neuropsychologists on mental capacity issues over the years, and we have learned from the different approaches and perspectives each profession takes. Due to this, we have taken a multi-disciplinary approach to the book to reflect a gold standard approach to mental capacity assessments, although we know that multidisciplinary assessments are not always possible in real life. Hopefully, the ideas and tips from those other professionals can help you improve your practice, even if you do not have access to them day-to-day. Case studies, examples, tips and cautions are included to bring the material to life, and hopefully you can relate them to people with whom you have worked. Semi-structured interviews, a multi-disciplinary team (MDT) questionnaire and other resources, which are mentioned in some chapters, are included in the appendices and on the accompanying website. These can be copied or downloaded and used for clinical cases to guide your practice. Other examples, information and tips are also available on the website for your use. Good luck with your cases! Any feedback about the book would be gratefully received on our website.

Website address: www.assessingcapacity.com

Areas covered in the book

- A summary of the mental capacity literature and research, as well as an overview of different mental capacity laws in the British Isles, and basic legal aspects of the MCA (2005)
- The basics of how to do a capacity assessment, including:

  o Taking into account psychosocial aspects and the person's functional, cognitive and communication abilities, and how to enhance the person's capacity with regard to all of these areas
  o How to find out the legal threshold of relevant information, or develop a reasonable threshold if there is no legal precedent, which is required for the person to be deemed to have capacity to make the specific decision
  o How to introduce a capacity assessment to ensure that the person knows the reason for it and the possible consequences of the outcomes but also to put them at ease and let them know their rights

○ Introducing a semi-structured interview and how to use it successfully or adapt it for your own assessment and how to document your outcomes.

• Relevant information for specific decisions and conditions, such as medical treatment; advance decisions/directives; care needs and accommodation/discharge destination; tenancy agreements; taking part in legal procedures; managing finances and making a lasting power of attorney or will; following swallowing advice; engaging in sexual relations and assessing capacity when someone has dementia

• Dealing with difficult situations such as when a person says one thing but does something different, capacity appears to fluctuate, the decision may lead to serious consequences or death or there is disagreement between parties during the capacity assessment or best interests decision-making process; also, what to do when someone refuses a mental capacity assessment, appears ambivalent about the process or the decision, or the decision needs to be made urgently

• Complex aspects of the MCA (2005) including Deprivation of Liberty Safeguards (DoLS) or Liberty Protection Safeguards (LPS), the best interests decision-making process and the interaction with other Acts such as the Mental Health Act (MHA) and the Sexual Offences Act (SOA)

• Additional information regarding tips on assessing capacity for the Court or as an independent practitioner and how to run a training course for other professionals as well as the consideration of ethical issues that arise when assessing capacity and making decisions on behalf of people who lack capacity.

Caution

This book cannot take the place of legal advice or clinical experience. While we appreciate that there are many ways to approach capacity decisions, the opinions and suggested practices provided are intended to offer a framework for this, based on our experience over many years, research findings and guidance from case law and established bodies. Hopefully, the book will help you to reflect on and enhance your practice and increase your confidence when assessing mental capacity and dealing with the outcome. If in any doubt, please seek professional supervision and, if necessary, seek legal advice and contact the local safeguarding team. Also, mental capacity laws are being reviewed and evolving so it is important to keep up to date with new developments.

References

Mental Capacity Act 2005. London: HMSO. Available at: www.legislation.gov.uk/ukpga/2005/9/contents

National Institute for Health and Care Excellence (2018). *Decision-Making and Mental Capacity* (NG108). Available at: www.nice.org.uk/guidance/ng108

Other useful resources

British Psychological Society (2019). *What Makes a Good Assessment of Capacity?* Professional Practice
    Board and Mental Capacity Advisory Group. Leicester: British Psychological Society. Available
    at: www.bps.org.uk/sites/bps.org.uk/files/Policy/Policy%20-%20Files/What%20makes%20
    a%20good%20assessment%20of%20capacity.pdf
Department for Constitutional Affairs (2007). *Mental Capacity Act 2005: Code of Practice*. London: The
    Stationery Office. Available at: https://assets.publishing.service.gov.uk/government/uploads/
    system/uploads/attachment_data/file/497253/Mental-capacity-act-code-of-practice.pdf
Farmer, T. (2016). *Grandpa on a Skateboard*. 2nd ed. Great Britain: Rethink Press.
Ruck Keene, A., Butler-Cole, V., Allen, N., Lee, A., Kohn, N., Scott, K., Barnes, K. and Edwards, S.
    (eds.) (2019). *A Brief Guide to Carrying Out Capacity Assessments*. 39 Essex Chambers. Available at:
    www.39essex.com/mental-capacity-guidance-note-brief-guide-carrying-capacity-assessments

Legal newsletters and websites for case law, updates and summaries

www.39essex.com
www.mentalhealthlaw.co.uk

Part 1

Getting started

Chapter 1

Mental capacity past, present and future

An overview

Reg Morris

In this chapter

This chapter provides on overview of mental capacity, looking at:

- The nature of mental capacity and factors that can affect it
- The evolution of legal systems to address the issues it raises
- The limitations of current mental capacity legislation and some of the steps being taken to improve its scope and operation
- The relationship between mental capacity and mental health legislation
- Current levels of knowledge and engagement with mental capacity legislation by service users, carers and professionals and measures to improve uptake of what the legislation offers
- Issues surrounding the assessment of mental capacity and the need for awareness raising and training of professionals to improve the process and outcomes of assessment.

Introduction

Decision-making is an integral aspect of everyday life. We make decisions about all kinds of things such as what to wear, what to eat and whom to socialise with, quite naturally and usually (but not always!) without effort or difficulty. On the other hand, there are more important decisions such as choosing a partner, accepting a particular medical treatment or buying a house that may take more reflection and research to accomplish. Like many human capabilities, most of us take our decision-making ability, and that of those around us, for granted. This makes it all the more difficult to deal with when things go wrong as a result of stressful or traumatic life events, physical or mental illness or injury. When this happens, a person may struggle to participate in decision-making and, in some cases, may not be able to participate at all. When a person cannot make decisions independently, she is said to have impaired mental capacity. This becomes particularly important when someone is facing a decision that must be made. For example, he may be in the process of being discharged from hospital and need to decide whether to go back home or into supported accommodation. Alternatively, he may have a serious illness requiring urgent medical treatment. Crucially, impaired mental capacity prevents a person from giving "informed consent" regarding what happens to her and, therefore, restricting her right to self-determination and autonomy. Informed consent is a legal requirement before professionals can perform health or social care assessments, make interventions or take action about placement, living arrangements or financial matters. Due to this, special legislation is required to protect those who lack capacity and those who act on their behalf without informed consent. Generally, such legislation can make four kinds of provisions:

- A person can make decisions in advance (advance decisions/directives) about refusing treatments – but not about deciding which treatment he wants.
- He can appoint someone in advance to make decisions for him (powers of attorney).
- Professionals can make decisions on his behalf – often, but not in all cases, based on the principle of 'best interests'.
- A court can appoint someone (a Deputy) to make decisions on behalf of the affected person.

Mental capacity is a significant and increasing issue in health and social care. Mental incapacity rates in older adults in long-term care settings ranged from 44% to 69% in a review of studies (Moye and Marson, 2007). In general, non-elective acute hospital inpatients rates of incapacity ranged from 37% to 40% (Etchells et al., 1999; Raymont et al., 2004). However, a lower, but still significant, rate of 26.7% was reported by Fassassi et al. (2009) in a general medical ward in Switzerland. A review of 99 studies of consent to treatment in older people found that age and lower educational standards were commonly associated with impaired ability to consent (Sugarman, McCrory and Hubal, 1998).

Factors that may affect mental capacity

Mental capacity depends on the core abilities of being able to assimilate, remember and process information and to communicate the decision. Any condition or life event that affects any of these core processes can affect capacity. Some include:

- **Intellectual disabilities**, often present from birth and caused by a range of factors from genes to adverse conditions or events
- **Dementia**, due to its impact on memory and reasoning
- **Brain injury and stroke**, which can affect cognition and communication

- **Mental health problems,** such as psychosis, depression and anxiety, as they can distort the way information is processed to arrive at decisions
- **Delirium** resulting from infections, drugs and intoxicants, which can temporarily affect mental capacity
- **Other causes** that prevent a person from thinking clearly and taking in information, such as severe traumatic events, grief or pain.

Summary: Factors that may affect mental capacity

- Health conditions or events that affect perception, thinking, memory or communication
- Cognitive abilities
- Communication ability
- Mood and emotional factors
- Support which presents information about the decision intelligibly and helps the person reach and communicate his/her decision
- The nature of the decision to be taken; more complex decisions are more demanding of the abilities underpinning mental capacity.

The history of mental capacity legislation in England and Wales

Mental capacity legislation has implications for a significant proportion of the population of all developed countries – probably over 10% if the carers of people with impaired decision-making are included. Moreover, the scope of mental capacity legislation is extremely broad, encompassing financial, health, welfare and social areas.

The social and ethical dilemmas posed by adults who lack the ability to make decisions for themselves have existed since the dawn of human groups and societies, and initially were determined by religious teachings. More recently, formal legal codes have been developed that address mental incapacity in a way that is systematic, open to scrutiny and revision and capable of being administered and enforced by the legal system.

In England and Wales, mental incapacity law dates back to the thirteenth century, when powers to deal with the estates and welfare of people who were incapable of making decisions was given to the king. Subsequently, the Chancellor's office gained powers to appoint a person to control the estates, affairs, health and welfare of those who lacked capacity. These powers lasted until the Mental Health Act 1959 abolished the Chancellor's powers over health and welfare. However, powers over health and welfare were subsequently reintroduced into the Mental Capacity Act 2005 (MCA) for England and Wales.

Limitations to mental capacity legislation

In 2006, the United Nations General Assembly adopted the Convention on the Rights of Persons with Disabilities, and this has since been ratified by the UK. This has the core purpose "to promote, protect and ensure the full and equal enjoyment of all human rights and fundamental freedoms by all persons with disabilities, and to promote respect for their inherent dignity". The convention states that treatment of disabled people (including those who lack mental capacity) should:

- Respect inherent dignity, individual autonomy and independence of all people, including the freedom to make their own choices
- Be non-discriminatory
- Allow full and effective participation and inclusion in society.

The Convention emphasises that *legal capacity* (the ability to hold rights and duties and to exercise these rights and duties) is a universal right that applies even for those without *mental capacity*. Therefore, it is important that mental capacity legislation does nothing to diminish legal capacity. In this respect, substitute decision-making by a healthcare practitioner or someone with powers of attorney using the principle of 'best interests' can be seen as discriminatory. The United Nations Convention on the Rights of Persons with Disabilities prioritises supporting the person in making her own decision and highlights the primacy of the wishes and preferences of the person without capacity. The notion of a 'best interests' outcome, as judged by a substitute decision-maker, has no place in this formulation. It is true that mental capacity legislation requires that a person should be supported to participate in decision-making and that his past wishes and preferences should be considered, but the United Nations Convention views the wishes of the person as paramount, rather than a third party's evaluation of what is in the person's best interests. In the British Isles, the mental capacity legislation of Scotland (2000) and the Republic of Ireland (2015) do not use the idea of best interests, but instead emphasise supporting a person to participate in decision-making and determining what she would want based on her principles, values and past history. (See Chapter 4 for further discussion of this topic).

Impaired mental capacity also evokes the crucial question of when (or if) a person's wishes should be overruled in order to protect him from harm or exploitation. For example, Section 4 of the MCA (2005) for England and Wales makes provision for the overruling of a person's wishes and the use of restraint if this protects her from harm, but neither the Act nor the Code of Practice (2007) are able to provide definitive guidance about the criteria for overruling a person's right to autonomous choice other than the general principle of preventing harm to the person. However, this has been refined by case law over several years; for example, emotional wellbeing, and not just physical wellbeing, must be taken into account when assessing harm to the person.

Closely linked to this debate is the need to restrict a person's freedom of movement (to deprive him of his liberty) in order to safeguard him from harm. For example, a person with a severe intellectual impairment who will not remain in a residence but is at risk of serious accidents when out unsupervised may need to be placed in a secure, locked facility. Such deprivation of liberty could be viewed as contrary to a person's basic human right to liberty, especially if it is long-term. In England and Wales, two amendments have introduced new authorisations and periodic review processes for people deprived of their liberty under the MCA (2005) – the Deprivation of Liberty Safeguards (Mental Health Act, 2007) and the Liberty Protection Safeguards (Mental Capacity [Amendment] Act, 2019). (See Chapter 28 for further discussion of this topic.)

A further criticism of the MCA (2005) is that its scope is too limited; it applies only to those whose capacity is impaired by a disorder of mind or brain, but there may be other reasons for impaired decision-making capacity and the restriction of individual autonomy. These include coercion, undue influence or lack of access to vital information. Consequently, it has been proposed that the requirement for having a disorder of mind or brain be removed and that the definition of mental incapacity should refer to *any* cause that impedes autonomous decision-making. This would encompass social reasons for impaired decision-making and include people who are under the influence of human traffickers or self-interested family members or who are affected by trauma or adverse life events. The mental capacity legislation of the Republic of Ireland has taken note of this and does not require a person to have an impairment of mind or brain (see Chapter 4).

Finally, mental capacity legislation and the associated codes of practice emphasise individual autonomy and rights. The primacy of individual rights is a feature of industrialised western societies, but it is less prominent in many African, Middle Eastern and Eastern societies where decision-making may be focused on the family or social unit rather than its individual members. The increasing trend for migration from less wealthy countries, or those divided by conflict, to more developed countries has created multicultural societies which may require greater flexibility in mental capacity legislation to recognise the cultural diversity of approaches to decision-making.

In working with current mental capacity legislation, professionals should be mindful that any legislation is not permanent and infallible (even if it is "the law"). Instead, mental capacity legislation is: 1) based on the prevailing system of belief and socio-cultural conventions; and 2) liable to change as conventions change. As an example, in recent times mental capacity legislation in England and Wales has been amended every 20 to 30 years or less (1833, 1862, 1890, 1913, 1934, 1959, 1983, 2005, 2007, 2019). Professionals and professional groups involved in implementing mental capacity legislation should be mindful of its limitations and proactive in identifying and publicising aspects that require amendment in response to social and cultural change.

Summary: Limitations to mental capacity legislation

- Mental capacity decisions made by someone else based on perceived 'best interests' are not fully compliant with human rights codes
- Restricting the freedom of a person without mental capacity is controversial and is subject to special safeguards
- Decision-making ability may be impaired when there is no disorder of mind or brain. The definition of mental incapacity needs to take this into account
- The primacy of individual autonomy is not embraced by all cultures
- Implementation of the Act should respect cultural diversity
- Mental capacity law depends on the social and cultural context, which changes every few decades. Professionals should be mindful of the need for change as it arises.

Mental health legislation and mental capacity legislation

There clearly is substantial overlap between mental health and mental capacity legislation. Both allow for decisions to be made for a person in some circumstances and for a person to be detained when he might come to harm. It is sometimes unclear which type of legislation should be used when a person lacks capacity as a result of mental illness. Since mental health and mental capacity legislation differ, there is potential for confusion. Consequently, there have been calls for the two types of legislation to be fused, and this has now happened in Northern Ireland (2016). However, the Northern Ireland legislation is in the early stages of implementation, and there may be significant hurdles before it can be used in practice. (See Chapter 4 for a more in-depth discussion of these points.)

Service users' and carers' appreciation of mental capacity and decision-making

User groups, such as the Alzheimer's Society, strongly supported the MCA (2005), and carers and service users with experience of mental capacity in decision-making also welcomed the principles and provisions of the Act (Manthorpe, Rapaport and Stanley, 2009). Unfortunately, there is poor awareness of mental capacity legislation in the general population (Das, Das and Mulley, 2006). Consequently, many people miss opportunities to benefit from Advance Decisions/Directives or appointing people with powers of attorney before losing capacity. A sample of service users and carers (Manthorpe, Rapaport and Stanley, 2009) felt that professionals should publicise the Act, something that is required of health care providers in the United States, and provide service users and carers with specific information about the Act's provisions.

Myron et al. (2008) identified several factors that encourage older people in mental health settings to become involved in decision-making about their treatment: Being listened to, having a choice of communication methods (verbal or written), being familiar with and trusting the staff involved and having pleasant environments and positive, friendly staff. Conversely, some factors made participation in decision-making less likely: Circumstances that did not build confidence to make decisions, prejudice and the assumption that people with some health conditions were incapable of decision-making. In addition, carers struggled to participate in decision-making when they knew that the person was different from his former self and when they felt accountable for decisions on behalf of another person.

Professionals and mental capacity

A House of Lords report in 2014 concluded that there was poor knowledge of the principles and provisions of the MCA (2005) and that they had not been sufficiently included in the practice of health and social care professionals. This supports the conclusions of research in the British Isles and North America regarding staff knowledge and confidence about mental capacity (Jackson and Warner, 2002; Myron et al., 2008; Schiff et al., 2006; Ganzini et al., 2004; Wilner et al., 2012, 2013; Marshall and Sprung, 2016). Emergency service workers in England had poor knowledge of the basic principles of the MCA (2005) – for example, that a competent person who refuses treatment should not be treated and that a relative's signature is not necessary to treat an incompetent person. In this study 33% of doctors, 90% of nurses and 100% of ambulance workers gave incorrect responses (Evans, Warner and Jackson, 2007).

It has been argued that medical practitioners lack the training and skills required for the complex nature of many capacity judgments (Silberfeld and Checkland, 1999). Myron et al. (2008) found that nearly all the staff in their study wished for more training and guidance on the operation of the Act. However, another study found that some healthcare staff did not subscribe to the principles of shared decision-making and service user autonomy and felt that the approach is unnecessary and impracticable (Gravel, Legare and Graham, 2006).

Manthorpe, Rapaport and Stanley (2009) noted staff concerns over the resources required to implement and monitor the MCA (2005) and the risks associated with any failings in its implementation. Full assessment of capacity, including consultations with family, friends or Independent Mental Capacity Advocates (IMCA), can be time-consuming. However, taking shortcuts could result in an incorrect outcome about someone's capacity to make a decision. Moreover, there is no provision in the Act to monitor whether decisions are genuinely in a person's best interests.

For people with intellectual impairments in residential care, Dunn, Clare and Holland (2008) demonstrated that important life planning and healthcare decisions for a person did generally follow the model proposed for best interests decisions by the MCA (2005). However, day-to-day decisions, such as choice of clothes or meals, were often taken spontaneously by staff without any attempt to obtain the person's views or to get informed consent. Dunn, Clare and Holland (2008) recommended that national standards for care should incorporate the provisions of mental capacity legislation and should be applied whenever decisions were required.

On a more positive note, although there is no specific qualification system for the MCA (2005) in England and Wales, as there is for the Mental Health Act (for example, responsible clinician qualification), healthcare providers in the UK have taken steps to improve staff awareness of mental capacity legislation through mandatory training of all relevant staff. However, training must be delivered in an appropriate manner: Wilner et al. (2013) found only limited benefit for classroom-based MCA (2005) training in learning disabilities settings. They recommend that classroom training is combined with actual experience of cases with opportunity for discussion with mentors and supervisors (see Chapter 33).

Summary: Staff and mental capacity

- Many staff have poor knowledge about mental capacity legislation and lack confidence in using it
- The provisions of mental capacity legislation are not routinely applied in health and social care services
- Most staff welcome training about mental capacity, but some do not agree that services users should be allowed to make their own decisions
- Staff are worried about the time and resources required to implement mental capacity legislation properly

- Important decisions often do follow the guidelines of mental capacity legislation, but day-to-day decisions and routine care often occur without consent or consultation
- Training about mental capacity is increasing, but it requires practical training as well as classroom sessions.

Assessment of mental capacity in practice

Most hospital staff find capacity assessment difficult and challenging in practice (Jayes, Palmera and Enderby, 2017). Reasons included time pressure, a perceived lack of knowledge or skills and concerns about poor practice. When making discharge decisions, members of multidisciplinary rehabilitation teams were uncertain about the capacity of approximately one-third of patients on average before a formal assessment had been completed; the uncertainty was most marked for those who were judged to lack capacity on formal assessment (Mackenzie, Lincoln and Newby, 2008).

There is evidence that mental capacity assessment for treatment decisions is not undertaken in the majority of cases where capacity is lacking. For example, an audit of capacity assessments in a general medical setting found only 7.5% of patients received an assessment – much less than the rate of incapacity. Moreover, all these assessments were when patients disagreed with the medical team about treatment! This suggests that many patients who lacked capacity received treatment without consent when they did not object to the clinicians' treatment recommendation (Sleeman and Saunders, 2013). This is supported by other studies, and it is likely that between around 60–70% of patients without capacity are treated without the benefit of an assessment of capacity (Rahman et al., 2012; Raymont et al., 2004; Sessums, Zembrzuska and Jackson, 2011).

Summary: Problems with assessment of mental capacity

- Mental capacity assessment is difficult and challenging in many services
- Staff are often uncertain about whether a person lacks capacity or not without a formal capacity assessment
- Many people without capacity who comply with treatments do so without being given a mental capacity assessment
- It is likely that many patients without capacity are treated without being able to give consent.

Agreement in mental capacity assessment

Mental capacity assessment can be complex (Raymont et al., 2007) so it is not surprising that agreement between practitioners is imperfect. Marson et al. (1997) found only near-chance agreement (56%) in the capacity assessments of five physicians for 29 patients with mild Alzheimer's disease. There were large differences in stringency of judgment (90% to 0% judged to lack capacity), and the physicians used different cognitive models in their assessments. Fassassi et al. (2009) found that physicians rarely said someone had capacity when a psychiatrist judged he did not, but they frequently said that a person lacked capacity when a psychiatrist said that he did in fact possess it. The agreement with the psychiatric assessment for other members of the healthcare team was even lower. Agreement may be affected by differences between physicians regarding the cognitive functions that are important for capacity. Earnst, Marson and Harrell (2000) found that physicians based their judgments on one or two specific cognitive functions (for example, memory, communication, orientation to time or place) and that these functions differed between physicians. Agreement rates also depended on the nature of the patient sample (Raymont et al., 2007); the 78.5% agreement between practitioners when assessing 40 acute general medical patients was much higher than the near-chance agreement for Alzheimer's patients reported by Marson et al. (1997).

It has also been shown that individual practitioners' assessments lacked agreement with assessments made by multidisciplinary teams. The assessment methods used by different physicians were varied and inconsistent and staff assessments did not agree with standardised assessments (Sullivan, 2004).

On a more positive note, it is likely that many of the issues with mental capacity assessment are due to inadequate or inconsistent training. It has been demonstrated that agreement about capacity assessment depends on staff knowledge and skill and that it improves with training (Marson et al., 2000).

Summary: Staff agreement in assessing mental capacity

- Professionals' agreement about mental capacity is often low
- This may be due to differences in understanding about what constitutes lack of capacity
- Training may help to increase agreement.

Conclusion

In this chapter:

- We have considered how decision-making ability is a vital part of our lives but, sadly, an increasing number of people in society lack this ability at some point in their lives due to physical, mental or social factors. Many, but not all, of these factors are health-related. They include brain diseases and injury, intellectual disabilities, severe mental health conditions as well as traumatic life events and social conditions. Many are not permanent.
- When decision-making is impaired, it may become difficult or even impossible for a person to make vital decisions about her welfare. In such cases she is said to lack mental capacity or decision-making ability.
- The implications of this can be sufficiently serious to require special legislation (mental capacity/incapacity laws) that provide ways of enabling the person's wishes to be fulfilled even when he is unable to fully participate in decision-making.
- However, the issues are complex and embrace current thinking about fundamental human rights and values, especially when the outcome may be restriction of liberty. So, as this thinking evolves nationally and internationally, mental capacity legislation must also evolve to keep pace. We have seen that the countries of the British Isles are recognising the defects of past legislation and are actively engaged in revising their mental capacity Acts.
- People with conditions that are likely to affect their mental capacity welcome legislation to protect them and help them to participate in decisions, but many are disappointed that the helpful provisions of the legislation are not better advertised and applied by professionals.
- Adherence to mental capacity legislation by professionals has historically been poor and has tended to remain so. However, there are signs that organisations and services are offering training that may improve this situation, but the training needs to be practical, with hands on experience, and staff need the time and resources to properly assess people and support them to make decisions.
- Agreement between staff about mental capacity can be low. There are several systems to help with assessment and improve agreement, but they all have limitations and there is a need for more research in this area.
- Perhaps the most promising route to improving assessment and appropriate interventions to support decision-making is to emphasise staff training and improve awareness of mental capacity legislation in professionals and the public. In this way, those with impaired mental capacity can be identified and helped to benefit from the many methods to support and assist them to participate in decision-making (see Chapters 9 and 11).

References

Adults with Incapacity (Scotland) Act 2000. London: HMSO. Available at: www.legislation.gov.uk/asp/2000/4/contents

Assisted Decision-Making (Capacity) Act 2015. Dublin: Irish Statute Book. Available at: www.irishstatutebook.ie/eli/2015/act/64/enacted/en/html

Das, A.K., Das, L. and Mulley, G.P. (2006). Awareness of living wills in the United Kingdom. *Age and Ageing*, 35, 543.

Department for Constitutional Affairs (2007). *Mental Capacity Act 2005: Code of Practice*. London: The Stationery Office. Available at: https://assets.publishing.service.gov.uk/government/uploads/system/uploads/attachment_data/file/497253/Mental-capacity-act-code-of-practice.pdf

Dunn, M.C., Clare, I.C.H. and Holland, A.J. (2008). Substitute decision-making for adults with intellectual disabilities living in residential care: Learning through experience. *Health Care Analysis*, 16, 52–64.

Earnst, K.S., Marson, D.C. and Harrell, L.E. (2000). Cognitive models of physicians' legal standard and personal judgments of competency in patients with Alzheimer's disease. *Journal of the American Geriatrics Society*, 48, 919–927.

Etchells, E., Darzins, P., Silberfeld, M., Singer, P.A., McKenny, J., Naglie, G., Katz, M., Guyatt, G.H., Molloy, D.W. and Strang, D. (1999). Assessment of patient capacity to consent to treatment. *Journal of General Internal Medicine*, 14, 27–34.

Evans, K., Warner, J. and Jackson, E. (2007). How much do emergency health careworkers know about capacity and consent? *Emergency Medicine Journal*, 24, 391–393.

Fassassi, S., Bianchi, Y., Stiefel, F. and Waeber, G. (2009). Assessment of the capacity to consent to treatment in patients admitted to acute medical wards. *Medical Ethics*, 10, 15.

Ganzini, L., Volicer, L., Nelson, W.A., Fox, E. and Derse, A.R. (2004). Ten myths about decision-making capacity. *Journal of American Medical Directors Association*, 5, 263–267.

Gravel, K., Legare, F. and Graham, I.D. (2006). Barriers and facilitators to implementing shared decision-making in clinical practice: A systematic review of health professionals' perceptions. *Implementation Science*, 1, 16.

House of Lords (2014). *Mental Capacity Act 2005: Post-Legislative Scrutiny*. London: House of Lords.

Jackson, E. and Warner, J. (2002). How much do doctors know about consent and capacity? *Journal of the Royal Society of Medicine*, 95(12), 601–603.

Jayes, M., Palmera, R. and Enderby, P. (2017). An exploration of mental capacity assessment within acute hospital and intermediate care settings in England: A focus group study. *Disability and Rehabilitation*, 39(21), 2148–2157.

Mackenzie, J.A., Lincoln, N.B. and Newby, G.J. (2008). Capacity to make a decision about discharge destination after stroke: A pilot study. *Clinical Rehabilitation*, 22, 1116–1126.

Manthorpe, J., Rapaport, J. and Stanley, N. (2009). Expertise and experience: People with experiences of using services and carers' views of the Mental Capacity Act 2005. *British Journal of Social Work*, 39, 884–900.

Marshall, H. and Sprung, S. (2016). Community nurse's knowledge, confidence and experience of the Mental Capacity Act in practice. *British Journal of Community Nursing*, 21(12), 515–622.

Marson, D.C., Earnst, K.S., Jamil, F., Bartolucci, A. and Harrell, L.E. (2000). Consistency of physicians' legal standard and personal judgments of competency in patients with Alzheimer's disease. *Journal of the American Geriatrics Society*, 48, 911–918.

Marson, D.C., McInturff, B., Hawkins, L., Bartolucci, A. and Harrell, L.E. (1997). Consistency of physician judgments of capacity to consent in mild Alzheimer's disease. *Journal of the American Geriatrics Society*, 45, 453–457.

Mental Capacity Act 2005. London: HMSO. Available at: www.legislation.gov.uk/ukpga/2005/9/contents

Mental Capacity (Amendment) Act 2019. London: HMSO. Available at: www.legislation.gov.uk/ukpga/2019/18/enacted

Mental Capacity (Northern Ireland) Act 2016. London: HMSO.

Mental Health Act 2007. London: HMSO. Available at: www.legislation.gov.uk/ukpga/2007/12/contents

Moye, J. and Marson, D.C. (2007). Assessment of decision-making capacity in older adults: An emerging area of practice and research. *Journal of Gerontology: Psychological Sciences*, 62, 3–11.

Myron, R., Gillespie, S., Swift, P. and Williamson, T. (2008). *Whose Decision? Preparation for and Implementation of the Mental Capacity Act in Statutory and Non-Statutory Services in England and Wales*. London: Mental Health Foundation.

Rahman, M., Evans, K.E., Arif, N. and Gorard, D.A. (2012). Mental incapacity in hospitalised patients undergoing percutaneous endoscopic gastrostomy insertion. *Clinical Nutrition*, 31, 224–229.

Raymont, V., Bingley, W., Buchanan, A., David, A.S., Hayward, P., Wessely, S. and Hotopf, M. (2004). Prevalence of mental incapacity in medical inpatients and associated risk factors: Cross-sectional study. *Lancet*, 364, 1421–1427.

Raymont, V., Buchanan, A., David, A.S., Hayward, P., Wessely, S. and Hotopf, M. (2007). The inter-rater reliability of mental capacity assessments. *International Journal of Law and Psychiatry*, 30, 112–117.

Schiff, R., Sacares, P., Snook, J., Rajkumar, C. and Bulpitt, C.J. (2006). Living wills and the Mental Capacity Act: A postal questionnaire survey of UK geriatricians. *Age and Ageing*, 35, 116–121.

Sessums, L.L., Zembrzuska, H. and Jackson, J.L. (2011). Does this patient have medical decision-making capacity? *JAMA*, 306, 420–427.

Silberfeld, M. and Checkland, D. (1999). Faulty judgment, expert opinion, and decision-making capacity. *Theoretical Medicine and Bioethics*, 20, 377–393.

Sleeman, I. and Saunders, K. (2013). An audit of mental capacity assessment on general medical wards. *Clinical Ethics*, 8(2/3), 47–51.

Sugarman, J., McCrory, D.C. and Hubal, R.C. (1998). Getting meaningful informed consent from older adults: A structured literature review of empirical research. *Journal of the American Geriatrics Society*, 46, 517–524.

Sullivan, K. (2004). Neuropsychological assessment of mental capacity. *Neuropsychology Review*, 14, 131–142.

United Nations (2006). *Convention on the Rights of Persons with Disabilities*. New York: United Nations. Available at: www.un.org/disabilities/documents/convention/convoptprot-e.pdf

Wilner, P., Bridle, J., Price, V., Dymond, S. and Lewis, G. (2013). What do NHS staff learn from training on the Mental Capacity Act (2005)? *Legal and Criminological Psychology*, 18, 83–101.

Wilner, P., Bridle, J., Price, V., John, E. and Hunt, S. (2012). Knowledge of mental capacity issues in residential services for people with intellectual disabilities. *Advances in Mental Health and Intellectual Disabilities*, 6(1), 33–40.

Chapter 2

Some basic concepts of the Mental Capacity Act (2005)
What you need to know

Kate Wilkinson

In this chapter

This chapter provides a very brief overview of the Mental Capacity Act (MCA, 2005) for England and Wales (a view of other capacity legislation can be found in Chapter 4). It summarises the basic points that anyone assessing capacity should be aware of. More detailed analysis and advice can be found in subsequent chapters.

A definition of capacity

Essentially *mental capacity* is the ability to use information in order to reason and make an informed decision. The MCA (Section 2 [1]) frames it in terms of a *lack* of capacity and defines it in the following way:

"A person lacks capacity in relation to a matter if at the material time he is unable to make a decision for himself because of an impairment of, or disturbance in the functioning of, the mind or the brain."

Mental capacity is time- and decision-specific

According to the MCA, mental capacity is both time- and decision-specific. Therefore, any assessment and subsequent opinion on capacity can only relate to the specific decision in question and to the time it is completed; however, the outcome is assumed to be valid until capacity is reassessed.

Tip

The decision in question should be clearly defined *before* any assessment takes place.

Cautions

- Beware of making blanket statements regarding capacity. It is still a common error for assessors to merely state, "Mr Sadiq does not have capacity" after assessing capacity about a specific matter. Another common error is for people to make assumptions about areas of capacity that have not been assessed, based on a person being found to lack capacity to make a specific decision about a separate matter. An example of this would be to assume that a person lacks capacity to decide where to live because an assessment found she lacked capacity to make decisions regarding whether or not to have an operation. The two are separate decisions and so need separate conclusions about the person's capacity to make them.
- Do not assume capacity remains stable over time. Ability to make decisions can change; therefore, the fact that a person has been found to lack capacity regarding a specific decision does not mean that she cannot regain capacity if circumstances change. Similarly, someone who has been found to have capacity can subsequently lose capacity if his decision-making abilities alter. (See Chapter 26 for an exploration of fluctuating capacity.)

What is covered by the MCA?

The MCA is concerned with decision-making and applies to everyone over the age of 16 living in England and Wales.

What is not covered by MCA?

There are a number of areas that fall outside the jurisdiction of the MCA in England and Wales, which instead are governed by existing case law and common law. The Act specifies that decisions cannot be made on someone else's behalf in these areas:

- Sexual relationships (ability to consent)
- Taking parental responsibility for a child
- Placing a child up for adoption
- Consent to fertility treatment
- Entering into marriage or a civil partnership
- Divorce
- Treatment or detention under the Mental Health Act (MHA, 1983).

Ability to give informed consent for a sexual relationship can also fall under the Sexual Offences Act (2003) and is discussed in more detail in Chapter 17. The MHA interacts with the MCA and the relationship between the two is discussed in more detail in Chapter 30. The other areas listed earlier are beyond the remit of this book and specialist guidance should be sought.

Other areas not mentioned by the Act in which case law must be considered alongside the MCA include:

- Ability to make a valid will (testamentary capacity) (see Chapter 18)
- Capacity to stand trial (see Chapter 20)
- Capacity to decide to enter into litigation (see Chapter 20).

Five principles of the Act

There are five fundamental principles that underpin the MCA.

---

5 Principles of the MCA (2005)

1   Presumption of capacity
2   Supported decision-making
3   The right to make an "unwise" decision
4   The principle of best interests
5   Considering less restrictive alternatives

---

1 Presumption of capacity

It should be assumed that a person has capacity, unless it is proven that he does not. The onus is on the assessor to prove the person does not have capacity (on the balance of probabilities), rather than the person to prove that he *does*.

2 Supported decision-making

A person must not be deemed to lack capacity to make a decision unless all practicable steps to help her have been taken without success. Therefore, it is the responsibility of the assessor to try and communicate, explain things and ask questions in the way most likely to help the person make an informed decision – for example, using interpreters, non-verbal communication and support with cognitive problems. (See Chapters 9 and 11 for more detail.)

3 The right to make an "unwise" decision

A person should not be treated as unable to make a decision just because others believe that he is making an "unwise" decision. As long as it is an informed decision (in other words, satisfying the functional test), it does not matter that others believe it to be unwise.

4 The principle of best interests

If someone is found to lack capacity, decisions and actions may need to be taken on her behalf. Any such actions or decisions *must* be made in her best interests. (See Chapter 29 for further information.)

5 Considering less restrictive alternatives

Any decision or action taken in the best interests of someone who lacks capacity must be the one that is least restrictive "of the person's rights and freedom of action" whilst fulfilling the original purpose of the decision.

Safeguards around assessment of capacity

The Act states that a person cannot be said to lack capacity to make a certain decision based solely on any of the following:

- Age
- Appearance (for example, physical indication of disability, skin colour or mode of dress)
- Assumptions about her condition (for example, physical disabilities, learning disabilities or illness linked to age)
- Assumptions about any aspect of his behaviour (for example, being introverted, extroverted or demonstrating risk-taking behaviour).

Assessing capacity and establishing a lack of capacity

The National Institute for Health and Care Excellence (NICE, 2018) guidelines on decision-making and mental capacity state that "effective assessments are thorough, proportionate to the complexity, importance and urgency of the decision, and performed in the context of a trusting and collaborative relationship" (p. 20). This section highlights some of the basics of assessment.

The "two stage" test of capacity

The "two stage" test of capacity mentioned in the MCA and the MCA Code of Practice (2007) is, at this stage in the life of the Act, probably best described as the *three* stage test, following various subsequent clarifications in case law.

The MCA Code of Practice (2007) originally defined and laid out the two stage test as:

Step 1: The diagnostic test

• Establish the presence of an impairment of, or a disturbance in the functioning of, the mind or brain.

Step 2: The functional test

A person is considered unable to make a decision if she is unable to do any one of the following:

• Understand information relevant to the decision
• Retain relevant information long enough to make a decision
• Use or weigh relevant information in the decision-making process
• Communicate her decision.

However, following rulings from the Court and more up-to-date advice, such as that found in the guidance on capacity assessment from 39 Essex Chambers (Ruck Keene et al., 2016), it is now commonly recommended that steps 1 and 2 are reversed and that a third step, of establishing the "causative nexus", is also required. (Steps 1 and 2 are reversed in the wording of the actual Act.)

Step 1: The functional test

Is the person unable to make a decision?

Step 2: The diagnostic test

Does the person have an impairment of, or a disturbance in the functioning of, the mind or brain?

Step 3: Establishing the causative nexus

Is the person unable to make a decision *because of* this impairment or disturbance of the mind or brain?

Case law has established the rationale for taking the steps in this order (*PC and NC v City of York Council* [2013], at paragraph 58; *Kings College NHS Foundation Trust v C and V* [2015], at paragraph 35). It attempts to address the concern that separating the establishment of the presence of a disorder or impairment and consideration of whether inability to make a decision is actually caused by the disorder will make the latter less carefully considered. It also seeks to reduce any potential discrimination against those with an impairment in, or disturbance of, mind or brain by making the reason for questioning capacity the inability to make an informed decision, rather than the presence of an impairment. There is the view that considering the diagnostic test first creates a bias in the assessment from the beginning and makes it more likely the person will be found to lack capacity (Ruck Keene et al., 2016).

Step 1: The functional test

Understanding relevant information

It is important to remember that a person does not have to understand every detail of the information you present to her. She just has to understand the information relevant to the decision in question – in other words, the salient points. In addition, you must not set the level, or threshold, of understanding too high. Chapter 7 explains how to establish what information is relevant to the decision and how to determine the level of understanding required.

Remember, you, or someone else, should present the relevant information to the person *before* the assessment begins. Never start with a 'blank canvas'. Chapters 9 and 11 detail ways of presenting information in order to support a person's decision-making.

Retaining relevant information

Again, the person only needs to retain relevant information and then only long enough to make the decision. The MCA is very specific about "the fact that a person is able to retain the information relevant to a decision for a short period only does not prevent him from being regarded as able to make the decision" (Section 3 [3]). However, the amount of time a person needs to retain information for will depend on the type of decision in question. Chapters 9 and 10 give specific guidance on establishing whether a person can retain information for a sufficient amount of time to make a decision.

Weighing and using relevant information

The person must be able to weigh information relevant to the decision and use it to come to a decision. The case of *PCT v P, AH & the Local Authority* [2009] describes this as "the capacity actually to engage in the decision-making process itself and to be able to see the various parts of the argument and to relate the one to another" (at paragraphs 34–35). It is arguably one of the most difficult areas to assess and is discussed in more detail in Chapters 3 and 22.

Communicating the decision

The person must be able to communicate his decision, but this can be by any means possible, as long it is reliable. For example, it can be verbal (in any language), sign language, gestures or eye movements. Chapter 11 has detailed guidance on supporting communication.

Step 2: The diagnostic test

You must answer the question: Does the person in question have an impairment of, or disturbance in, the functioning of her mind or brain? Only if she does can you potentially conclude that she lacks capacity under the MCA. This can involve a formal medical diagnosis, such as:

- Dementia
- Acquired brain injury
- Significant learning disability
- Psychosis
- Severe depression
- Severe anxiety.

However, there does not need to be a formal diagnosis as such, as long as there is a sound basis for believing the person has an impairment or disturbance of mind or brain. Examples of this might include:

- Apparent cognitive problems in the absence of a formal diagnosis
- The effects of alcohol or drugs
- Drowsiness caused by a medical condition or other medication.

The MCA states that the impairment can either be temporary or permanent. If it is temporary, it is only appropriate to do a capacity assessment if the decision cannot wait until the impairment has resolved (for example, when someone is drunk). For more information on urgent decisions and fluctuating capacity see Chapters 24 and 26.

Step 3: Establishing the causative nexus

This is the final part of the process of establishing capacity. Once you have ascertained that the person is unable to make a decision (following the functional assessment) and has an impairment or disturbance of mind or brain, you must form an opinion on whether this lack of ability to make a decision is directly *because of* the impairment. Only if this is the case can you conclude that the person lacks capacity to make the decision in question. The causative nexus is discussed further in Chapters 3 and 5.

Take-home point

All three of these components must be satisfied for a person to be said to lack capacity.

Pre-assessment checklist

Here is a basic guide of things to consider before carrying out a capacity assessment. More details on each point can be seen in other chapters of this book.

About the decision

- Identify the decision in question. Is there more than one? (See Chapter 3.)
- Ensure you and the person being assessed have the details of the choices available to the person.
- List all the most important aspects of the decision (salient information) that the person would need to show she had understood, whilst ignoring the irrelevant or peripheral details. (See Chapter 7.)
- Ask yourself whether this decision should be made by you or someone else – for example, an attorney with Lasting Power of Attorney or a Court appointed Deputy. (See Chapters 14 and 18.).

About the person

Any information gathered should be used to try and enhance capacity in addition to informing assessments.

- Identify possible sources of evidence.
- Ask yourself, is there a family member or another professional that could provide useful information about the person's decision-making, communication style, cognitive difficulties and so on?
- Establish the nature of any cognitive impairment and consider how this might affect the person's capacity and what you could do to minimise this. (See Chapter 9.)

- Consider whether the assessment should be delayed pending further recovery or to allow the assessment to take place in an optimal environment.
- Establish whether there are any functional issues or risks specific to the person that would be relevant to the decision – for example, is the person currently following advice given or prepared to use aids? (See Chapter 6.)
- Identify the person's communication profile – do they need hearing aids? Writing materials? Picture prompts? If this is not possible, what easy words and questions will you use to introduce, explain and discuss the decision? (See Chapters 9 and 11.)
- Consider questions you could ask as prompts or alternatives if the person does not understand the first time – for example, closed or forced-choice questions. (See Chapters 9 and 11.)
- Establish whether there are any psychosocial factors that might distort the person's decision-making – for example, low mood or a history of abuse. Consider what could be done to address or minimise the impact of these. (See Chapter 5.)

About the environment and wider context

- Identify a quiet, communication-friendly environment where you can conduct your assessment. (See Chapters 9 and 11.)
- Consider whether the person might be overly influenced by others in this process – for example, family or professionals. Decide on a strategy to minimise any concerns. (See Chapter 5.)

About you

- Reflect on your communication style – how can you modify or adapt it to communicate more easily with the person? (See Chapter 11.)
- Identify your biases/preferences in this case and consciously put them aside as much as possible. (See Chapter 23.)

The balance of probabilities

The standard of proof required by the MCA for lack of capacity is "the balance of probabilities", rather than "beyond reasonable doubt", which is the case in criminal court cases. Therefore, an opinion on capacity should be reached "on the balance of probabilities". This means the assessor should be able to show, with evidence, that it is more likely than not that the person in question lacks capacity (MCA Code of Practice, 2007, at paragraph 4.10).

Summary

This chapter focused on the MCA (2005) for England and Wales and takes a very brief overview of the "basics" of the Act. Chapter 4 provides an overview of capacity legislation in other areas. Chapter 3 takes a more detailed look at some of the issues detailed in this chapter and how these can be misinterpreted or incorrectly applied. The other chapters in the book provide further guidance on the assessment of capacity and mental capacity in general.

References

Department for Constitutional Affairs (2007). *Mental Capacity Act 2005: Code of Practice*. London: The Stationery Office.

Department of Health (2005). *Mental Capacity Act*. London: HMSO. Available at: www.legislation.gov.uk/ukpga/2005/9/pdfs/ukpga_20050009_en.pdf

Department of Health (1983). *Mental Health Act*. London: HMSO. Available at: www.legislation.gov.uk/ukpga/1983/20/contents

National Institute for Health and Care Excellence (2018). *Decision-Making and Mental Capacity* (NICE Guideline 108). Available at: www.nice.org.uk/guidance/ng108

Ruck Keene, A., Butler-Cole, V., Allen, N., Bicarregui, A., Kohn, N. and Akhtar, S. (2016). *Mental Capacity Law Guidance Note: A Brief Guide to Carrying Out Capacity Assessments*. 39 Essex Chambers. Available at: www.39essex.com/mental-capacity-guidance-note-brief-guide-carrying-capacity-assessments

Sexual Offences Act 2003. London: HMSO. Available at: www.legislation.gov.uk/ukpga/2003/42/contents

Case law

Kings College NHS Foundation Trust v C and V [2015] EWCOP 80

PC and NC v City of York Council [2013] EWCA Civ 478

The PCT v P, AH & the Local Authority [2009] EW Misc 10 (COP)

Chapter 3

Legal perspectives on practical capacity concerns

Emma Fowler

In this chapter

Research suggests that practitioners can feel unsure about how to apply knowledge of the Mental Capacity Act 2005 (MCA) in their practice (Williams et al., 2012; Mental Health Foundation and The Mental Capacity Forum, 2016). This chapter will explore aspects of mental capacity that can present challenges to professionals in practice and discuss legal perspectives that can clarify some of these issues. It might be helpful to think of this chapter as a framework for the whole process, whilst other chapters will provide more detail on specific aspects of capacity work.

Do you really need to undertake an assessment?

Capacity should be assessed when there is doubt about a person's ability to make a decision and all practical and appropriate steps to support him have not been successful.

Doubt about a person's ability: The onus is on us to assess capacity when we doubt someone's ability to make the decision for himself (Department for Constitutional Affairs, 2007, p. 52). "Risky" or unusual decisions might give rise to concern, but the concept here is broader and is about the person's ability to make sense of the decision. Moreover, we are more likely to know we are doubtful about someone's capacity if we have honoured the person's right to be supported in making her decision (MCA, 2005).

Myth-busting

Myth 1: Someone with a mental impairment who wants to make a "risky" decision will need a capacity assessment.

Everyone has the right, under the Act, to make unwise decisions. However, many professionals instinctively feel that such decisions should lead to an assessment of capacity (Williams et al., 2012). "Unwise decisions" are

---

often conflated with decisions at odds with a course of action others would prefer. Refusing assistance with personal hygiene, drinking alcohol, smoking or declining treatment are typical examples.

Myth 2: You don't need to do a capacity assessment if the person is going along with the decision, or action, you think is best.

The opposite, but equally misplaced belief, is that you are always exempt from considering capacity if someone is compliant with a course of action that others believe to be appropriate.

The consequence of acting in line with Myth 1 is to potentially engage in discriminatory practice against a disabled person by imposing an assessment when it might not be required. Acting in line with Myth 2 could result in having no protection from liability if you have failed to take steps to assess capacity (and properly record it) when there has been reason to doubt the person's ability to make the decision (Department for Constitutional Affairs, 2007).

Someone *needs to have a decision to make* in order for an assessment of capacity to take place. In recent years, participants attending our training have raised capacity questions that have had a common theme – confusion has arisen because there was, in fact, no decision to make. Consider the following examples:

• Someone with dementia has been treated in hospital and is ready to go home without the person, professionals or family members considering any changes in his support system to be necessary
• A person with a learning disability has been arrested on suspicion of committing a crime and is going to be interviewed by a police officer.

These are examples in which professionals believe that a capacity assessment is required, but what is the decision that needs to be made? The overuse of capacity language in some contexts has meant that it is occasionally generalised to situations where it does not apply. An assessment requires someone to have a *genuine decision to make between at least two options*. The examples described here represent circumstances in which someone might need something explained to her in a way that she can understand, but she does not require an assessment of capacity as there are no options from which to choose and no decision to make (Department for Constitutional Affairs, 2007).

Pause to consider:

• What was your motivation for doubting capacity the last time you undertook an assessment?
• Have there been situations in your practice when you perhaps should have undertaken an assessment but did not? If so, what were the reasons?

Who should assess capacity?

This is a question we are often asked, and it is a tricky one to answer as it usually depends on the situation and/or the decision. In England and Wales, for example, the Mental Capacity Act Code of Practice (2007) provides some guidance but, in most instances, it is not prescriptive. It is probably helpful to start with the situations/decisions that do require assessment by a specific person:

- If someone else has been granted decision-making powers – for example, a Lasting Power of Attorney or a Court Appointed Deputy – and the decision comes within the scope of his remit, that person decides when the person in question is unable to make a decision and what is in her best interests. This does not mean that this person cannot be assisted; in fact, many people in these roles appreciate some support and guidance. But it does mean that person has the final say. It is also important to remember that these decisions should be discussed with the person in question and made in partnership with her
- In instances where treatment is being proposed, it is typically the case that the person responsible for the treatment should assess capacity
- In England and Wales, legal transactions have to be assessed by a legal professional such as a solicitor
- If there is disagreement about someone's capacity that cannot be resolved, then it might be appropriate for a Judge (for example, in the Court of Protection) to make the final decision about the person's capacity.

Outside of these circumstances it is useful to keep guiding principles in mind:

- For most day-to-day decisions, *someone who knows the person best* is the right person to assess capacity. This makes sense when we consider how many people with mental impairments are being cared for and supported informally and might not even be in contact with services.
- For most complex decisions, *the person intending to make or carry out the decision if the person is found to lack capacity* should make the final decision about capacity.

Cautions

- Independent Mental Capacity Advocates (IMCAs) should not be asked to undertake capacity assessments. This is not their role.
- IMCAs might challenge the validity or quality of a capacity assessment if they are commissioned to support someone at the best interests stage, but they would neither make the decision nor provide a second assessment.

Where decisions are complex, the person responsible for the decision may need advice or opinions from others, but she will still be responsible for ultimately deciding whether, on balance, the person lacks capacity. In such cases, it would be good practice to carry out a joint assessment between an "expert" in capacity assessment and a professional who knows the person well, such as his regular nurse or a key worker.

Tips

- If you are struggling to describe a decision, consider how you might describe it if it were your decision or that of a friend.
- Once you have described the decision, remember to actually ask the person what he would choose to do.

Preparing to undertake an assessment

Have any of these scenarios ever applied to you?

- An assessment that was intended to consider where a client lives ends up being a conversation about the person's favourite soap opera or another unrelated topic
- You return to the office after undertaking a capacity assessment and realise you did not cover a crucial aspect of the decision
- It has been difficult to complete the "use and weigh" aspect of your capacity record as all of the evidence you appear to have collected relates to risk, problems or general "downsides" of the decision.

In most cases, these situations can be avoided through effective preparation, which can be distilled into two key points:

1 What is the decision?
2 What information would someone need to have, or be aware of, to make an informed decision?

What is the decision?

It is important to be clear about what the decision is *before* you undertake an assessment. Any description of a decision should be accurate and succinct (one or two sentences maximum). Think of it as a newspaper-like headline that summarises the issue without going into excessive detail. Here are some ideas:

- Whether to join a dating website or not
- Whether to have some care at home and, if so, what sort of care

      ○   What type of holiday to go on this summer
      ○   Whether to consent to a blood test to check for anaemia.

Articulating the exact nature of a decision can be problematic, especially when the decision is complex or presents potential risks to the person.

    In what ways might the following descriptions be flawed, imprecise or inaccurate?

1   Whether **Ruth** understands the risks of going on holiday on her own
2   **Maria** needs to understand the consequences of not taking her medication
3   Whether **Nitin** can refuse carers at home
4   Whether **Jayden** can manage his finances

Experience shows that most of the problems associated with poor decision descriptions can be categorised into four themes:

1   *The decision focuses exclusively on risk.* Decisions couched purely in terms of risk (like **Ruth's**) will, not surprisingly, often lead to a capacity assessment being indistinguishable from a risk assessment, which is not what we are aiming to achieve. Decisions usually involve a range of factors, which can include negative foreseeable consequences (for some options) but also potentially positive outcomes as well as practical considerations. Some aspects of a decision might be subjective or be given more weight by a client ("Eating Mars bars for breakfast everyday makes me happy!"), but that does not mean they can be dismissed by professionals. Case law has shown that it is legitimate for people to give *different weight to different factors*, which should be distinguished from demonstrably false beliefs (*CC v KK & STCC* [2012]).

2   *The decision implies that the person is required to prove something.* As in the description of **Maria's** decision, many decisions indicate that someone *has* to understand certain factors or demonstrate specific skills in order to be deemed to have capacity. The emphasis here is wrong. The law is clear that the person does not have to prove anything – *we* have to determine whether the evidence we have gathered in the course of the assessment is enough, on balance, to displace the presumption of capacity (MCA, 2005).

    In other words, do you have sufficient evidence to show the person *does not* have capacity to make the decision? It is not about whether you have enough evidence to show that she *does* have capacity, or whether the person has given you enough evidence to show that she *does* have capacity, as we are supposed to start with the premise that the person can make any decision. It is not like passing your driving test or a job interview. It is more like the judicial process except that, in court, the prosecution has to prove that you *have done something* and with capacity assessments we have to prove that *the person (on balance) cannot do something*.

For example, Maria has dementia, and in recent weeks, she has not been taking her medication. This might, understandably, be concerning for the people who support her. The correct approach would be to explore with Maria why she might not have taken the medication (it would be an assumption to think it is because of her dementia) and consider ways in which she could be supported (principle 2 of the MCA – the right to be supported to make a decision). When asked, she reported that she cannot remember why she has to take her medication and so does not want to. She added that she seems to be forgetting things more often than she used to.

Following this, strategies to support Maria's memory were implemented, for example, explaining the reasons in simple terms, giving a written reminder of the main points or getting her to write them down and attaching this reminder to the medications. If everything practical has been done to support her with this and she still cannot remember why she needs to take her medication and so continues not to take it, then we have begun to gather evidence to suggest that Maria might be *unable* to make the decision – because she is struggling to retain relevant information. This example also illustrates the central importance of principle 2 of the MCA – it is difficult (often impossible) to adequately evidence that someone cannot make a decision unless we have tried to help her to do so and that support has not succeeded.

3   *The description of the decision is too narrow.* Consider **Nitin's** decision (whether to refuse carers at home). Would Nitin describe his decision in this way? It is likely that "refusing carers" is just part of a wider decision that has arisen for Nitin about how (and whether) his care needs could be met. One option might be the proposed carers at home, but there might also be others that have not been envisaged or explored.

4   *The description of the decision is too broad.* It is always worth reflecting on whether a decision like **Jayden's** (whether he can manage his finances) can be broken down into smaller units. For example, someone might lack capacity to manage a large compensation fund but have capacity to manage weekly benefits or decide to sell his flat. Failing to refine decisions to their smallest denominators can result in people being inappropriately denied the right to make decisions for themselves.

These examples illustrate how assessor bias and attitudes can affect the assessment. Fears about risks posed to a person, or frustration with a situation, are often understandable but need either to be acknowledged and set aside or positioned proportionally within the full context of the decision.

What is relevant for the assessment?

You also need to establish what the person needs to know. Legislation describes this as "relevant" or "salient" information (*LBJ v RYJ* [2010]). Identifying relevant information need not take long and, if it is a category of decision that you are often called on to assess (for example, care, accommodation or a specific treatment), your ideas and conclusions about relevant information can inform future assessments (see Chapter 7).

The MCA Code of Practice (2007) says that relevant information includes:

- The nature of the decision
- The reason why the decision is needed, and
- The likely effects of deciding one way or another or of making no decision at all.

Take home point

Notice that the language used is that of "likely effects". Legislation also refers to "reasonably foreseeable consequences". This is distinct from "good or bad" consequences of a decision and from the idea of risk. It offers a more neutral way of considering a decision and should enable you to employ more objectivity in your identification of relevant information.

Does any case law apply to your decision?

Applying the concept of what the "average person on the street" needs to know in order to make an informed decision is useful but can take time and might not be the best thing to do if case law already exists about the decision that could form the basis of your "relevant factors". For example, there is existing case law relating to sexual relations and marriage, accommodation and care and to health and treatment (*London Borough of Southwark v KA and Ors* [2016]; *LBX v K, L and M* [2013]; *Montgomery v Lanarkshire Health Board* [2015]; see Chapter 7 for more detailed information).

Important factors in forming an opinion on capacity

The concept of "retaining"

Myth-busting

Myth 3: People only ever need to remember information for a short time.

Most of us are aware that we should not automatically assume someone is unable to make a decision if she can only hold information in her mind for a short time (Department for Constitutional Affairs, 2007, p. 47). Many decisions can be taken over a relatively short period (for example, consenting to a blood test or having a tooth filled), or memory can be scaffolded to ensure that people can remember information or draw on it when needed (see Chapter 9). However, there are circumstances in which people have to make decisions over a longer period, or on an ongoing basis, and support to help them to remember relevant information over this time has failed, for example, in relation to administering medication or the management of household bills. What should be the test of retention in these circumstances? The Code of Practice gives us some direction, in that it describes how someone "must be able to hold information in their mind long enough to use it to make an effective decision" and that this depends on "what is necessary for the decision in question" (Department for Constitutional Affairs, 2007, p. 47).

"Use and weigh" information as part of the decision-making process

This area of functioning is often the most difficult to assess and is perhaps the most complex concept to translate into practice (see Chapters 10 and 22 for more information). For the purpose of this chapter we will consider a few potential pitfalls that are important to be aware of and avoid.

Caution

Be careful not to interpret this aspect of the test as being exclusively about "weighing up".

There are two distinct functional skills contained within this aspect of the test. In practice, however, these two ideas are frequently conflated into one (weighing). The person has to be able to *use* the relevant information in the moment when the decision is required. This is more difficult to assess when the decision is ongoing, such as capacity to manage her benefits. The Code of Practice provides some useful examples of impairments that might give rise to an inability to use information, including impulsivity resulting from a brain injury (Department for Constitutional Affairs, 2007).

Caution

Make sure to include the least restrictive option as part of your capacity conversation.

In order to weigh the options available, the person needs to be aware of all the options available. In practice, however, the least restrictive option is often omitted or ignored by professionals as it presents too high a level of risk to the person's wellbeing to be considered legitimate. A typical example might be returning home from hospital without support when professionals believe that this is ill advised.

Caution

Be careful not to focus on only "weighing the risk".

In order to weigh up information when making a decision is it necessary to consider both the potential positive and negative consequences.

Caution

Be careful not to confuse making an "unwise" decision with inability to make a decision.

One of the five key principles of the MCA is a person's right to make "unwise" decisions. The fact that the person does not agree with professionals does not mean she is necessarily unable to make the decision, especially if she is weighing up the information to come to that decision. People give weight to different aspects of the relevant information depending on their beliefs and experiences, and so what is most important to the person may be different from what you might expect.

The "causative nexus"

If the person you are assessing is unable to make the decision, it must be *because of her impairment*. This is what the causative nexus is concerned with. For example, where someone is experiencing domestic abuse to such a degree that it is impairing her ability to process information, it might be her circumstances that are preventing her from making an informed decision and *not a mental impairment*. In such circumstances the causative nexus would not be satisfied, and the person would not lack capacity under the MCA (Department for Constitutional Affairs, 2007). Of course, it might be the case that the person is experiencing poor mental health as a result of her circumstances (which may amount to an impairment), but this should not be assumed.

Recording assessments

It is essential that you make a proper, contemporaneous (made at the time) record of your assessment and that people are able to follow your reasoning. You must evidence how (on the balance of probabilities) you came to your opinion on capacity.

Tip

Consider how your assessment would stand up to scrutiny if it were examined in the Court of Protection.

Your record should include:

- Person's name and other identifiers, such as date of birth and NHS number
- Person's first language and whether an interpreter was used
- The number of sessions the assessment was carried out over
- Date, time and location of the assessment(s)
- People present during the assessment(s) – names and job titles
- A clear statement of the decision that needs to be made
- The reason for the assessment – why the person's capacity is being questioned and what support has been tried unsuccessfully
- The options available to the person
- The salient factors you have identified; in other words, what is the relevant information? (When describing the salient factors, it is advisable to be explicit in your record about what informed your list if possible, for example, the MCA Code of Practice and a specific case.)
- The people consulted in order to gather information before the assessment
- Additional factors that may impact on the person's capacity – for example, low mood affecting engagement or coercion from others
- The measures taken to enhance the person's capacity and support decision-making (Does the person have any difficulties that require support? How was relevant information presented? Were any special adjustments made?)
- Examples of the questions you asked (verbatim where possible) and the answers the person gave to each (verbatim where possible) within your report and preferably attach your structured notes as an appendix

- A consideration of each part of the two-stage test, supported by evidence you have gathered (including direct quotes):

  - The diagnostic test

    - ○ Does the person have an impairment of, or disturbance in the functioning of, the mind or brain, and what is the nature of this?
    - ○ Is the impairment or disturbance permanent or temporary? If it is temporary, state the reason why the decision cannot be delayed.

  - The functional test

    - ○ Is the person able to understand the relevant information and why the decision has to be made? If not, why not?
    - ○ Is the person able to retain the relevant information for long enough to make the decision? If not, why not?
    - ○ Is the person able to use and weigh the relevant information in order to make a decision? If not, why not?
    - ○ Is the person able to communicate his decision? If not, why not?

- Your opinion, formed on the balance of probabilities (making it clear that it is your opinion and not a statement of fact). This should include:

  - ○ A statement addressing the causative nexus, in other words that the person's inability to make an informed decision is due to his impairment of mind or brain
  - ○ A sentence stating that the person does not have the capacity to make this decision at this point in time and, if you think that he will regain this capacity, state when this may be

- Recommendations, whether or not the person has capacity to make the decision, for example, if and when capacity for this decision should be reassessed, who should be involved in a best interests meeting or other actions to be taken, such as a risk assessment and risk management strategies
- The decision the person actually came to (regardless of whether or not you consider her to have capacity)
- Contact details of the assessor(s).

Additional advice on recording your opinion

In terms of written conclusions, the following example is a common error:

"Joe was unable to demonstrate an understanding of relevant factors."

Remember, Joe does not need to demonstrate *anything,* as he is protected by the principle of the presumption of capacity. If someone has been unable to demonstrate understanding to a prescribed threshold, then be accurate in your description of this. For example:

> "Joe was unable to understand (x and y relevant factors) to the extent that I am satisfied the presumption of capacity is displaced."

In addition, consider how your assessment reflects the burden of proof in the context of capacity. For example, using the phrase *on balance* in concluding statements reflects that you understand that both stages of the test are assessed on the balance of probabilities.

Summary

Being familiar with the basics of the MCA and undertaking some basic preparation can be effective ways to improve the quality of your assessments. Small adjustments, such as accurately defining the decision and spending a few minutes articulating relevant factors, can pay dividends and help to break assessments down into sequential steps. It is essential that you make a detailed recording of your assessment and opinion that will stand up to external scrutiny.

At the end of this chapter is a list of sources that we have found useful and reliable and which can help professionals stay up-to-date with legislative developments.

References

Department for Constitutional Affairs (2007). *Mental Capacity Act 2005: Code of Practice*. London: The Stationery Office.

Law Commission (2017). *Mental Capacity and Deprivation of Liberty* (Law Com No. 372).

The Mental Capacity Act 2005. London: The Stationery Office.

Mental Health Foundation and The Mental Capacity Forum (2016). *The National Mental Capacity Forum Chair's Annual Report*. London. Available at: www.scie.org.uk/files/mca/directory/forum/chair-report-2016.pdf

Williams, V., Boyle, G., Jepson, M., Swift, P., Williamson, T. and Heslop, P. (2012). *Making Best Interests Decisions, Norah Fry Research Centre, University of Bristol*. Available at: www.mentalhealth.org.uk/publications/bids-report

Case law

CC v KK & STCC [2012] EWHC 2136 (COP)

London Borough of Southwark v KA and Ors (Capacity to marry) [2016] EWCOP 20

LBJ v RYJ [2010] EWHC 2664 (Fam)

LBX v K, L and M [2013] EWHC 3230 (Fam)

Montgomery v Lanarkshire Health Board [2015] UKSC 11

Useful sources of information and support

The MCA Code of Practice (2007)

The Code of Practice usually provides a helpful starting point with any practice quandary. Given its value, I am often surprised how rarely colleagues use it as a resource; preferring to seek guidance from colleagues or to "save" questions up for future training sessions. I want to encourage you to consult and use the Code of Practice to full advantage; it is easy to use and read, and it is useful.

Legal newsletters, webinars and databases

There are many excellent online resources that can support your practice. Three of our favourites, and where you can find many useful legal perspectives on complex questions relating to capacity work, include:

a) Mental Health Law Online (mentalhealthlaw.co.uk): This can be used to find case law relating to specific legal areas (e.g., capacity or best interests) or to particular decision domains. The site provides a summary of the case and usually a link to the transcript and/or to articles or commentary. It's comprehensive, updated regularly and worth exploring.

b) 39 Essex St Chambers (www.39essex.com): Provides a range of useful written resources, including a monthly newsletter that summarises and appraises Court of Protection cases for that period.

c) Browne Jacobson legal services (www.brownejacobson.com): If you do not always have the time or inclination to read legal articles or newsletters, this site hosts regular webinars facilitated by solicitors that can be used as a forum to listen to an account of recent cases and to explore them with health and social care colleagues.

Chapter 4

International perspectives on mental capacity law

Helen Claridge

In this chapter

This chapter explores the law in relation to mental capacity from jurisdictions other than England and Wales. Consideration is given to the ways in which mental capacity and decision-making are approached by Scotland, Northern Ireland and the Republic of Ireland, but also countries further afield. Finally, the unifying themes behind capacity law are discussed, with a nod to likely future progression.

Scotland

Scotland's legislation for mental capacity and decision-making predates that of England and Wales. The Adults with Incapacity (Scotland) Act 2000 ("the Scottish Act") sets out a two-pronged approach in relation to the welfare and finances of those whose decision-making ability is in question.

Much like the Mental Capacity Act 2005 (MCA) in England and Wales, the Scottish Act starts with the general principles intended to influence all actions and considerations under the act. These are (section 1(2)-(5)):

1   **Benefit** – any intervention under the act must benefit the person and be necessary in order to achieve that benefit
2   **Minimum intervention** – any intervention must be the least restrictive option in relation to the freedom of the adult whilst meeting the purpose of the intervention
3   **The adult's wishes and feelings** – present and past wishes and feelings of the person should be taken into account, so far as they can be ascertained, and the person must be offered help to communicate his views
4   **Consultation with relevant others** – the views of people with an interest in the person's welfare, for example, the nearest relative and the primary carer, must be taken into account so far as is reasonable and practicable

5   **Encourage the adult to exercise whatever skills she has** – the person should be encouraged to make decisions, manage her own affairs and develop new skills in order to do so, in so far as is reasonable and practicable.

The Scottish Act sets out that a person is "incapable" of making a certain decision if they are incapable of:

(a)   acting; or
(b)   making decisions; or
(c)   communicating decisions; or
(d)   understanding decisions; or
(e)   retaining the memory of decisions,

by reason of mental disorder or inability to communicate because of a physical disability (section 1 (6)).

Whilst the least restrictive principle and the majority of the factors to be taken into account when assessing capacity have clear equivalents in the MCA, there are noticeable differences between the two Acts. Perhaps the most striking difference is the absence of the best interests principle in the Scottish Act. This is not a casual omission or a failure to appreciate how the law would likely develop in other jurisdictions but a conscious choice by the legislators. Shortly before the first bill was produced, the Scottish Law Commission (1995, at paragraph 2.50) commented on this as follows:

> We consider that "best interests" by itself is too vague and would require to be supplemented by further factors which have to be taken into account. We also consider that "best interests" does not give due weight to the views of the adult, particularly to wishes and feelings which he or she had expressed whilst capable of doing so. The concept of best interests was developed in the context of child law where a child's level of understanding may not be high and will usually have been lower in the past. Incapable adults such as those who are mentally ill, head injured, or suffering from dementia at the time when a decision has to be made in connection with them, will have possessed full mental powers before their present incapacity. We think it is wrong to equate such adults with children and for that reason would avoid extending child law concepts to them. Accordingly, the general principles we set out below are framed without express reference to best interests.

So how does this rejection of best interests look in practice? In terms of medical decision-making in relation to "incapable" adults, the doctor primarily responsible for treatment must issue a certificate giving authority to treat that person under section 47 of the Scottish Act. Nurses, dentists and ophthalmologists can complete section 47 certificates as well, but these will only be valid for treatment in their relative specialities. The professional providing the certificate has to have had the appropriate training (Adults with Incapacity (Requirements for Signing Medical Treatment Certificates) (Scotland) Regulations, 2007). The certificate has a prescribed form, and the authority cannot exceed one year, although there are exceptions to this (Adults with Incapacity (Conditions and Circumstances Applicable to Three Year Medical Treatment Certificates) (Scotland) Regulations, 2007).

In completing a section 47 certificate, the healthcare practitioner confirms that the patient lacks capacity to make a decision about a specified treatment and that it is appropriate for the authority to treat to be granted. A specific Code of Practice provides guidance on the use of these certificates and states as follows:

> Part 5 [of the Act] means that **provided** a certificate of incapacity is issued for the treatment in question and **provided** the general principles of the Act are observed, the treatment may be given. In deciding whether to issue such a certificate, the healthcare practitioner must apply the general principles of the Act. The healthcare practitioner issuing the certificate should be responsible for the provision of the proposed treatment or in a position to delegate appropriately the responsibility for the provision of the treatment.
> (Health and Social Care Integration Directorate, 2010)

Medical treatment "*includes any procedure or treatment designed to safeguard or promote physical or mental health*" (section 47(4)). This is broad definition, which imposes a considerable burden on those treating. However, it is clear that a separate certificate is not required for every single intervention. For instance, the Code of Practice is supportive of appending treatment plans to a certificate when a number of interventions are intended.

There are a number of areas which cannot be covered by the power to treat conveyed by a section 47 certificate – for example, where there is a conflicting court decision, where there is a proxy with powers to consent on behalf of the patient (such as a welfare attorney or guardian) or where there are treatments requiring force or detention. There are certain treatments, including abortion and electroconvulsive therapy, which are subject to increased requirements.

Unless one of these exemptions applies, a valid section 47 certificate conveys an "authority to do what is reasonable in the circumstances, in relation to (the medical treatment in question), to safeguard or promote the physical or mental health of the adult" (Adults with Incapacity (Scotland) Act 2000, section 47(2)). This explicit power to treat is technically different from the MCA, which does not provide a power to treat but does protect an individual from liability if she carries out an act in connection with the care and treatment of the person in question if she reasonably believes that the person lacks capacity and that it is in his best interests. However, the practical effect is the same in that they both provide a lawful way to treat an adult who lacks capacity.

Interestingly, although the clear focus behind the legislation is on prioritising the wishes and feelings of the individual, there is no explicit reference to these in the prescribed form for the section 47 certificate. There is, however, a declaration in the form that the principles of the Scottish Act have been adhered to.

In summary, it is clear from the earlier comments that the Scottish legislators took a conscious step away from best interests and that the procedural requirements differ significantly between the MCA and the Scottish Act. However, the difference between a protection from liability when acting on the assessment of *best interests* versus the power to do what is *reasonable in the circumstances* is the subject of debate, and there is both case law and academic discussion about the extent to which these differ in practice (Ruck Keene and Ward, 2016).

Please note that, at the time of writing, there is an ongoing review of the Adults with Incapacity (Scotland) Act 2000, which is expected to lead to significant reform.

Northern Ireland

Northern Ireland has taken a radical step in its approach to mental capacity law. The Mental Capacity Act (Northern Ireland) 2016 ("the NI Act") received Royal Assent on 9 May 2016. This Act introduces legislation in relation to mental capacity to the country for the first time. However, whilst Northern Ireland could be seen as a late starter in this respect, it simultaneously amalgamates mental capacity with mental health into one piece of legislation including criminal justice provisions as well. This is the first time in the world this has been done.

As with both the MCA and the Scottish Act, the preliminary sections of the NI Act are devoted to general principles. These can be summarised as follows (Mental Capacity Act (Northern Ireland), 2016, section 1(2)–2(2)):

1   Presumption of capacity unless lack of capacity established
2   Lack of capacity is established by reference to provisions in this Act and not determined only on the basis of any condition/characteristic
3   A decision cannot be taken on a person's behalf unless all practical help and support to enable the person to make their own decision has been given without success
4   An unwise decision does not necessarily mean a lack of capacity
5   Where an act is done or a decision made on behalf of a person who lacks capacity, it must be in that person's best interests.

All of these principles have clear mirrors in the MCA principles with the exception of the second principle, although this is also embodied in the MCA. Unlike in the MCA, the NI Act does not have a least-restrictive principle. However, this is included in the best interests criteria, so it is a difference in priority as opposed to approach.

The test for capacity sets out that a person (16 or older) lacks capacity in relation to a matter if, at the material time, the person is unable to make a decision for himself about the matter because of an impairment of, or a disturbance in the functioning of, the mind or brain. A person is unable to make a decision if he cannot:

1   Understand the information relevant to the decision
2   Retain the relevant information for long enough to make the decision
3   Appreciate the relevance of that information and use and weigh that information as part of the process of making the decision; or
4   Communicate his decision by any means.

The NI Act test for capacity clearly borrows much from the MCA but adds that an individual must be able to appreciate the relevance of information to a particular decision as well as use and weigh the information, which adds an important practical consideration.

In short, there are clear parallels between the NI Act and the English and Welsh legislation. However, the decision to "fuse" mental health and mental capacity is unprecedented. The basis for this decision is explained in the review that founded the reform as follows (Bamford, 2007):

> The Review considers that Northern Ireland should take steps to avoid the discrimination, confusion and gaps created by separately devising two separate statutory approaches, but should rather look to creating a comprehensive legislative framework which would be truly principles-based and non-discriminatory.

According to this same review, the system proposed (and now in legislation) demonstrates how "A principled, human rights-based approach moves from public protection as the priority towards safeguarding the rights and dignity of people with a mental disorder or a learning disability."

Health Minister for Northern Ireland, Simon Hamilton, has said that this new legislation is "about reducing the stigma still felt by many people suffering from mental disorder. It will introduce a new rights-based legal framework that applies equally to every adult where there is a need to intervene in their lives on health grounds. . . . [It] will allow for no more separate rules for those with mental health disorder; instead we will have rules that recognise every adult's fundamental right to make decisions for themselves, if they have the capacity to do so" (Department of Health, 2016).

This seems generally to have been well received, with comments that this "fusion approach" is a simplification of a previously "anomalous, confusing and unjust" situation (Harper, Davidson and McClelland, 2016).

> The proposal builds on the strengths of the two existing regimes. Existing capacity-based legislation's strength in giving due weight to autonomy is nearly always counterbalanced by a number of weaknesses. These lie in the lack of sufficient attention to emergency treatment, non-consensual treatment and detention in hospital. But these are exactly those areas in which civil commitment schemes are strong; detention and the use of force are clearly authorised and regulated.
>
> (Szmukler, 2014)

However, there are also concerns about the practicalities of the NI Act. Whilst it has received Royal Assent, at the time of writing it is not yet clear when the NI Act will be implemented in full, although certain provisions were commenced in 2019. Significant secondary legislation is envisaged, and it will need to be supported by a detailed Code of Practice. A report from January 2016 (Northern Ireland Assembly, 2016) set out the predicted costs associated with the Bill as it then was. The report sets out that there will be significant financial implications of this change including staff training, recruitment, an impact on legal aid and the establishment of necessary bodies such as the Office of the Public Guardian. The report set out the estimate of costs as between £76.4 million and £84.7 million for implementation in the first year, with £68.6 million to £76.9 million for recurrent costs.

In summary, the NI Act comes from behind to take a radical step in relation to capacity law. Reception of this ambitious plan has been positive, but the practicalities in implementing it raise concerns about its future.

Republic of Ireland

Until relatively recently the mental capacity legislation in the Republic of Ireland was the Lunacy Regulations (Ireland) Act 1871. This set out a crude system whereby people who were held not to be able to make decisions for themselves were made wards of court and thereby lost the right to make decisions on a wide range of issues.

The Assisted Decision-Making (Capacity) Act 2015 ("the RI Act") was signed into law in December 2015.

The guiding principles of the RI Act for any intervention in respect of a relevant person can be summarised as follows:

1 Presumption of capacity unless proved otherwise.
2 All practicable steps must be taken to assist a person to make a decision for herself.
3 An unwise decision does not equate to a lack of capacity in relation to that decision.
4 An intervention must be necessary in the person's individual circumstances.
5 Any intervention must:

  - Be least restrictive of that person's rights and freedom of action
  - Respect that person's rights
  - Be proportionate to the significance and urgency of the subject matter, and
  - Be applied for the least time possible.

6 The intervener will:

  - Encourage the person to participate as fully as possible in the intervention
  - Give effect to past or present wishes as far as is practicable
  - Take into account the beliefs and values of the person and any other factors the person would be likely to consider
  - If appropriate and practicable, consider the views sought from any person named or nominated to assist in the decision
  - Act at all times in good faith and for the benefit of the relevant person, and
  - Consider anything else which it would be reasonable to regard as relevant.

7 The intervener may consider the views of any person engaged in caring for the relevant person including anyone with a bona fide interest in the relevant person and healthcare professionals.
8 Regard shall be had to the likelihood of recovery of capacity by the relevant person and the urgency of the intervention.
9 The intervener shall not obtain information that is not reasonably required for making a relevant decision and shall take reasonable steps to protect that information from unauthorised access and shall dispose of it when no longer required.

Under the RI Act a person's capacity is assessed on the basis of her ability to under-stand, at the time that a decision is to be made, the nature and consequences of the decision in the context of the choices available at that time. A person lacks capacity if she cannot:

- Understand the information relevant to the decision
- Retain the information long enough to make a voluntary choice
- Use or weigh the information as part of the process of making the decision, or
- Communicate his or her decision by any means.

There are clear echoes in this legislation of the MCA; however, there are a num-ber of key differences. An interesting addition to the principles is the informa-tion governance provision (see number 9), which has no equivalent principle in the MCA. In addition, the RI Act applies only to those 18 and over, as opposed to 16 and over as in the MCA. The Act also avoids "best interests" terminology, instead stressing that an intervener must act "in good faith and for the benefit" of the relevant person (section 7(8)(e)). Perhaps the most striking difference in the RI Act, however, is the absence of the diagnostic element of the test for capacity. This is starkly emphasised in the RI Act with the relevant section of the legislation entitled "Person's capacity to be construed functionally". It is envisaged that the assessment will be less a medical test and more a multi-faceted process with input from a range of sources.

The RI Act sets out detailed provisions as to how decisions are made in relation to a relevant adult. The emphasis is on assisting that individual to make a deci-sion, and the RI Act introduces the roles of Decision-Making Assistant (appointed by the relevant person when he considers that his capacity may be in question, to advise and assist him to make a decision) and Co-Decision Maker (appointed by the relevant person when she considers that her capacity may be in question, jointly to make decisions with her). If the relevant person cannot appoint any such assistance, the Court (Circuit Court) can make either a decision-making order or an order appointing a Decision-Making Representative. This representative could be a family member or a friend of the relevant person or someone from a special-ist professional panel. The RI Act also provides for Enduring Powers of Attorney and Advance Healthcare Directives as well as the appointment of a Director of the Decision Support Service, who will oversee and guide the function of the legislation.

Interestingly, there is no explicit power to treat or protection from liability set out in the Act for clinicians proceeding with treatment of those who are not able to make treatment decisions and have no appointed proxy or relevant Advance Directive. This issue will therefore continue to be covered by the common law, although the RI Act does include some limitations to this; for instance, a decision as to the donation of an organ must be referred to the Court.

Whilst the RI Act has been signed into law and certain sections have been commenced, at the time of writing, it is not clear when the provisions of the Act will be implemented in full. As with the NI Act, much work is required to support the operation of the RI Act.

In summary, the Republic of Ireland has also refused a best interests approach. The gateway is an assessment of capacity that is purely functional, and the approach of the Act is to assist the relevant person to make a decision as opposed to automatically empowering an alternative decision-maker. The Act is not yet fully in force, and it will be interesting to see what the practical impact of this law will be, especially in the early days when patients are unlikely to have made the directives or agreements envisaged in the legislation.

A summary of mental capacity law in the British Isles

It is clear that, even in the British Isles, there are a number of approaches to mental capacity law, which are summarised in Table 4.1.

Table 4.1 Summary of mental capacity law in the British Isles

	Mental Capacity Act 2005 England and Wales	Adults with Incapacity (Scotland) Act 2000	Mental Capacity Act (Northern Ireland) 2016	Assisted Decision-Making (Capacity) Act 2015 Republic of Ireland
Diagnostic test for capacity	✓	✓	✓	✗
Best interests principle	✓	✗	✓	✗
Explicit power to treat without consent	✗ (but protection from liability)	✓	✗ (but protection from liability)	✗
Amalgamation of mental health and mental capacity law	✗	✗	✓	✗

UN Convention of the Rights of Persons with Disabilities

One reason behind the different approaches, particularly in relation to best interests and the diagnostic element to a capacity test, is the Convention of the Rights of Persons with Disabilities (CRPD). The CRPD was formed with the purpose of guarding against the "stripping away of a person's rights through a finding of mental incompetence or by placing people with an intellectual disability under guardianship without process" (Department of Mental Health and Substance Dependence, World Health Organisation, 2004).

The CRPD was adopted by the General Assembly of the United Nations in December 2006 and came into force on 3 May 2008. The UK ratified it in 2009, choosing also to sign up to the Optional Protocol and thereby empowering the Committee to examine individual complaints and undertake inquiries in relation to alleged violations of the Convention. The Republic of Ireland signed up to the CRPD in 2009 and ratified it in 2018.

Article 12 of the CRPD sets out that States Parties reaffirm that persons with disabilities have the right to recognition everywhere as persons before the law and enjoy legal capacity on an equal basis with others in all aspects of life. Article 14 sets out that disability, including mental disability, should not be a criterion for detention.

The CRPD is monitored by the Committee on Rights of Persons with Disabilities. This Committee has commented that "the 'best interests' principle is not a safeguard which complies with article 12 in relation to adults. The 'will and preferences' paradigm must replace the 'best interests' paradigm to ensure that persons with disabilities enjoy the right to legal capacity on an equal basis with others" (United Nations Office of the High Commission Human Rights, 2014, at paragraph 21).

The Committee also comment that a person's status as a person with disability or impairment must never be grounds for denying legal capacity. Clearly, the legal capacity at issue here is wider than that as earlier discussed for the main part. However, the comments are as starkly against a diagnostic differential as they are against a best interests approach.

When reviewing the various legal frameworks for mental capacity and decision-making in tandem with the CRPD, it is clear that the CRPD has influenced the evolution of mental capacity law on an international level. The Republic of Ireland has made much of their new legislation to ensure compliance with the CRPD.

Further afield

Looking further afield, the range of approaches to mental capacity and decision-making continues to be striking.

There are many areas that do not have legislation in relation to a test for capacity and operate only on the basis of common law and professional guidance. One such area is Western Australia (although interestingly, some of the other Australian states and territories have brought in legislation for this purpose). A further notable difference in approach is their use of a surrogate decision-maker to provide consent to treatment of an individual without capacity. Legislation sets out a hierarchy of decision-makers (spouse or partner, then unpaid carer, then nearest relative who maintains a close relationship with the person, then any other person who maintains a close relationship with the person) from whom clinicians will take consent for medical treatment of a person without capacity in circumstances where that person had not previously made arrangements either for an Advance Health Directive or a Guardian (*Guardianship and Administration Act, 1990*).

Western Australia is not alone in automatically turning to a specified person as a surrogate decision-maker. Similar provisions operate in many states of America, France and South Africa to name but a few.

It is clear that the approaches to mental capacity and decision-making are many and varied. If the aim is an internationally uniform approach that is consistent with the CRPD, there is still much work to be done.

Conclusion

There have been a number of changes in relation to mental capacity law and the approaches adopted by different countries in recent years. Until very recently, several jurisdictions have had significant gaps in their legislation in relation to capacity and decision-making. Change is not complete, and it will be very interesting to see how the law evolves in various jurisdictions and the impact this has on the law of England and Wales. Under the influence of the CRPD, it may be that the future for mental capacity law is a removal of the diagnostic test, an increased focus on supported decision-making stepping away from a best interests approach and a fusion with mental health law. Whether and how well such a legislative framework operates on the ground remains to be seen.

References

Adults with Incapacity (Conditions and Circumstances Applicable to Three Year Medical Treatment Certificates) (Scotland) Regulations 2007. Available at: www.legislation.gov.uk/ssi/2007/100/resources

Adults with Incapacity (Requirements for Signing Medical Treatment Certificates (Scotland) Regulations 2007). Available at: www.legislation.gov.uk/ssi/2007/105/contents/made

Adults with Incapacity (Scotland) Act 2000. London: The Stationery Office.

Assisted Decision-Making (Capacity) Act 2015. Dublin: Irish Statute Book.

Bamford, D. (2007). *The Bamford Review of Mental Health and Learning Disability (Northern Ireland): A Comprehensive Legislative Framework.* Belfast: Department of Health, Social Services and Public Safety.

Department of Health (2016). *Global First Legislation to Reduce Mental Health Stigma Passes Final Stage.* Available at: www.health-ni.gov.uk/news/global-first-legislation-reduce-mental-health-stigma-passes-final-stage. Accessed 4 December 2019.

Department of Mental Health and Substance Dependence, World Health Organisation (2004). *The Role of International Human Rights in National Mental Health Legislation*. Switzerland: World Health Organisation.

Guardianship and Administration Act 1990. Western Australia: State Law Publisher.

Harper, C., Davidson, G. and McClelland, R. (2016). No longer 'anomalous, confusing and unjust': The Mental Capacity Act (Northern Ireland). *International Journal of Mental Health and Capacity*, 22, 57–70.

Health and Social Care Integration Directorate (2010). *Code of Practice for Practitioners Authorised to Carry Out Medical Treatment or Research Under Part 5 of the Act* (Paragraph 2.2). Available at: www.gov.scot/publications/adults-incapacity-scotland-act-2000-code-practice-third-edition-practitioners-authorised-carry-out-medical-treatment-research-under-part-5-act/pages/2/

Mental Capacity Act 2005. London: HMSO. Available at: www.legislation.gov.uk/ukpga/2005/9/contents

Mental Capacity Act (Northern Ireland) 2016. London: The Stationery Office.

Northern Ireland Assembly (2016). *Add Hoc Joint Committee of the Mental Capacity Bill Report of the Mental Capacity Bill* (Report: NIA 252/11–16). Belfast: Northern Ireland Assembly.

Ruck Keene, A. and Ward, A. (2016). With and without 'best interests': The Mental Capacity Act 2005, the Adults with Incapacity (Scotland) Act 2000 and constructing decisions. *International Journal of Mental Health and Capacity Law*, 22, 17–37.

Scottish Law Commission (1995). *Report on Incapable Adults* (Scot Law Com No. 151, Paragraph 2.50). Edinburgh: HMSO.

Szmukler, G. (2014). *A Defence of 'Fusion' Law*. Available at: www.mentalcapacitylawandpolicy.org.uk/a-defence-of-fusion-law. Accessed 4 December 2019.

United Nations Office of the High Commission Human Rights (2014). *Committee on the Rights of Persons with Disabilities* (General Comment No. 1).

Part 2

Factors to consider

Chapter 5

Psychosocial aspects of decision-making and the assessment of mental capacity

Dan Ratcliff

In this chapter

We tend not to think too hard about how people make decisions or the processes by which people decide on a particular course of action. As we start to think about this, it becomes clear that there are many influences on our ability to make decisions. Some of these are relevant to the person specifically, and some may be relevant to his physical and social environment. This chapter will help you, as an assessor, think of areas that may influence a person's ability to make a decision and help you think of the right questions to ask.

When people talk about "psychosocial", what do they mean?

All human decision-making, however simple or complex, is influenced by many factors. Assessors think first about a person's cognitive skills. (For example, can she remember what she has been told? Does she understand the words that have been used?) However, there are lots of other factors that may influence a person's ability to make a decision. This chapter uses the umbrella term *psychosocial* to refer to these other factors. This includes not just psychological or personal characteristics of the person, but also the type of environment in which the person has to make decisions.

Capacity assessment as an "explanation" of decision-making ability

As a psychologist, I am often asked to provide explanations for why people behave in a particular way, and this almost always requires me to look at a range of personal and environmental factors and how these interact. Mental capacity assessments are no different, and it is always helpful to think of them not just as a process providing a yes or no answer, but as a way of understanding the influences upon a person's decision-making ability. Linking an adult's personal and social experiences to questions about their decision-making capacity is required to differentiate between adults who may be different or "eccentric" (and make what others consider to be "unwise" decisions) and those who genuinely lack mental capacity (Newberry and Pachet, 2008). We must also not forget that we have a legislative and ethical requirement to understand what the barriers to capacity are and whether these can be removed or reduced to maximise someone's capacity. Capacity assessments will therefore require you, like a good detective, to ask the right questions that will allow you to sufficiently explain why the person has reached a particular decision.

Consider the person's mental health and emotional reactions

Difficulties with mental health can cover a wide range of experience, with differences in the intensity and frequency of symptoms that people encounter. People also differ in the intensity with which they experience, express and regulate their emotions. Some people may suffer from mental health conditions such as anxiety, depression and psychosis where this is the primary diagnosis. Other people may suffer mental health conditions in conjunction with another condition – for example, a person with a learning disability, a long-term health condition such as HIV or a physical disability like spina bifida who also experiences periods of anxiety and depression. In addition, there may be people who will have an intense emotional reaction that is situational and only arises in response to a particular situation – for example, a person with an extreme phobia of needles.

Regardless of whether the person has a mental health condition or a more temporary situational response, the question you have to ask yourself is the same: Does this emotional state (including the person's feelings and beliefs) result in an inability of the person to adequately consider and/or weigh up the necessary information resulting in a disturbance of the mind? The following questions should therefore be considered:

Can the person adequately process information presented to him?

A person's mental state may make it difficult or impossible for him to maintain attention sufficiently or to remember the information in order to make a decision. In some cases, he may have developed extreme avoidance – for example, a person who has developed Post-Traumatic Stress Disorder (PTSD) from a stay in Intensive Care will avoid hospitals or any discussion around this. It may, however, be necessary to discuss this during a capacity assessment, for example, if the person needs to be admitted to hospital for an operation.

If the person can understand and retain the information, can she then weigh it up in a balanced way?

A person's emotional state may lead her to hold very rigid beliefs that are difficult to change even when presented with information or evidence that is contrary to those beliefs (Halpern, 2012). This may result in people placing too much emphasis on some information and too little emphasis on other factors, resulting in an inability to weigh these up adequately. For example, people suffering from depression may be more likely to focus on the likelihood of risks or problems occurring and are less likely, because of "depressive hopelessness", to consider the possible benefits that may occur from making a particular decision (Sullivan and Younger, 1994). Alternatively, in cases where a person has an elevated mood or there is a disturbance with impulse control (for example, mania, frontal lobe injuries and intoxication) he may respond to risks in an overly casual way, giving them insufficient consideration (Hotopf, 2013).

Is the person out of touch with reality?

A person may hold particular beliefs that simply do not reflect reality and distort her ability to weigh up information – for example, a person with severe depression who believes that his partner would be better off if he were dead or a person with psychosis who believes that her treating doctor is trying to harm her and does not believe the medical information that is being given to her.

However, it is important that the beliefs are *directly* linked to the decision in question, as it is possible to have a delusional belief or range of beliefs that do not impact on the specific decision – for example, just because a person holds a delusion that his neighbour is trying to harm him does not necessarily mean he lacks capacity to manage his benefits.

Tip

There is a range of mental health conditions, some of which show complex presentations. It may be helpful to seek advice from people with specialist condition-specific knowledge to assist or advise you in assessing capacity (National Institute for Health & Clinical Excellence, 2017).

Consider the person's decision-making environment

We do not make decisions, for the most part, in a social vacuum. Decisions are often made within a particular social context where other people, including carers, family members and friends are either physically present in the person's life or are a major consideration for the person when she is making the decision. Whilst the influence of others may be positive, assessors should always be aware of the possibility of coercion or undue influence. This can take many forms, from the obvious use of threats and intimidation to less obvious and more subtle forms of persuasion. Such scenarios may be less obvious and will only become clear through careful questioning based upon knowledge of the person's unique social circumstances. As an example, consider John, a man with a learning disability who lives with his mother, but who now wants to move out and live independently in his own home. His mother, who has health problems, does not want him to leave and makes frequent statements such as: "We look after each other; what would happen to me if you left?" Whilst this is not a direct threat, the message that underlies this could be reframed as: "If you leave me then something bad will happen to me."

Most people, regardless of their mental capacity, are subject to some degree of influence from others. However, the question of where the threshold lies for "undue influence" is difficult to work out in practice. Courts have considered the following three questions in helping to decide this. Can the person:

- Take the advice?
- Consider the advice?
- Act upon the advice given?

These three stages make up a process that, depending on the decision in question, may be quite lengthy. For example, there may be several months between John considering the options of housing away from the family home and physically moving out. The period in between may make him particularly vulnerable to the influence of family members (even though they may be well-meaning and have no ill intent).

Consider the person's own characteristics

The impact of the influence of others, however extreme or subtle, cannot be established without some thought given to the person's own style of interacting with others. Individuals may be more susceptible to the influence of other people if one or more of the following are present:

- The person tends to agree with other people or to say "yes" to questions (also called acquiescence)
- The person appears very passive and tends not to express an opinion
- The person expresses negative views about herself or her ability to make changes in her life

- The person changes his views or opinions easily, possibly saying what he thinks the assessor or other people, such as family members, want to hear
- The person defers easily to others generally, or to specific individuals in particular.

In addition to personal characteristics, a person's mental health state may also make her more susceptible to undue influence; for example, a depressed person may show significant passivity. As an assessor, the extent to which you get to know the person will vary greatly. However, in addition to the time you spend with the individual (which may be limited), you may get a sense of the person's interaction style from talking to others or from observations that other people have made.

Don't forget: You must link the person's incapacity to her impairment

It is not sufficient to simply argue that someone lacks capacity because he has been subject to the influence of others. After all, this applies to many people whose capacity we would not query (for example, people without an impairment in mind or brain who are subject to domestic violence). You must conclude that the impairment of mind or brain is the effective, or primary, cause of his inability to make an informed decision, otherwise known as the *causative nexus* (*PC and NC v City of York Council* [2013]). This does not mean that the issue of undue influence is now irrelevant; rather it requires you to answer the following question:

Is the person unable to resist the influence of another BECAUSE OF his impairment or disturbance in the mind or brain?

This question may be less relevant in those cases where it is clear that the impairment of mind or brain causes the incapacity (for example, later stage dementia) even if other factors, such as undue influence, were not present. However, where the causal influences are less clear, the assessor needs to provide an answer to this question. This may be difficult and will likely rely heavily on the professional judgment of the assessor.

The following questions may be helpful to think about:

- Does the person's impairment make it difficult for her to access information relevant to the decision in question? For example, someone with a learning disability may rely on other people (such as care staff or family members) to support her to physically access services or to act as gatherers of information. If carers are obstructive in this process, then the person may not have sufficient access to the required information to help her understand it and weigh it up.

- If the person has sufficient access to the relevant information, is he able to consider it in a way that does not become distorted by the influence of others? For example, a person with cognitive limitations or who is subject to extreme emotional reactions may uncritically accept the opinions of other people and change his mind to fit these alternative views. Furthermore, the person may provide different answers or opinions to different people depending on how these people (including assessors) present information to him.

Tips

- Try to have an understanding of the person's social context prior to the start of the assessment.
- Ask the person about her social networks during the assessment, including her family, friends, contacts and who she regards as being important in her life.
- It is appropriate to enquire of the person what "others" (whoever they may be) think about the decision.
- Consider the "what if" question: "If [person x] was not here what would you do?"
- Does the person have any history of abuse or vulnerability that could provide additional information to support your conclusion?
- Have other people observed any interactions between the person and others that would indicate undue influence?
- When you are undertaking a capacity assessment, think carefully about who you want to be present and where you want the assessment to take place.

Does the person being assessed need to appreciate other people's feelings?

This question may or may not be relevant. Making a decision about having a blood test does not require the person to have any such understanding. Whilst the nurse or doctor may be disappointed with a decision to refuse a blood test, her feelings on the matter are largely irrelevant. However, there are decisions where the person will have to demonstrate, at some level, an appreciation of the impact his actions or decision will have on others. For example:

- A person with dementia having an awareness of the potential stress that her behaviour has on her carer, and the impact this will have on their relationship, when considering where her care needs will be best met

- A person making a will giving away his entire estate to one person at the expense of the other potential beneficiaries must appreciate the impact of this decision on these people (*Banks v Goodfellow* [1870]). As an example, if a person has made a will, leaving his entire estate to only one of his four children, the person must be able to appreciate the impact or effect that this will have on all of the children

- In cases where a person is giving a gift or bequeathing something in a will, the extent of the person's appreciation of others may vary. If the gift is small, then the impact on others is of less importance. However, if the gift is substantial, for example, giving away her house or all of her substantial savings to a close friend, then the person should have an understating of the impact this will have on the other potential donees (*Re: Beaney* [1978]) – for example, how her children will feel and how this will affect their relationship.

The ability to "put yourself in someone else's position" is an area of social cognition that may be impaired in a number of conditions, including autistic spectrum disorder, schizophrenia, acquired brain injury and dementia.

Tips

- Ask the person who this decision would affect. Can he at least recognise that it may impact others?
- If the person cannot identify anyone, and it is relevant, present her with the names and/or photos of people who may be potentially affected and ask her how they would feel or what they would think about the decision.
- Consider using visual supports where there is difficulty with verbal communication or when gathering views from the person is difficult. For example, use visual categories of "happy", "sad", "angry", or "neutral" in which people likely to be impacted by the decision can be placed and people unlikely to be impacted by the decision can be placed. You can then use this as a basis to open up discussion further.

Values and belief systems: What are they and are they relevant?

As well as idiosyncratic beliefs held as a result of a mental health condition (for example, psychosis or depression), people may hold a range of beliefs and values that guide their decision-making. In practice, these can fall into several categories, as follows:

Religious beliefs and values

There is a general understanding, supported by case law, that a decision that might be influenced by religious beliefs should be respected. This is made more straightforward when assessors have a clear understanding of the principles on which the belief system is based (Jacob and Fistein, 2013). For example, in the case of *Re:T* [1992], the Court dealt with the refusal of a blood transfusion by a Jehovah's Witness on religious grounds.

Culturally held beliefs or values

There may be instances where a person holds particular values or beliefs that are not part of established religious doctrine but have arisen in other ways and which are impacting on her decision-making ability. For example, an older woman with moderate dementia who has been brought up to assume that males will always manage the finances in a family insists that her son should continue to manage her money despite evidence of financial abuse (British Psychological Society, 2006). However, this is not a reason to conclude a lack of capacity unless the functional test of capacity is not met and the causative nexus is proven.

Beliefs arising from specific experiences

Individuals may have developed beliefs linked to specific life events that guide their decision-making. These beliefs may, in some circumstances, distort a person's ability to accept, understand and weigh up information. For example, a man with dementia who was physically and sexually abused in a children's home believes with absolute certainty, on the basis of this historical experience, that he will be similarly abused in a care home. This information provides the assessor with some insight into his thought processes. However, whilst this distorted belief may prevent him from weighing up information in a balanced way, once again, this cannot be used to conclude a lack of capacity unless the causative nexus is proven. It has been established in case law that a decision based on a value system or belief (in the absence of a diagnosed condition) cannot be labelled "irrational" and therefore rejected, simply because the majority of people faced with a similar situation would make a different decision (*St George's Healthcare NHS Trust v S, R v Collins* [1998]).

Tips

- Ask the individual if she has any religious, cultural or spiritual beliefs that are guiding her decision-making.
- Ask the individual, or explore by other means, whether he has had any key life events that may explain his decision-making.

- If the impairment is a developed condition – for example, dementia – is there evidence that the guiding belief(s) existed prior to the impairment?
- Try testing out the strength of the person's idiosyncratic belief or her ability to think flexibly. For example:

    o   Offer alternative possibilities or scenarios relevant to the decision and gauge the person's level of recognition or acceptance of these. For example, for a neurological patient with the belief that grass was growing from his torso: "You have told me that you have grass growing on your body but cannot see it. What do you think about this?" or "The doctors have said this feeling is likely to do with the problem with your nerves. Is this possible?"

    o   Establish how likely the person regards a particular outcome. For example, use a scale of zero to 100 where 100 is absolutely certain to occur and zero is certain not to occur. Alternatively, provide a small number of options such as "definitely will happen", "may happen", and "won't happen". This can be written down to aid recall, or it can be presented in a visual manner (see Figure 5.1).

    o   Ask the person what would have to happen to change his belief.

    o   Ask the person what other people would think or believe and, if there is a difference between their opinion and the person's, what is the reason for this difference.

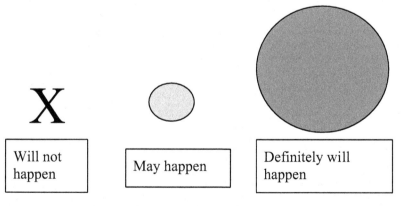

| Will not happen | May happen | Definitely will happen |

Figure 5.1 Visual aid to support establishing how likely a person regards a particular outcome

Summary

A person's decision-making capability can be influenced by a large number of factors. It is important to at least consider the possible existence of such influences and to explore them further as part of a holistic assessment. In addition to considering the possible influence of such factors, think about the following:

- Psychosocial factors are not always obvious and may need to be elicited with particular questions or from wider sources. If a particular belief or value is guiding the person, try to explore the basis for this and its strength.
- If particular beliefs or factors exist that are making it difficult for a person to fulfil the functional test of mental capacity, you must always provide an opinion as to whether this is linked directly to an impairment or disturbance in the functioning of the person's mind or brain (the causative nexus).
- Integrating a range of information helps us not only to determine a person's mental capacity, it also allows us, in some cases, to potentially make changes to maximise capacity (see Chapter 9).

References

British Psychological Society (2006). *Assessment of Capacity in Adults: Interim Guidance for Psychologists.* Leicester: The British Psychological Society.

Halpern, J. (2012). When concretized emotion-belief complexes derail decision making capacity. *Bioethics*, 26(2), 108–116.

Hotopf, M. (2013). The assessment of mental capacity. In Rebecca Jacob and Anthony Holland (eds.), *Mental Capacity Legislation: Principles and Practice.* 1st ed. London: Royal College of Psychiatrists.

Jacob, R. and Fistein, E. (2013). Clinical ambiguities in the assessment of capacity. In Rebecca Jacob and Anthony Holland (eds.), *Mental Capacity Legislation: Principles and Practice.* 1st ed. London: Royal College of Psychiatrists.

National Institute for Health & Clinical Excellence (2017). *Decision Making and Mental Capacity.* Draft for consultation.

Newberry, A.M. and Pachet, A.K. (2008). An innovative framework for psychosocial assessment in complex mental capacity evaluations. *Psychology, Health & Medicine*, 13(4), 438–449. doi:10.1080/13548500701694219.

Sullivan, M.D. and Younger, S.J. (1994). Competence and the right to refuse lifesaving medical treatment. *American Journal of Psychiatry*, 151(7), 971–978.

Case law

Banks v Goodfellow [1870] LR 5 QB 549

PC and NC v City of York Council [2013] EWCA Civ 478

Re: Beaney (Deceased) [1978] 2 All ER 595

Re: T (Adult) [1992] 4 All ER 648

St George's Healthcare NHS Trust v S, R v Collins, ex parte S [1998] 44 BMLR 160 (CA)

Chapter 6

A functional perspective to information-gathering, risk assessment and insight-building

Sam Jones

In this chapter

When gathering the relevant information before a capacity assessment, the individual's level of functioning, along with the foreseeable risks and consequences of the various options, must be taken into account. Often, the benefits of certain options are obvious to the person and his family, but it may require further assessment for the risks to be revealed. This chapter will highlight important aspects to consider in relation to information-gathering and risk assessment. It will also explain the role of an occupational therapist (OT) and how an OT can be invaluable in supporting the individual to develop the skills she needs to increase independence and insight into her difficulties, which will optimise engagement in specific capacity assessments and decisions.

Information-gathering and risk assessment

Understanding the person's current and previous levels of functional performance and her normal physical and social environments allows the professional completing the capacity assessment to construct a baseline against which any changes can be measured. Multi-disciplinary team (MDT) reports and assessments are invaluable here to highlight issues and provide evidence and rich detail to support the process. If you are working alone, it is important to identify the areas in which the person is struggling and consider, if appropriate, postponing the process until supporting evidence from relevant professionals can be gathered. From a functional perspective, this would include an assessment of the various contexts within which the person operates, such as her home or the local community, and whether the person was independent, struggling to cope or dependent on others for support and to what degree.

Understanding the context in which a person functions is essential and is a key part of the assessment process. Information-gathering should incorporate the perspectives of other people in the person's life prior to the assessment to offer greater detail of her situation. An OT may also complete a visit to the person's home environment to identify any factors that will impact on discharge or her continuing ability to manage at her current level. These may include physical elements such as steps, stairs and trip hazards, which may provide challenges due to changes in mobility, and risk factors due to changes in her cognitive abilities, such as the presence of a gas cooker, an over-stimulating environment, a busy main road and location of amenities. The condition of the property may also indicate how the person was managing prior to her admission to hospital.

Whether the individual is an inpatient or seen by an OT in the community, functional assessment within the home context is normally considered to be dependent on risk factors and offers a fuller understanding of the difficulties a person may encounter and her own insight into these. OTs may complete home visits and further interventions jointly with other professionals to gain additional perspectives on potential risks and promote joint decision-making. (See Box 6.1 for examples of situations in which to involve an OT.)

Box 6.1   Indicators for involving an occupational therapist

- When illness, injury or a deterioration in a person's health results in difficulty completing day-to-day tasks or activities of daily living (ADLs)
- When, as a consequence of health changes, the person is unable to function independently, putting her at risk of harm due to a range of factors
- When there is a need to identify risks resulting from a deterioration in function, including physical harm, such as falls; emotional difficulties, including low mood which may lead to self-neglect; vulnerability to abuse or safety issues due to cognitive impairments.

A functional approach to assessment

As assessors of capacity, it is essential to gather information from a range of sources; this may include the outcome of a functional assessment by an OT. The central focus of an OT assessment is to determine a person's strengths and difficulties through observation within a particular task. This should be an activity in which a person normally engages and is therefore meaningful to him (Wilcock, 2006). OTs use function as a means to assess the difficulties the person may now encounter as a result of ill-health and also as a means to remedy them (Wilcock, 2006). The task may be graded to both support engagement and challenge and stimulate the person, whilst being achievable within his current functional abilities (COT, 2014). Consequently, OTs require a broad understanding of the skills required to complete day-to-day activities from a physical, cognitive, sensory and psychosocial perspective (WFOT, 2010). During intervention, OTs will employ a range of approaches to optimise and support learning, skill acquisition and adaptation to overcome barriers to engagement (Grieve and Gnanasekaran, 2008; COT, 2014). (See Box 6.2 for factors to be considered in functional assessments.)

Whilst difficulties stemming from a range of impairments will be explored in a functional context, it is the presence of cognitive and psychosocial issues that are most likely to impact on the person's facility to recognise his difficulties and adapt to a change in his functional status. Problems with insight (or self-awareness) will impact on the person's ability to adapt or understand the need for support (see Chapters 9 and 10 for more information).

Cognitive difficulties impact upon every aspect of a person's life and will influence his ability to complete functional activities, re-learn skills, recognise risks, understand the need for therapy and engage in therapy (Grieve and Gnanasekaran, 2008). If a person is unaware of the shortfall that may exist between his abilities and the demands of the task, this is likely to expose him to being unable to manage and increase the likelihood of harm.

Box 6.2   Key considerations within functional assessments

- What is the task being completed? Is it meaningful to the person? Can the complexity of the task be graded according to the person's ability, for example, can the challenges be increased or reduced?
- How will the environment influence the activity, and can it be adjusted? If the person fatigues, can he sit during the task? Is he able to reach/see/grip items? Is he distracted by noise and activity around him?
- Whilst completing the task, does he need assistance, for example, lifting or reaching objects or having items brought to him? Does he need prompting to initiate the task, to stay on track, sequence and problem-solve, take rests or correct mistakes?
- What can the person do for himself, and where does he need assistance?
- Does he recognise when he needs help? Does he respond to performance errors, correct them and demonstrate new learning?
- What, if any, risks exist when the person performs this task?

During assessment and intervention, an OT will consider:

- The difficulties the person encounters and the strengths he has to overcome these
- How this will impact on his ability to function in other activities
- How to grade the demands of the task and modify the environment to support his continuing engagement, and
- Whether, through further practice, he may regain skills required for independence.

Even at the initial stages of input, the OT will be able to provide the family, carers and the MDT with details of the current level of support a person requires to perform an activity. This may include the need to set up his environment to complete his personal care or provide supervision whilst making a hot drink. These details can support the capacity assessment process, including indicating any risks which are likely to be present should the person be unable to access the appropriate level of support (see Box 6.3). This can help to raise the person's insight, and that of his family, regarding the reality of the different options. It will also help the assessor know what questions to ask in order to determine whether or not the person has the capacity to make the specific decision.

Box 6.3   Information that functional assessments can provide to support the capacity assessment process

- The person's previous level of functioning, habits and routines, support received, and the challenges and demands of the physical and social environments in which he normally operates
- The person's new or altered level of ability following illness or injury including physical, cognitive and psychosocial difficulties. Details of his level of independence and current support requirements within identified activities of daily living
- Risk factors relating to potential options available, including specific examples to indicate difficulties the person experienced within a functional context, which would provide useful evidence for the capacity process
- Ways in which the person's preferred option for the decision have been explored and details of attempts to make it viable, including management of any risks where possible
- Evidence of the support, information and education provided to the person prior to commencing the capacity assessment process, including opportunities to learn in context and insight-building.

Intervention

Rehabilitation

Following a deterioration in someone's functional abilities, rehabilitation offers those with the potential to improve the opportunity to regain skills and/or adjust and develop insight into their changed needs and circumstances. It can also allow time for significant decisions, such as whether a person should go into care, to be made with all due support and consideration. Rehabilitation ensures the person is offered every opportunity to return to her previous level of function, or achieve greater independence, and a referral should be considered by professionals involved in assessing capacity. OTs are employed in a wide range of settings and can provide rehabilitation independently or as part of an MDT at an inpatient or community level, dependent on the person's needs and situation.

Rehabilitation may offer, for example, the opportunity for a person to regain the skills to return home following a hospital admission or to reduce the level of care required to complete activities. It may also allow the person time to recognise, within a supportive environment, her difficulties and the impact on her independence. If a person is struggling to recognise her difficulties, therapists are able to grade the challenges set to support insight and adjustment (Malia and Brannagan, 2012).

Very often, a person with insight difficulties perceives that she is limited only by being in an unfamiliar hospital environment and believes that she will be independent once at home. As part of the rehabilitation process, the OT is able to explore how the person functions within her normal environments (if this is appropriate) in order to provide further insight-building into her difficulties and dynamic learning opportunities to support the capacity assessment process.

Insight-building

It is essential for the MDT to enhance a person's insight as part of rehabilitation to ensure a collaborative approach to the capacity assessment process. If a person has limited insight, he is unlikely to recognise the need to adjust and engage with the process. A crucial aspect of the capacity process requires giving the person relevant information so he can participate in any decision affecting him (Mental Capacity Act (MCA) Code of Practice, 2007). This includes the opportunity to understand his difficulties, the impact these may have on his independence and where risks may occur.

In order for a person to understand how his abilities have been affected following illness, and the impact this will have on his independence, it is crucial to provide the opportunity for him to test them (and to fail in a safe environment) in order to build insight (Malia and Brannagan, 2012). This process can support the person to develop insight into his difficulties, the need to form new skills or, failing that, to adapt and compensate. In addition, it ensures the person is provided with rich information, *in context*, regarding his difficulties and how they may impact on the decision being made during the capacity assessment process.

Insight is developed through the complex interplay of high-level cognitive skills which may be affected by a person's illness or injury. It may also be influenced by denial, a normal emotional response to significant change and loss of function. Cognitive and psychological skills allow a person to understand his current abilities and limitations, to set realistic goals based on these and to recognise and respond to performance errors as they occur.

Risk management

If a person's rehabilitation potential is limited or she has been unable to return to her previous level of functioning, consideration should be given to how she may compensate for her difficulties and manage the risks associated with the decision being made. Risk management approaches can reflect a growing risk-averse culture in services and fear of any potential harm; however, it is recognised that people have the right to make choices and have control over their lives. Such freedoms can involve a degree of risk, but trying to remove potential harm altogether can outweigh the benefits and limit a person's quality of life (DoH, 2007). It is important to consider a person's emotional wellbeing as well as her physical wellbeing when implementing risk management strategies. A key role of professionals working with people undergoing a capacity assessment is to help them understand the implications and consequences of their choices, including relevant risks (MCA Code of Practice, 2007; DoH, 2007).

A core skill of the OT is the assessment and management of risk whilst simultaneously working towards realisation of a person's preferred option (RCOT, 2018). When this aim is to return home or engage in a particular activity, it is the OT's role to identify the intrinsic risks dependent on the person's difficulties and manage them where possible. This may include using alarms or signs to remind the person to take her medications, providing a frame or rail to support bath or shower transfers to reduce the risk of falls or considering the level of support a person receives when completing a specific task and ensuring this is available.

However, not all risks are so easily recognised and managed. A person with cognitive problems may be able to discuss potential difficulties with the MDT before completing an activity but, whilst engaged in it, be unable to recognise and respond to any risks as they arise. An example of this may be demonstrated during a kitchen assessment when bread becomes stuck in the toaster. Prior to the assessment, the person may be able to explain what to do in this circumstance and the potential risks attached; however, when the problem occurs in reality, she may be unable to recognise the risks involved, respond safely or resolve it independently. This may be due to reduced insight and self-monitoring and can indicate difficulties with impulsivity, reduced attention or problem-solving, especially if the problem is slightly different from one she has dealt with before. Immersing the person in this situation would offer the opportunity for the therapist to provide direct feedback and explore these risks in context. It may also provide evidence of the mismatch between the person's perceived and actual abilities. This is a key consideration in the capacity assessment process and requires professionals to ensure that contributing information to the process is robust and gathered from a range of sources, including evidence of the person's actual capabilities, rather than relying solely on the person's own account. (See Chapter 22 for more information.)

An important aspect when considering the person's preferred option during the capacity assessment process, and a key part of OT practice, is the role of positive risk-taking. *Positive* refers to the outcome rather than the risk itself, and enabling these opportunities as part of the therapeutic process can be essential to learning a new skill and making the necessary progress for a person to achieve her goal, for example, to return home (RCOT, 2018). Positive risk-taking is only exercised against a background of significant preparation to adequately reduce the likelihood and impact of harm to the individual (COT, 2015).

OTs have long employed a creative approach to managing risks using a broad range of tools and resources which centre around the person's particular needs and set of circumstances. These include the use of equipment, adaptations and assistive technology, and accessing dynamic packages of support. Managing the risks related to the person's preferred option may make it viable and allow the person to retain or regain greater independence. (See Box 6.4 for more information about accessing OT input.)

It is important to note that risk is not the only factor to be considered in balancing the pros and cons during a capacity assessment. Other important factors, including the person's past and present values, beliefs and wishes, must be given due weight. This can make the assessment process difficult for lone-working professionals. It is, therefore, essential for complex cases and decisions to include information-gathering from a broad range of sources and, where possible, the involvement of other professionals to support the assessment process.

Box 6.4   Accessing occupational therapy input

- OTs work in a wide range of health and social settings, including children and adult services, physical and mental health and learning disabilities.
- OTs can provide assessment in the person's home and community, in hospital and specialist inpatient rehabilitation settings, dependent on the level of difficulty and support she requires.

- OTs with specialist knowledge and experience of working with a particular client group should be considered, where possible, dependent on the person's diagnosis, for example, dementia services or neurology.
- If decisions are to be made regarding a person's functional abilities, for example, whether she requires care or is able to return home, OTs are well-placed to provide opportunities for an individual to develop awareness of her needs and the supporting evidence to enhance the capacity assessment process.
- Finding an OT: www.rcot.co.uk/about-occupational-therapy/find-occupational-therapist or www.hcpc-uk.co.uk/

Summary

- When assessing a person's capacity to make a decision, it is important to gain information from a range of sources
- One fundamental area to consider is a person's functional abilities, especially if they have recently changed due to an illness or injury
- OTs are well-placed to assess a person's functional abilities in her own environment
- OTs can also help build a person's insight and increase his functional skills through rehabilitation to help him realise his goals, as well as enhancing decision-making ability
- Information gathered during assessment and rehabilitation of functional skills will provide you with information relevant to the decision in question and will inform your assessment of capacity
- Important relevant information will include the person's functional strengths and weaknesses, as well as the potential risks of the options under consideration in light of these. It should also include ways to make the person's choice viable through risk management.

References

College of Occupational Therapists (2014). *College of Occupational Therapists' Learning and Development Standards for Pre-Registration Education*. London: College of Occupational Therapists.

College of Occupational Therapists (2015). *Code of Ethics and Professional Conduct*. Rev. ed. London: College of Occupational Therapists.

Department for Constitutional Affairs (2007). *Mental Capacity Act 2005: Code of Practice*. London: The Stationery Office. Available at: https://assets.publishing.service.gov.uk/government/uploads/system/uploads/attachment_data/file/497253/Mental-capacity-act-code-of-practice.pdf

Department of Health (2007). *Independence, Choice and Risk: A Guide to Best Practice in Supported Decision-Making*. London: Department of Health.

Grieve, J. and Gnanasekaran, L. (2008). Occupation & cognitive rehabilitation. In *Neuropsychology for Occupational Therapists: Cognition in Occupational Performance*. 3rd ed. Oxford: Blackwell Publishing.

Malia, K.B. and Brannagan, A.E. (2012). *Insight Workshop Course Notes*. Brain Tree Training. Available at: www.braintreetraining.co.uk

Royal College of Occupational Therapists (RCOT) (2018). *Embracing Risk: Enabling Choice. Guidance for Occupational Therapists*. 3rd ed. London: Royal College of Occupational Therapists.

Wilcock, A. (2006). *An Occupational Perspective on Health*. Thorofare, NJ: SLACK Incorporated.

World Federation of Occupational Therapists (2010). *Statement on Occupational Therapy*. Available at: https://wfot.org/resources/statement-on-occupational-therapy

Chapter 7

Information relevant to the decision

Deciding what the person needs to know, and to what extent, in order to be able to make a decision

Kate Wilkinson and Emma Fowler

In this chapter

This chapter examines what constitutes relevant information in terms of decision-making and mental capacity assessment, as well as the extent to which a person needs to be able to understand, retain and weigh up this information in order to be considered able to make a decision. Using practical examples and guidance from the Mental Capacity Act (MCA) Code of Practice (2007) and existing case law, it aims to provide support in deciding what information is relevant to the specific capacity decision and where to set the threshold. It also examines the concept of retaining information, how difficulties with memory can impact on decision-making and how different types of decision require different thresholds for retention of relevant information.

Introduction

Important questions to consider before carrying out an assessment of mental capacity are:

- What information is relevant to the specific decision?
- To what extent does the person need to understand the relevant information in order to make an informed decision?

In other words, where do we set the bar? What is the threshold for demonstrating capacity? Often these answers are not clear-cut, and it is you, as the assessor, who must decide. Exceptions to this are certain decisions where there has been a judgment from the Court of Protection on a specific issue. In these cases, you can use case law to guide you on what the salient points of a decision are and where the bar should be set (see the following content for examples of these).

What information is relevant?

In the absence of any case law, how do you decide what information is relevant to the decision? There is some guidance in the MCA Code of Practice (2007), which states that relevant information includes:

- The nature of the decision
- The reasons why the decision has arisen/needs to be made
- The foreseeable consequences of deciding one way or another or making no decision (for example, the risks and benefits), and
- Relevant information on all the options available.

Caution

It is important to remember that people only need to be aware of "reasonably foreseeable" consequences of their decisions, rather than every possible eventuality (which would be a case of "setting the bar too high"). This requirement has been established in case law (see *LBX v KLM* [2013]).

Tip

Often it is advisable to get specialist advice, where possible, when deciding on relevant information. Depending on the decision, it may be a good idea to seek the opinion of treating clinicians, doctors, occupational therapists or solicitors. For example, for someone making a decision about care needs after discharge from hospital, the treating team will be able to advise you on most, if not all, of the information relevant to the decision being made (that is, the person's specific difficulties and what help she may need).

The threshold for capacity: Where should the bar be set?

An important principle of the MCA (2005) is that the threshold for understanding and weighing up must not be set higher than we would expect from any member of the general public. Judgments in the Court of Protection, such as *PH and A Local Authority v Z Limited and R* [2011], make it clear that it is unacceptable to set the bar so high that a person with no "disturbance of mind", or someone who has not had her capacity questioned, would struggle to reach it.

So how high *should* the bar be set? If there is no case law to guide you, then it is up to you, as the assessor, to set the threshold before the capacity assessment. To do this, you need to use the "average person on the street" test, as mentioned earlier. In effect, this means that the person does not need to understand all the minute details, but must be able to grasp the "salient facts" (see *LBJ v RYJ* [2010]). The salient facts should be established using guidance from this chapter or case law prior to assessment. An example of a possible threshold for admission to hospital for care and treatment can be seen in Appendix 1.

A helpful exercise

Try this exercise, which is designed to explore the process of deciding on salient points and where to set the bar. Consider the scenario in Box 7.1.

Box 7.1   Case study

Mary is 62 years old and has recently been diagnosed with vascular dementia. She experiences some difficulty with her short-term memory and struggles to find her way around new places. Mary also has high blood pressure and takes medication for this every day but requires prompting to do so. Mary thinks that it would cheer her up to go to Malaga on holiday, as she enjoyed many happy trips there with her late husband. She wants to do this on her own. Her adult daughters are worried about her doing this. They are concerned that she may get confused, for example, at the airport, be vulnerable to exploitation from strangers and forget to take her medication. Mary has agreed to talk to her GP about this decision. Her local practice nurse provided some ideas on how to support her short-term memory and general cognition; however, these strategies have proved to be ineffective so far. A decision has been taken, therefore, to undertake a formal assessment of her capacity to make a decision to go on holiday alone.

Assuming that the decision in this case can be described as, "whether to go on holiday alone" write down on a piece of paper EVERYTHING that might be relevant to this decision and categorise your points using these three headings (try to do this before looking at Figure 7.1.):

• Nature of the decision
• Purpose/Reason why the decision is needed
• Reasonably foreseeable consequences of deciding one way or another or of making no decision at all

Relevant factors

Nature of the decision:

This decision is likely to include booking a flight and a hotel

Packing medication, documents, and clothing

Deciding how you will pay for things

Getting to the airport then to the hotel

Getting around the hotel complex and local area

Communicating with new people

Remembering to take medication

Getting to the restaurant in time for meals

Getting to the airport on time for the flight home

Getting home from the airport

Why the decision is needed:

Mary wants to go on holiday alone
Her daughters have expressed doubt about her ability to understand some aspects of the decision
Support, to date, to make the decision has not been effective

Whether to go on holiday alone

Likely effects (or reasonably foreseeable consequences) of deciding one way or another or making no decision:

Go on holiday alone

Pros: Mary would like a break

She has chosen a place that she loves which has fond memories for her

Mary could have a positive experience and enjoy herself

She could meet new friends

Cons: Mary could be taken advantage of on holiday and, for instance, experience financial or emotional exploitation

She could have a negative experience on holiday, for example, feeling lonely or sad at being away on her own

Mary might forget to take her medication, leading to health problems

She might forget to go for meals at the right times and need to find a solution to this problem

Mary could get lost or disorientated whilst at the airport or at the holiday resort

There would be a financial cost to Mary going on holiday

Do not go on holiday alone

Pros: Mary will save the cost of the trip

There will be fewer risks in relation to remembering medication or travelling alone

Cons: Mary will not have the opportunity to revisit a place she loves which has sentimental value

Mary will not meet new people at the resort or have a break in a different country

There may be consequences to her sense of personal agency and confidence

Figure 7.1 Case study

As mentioned previously, considering what information someone, or an "average man" (*Healthcare at Home Limited v The Common Services Agency* [2014]), might need in order to make a specific decision is a useful tool from the legal sphere and helps to ensure that:

(i)   We include a complete list of "foreseeable consequences". (Notice that the lists in Figure 7.1 include factors that could have either positive or negative consequences for Mary's wellbeing.)
(ii) We do not explore information, or expect a level of understanding, within the context of a capacity assessment that would be considered irrelevant by a non-disabled person making the same decision.

It is important to check your list to clarify whether it is free of irrelevant information and whether your thresholds are appropriate (*PH and A Local Authority v Z Limited and R* [2011]). Thoughtful reflection on the following questions might help your thinking when you analyse your list:

1   Is every factor truly relevant to this decision?
2   Would someone need to understand every nuance and detail of each item on the list, or would a general or broad understanding be sufficient?

If you identify a factor that is not relevant, strike a line through it. If you are unsure, try reframing the question; for example, "If someone were unable to understand a particular factor I've identified, would it matter?" or "If I were making this decision, would I consider this factor to be salient?" Do not be afraid to seek opinions from colleagues to check your reasoning.

It is this list that becomes your "relevant factors" when considering whether a person is unable to understand, retain, use or weigh information as part of the decision-making process.

Tips

- Construct your questions around your "relevant factors" list to ensure that you have covered everything you think is relevant. (See Chapters 3 and 12 for ideas and inspiration for how this could be done.)
- Keep your lists for future assessments that may be similar, particularly ones that crop up again and again. It is unlikely all factors will be identical, as everyone's circumstances are different, but adapting existing lists should be more efficient than starting from scratch.

What does the law say? Case law, relevant information and setting thresholds for specific decisions

There is now extensive case law that can be referred to for help in deciding what information is and is not relevant for various decisions. Some of these, such as consent to sexual relations and the capacity to decide about contact with others, where to live and care are discussed in other chapters (see Chapters 16 and 17). Two that have not been discussed elsewhere are the capacity to decide to marry and the capacity to use the Internet and social media; these are set out next. The document "A Brief Guide to Carrying Out Capacity Assessments", prepared by 39 Essex Chambers (Ruck Keene et al., 2019), and the original legal rulings were used as source material when compiling this information.

Caution

A Court of Appeal ruling (*B v A Local Authority* [2019]) stated that case law rulings on the relevant information for a decision should be "treated and applied as no more than guidance to be expanded or contracted or otherwise adapted to the facts of the particular case" (at [62]). This means that all of the aspects of the case law threshold may not apply to the person you are assessing or that there may be other aspects not included in the case law that may be relevant to the person's specific circumstances.

Marriage

The test for capacity to marry is relatively simple, as the Courts have emphasised that (similar to sexual relations) the bar must not be set so high as to result in discrimination against people whose capacity has been questioned (*Sheffield City Council v E* [2004]).

Case law has also determined that in order to have capacity to enter into marriage, the person must not lack capacity to consent to sexual relations (*LB Southwark v KA (Capacity to Marry)* [2016]).

Relevant:

(These points have been taken from the case *LB Southwark v KA* [2016].)

1   The broad nature of the marriage contract
2   The duties and responsibilities that normally attach to marriage, including that there may be financial consequences and that spouses have a particular status and connection with regard to each other

3   That, at its core, marriage is for two people to live together and to love one another.

Not relevant:

1   Who the person wants to marry; the test for capacity is status-specific, rather than person-specific. Case law holds that the "wisdom" of the marriage is also irrelevant (*A, B and C v X and Z* [2012])
2   The notion that, in a family that practices arranged marriage, the person is much more likely to find a spouse than if he were to attempt this without help (*LB Southwark v KA* [2016])
3   How divorce law and procedure work; a person who lacks capacity to conduct proceedings in relation to any financial aspects of divorce proceedings does not necessarily lack capacity to marry (*LB Southwark v KA* [2016])
4   That, in relation to immigration law, a non-resident spouse may require entry clearance to come to the country the person lives in (*LB Southwark v KA* [2016]).

Social media and the Internet

The use of the Internet and social media were described as "inextricably linked" in two linked judgments and recognised as separate to decisions around contact and care (*Re A (Capacity: Social Media and Internet Use: Best Interests)* [2019]; *Re B (Capacity: Social Media: Care and Contact)* [2019]). Therefore, the relevant information here applies to the use of both the Internet and social media but can be contracted or expanded, as appropriate, to the person's circumstances.

Relevant:

1   Information and images (including videos) that you share on the Internet or through social media could be shared more widely, including with people you do not know, without you knowing or being able to stop it
2   It is possible to limit the sharing of personal information or images (and videos) by using privacy and location settings on some Internet and social media sites (see the next paragraph)
3   If you place material or images (including videos) on social media sites which are rude or offensive, or share those images, other people might be upset or offended (see the next paragraph)
4   Some people you meet or communicate with ("talk to") online, who you do not otherwise know, may not be who they say they are (they may disguise, or lie about, themselves); someone who calls himself a "friend" on social media may not be friendly
5   Some people you meet or communicate with ("talk to") on the Internet or through social media, who you do not otherwise know, may pose a risk to you;

they may lie to you or exploit or take advantage of you sexually, financially, emotionally and/or physically; they may want to cause you harm

6   If you look at or share extremely rude or offensive images, messages or videos online you may get into trouble with the police because you may have committed a crime (see the next paragraph).

Mr Justice Cobb added some further points to clarify the threshold described earlier:

1   In-depth knowledge of privacy settings is not required but the person must be "capable of understanding that they exist and be able to decide (with support) whether to apply them" (at [29])
2   *Sharing* means "sending on an email, offering on a file sharing platform, uploading to a site that other people have access to, and possessing with a view to distribute" (at [29])
3   The words *rude or offensive* were chosen because they could be "easily understood by those with learning disabilities as including not only the insulting and abusive, but also the sexually explicit, indecent or pornographic" (at [29])
4   The last point (number six) is not meant to be a statement of criminal law but highlights the understanding that one should not go searching for this material and should move away from it if one comes across it accidentally. "A person should know that entering into this territory is extremely risky and may easily lead a person into a form of offending" (at [29]). It may be more relevant to general Internet use but can be relevant to using social media as well.

Not relevant:

1   That Internet use can be addictive
2   That viewing extreme information, images or videos online could cause the viewer distress.

Providing relevant information

> **Caution**
>
> Once you have established what information is relevant to the decision and determined where the bar should be set, do not forget to provide all of it to the person *before* you undertake the capacity assessment. The information should be provided in the manner best suited to the person in order to enhance her decision-making ability. (See Chapter 9 for more guidance on how to do this.)

Retaining information

As with understanding and weighing up, retention can also be a matter of degree. A question to ask in every assessment is: How long does a person have to be able to retain salient information? This is a particularly important consideration when assessing people with memory problems. The answer is often that it depends on the decision, especially whether it is a one-off decision or an ongoing one. Both scenarios will be considered here.

A one-off decision

Examples of one-off decisions include discharge destination on leaving hospital, who to leave money to in a will or whether or not to have an operation.

Myths

- A person must be able to retain information between capacity assessments or for at least a few days.
- A person does not have capacity if she cannot remember having the conversation the next day or later the same day.

In the case of a one-off decision, a person only has to remember information long enough to weigh it up during the assessment and use it to make a decision. It does not matter if he cannot remember being asked about it next day, or even an hour later. However, in such cases, the assessment would need to be repeated to demonstrate that he comes to same decision, using similar reasoning, each time. In other words, that his reasoning is consistent.

Ongoing decisions

Examples of ongoing decisions include whether or not to accept care from support workers (as this is a decision made every day or several times a day when the carers call), whether or not to take a certain medication and managing your finances.

Caution

Unlike one-off decisions, in the case of ongoing decisions, ability to retain information for longer than a few hours or several days may be necessary.

As ongoing decisions are effectively being made repeatedly, every day, they would require the person to be able to retain the relevant information (for example, why she needs support or why she needs the medication) over time. Otherwise, the information would need to be provided every time a decision had to be made, which may not be practical.

Take home points

- Even severe memory problems do not necessarily mean someone cannot make an informed decision on a one-off basis.
- Support can be provided for one-off decisions, but this is often not practical for ongoing decisions.

Other implications of memory problems

We have just examined how anterograde memory problems (difficulty making new memories since the onset of a dementia or a brain injury, such as remembering what happened yesterday or this morning) impact on a person's capacity. Retrograde amnesia (for example, poor memory for things that happened before a brain injury) can also impact on capacity. In some circumstances (but not always), a person will need to remember past events in order to make an informed decision in the present.

The following case study (Box 7.2) illustrates this in the context of a decision about discharge destination.

Box 7.2 Case study

Bob had a severe hypoxic brain injury after a heart attack. He is currently in a rehabilitation unit and is being asked to make a decision about discharge destination. At the time of his injury, he was living alone in a flat after he and his wife separated 12 months previously. His wife and teenage children have been supportive during his time in the unit and have visited, but his wife does not want to resume their relationship. Unfortunately, Bob's brain injury has left him unable to clearly remember the past 18 months of his life. Therefore, he does not remember that he and his wife have separated and, although he is reminded, it is not something he is able to retain.

The discharge options he is being asked to consider are:

- Home (where he lived at the time he was admitted to hospital) with four care calls per day
- A supported living house with other people who have had a brain injury.

So, what information would Bob need to understand and retain to make this decision? First, he needs information on the supported living home and what support would be offered there, as well as what he needs support for. However, he also needs to understand what "home" means now. His inability to remember his separation and where he was living at the time of admission means he thinks "going home" means going home to live with his wife and children in their family home, but what it really means is he will be returning to a one bedroom flat with carers calling in briefly four times a day to offer support. During the capacity assessment, his inability to retain information about his change in circumstances (even with support), impacted on his ability to weigh up the options and, therefore, he was determined not to have capacity to decide on discharge destination.

The following case study further illustrates the importance of memory for past events.

Box 7.3   Case study

Marjorie has dementia. A capacity assessment about her ability to manage her daily finances was carried out, and she was found to lack capacity in this respect. Therefore, she decided to create a Lasting Power of Attorney (LPA) to let someone else look after her finances but, following discussions, there were some concerns about her memory and how this would affect her decision-making. An assessment to determine whether or not she has capacity to make this decision was undertaken.

Marjorie was adamant that she would like her son to take care of her finances. However, staff and other family members were concerned about this, as Marjorie's son had stolen money from her in the past and Marjorie was very upset by this at the time. Unfortunately, due to her advancing dementia, Marjorie could not remember these events and denied that it had happened when she was reminded, which meant that she was using inaccurate information to make her decision. Due to this, it was decided that Marjorie did not have capacity to make this decision.

Summary

- It is the job of the person assessing capacity to determine what information is relevant to the decision in question.
- The assessor must often decide to what extent the person needs to be able to understand, retain and weigh up the information in order to be able to use it to make a decision.

- Case law exists which states what constitutes relevant information and thresholds for a number of specific decisions. If your assessment relates to one of these decisions, then you should follow this guidance and adapt it as necessary to the specific situation relating to the person whose capacity you are assessing.
- The Code of Practice states that relevant information includes the nature of the decision, the reasons why the decision has arisen, the reasonably foreseeable consequences of deciding one way or another or making no decision (for example, the risks and benefits), and relevant information on all the options available. In the absence of case law, the assessor will need to decide the detail of this relevant information.
- Often it is advisable to get specialist advice, if possible, when deciding on what information is relevant to the specific decision.
- The threshold for how long a person has to retain relevant information varies depending on the nature of the decision, particularly whether it is a one-off or ongoing decision.
- Memory problems and problems retaining information can also have an impact on a person's ability to understand and weigh up relevant information in order to make a decision.

References

Department for Constitutional Affairs (2007). *Mental Capacity Act 2005: Code of Practice*. London: The Stationery Office.

Ruck Keene, A., Butler-Cole, V., Allen, N., Lee, A., Kohn, N., Scott, K., Barnes, K. and Edwards, S. (eds.) (2019). *A Brief Guide to Carrying Out Capacity Assessments*. 39 Essex Chambers. Available at: www.39essex.com/mental-capacity-guidance-note-brief-guide-carrying-capacity-assessments

Case law

A, B and C v X and Z [2012] EWHC 2400 (COP)

B v A Local Authority [2019] EWCA Civ 913

Healthcare at Home Limited v The Common Services Agency [2014] UKSC 49

LB Southwark v KA (Capacity to Marry) [2016] EWCOP 20

LBJ v RYJ [2010] EWHC 2664 (Fam)

LBX v KLM [2013] EWHC 3230 (Fam)

PH and A Local Authority v Z Limited and R [2011] EWHC 1704 (Fam)

Re A (Capacity: Social Media and Internet Use: Best Interests) [2019] EWCOP 2

Re B (Capacity: Social Media: Care and Contact) [2019] EWCOP 3

Sheffield City Council v E [2004] EWHC 2808 (Fam)

Chapter 8

Introducing a capacity assessment to the person, family and carers

Dan Ratcliff

Introducing and explaining a capacity assessment could reasonably be expected to be relatively straightforward. However, in reality, it is one of the more difficult aspects of assessing mental capacity and can often feel particularly awkward. The following points are a guide to help address some of the tensions that can arise at this early stage of assessment.

Introducing the assessment to the person

First, you must allow sufficient time at the start of the assessment to explain the process and make the person feel at ease. Starting the "core questions" too early will risk producing inadequate or unreliable information. How you explain the nature and process of mental capacity assessments will be different depending on the person's level of functioning. This is information you should, ideally, have before walking into the room with the person. However, regardless of how you "pitch" the explanation, you must at least inform the person of the decision to be addressed. The explanation should also reflect the aim of the assessment, which is to decide on whether the person has the ability to make the decision. You should therefore be careful not to give such "woolly" explanations that completely hide the purpose of the assessment, for example, simply saying to the person: "I want to talk to you about where you would like to live". This may make the assessor and the person feel OK, but it is far from transparent.

It is preferable to try and be clear about the purpose of the assessment: "I have been asked to assess your capacity/ability to make decision X". You can then follow this up with further explanation that is more person-centred, for example: "It is important that I understand your views about X".

It is vital that you give the person permission to talk about risks associated with decisions. Many people believe that talking about risks is a bad thing and will "go against them". The opposite is true, and this should be made clear to the person: "It is important that you tell me the bad things/risks as well as the good things about

X. This is important as it helps me understand if you can make the decision". Similarly, people may be reluctant to tell you the good things about a decision-making option, for fear that this will be taken by others as them expressing a preference for that option. Therefore, you should also make it clear at the start of the assessment, that it is important that the person tells you about the benefits of *all* options. Furthermore, you should make it clear that talking about benefits of an undesirable outcome (for example, if the person does not want to live in a care home), does not mean that this will be seen as the person's preferred choice.

It is not absolutely necessary to explain the details of the law and any requirements from relevant case law. However, if you feel the person would grasp this and it may aid the process, then this would be reasonable.

Introducing the assessment to family and carers

Many family members or carers struggle with the mental capacity process and, in particular, the concept of "unwise" decision-making. Parents or carers of younger adults also struggle with that transition from making decisions for their child to the mental capacity and best interests process relevant to them as new adults. It is important from the outset that you explain the legal requirements in simple language and your role as an assessor within this. There is a risk of depersonalising the experience for carers through excessive legal "justification" and to come across as ignoring their concerns. Therefore, it is important to explore their concerns and discuss potential response options – for example, if someone is found to have capacity to stay living at home (as opposed to moving into a care home), telling his family the ways in which services could look at helping to mitigate risks. Similarly, if a lack of capacity is found, then the best interests process will take into account a range of views, including those of the family. Being made aware that there is a process to support both "yes" or "no" outcomes to a mental capacity assessment can ease tension from the outset.

Carers or relatives may ask to be part of mental capacity assessments as they know the person and can help with understanding, communication and reducing anxiety. Assessors need to think carefully about this. In some cases, this may be helpful; however, in many situations this is not advisable, as the presence of a carer may influence the person's reporting.

Should assessors be independent?

Is a mental capacity assessment better or more reliable when delivered by a practitioner who knows the person well or by a person who is unknown? Again, whilst knowing the person may bring benefits for aiding communication and making the person feel relaxed, there are pitfalls. For example, the person may feel a desire to give answers that she thinks will please the assessor. Furthermore, there is evidence that assessors who know the person well may, consciously or unconsciously, make decisions on capacity not purely on her functional ability, but will make a determination on capacity that fits with what they think is best for the person. For example, finding a lack of capacity so that a best interests decision can be made in order to protect the individual (Ratcliff and Chapman, 2016). In decisions that are significant or contentious, some services recommend that two assessors attend, one who knows the person and one who is independent (Farmer, 2016). Whilst this may be helpful, it is likely that in cases where mental capacity is "borderline" or difficult to work out, the important issue is producing a robust mental capacity assessment that can stand up to scrutiny. This will not necessarily be accomplished by simply having two assessors present. From my experience, the more important issue is having an assessor with the relevant expertise who can ensure the functional test is fully evidenced and that the person's capacity has been maximised to an extent reasonably achievable in the time frame. In contentious or difficult cases, having assessors involved who can add sufficient expertise in this area, for example, a clinical psychologist or a speech and language therapist, will prove helpful.

References

Farmer, T. (2016). *Grandpa on a Skateboard*. 2nd ed. Great Britain: Rethink Press.

Ratcliff, D. and Chapman, M. (2016). Health and social care practitioners' experiences of assessing mental capacity in a community learning disability team. *British Journal of Learning Disabilities*, 44(4), 329–336.

Chapter 9

How to provide relevant information and enhance mental capacity

Kate Wilkinson

In this chapter

This chapter examines how to enhance a person's decision-making, and therefore mental capacity, by careful consideration of methods of providing relevant information and assessment techniques. It highlights the importance of tailoring any adjustments made to the person's particular circumstances and abilities, for example, providing information in the most appropriate format to support decision-making such as verbal, written or pictorial forms. It also highlights the importance of timing and location of assessments and discusses how to make appropriate adjustments to enhance a person's capacity, taking into account sensory issues, physical problems (for example, pain) and speaking English as a second language. It also goes into detail regarding methods of overcoming cognitive and communication problems. (See Chapter 11 on communication for additional guidance on this.) Finally, it provides guidance on engaging the person in the process and ways of getting the best from him. This includes, rapport-building, the pros and cons of having a second person present for support and overcoming barriers to engagement such as anxiety or fixed beliefs regarding the issues in question.

Introduction

Principle two of the five statutory principles of the Mental Capacity Act 2005 (MCA) states that, "A person is not to be treated as unable to make a decision unless all practicable steps to help him to do so have been taken without success" (Section 1(3)). Therefore, when assessing mental capacity, you should make as much effort as possible to enhance the person's capacity. In addition, Section 3(2) of the MCA states, "A person is not to be regarded as unable to understand the information relevant to a decision if he is able to understand an explanation of it given to him in a way that is appropriate to his circumstances (using simple language, visual aids or any other means)."

In other words, the steps taken to enhance capacity must meet each individual's specific needs. Ways of providing information and carrying out assessments that support a person's decision-making ability, with reference to the MCA Code of Practice (2007), are detailed next.

Providing relevant information

An important starting point for any assessment is providing the right information. It is essential that a person is provided with all the relevant information necessary for him to make the decision *before* the assessment. The way we provide this information can enhance an individual's capacity and has the potential to hamper his decision-making if we do not get it right.

Cautions

- Never assume that the person has all the information he needs to make an informed decision, even for a simple decision or a decision he has made before – for example, to have a flu jab. Always ask why he said yes or no.
- Remember, relevant information includes information about *all* alternatives if there is a choice to be made (MCA Code of Practice, 2007).

Guidance on what information is relevant to a particular decision can be found in Chapter 7, along with insights regarding the extent to which a person needs to understand and weigh up the information (thresholds for capacity).

Any information should be provided in the format best suited to support a person's understanding and reasoning. Some important points to remember:

- Information should be conveyed in simple language (either written or verbal). For written, it should be in an "easy read" format.
- It should be in a person's first language (for those with English as a second language). Note, this is not always necessary if the person remains fluent in English.
- In many circumstances it is good practice to give information verbally, then follow up with written information (unless people have literacy problems). This is particularly relevant for those with memory problems as it allows them to refer back to it after information-giving sessions.
- For people who cannot read well or have a condition where written or verbal information is difficult to understand, pictures can be used alongside verbal

communication. (See Chapter 11 for detailed information on how visual support can be used to enhance capacity.)

- o   For example, some people with memory problems can remember visual information better than verbal. They may have had a cognitive assessment completed that provides this information (make sure you request a summary of the results of any such assessments to help you). Others may have family members or carers who might be able to tell you which they prefer.

- For people with specific sensory problems such as sight and hearing difficulties, you will need to make the relevant adjustments. For example, providing an audio recording of you explaining information for them to review after the session.
- Information-giving sessions should be repeated as many times as necessary, provided the person is making progress in his understanding and reasoning and you believe he has potential to demonstrate capacity. Time consideration should not be a barrier unless the decision is an urgent or time-limited one.

When and where to assess

The "when" of assessments is important. People with conditions affecting cognition or fatigue levels (for example, dementia or multiple sclerosis) can often function differently at different times of day.

Tips

- Find out when the person normally functions best and try to carry out the assessment then. If you cannot find this out, then it is a good idea to repeat the assessment at a different time of day to see if this improves his decision-making ability.
- When scheduling appointments, try to avoid the introduction of any time pressure, however subtle. For example, the knowledge that a mealtime or outing is approaching can impact on a person's ability to engage with and focus on the capacity assessment.

It is also important to take into account the effect of any medications and the timings of these. Some medications reduce cognitive ability (for example, by having a sedative affect) and some improve it (for example, pain medication or Parkinson's medications). Get advice from family or medical staff on appropriate timing around the person's medication regime. (See Chapter 26 for more detail on fluctuating capacity.)

It is good practice to do more than one assessment before forming your opinion, unless the decision is very urgent or it is an emergency situation. There are a number of reasons for this:

- You may have caught the person on a "bad day" or her capacity may fluctuate due to an unstable medical condition. As laid out in the MCA, you need to give people as much opportunity as possible to demonstrate capacity, so it is often not good practice to conclude that a person lacks capacity after only one session. (See Chapter 26 for further information regarding fluctuating capacity.)
- Repetition allows you to check carry-over of information from session to session, as well as consistency in responses, ensuring that she is reaching the same decision each time (and in a broadly similar way). This is especially important with ongoing decisions, such as managing finances and accepting support for daily living.
- Sometimes an initial assessment, in which you conclude the person lacks capacity, can give you ideas on ways to support a person in a subsequent assessment in order to overcome some of the difficulties she is experiencing and thus support her to demonstrate capacity.

The "where" is also important. The assessment should take place somewhere quiet with no distractions and somewhere the person will be more at ease (Myron et al., 2008). This may be her own home (remember to turn off the television or radio or any other background noise to maximise ability to concentrate and take in information) or in a hospital ward or other busy place (in which case, a side room should be used if possible, for the same reasons). (See Chapter 11 for more details on creating a "communication and cognition friendly environment".)

Privacy is also important, so the person has the opportunity to speak freely. Whether or not to include someone who the person knows well in the assessment will be discussed in the section that follows.

Making appropriate adjustments

Use the following points as a guide:

- Check to see if a person has sensory difficulties and adjust the assessment accordingly. Ensure glasses and hearing aids are worn where needed. In one situation, a person with mild dementia was deemed not to understand information because he did not have his hearing aid in! Equally, if a person has problems with hearing in one ear or sensory inattention, make sure you sit on his "good side".
- Think about whether there are any other physical problems that may impact on capacity. For example, is the person in pain? If so, try to ensure pain relief is given prior to any assessment where possible.
- Is English the person's first language and, if not, does she need an interpreter?

Myth-busting

You do not need an interpreter if a person has spoken English well for a number of years, even if it is not his first language.

It is good practice to use an interpreter regardless. When someone develops cognitive problems (either due to injury or illness, including dementia), he can often retain better thinking skills and understanding in his "mother tongue", as this is more robust in the face of cognitive decline. This may not be obvious at first, and the person may decline an interpreter, thinking he is fine using English. However, the concepts discussed in a capacity assessment are often abstract and sometimes difficult to understand, and so even people with reasonable day-to-day English may struggle to understand the words being used or miss details in the explanation. However, if someone is managing well an interpreter may not be required.

Tip

If a person with English as a second language is found not to have mental capacity for a certain decision, repeat the assessment with an interpreter to check whether this changes when using her original language.

Myth-busting

You do not need to use an interpreter if the person has a family member or friend to translate for her.

It is good practice to use an independent interpreter to avoid any bias or potential undue influence on the person being assessed. It is possible that the family member may be "filling in" any gaps in the person's reasoning and covering up any difficulties with understanding, memory or weighing up. Bear in mind you would be unaware of any bias or undue influence due to the language barrier. However, it is also useful to discuss the point of the capacity assessment with the independent interpreter beforehand so that questions and answers are interpreted directly and there is no cultural influence exerted on the person by the interpreter. Assessing whether a person is making a decision free from third-party influence is an essential part of a capacity assessment.

Overcoming cognitive problems

Cognitive problems can often be remedied before, during and after the capacity assessment. (See Chapter 10 for more information on cognitive problems). Bear the following general points in mind. (See Appendix 2 for a list of possible strategies to try to overcome common cognitive and other problems that impact on capacity.) They are also relevant to people with language difficulties. (See Chapter 11 or more information on overcoming such problems.)

- You will need to repeat information a number of times to give the individual the best chance of demonstrating capacity, particularly if she has memory problems.
- Be careful not to overwhelm her with too much information. Only include what is necessary to make an informed decision. Be concise.
- Avoid complex questions or "compound" questions (two or three questions in one). This is good practice in capacity assessments anyway, but it is particularly important when people have cognitive or language difficulties.
- During the assessment use simple language and speak slowly enough for the person to understand you and take in all the relevant details (especially important if a person has slowed processing speed). Give her plenty of time to process your question and form a response before she replies.
- Break verbal information down into small, "digestible" chunks, and ask her to repeat back information to check she has taken it in.

Caution

A person with very significant cognitive difficulties can often repeat or echo your words, but this does not mean she has understood the information or is weighing it up to make a decision. In fact, it can mean she is having difficulties and that this is a strategy she has developed to mask them. You will need to ask further questions to check this.

Reducing the abstract nature of decisions

Some people have difficulties with abstract thinking due to cognitive problems. For example, some people struggle with imagining or placing themselves in a situation they have never experienced. In case law, the ruling from *LBX v KLM* [2013] emphasises the importance of using tangible techniques (things people can see or touch) to support people grappling with abstract concepts.

Tips on how to reduce the abstract nature of decisions:

- Consider the case of deciding where to live. If you were considering moving house, imagine how important it would be for you to visit first and how difficult such a decision would be without seeing it. Therefore, prior to assessing capacity for such a decision, the person should be taken to view the house/ home if a specific one has been chosen. If this is not practical, consider whether taking photos or a virtual video tour would support her decision-making.
- Consider the more complex decision of someone who has experienced a dramatic change in abilities due to a sudden cause (for example, a traumatic brain injury) needing to make decisions about discharge destination and care needs. People often understand and accept that they have difficulties that require care and certain facilities when they are in the hospital but think they will be fine when they go home, as they have not experienced being at home with their current difficulties. This may be due to a newly acquired difficulty with thinking in the abstract (although it could also be due to psychological denial or holding out hope for such a change). A way to support the person's reasoning would be to organise a home visit so that she can experience her new difficulties in her previous environment.
- The use of mime and non-verbal demonstrations can help someone understand what is being discussed. For example, during a joint assessment, an occupational therapy colleague demonstrated falling out of a wheelchair and attempting to get up (while recreating the person's physical problems). This was for a person who was at risk of falling, but who had not experienced this and was struggling to imagine it.

Increasing the level of structure of assessments

This can often help a person with cognitive problems, particularly if he has difficulties with executive functioning. There are a number of ways of doing this, including using closed questions.

Myth-busting

You cannot use closed questions in a capacity assessment.

People with cognitive problems, particularly executive functioning difficulties, often find open questions difficult (and sometimes impossible) to answer. This is due to the lack of structure and the difficulty searching for information in their heads. People with speech and language problems can also struggle with open questions. It is true that it is good practice to begin with open questions and that you need to avoid asking leading questions. However, do not be afraid to try closed questions if the person appears to be struggling. The best technique for this is often the "funnel" technique, where you begin with open questions and narrow them down as needed until you are at closed questions. Sometimes, if a person has verbal communication difficulties, you may be asking questions that only require a yes or no answer. In such cases it would be good practice to seek advice from a speech and language therapist. (See Chapter 11 for examples of the funnel technique and further guidance on asking closed questions.)

Caution

If you are using yes or no answers or closed questions you need to guard against leading the person and against affirmative bias. Affirmative bias is a tendency for people to agree/say yes to people in positions of power and authority. You can avoid this by repeating a question but rephrasing it in a way that requires the opposite answer and checking the consistency of the person's answers. For example:

- Do you need help with getting dressed?
- Are you able to get dressed on your own?

If the person answers yes to both questions, he may not understand the question or know the correct answer.

Other ways of increasing structure include:

- Using decision trees, which can be helpful as a visual aid. They can help make the decision less abstract and mean that the person has to hold less information in his mind at one time so that he can follow the decision through to possible consequences. (See Figure 9.1 for a simplified example. This is not the same as a list of pros and cons.)
- Providing multiple-choice options for questions, including providing written lists of answers for the patient to choose from – for example, a list of tasks that a person finds difficult or needs support with or a list of potential risks

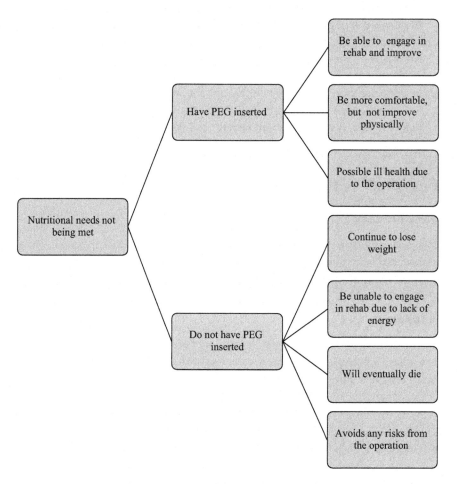

Figure 9.1 A simplified decision tree for the decision of whether or not to have a PEG (feeding tube) fitted

that he can select from. Having written information to refer to can reduce the cognitive load of having to keep lots of information in his head at one time. If doing this, it is a good idea to have some distractor items on the list which you know the person does not have problems with; this will help to check the accuracy and consistency of his responses. (See an example of such a list in Appendix 3.)

•   Providing a written or verbal list of pros and cons for the decision in question and asking the person to select the ones that are relevant to him or that he agrees with so that he can then weigh them up.

Myth-busting

People need to generate their own pros and cons to demonstrate capacity.

This is not the case. Generation of pros and cons for the different options of a decision can be very difficult for a person with cognitive problems. It is fine to generate a selection for him and discuss whether or not he considers these to be accurate and relevant benefits and disadvantages of his situation.

Engaging the person effectively in the process

Transparency

It is good practice to be transparent and tell the person the nature and purpose of your assessment before you start. You should do this using simple, jargon-free language. (See Chapter 8, on introducing capacity assessments for more detail on how to do this.)

Rapport

You do not always know the person you have been asked to assess, and you may never have met her before. In these cases, you will need to make a connection and build a rapport quickly in order to gain her trust and so get the best out of her in terms of capacity. Rapport has been shown to be an important factor in enhancing capacity (Myron et al., 2008). Some ways of doing this include:

- Introducing yourself and explaining the purpose of the assessment. (See Chapter 8 on introducing capacity assessments for further detail.)
- Having a little conversation first, unrelated to the assessment. Try to find out things she enjoys or is interested in to give you something to talk about. If possible, try and find something you have in common (but only if this is genuine).
- Trying to stay friendly and approachable, despite the serious nature of the assessment. Reducing the power imbalance as much as is possible will help with rapport-building, as will adopting an open, non-judgmental stance.
- Using active listening skills to hear any concerns or opinions she has about the process and the decision in question.

Overcoming the impact of anxiety

Often people will be anxious, often very much so, particularly if the stakes are high (for example, if they have strong feelings against what is being suggested as one of the options, such as moving out of home or accepting help with finances). This can have a huge impact on a person's thinking processes, particularly if he is already cognitively impaired. It is important to recognise when someone is very anxious and to support him to feel calmer. Attempting to establish good rapport and a feeling of trust between you will help. It is also a good idea to acknowledge and normalise feelings of anxiety, as well as taking regular breaks and checking how he is feeling. You could also teach him simple breathing and relaxation techniques to try and reduce his level of autonomic arousal. Sometimes having someone a person knows well with him may help. However, this is not always appropriate, see below for further discussion.

Privacy vs. having someone accompany the person

People should always have the opportunity to choose to have a capacity assessment alone. However, in some circumstances it can be helpful for a person to be accompanied by someone who knows her well and who is able to support communication or reduce her anxiety (for example, a speech and language therapist or family member). Indeed, the MCA Code of Practice (2007) suggests involving someone the person trusts and who knows her well as a way of enhancing capacity. However, caution should be exercised here, as privacy can be very important. Depending on who is with her, this could increase anxiety or make it difficult for her to say what she needs to for fear of what the other person might think. This can include an interpreter from her own culture or of a different gender. Remember the Act states that to conclude someone has capacity, you must be confident that her decision-making is free of undue influence from others. Therefore, you must balance this concern with the potential benefit of having someone there to support her. It might be necessary to assess twice, once with and once without support, and compare the two sessions. An additional concern is that sometimes the person looks to her companion to answer questions and allows him to do this because it is easier than engaging with the process herself.

You will need to assess the individual's circumstances and make a decision on what is most likely to help her make a decision.

Getting the best out of someone

Some people can find capacity assessments a challenge to their independence and sense of identity, and they may react in a way that hampers their ability to demonstrate capacity. Some of them may struggle to engage with the process at all, for example, thinking that you are trying to "put them in a home". (See Chapter 25 for further ways to engage people who appear to be unwilling to take part in the assessment.)

In such instances the following tips may help:

- Try to "sell" the capacity assessment as a chance for a person to get his side of the story across and show that he has considered the issues.

- Make sure you explain that the person has the right to make what other people consider an "unwise" decision, as long as he understands the consequences, and this process is a way for you to find this out.
- Give the person permission to talk about risks of her preferred option and benefits of her non-preferred option, without fear that options acknowledged to be risky will be discounted or acknowledgement of benefits be taken for preference. (See Chapter 8 for more details on how to approach this.)

When someone is finding engaging with a capacity assessment difficult or being inflexible in his thinking, asking the right follow-up questions is important. You should check for any core beliefs or anxieties that may be impacting on reasoning. These may not be immediately obvious, and you may need to "dig" to find them. You should check the reasons for his choice when considering his ability to weigh up information. This can lead to more options or choices being put forward. For example, refusal to go for an important hospital appointment may actually be due to fear of using the bus. It may be that suggesting a taxi supports the person to change his decision. Alternatively, the underlying reason could be related to a fear of hospitals, due to the previous death of a relative and development of a core belief that hospitals are dangerous. In this case, education on the nature of the appointment and reassurance that this is low risk (if indeed, it is), compared to the relative's experience, may work to help a person's reasoning.

Summary

- The MCA stresses the importance of taking "all practicable steps" to support someone before concluding that she lacks mental capacity to make a certain decision. It also states that the attempts to enhance capacity must meet each individual's specific needs.
- It is essential that a person is provided with all the relevant information necessary for him to make the decision *before* the assessment; the way we provide this information can enhance an individual's capacity and has the potential to hamper his decision-making if we do not get it right.
- Any information should be provided as many times as necessary, in the format best suited to support a person's understanding and reasoning. This includes being in simple language, in both verbal and visual (written or pictorial) formats and in her first language (if she does not speak English or it is her second language). Time consideration should not be a barrier unless the decision is an urgent or time-limited one.
- When attempting to enhance capacity, it is important to carefully consider the timing of assessments and the environment in which they take place. Get advice from family or care staff on timing and make sure any assessment environment is quiet, private and, if possible, familiar.

- Try to make adaptations to the assessment to take into account any sensory or physical difficulties and always use an impartial interpreter if the person does not speak English or speaks English as a second language.
- Someone with cognitive and/or communication problems can be supported by speaking slowly, in simple language to provide concise information in small, "digestible" chunks and repeating information a number of times. In addition, reducing the abstract nature of some decisions, and increasing the level of structure within an assessment will also enhance a person's capacity.
- Engaging the person effectively in the process should also enhance decision-making. This involves attempting to reduce any barriers to engagement by building a good rapport, helping her to manage any anxiety and identifying and addressing any fixed beliefs regarding the issues in question.

References

Department for Constitutional Affairs (2007). *Mental Capacity Act 2005: Code of Practice*. London: The Stationery Office.

Myron, R., Gillespie, S., Swift, P. and Williamson, T. (2008). *Whose Decision? Preparation for and Implementation of the Mental Capacity Act in Statutory and Non-Statutory Services in England and Wales*. London: Mental Health Foundation.

Case Law

LBX v KLM [2013] EWHC 3230 (Fam)

Chapter 10

Capacity assessment and cognitive impairment

Janice Mackenzie

In this chapter

This chapter will explore what is meant by *cognition* and look at the separate aspects in more detail, especially how they can affect someone's capacity to make a decision. It will also discuss the usefulness of cognitive assessments in relation to mental capacity assessments. A significant part of assessing capacity is making sure that you enhance the person's capacity first so, once you have identified what cognitive problems a person may have, you can use some of the strategies in Chapter 9 and Appendix 2 to try to do this.

What is cognition?

A broad definition of *cognition* is "to think and then act". It is a general term for thinking skills such as:

- Memory
- Attention
- Executive functioning
- Speed of information processing
- Language use
- Visuo-spatial perception
- General intellectual skills
- Orientation.

The first three aspects of cognition above have the strongest influence on the ability to make decisions (Dreer et al., 2008; Dymek et al., 2001; Marson et al., 1997). Other important factors are orientation in time and place and a person's insight into her difficulties. However, someone may need to use different aspects of cognition depending on the situation she is faced with and the difficulties that arise in everyday life. This makes assessing cognition – both in function and using paper and pencil tests – an important part of a mental capacity assessment for ongoing decisions, such as level of care required after discharge from hospital or managing everyday finances. Due to the varying nature of cognitive difficulties across conditions, and between people with the same condition, cognitive strengths and difficulties can never be assumed as they are sometimes hidden. A cognitive assessment alone can never be taken as an assessment of a person's capacity and, although it can be a useful addition in some cases, it is not always necessary. A formal assessment through the use of a semi-structure interview and observations remains the best approach to assessing an individual's capacity for complex decisions (see Chapters 6 and 12 for further information).

Cognition and mental capacity

Decision-making is a complex process requiring a variety of cognitive abilities including most of the aspects of cognition discussed here, as can be seen in Table 10.1, which relates cognitive functions to the Mental Capacity Act (MCA, 2005).

The Adults with Incapacity Act (Scotland, 2000) states that the factors required to have mental capacity are to understand, make and communicate the decision, retain the memory of the decision, and act on the decision. This last point is important, as a person can appear to be able to make a decision but then cannot put the decision into practice due to problems with executive functioning (George and Gilbert, 2018; see Chapter 22), and the structure of a capacity assessment can hide these problems (ABI and MCA Interest Group, 2014). Although the law in England and Wales (MCA, 2005) states that a person lacks capacity to make a decision if he is unable to "use *or* weigh" the relevant information, often in practice the terms are used together so the person lacks capacity if he is unable to "use *and* weigh" the

Table 10.1 Aspects of cognition linked to mental capacity

Factors required to have capacity in the MCA (2005)	Cognitive functions
Understand the decision and why it needs to be made	Language, insight, orientation
Understand the information relevant to the decision	Language, insight, attention, memory, executive functioning
Retain the information	Memory
Use and weigh the information to make a decision	Memory, attention, executive functioning (including inhibition and initiation)
Communicate a decision	Language, including non-verbal

information. But the law is clear that a person who can use the information but not weigh it, or vice versa, would be found to lack capacity to make the decision (Ruck Keene et al., 2019). This is sometimes difficult to assess using only an interview, and so functional assessments must also be used (see Chapter 6).

Several cognitive abilities have been found to correlate with decision-making capacity, including higher-level decision-making and judgment (executive functions), memory, comprehension, verbal fluency, mental flexibility, visual and auditory attention and ability to reason abstractly (Gurrera et al., 2006; Marson et al., 1996; Moye and Marson, 2007; Okonkwo et al., 2007). When evaluating the ability of people with intellectual disabilities (ID) to weigh up information in two tests of financial reasoning, Willner et al. (2010) found that performance in both decision-making tasks was related more strongly to executive functioning than to IQ. They concluded that difficulty in weighing up information may be a general problem for people with ID. Executive functioning has also been found to be important with regards to mental capacity in other populations (Casarett, Karlawish and Hirschman, 2003; Dreer et al., 2008; Dymek et al., 2001; Marson and Harrell, 1999).

It is important to remember that capacity is time-specific and is recognised to fluctuate (MCA Code of Practice, 2007), especially when cognition is improving after a stroke or head injury, declining due to a dementia or fluctuating due to significant mental health problems (see Chapter 26). Capacity is also decision-specific, and people lacking capacity in one area may retain it in another, even if the decisions are related and appear to be similar (Maxmin et al., 2009). Therefore, you cannot generalise the outcome from one assessment of capacity to another, even if there has been no change in cognition.

Different aspects of cognition and their effect on mental capacity

All aspects of cognition interact and rely on each other. Memory problems are the most common complaint of people seeking help for cognitive problems; however, they may not have a specific problem with their memory, per se. For example, someone with attentional problems may find it difficult to remember things, even though her memory is intact, due to finding it difficult to pay attention to information in order to store it in her memory. Alternatively, someone with executive functioning problems may find it difficult to organise information in his mind in order to store it in his memory efficiently and so, when he comes to try to retrieve the information, he cannot find it; however, he can recognise it when he sees or hears it later.

When we talk about memory, attention or executive functioning, we are not talking about a single ability that is or is not impaired. Each of these aspects of cognition contains several other components (see Tables 10.2, 10.3 and 10.4), which can be individually impaired with others left intact. This is important when it comes to enhancing capacity, as you can use the person's strengths to help overcome her weaknesses (see Chapter 9). Also, being aware of these issues can help you to understand what difficulties the person may have if she chooses certain options available to her, and so risk management strategies could be put in place to make a less restrictive option viable.

Examples of memory strengths and weaknesses that could affect a capacity assessment

- Someone may have problems with auditory memory but not with visual memory or vice versa (see Table 10.2 for definitions)
- Most people find it easier to recall information immediately after being told it than after a delay
- Some people may not be able to recall information but can recognise it, which may be enough for them to have the capacity to make a one-off decision with support
- Most, although not all, people learn information better through repetition
- Some people may not be able to remember the verbal instructions of a task and therefore are unable to tell you how they will do it, but they are able to remember how to do it practically and can therefore demonstrate it. Other people may remember the verbal instructions but cannot remember how to carry out the task – for example, making a cup of tea (procedural versus declarative memory) – hence observations can be invaluable. The latter can also be due to executive functioning issues, such as planning, sequencing and initiation
- Some people may not be able to tell you who the prime minister is but can remember important information about their own lives, and others may remember information people have told them but have no recollection of it happening
- Retrograde amnesia, forgetting events in the past, can occur after a brain injury and can vary from days to years, depending on the severity of the damage. If someone cannot remember important events in relation to the decision, for example, that she got divorced last year, then it can affect her capacity to make that decision
- Prospective memory is often essential in everyday life, but it can be supported through aids. It can be difficult to assess, but functional tasks simulating a future situation can help – for example, seeing whether someone can come to the nurses' station at the right times for his medications without being prompted to help determine whether he will remember to take his medications following discharge
- The person has to remember the relevant information for long enough to make the decision, and with consistency across different time points if her memory span is very short. She may have no memory of you visiting her two days ago or the discussion you had, but if she reasons through the decision in

the same way that she did two days earlier, then she could be said to have the capacity to make that decision. The exception to this rule is when the decision is an ongoing decision, as she would have to be able to retain the information to be able to use it consistently every time a decision is required to be made, and so this would need to be assessed across different time points.

Table 10.2 Different aspects of memory

Aspect of memory	What this means	Examples
Auditory (verbal) memory	Remembering information you hear	Remembering conversations, names or information you hear on television
Visual (non-verbal) memory	Remembering information you see (although we often put verbal labels on these too, helping to spread the memory across two systems)	Remembering faces, routes, objects or pictures
Immediate memory	Remembering information shortly after its presentation	Being able to repeat back several groceries you need to buy after your partner has told you what is required
Delayed memory	Remembering information for a period of time, ranging from several minutes to several days, after it is presented	Remembering what you need to buy once you get to the shop
Recall	Bringing information to mind yourself	Remembering what is on your shopping list without prompts
Recognition	Matching information in your mind to an external stimulus	Only remembering that you need to buy milk when you see it in the shop
Single-trial learning	Only hearing or seeing information once (although you may repeat it to yourself)	Finding your way back to a place you have only been to once before
Learning through repetition	Hearing or seeing information several times	Learning times tables by rote

(Continued)

Table 10.2 (Continued)

Aspect of memory	What this means	Examples
Procedural memory	Subconscious processes that our bodies remember how to do	Remembering how to ride a bike or put in a door code
Declarative memory	Being able to tell someone the information	Telling someone the door code without re-enacting it with your fingers or telling someone the date of the Battle of Hastings
Semantic memory	Remembering facts without having to have any memory of the event	Remembering the name of your primary school, who won the general election or the capital of France
Episodic memory	Remembering episodes from your life, rather than facts someone else has told you (this helps you believe information about yourself, unless you interpret it differently from other people who were there)	Remembering a hospital admission when you were a child, watching the general election or having dinner last Sunday
Prospective memory	Remembering to do something in the future	Remembering to attend appointments, take medications or telephone your power supplier during opening hours

Examples of attention strengths and weaknesses that could affect a capacity assessment

- As with memory, depending on the location of the brain injury or the type of condition, some people may have problems with auditory attention but not spatial attention and vice versa (see Table 10.3 for definitions)
- It is easier to pay attention to straightforward information than to keep information in your head and manipulate or use it
- Knowing how long someone can sustain his attention or knowing what his attentional capacity is can be useful for adapting your capacity assessment
- Selective, switching and divided attention tasks are the most challenging for everybody and can be impossible for people after a brain injury, so it is important to consider how and where you carry out your capacity assessment.

Table 10.3 Different aspects of attention

Aspect of attention	What this means	Examples
Auditory (verbal) working memory	Ability to remember information you hear for a few seconds and be able to keep information in your mind in order to manipulate and use it – linked more to attention than memory as most people think of it	Repeating a phone number to yourself long enough to dial the number but forgetting it straight afterward or remembering numbers while trying to add them up
Spatial (visual) working memory	As auditory working memory, but for spatial information that you see	Looking at a map and remembering the next few directions on a route before having to check again (without verbalising it) or copying complex dance steps after watching someone else
Attentional capacity	The amount of information that you can take in at one time – this is usually +/- 7 short pieces of information, such as digits	Feeling overwhelmed when someone is telling you too much information and feeling the need to write it down as you hear it
Sustained attention	Ability to pay attention or concentrate for a reasonable period of time until you are "full" or cognitively fatigued	Watching television, listening to a speech, or reading a book
Selective or focused attention (verbal or visual)	Picking out specific information that you hear or see when there are distracters present	Listening to a conversation while the television is on or finding your glasses on a messy table
Attentional switching	Having the flexibility to switch your attention from one task to another (and being able to switch it back again)	Cooking a complex meal with several different aspects to monitor or being interrupted by a phone call when writing an email
Divided attention	Being able to do more than one task at the same time	Watching television while cooking or talking and driving at the same time

Examples of executive functioning strengths and weaknesses that could affect a capacity assessment

- Problem-solving, use of strategies, planning and organising abilities may not affect the capacity assessment, but they can have a large impact on how the person will cope in different situations and they can affect how she weighs up and uses information (see Table 10.4 for definitions)
- It is important to be aware of ways of helping someone who has problems with perseveration during the capacity assessment, as he may start telling you something sensible but then is unable to move off the topic without a prompt. Alternatively, he may, for example, get stuck on saying he wants to go home, which stops him from considering other options
- Confabulation can catch out assessors if they are not aware of the facts, as the person can sound very convincing
- Disinhibition and impulsivity may cause problems both during the capacity assessment and in everyday life, as the person may not think things through before acting. However, if the person is aware of them, strategies can be put in place to reduce the impact of these difficulties. It is important that these are assessed for effectiveness before the end of the capacity assessment, as someone may be able to say the right things but then not stop herself from doing something risky (see Chapter 22)
- Initiation and goal maintenance can also affect the capacity assessment and everyday life but, again, strategies can help (see Chapter 9 and Appendix 2).

Table 10.4 Different aspects of executive functioning

Aspect of executive functioning	What this means	Examples
Problem-solving and use of strategies	How you approach a problem you come across and whether you are able to learn and use effective strategies; also, whether you are able to deal with novel situations and transfer skills to different circumstances	Finding that you do not have the right ingredients for the meal you were about to cook and solving this problem (possible strategy: Plan meals in advance and write a shopping list.)
Planning and organisation	Whether you plan how to do a task beforehand or jump straight into it and how you organise your time and resources; also involves thinking about the consequences of your actions	Reading about a holiday destination and planning your itinerary well in advance vs. booking a holiday to somewhere you know nothing about or trying to read about it the night before you go

(Continued)

Table 10.4 (Continued)

Aspect of executive functioning	What this means	Examples
Perseveration	Getting stuck on doing or saying something, repeating it and not being able to move off the subject without being prompted	Telling the same story several times in a conversation or shaving the same side of your face repeatedly until it bleeds
Confabulation	Your brain fills in the gaps in your memory by making up a false memory, although you are not aware that it is false and so it is different from lying	An inpatient tells you that she has been to the hairdresser that morning when she has not left the ward
Disinhibition	Having difficulty stopping yourself from doing or saying things that are inappropriate for the task or situation	Swearing in front of a person in authority or making sexually explicit remarks to someone you find attractive in a shop
Impulsivity	Acting without thinking and often regretting it afterward	Getting up to walk to the toilet even though you remember that you have been told that it is not safe or buying a very expensive item that you do not need and cannot afford
Initiation	Having difficulty starting a task without a prompt, even though you want to do it (not to be confused with lack of motivation or procrastination)	Example problem: Not getting up to walk when you want to go to the toilet until someone says "Let's go" or takes your arm
Goal maintenance	Being able to remember what you are doing and stay on track without prompts	Example problem: Starting to reply to emails that have arrived in your inbox while you are in the middle of writing a report

Other aspects of cognition, and abilities linked to cognition, that are useful to investigate include a person's insight into her problems, the level that she was functioning at previously, the level of effort that she puts into the assessments and her orientation, speed of information processing, language abilities and visuo-spatial perception.

Pre-morbid estimate of functioning

It is important to know the level at which a person was functioning before he started to experience cognitive problems (as opposed to a developmental disorder which he has had since birth or early childhood). If you are unaware of this, then you cannot be sure whether or not there has been a change in his functioning. There are cognitive tests and formulae to help estimate this, which take into account the person's educational and employment history. It is also useful to gain an idea of his functional abilities prior to the onset of his difficulties, to see what he was able to do in everyday life and the amount of support he required to carry out these tasks.

Orientation

A person does not necessarily have to be orientated to the exact day and know the name of the place that she is in to have mental capacity to make a decision, but she needs to have a general idea of time and place so that she knows, for example, that she is in hospital and lives alone because her husband died last year. Orientation in time can cause problems when, for example, an older adult thinks that she is a young adult still living with her parents.

Speed of information processing

Speed of information processing should be considered during a capacity assessment, as it will affect the person's ability to take in and process information that is given to him. For example, he may not be able to process everything that has been said to him in the session and make a decision quickly but may be able to think it over and come to a conclusion later. This is one reason that a repeat assessment is recommended where possible.

Language abilities

Language abilities are important when assessing mental capacity, as you need to be sure that you are communicating with the person in a way that she can understand and that you are able to understand what she is trying to say. Consulting a Speech and Language Therapist (SLT) before the capacity assessment would be recommended if the person has any speech or language difficulties. Doing a joint assessment with a SLT would be recommended for people with more significant communication difficulties. (See Chapter 11 for more on communication.)

Visuo-spatial perception

Visuo-spatial perception refers to how your brain makes sense of your environment as you see it, rather than a problem with your eyesight, such as short-sightedness. This may not be as important for the capacity assessment itself but could be very important when assessing the risks associated with the different options available – for example, someone wanting to return to his home to live alone. Visuo-spatial perceptual problems alone may not affect the person's ability to go home but, when combined with other cognitive problems such as memory problems and impulsivity, they may add up to a significant risk. Aspects to consider are:

- The ability to identify objects (although he does not have to be able to think of the names)
- The ability to find things in space (for example, reaching for a cup and making contact in a safe manner rather than reaching ten centimetres to the left and knocking it over)
- Visual inattention, also known as visual neglect. (This condition occurs when the person is unaware of a portion of space, most commonly on the left. Depending on the severity of the inattention he may not be aware of someone approaching him on that side, may not eat one half of what is on his plate or walk into walls, doors and people on the affected side. Brains are good at filling in gaps, and so the person will be unaware that he is not paying attention to a proportion of the space around him. This is in contrast to hemianopia, which is a visual problem when the person cannot see half of space but is aware of this problem. Some people can have both a hemianopia and visual inattention.)

Occupational Therapists (OT) often assess aspects of visual perception on tests and during functional tasks.

Insight

Insight relates to being aware of your difficulties and how they will affect you when carrying out different tasks. It can be affected by damage to the brain, and problems with insight are common after traumatic brain injury, especially in the acute phase (Robertson and Schmitter-Edgecombe, 2015). For example, someone may not be aware that he has planning problems that affect his ability to make a cup of tea or someone else may be unaware of her risk-taking behaviour when crossing roads. Crosson et al. (1989) proposed the first multi-dimensional model, which split insight into different hierarchical levels:

- Intellectual awareness – being aware that a specific function is impaired
- Emergent awareness – ability to monitor performance and recognise a problem when it is occurring during a task
- Anticipatory awareness – ability to anticipate that a particular problem may be experienced in a specific situation due to the functional impairment.

The last two aspects are sometimes referred to as "online" awareness as they occur during and immediately after a task. Toglia and Kirk (2000) proposed a dynamic, non-hierarchical model of insight which takes into account:

- The knowledge and beliefs the person brings to the task (off-line awareness)
- Self-monitoring of errors, ability to change behaviour in response to the task and errors noted, self-evaluation of performance and appraisal of the task (online awareness)
- The effect of the demands of the task and context of the situation, so that someone could have insight in one situation but not another.

Insight is possibly the most important aspect of thinking relating to the ability to make decisions. If a person is not aware of, or does not believe, the difficulties that she is having, or will have, then she will find it very difficult to understand that the salient information is related to her and to use and weigh it up in relation to the options available. However, someone can have insight into some aspects of her problems but not others, and so this should be investigated during the capacity assessment. Insight should be thought of as separate from denial, which is a psychological defence mechanism that comes into play, consciously or subconsciously, when there is a threat, for example, to your self-image or self-esteem, and affects awareness of your deficits. (See Chapters 6, 9 and 25 and Appendix 2 for ideas on how to work with insight difficulties and denial.)

Effort

When administering cognitive assessments, it is important to consider the amount of effort the person is putting into the tests, and this also applies to capacity assessments. For example, if someone is saying "I don't know" a lot, it might indicate that she is not trying her best to answer the questions. Effort can be affected by lots of factors including low mood, anxiety, fatigue, pain, and low motivation, as well as potential secondary gain.

Assessing cognition

A thorough cognitive assessment will evaluate all aspects of cognitive function in detail, including assessing the level at which the person was functioning before he started to notice cognitive problems. However, it is not always possible, or necessary, to administer a full cognitive assessment, or you may not have access to a clinical neuropsychologist who would do such an assessment. In these cases, cognitive screens can be useful – for example, the Montreal Cognitive Assessment (MoCA; Nasreddine et al., 2005) or the Addenbrooke's Cognitive Examination (ACE III; Hsieh et al., 2013) – if administered correctly and if each aspect of the screen is interpreted by a professional with experience of cognitive assessments. The overall score is rarely useful with regard to capacity assessments; for example, someone with significant language difficulties may not pass most of the subtests but can still understand concrete information relating to his own situation. The Mini-Mental State Examination (MMSE; Folstein, Folstein and McHugh, 1975) has been found to be "no better than chance" at finding cognitive problems in a stroke population, especially around executive functioning and visual perception/construction (Nys et al., 2005). As has been mentioned in other chapters, a functional approach to assessing a person's cognitive problems and care needs is recommended when thinking about mental capacity. A more ecologically-valid assessment, such as the Multiple Errands Test (MET; Shallice and Burgess, 1991) can provide useful information, or an OT can assess cognitive abilities during functional tasks. The MET has also been adapted for use in a hospital setting and so can be used with people before they are discharged (Knight, Alderman and Burgess, 2002).

Usefulness of cognitive assessments in mental capacity assessments

Although some studies have found certain aspects of cognition linked to mental capacity, decision-making ability does not only rely on cognitive abilities, and some studies have found that neither general nor specific measures of cognitive functioning accurately predicted decision-making capacity for particular decisions (Freedman, Stuss and Gordon, 1991; Murphy and Clare, 2003). In addition, Mackenzie, Lincoln and Newby (2008) found no significant difference in any aspect of cognitive functioning between groups of stroke patients with capacity to make a decision about discharge destination and those without. However, the lack of differentiation may have been due to the tests of executive functioning used, as they may not have tapped into the specific aspects of executive functioning required for decision-making, such as conceptualisation and reasoning (Dymek, Marson and Harrell, 1999). A combination of cognitive problems may have been a better predictor, but the sample size was not large enough to do further statistical tests. This is an important reminder that you need to take a holistic view of a person when assessing mental capacity. Two examples demonstrate this (Mackenzie, Lincoln and Newby, 2008):

- Francis passed all of the cognitive assessments and was able to report information that staff had told him but, when asked if he thought it applied to him, he stated that he did not and that he would be fine, showing intact cognition but impaired insight. Francis was found not to have capacity to make a decision about his discharge destination.
- Betty had significant expressive language problems but no receptive language problems. She failed several of the cognitive assessments due to her language difficulties, but she had good insight into her physical and cognitive difficulties and was able to answer closed questions with the use of gesture and mime. Betty was found to have capacity to make a decision about her discharge destination.

Although a capacity assessment should never be based on the results of a cognitive assessment alone, and caution should be used when interpreting the results of cognitive assessments in relation to capacity, they can be useful for:

- Adapting the level of the assessment to enhance capacity, such as simplifying the language used (Arscott, Dagnan and Kroese, 1999)
- Understanding the general functional abilities underlying specific decision-making abilities in borderline cases and remediating the difficulties (Sullivan, 2004), for example, through the use of memory aids or decision trees
- Informing the decision to postpone the capacity assessment, if possible, when improvements are noted on consecutive cognitive assessments.

(See Chapter 9 and Appendix 2 for further information on enhancing capacity.)

It is not always necessary, or possible, to do a cognitive assessment before a capacity assessment, and it is just one of a variety of different sources of information you would hope to gather before commencing a capacity assessment. Others would include:

- Information on abilities, insight, behaviour and potential risks from the staff or multi-disciplinary team (MDT) working with the person and from the person's family or friends
- Changes in the person's cognition and behaviour reported by family and close friends
- Qualitative observations during a cognitive assessment, in function and during the capacity assessment.

Summary

It is likely that the majority of the people you see in order to assess their mental capacity will have cognitive problems. Although this is a complex and, at times, confusing area, being aware of the issues mentioned in this chapter will help you understand why someone may be presenting as she is and to gently question areas in more depth to gain clarity regarding her mental capacity. It will also help you to think about what aspects of cognition need to be remedied to enhance someone's mental capacity, as can be seen in Chapter 9. OTs are often useful professionals to talk to about a client's cognitive problems as well as clinical psychologists and clinical neuropsychologists.

References

Acquired Brain Injury and Mental Capacity Act Interest Group (2014). *Acquired Brain Injury and Mental Capacity: Recommendations for Action Following the House of Lords Select Committee Post-Legislative Scrutiny Report into the Mental Capacity Act: Making the Abstract Real.* Available at: https://empowerment mattersweb.files.wordpress.com/2014/11/making-the-abstract-real.pdf

Adults with Incapacity (Scotland) Act 2000. London: HMSO. Available at: www.legislation.gov.uk/asp/2000/4/contents

Arscott, K., Dagnan, D. and Kroese, B.S. (1999). Assessing the ability of people with a learning disability to give informed consent to treatment. *Psychological Medicine*, 29(6), 1367–1375.

Casarett, D.J., Karlawish, J.H.T. and Hirschman, K.B. (2003). Identifying ambulatory cancer patients at risk of impaired capacity to consent to research. *Journal of Pain and Symptom Management*, 26(1), 615–624.

Crosson, B., Barco, P.P., Velezo, C.A., Bolesta, M.M., Cooper, P.V., Werts, D. and Brobeck, T.C. (1989). Awareness of compensation in postacute head injury rehabilitation. *Journal of Head Trauma Rehabilitation*, 4, 46–54.

Department for Constitutional Affairs (2007). *Mental Capacity Act 2005: Code of Practice.* London: The Stationery Office. Available at: https://assets.publishing.service.gov.uk/government/uploads/system/uploads/attachment_data/file/497253/Mental-capacity-act-code-of-practice.pdf

Dreer, L.E., DeVivo, M.J., Novack, T.A., Krzywanski, S. and Marson, D.C. (2008). Cognitive predictors of medical decision-making capacity in traumatic brain injury. *Rehabilitation Psychology*, 53(4), 486–497.

Dymek, M.P., Atchison, P., Harrell, L. and Marson, D.C. (2001). Competency to consent to medical treatment in cognitively impaired patients with Parkinson's disease. *Neurology*, 56, 17–24.

Dymek, M.P., Marson, D.C. and Harrell, L. (1999). Factor structure of capacity to consent to medical treatment in patients with Alzheimer's disease: An exploratory study. *Journal of Forensic Neuropsychology*, 1(1), 27–48.

Folstein, M.F., Folstein, S.E. and McHugh, P.R. (1975). 'Mini-mental state': A practical method for grading the cognitive state of patients for the clinician. *Journal of Psychiatric Research*, 12(3), 189–198.

Freedman, M., Stuss, D.T. and Gordon, M. (1991). Assessment of competency: The role of neurobehavioral deficits. *Annals of Internal Medicine*, 115, 203–208.

George, M. and Gilbert, S. (2018). Mental Capacity Act (2005) assessments: Why everyone needs to know about the frontal lobe paradox. *The Neuropsychologist*, 5, 59–66.

Gurrera, R.J., Moye, J., Karel, M.J., Azar, A.R. and Armesto, J.C. (2006). Cognitive performance predicts treatment decisional abilities in mild to moderate dementia. *Neurology*, 66, 1367–1372.

Hsieh, S., Schubert, S., Hoon, C., Mioshi, E. and Hodges, J.R. (2013). Validation of the Addenbrooke's cognitive examination III in frontotemporal dementia and Alzheimer's disease. *Dementia and Geriatric Cognitive Disorders*, 36(3–4), 242–250. ACE III available at: https://sydney.edu.au/brain-mind/resources-for-clinicians/dementia-test.html

Knight, C., Alderman, N. and Burgess, P.W. (2002). Development of a simplified version of the multiple errands test for use in hospital settings. *Neuropsychological Rehabilitation*, 12(3), 231–255.

Mackenzie, J.A., Lincoln, N.B. and Newby, G.J. (2008). Capacity to make a decision about discharge destination after stroke: A pilot study. *Clinical Rehabilitation*, 22, 1116–1126.

Marson, D.C., Chatterjee, A., Ingram, K.K. and Harrell, L.E. (1996). Toward a neurologic model of competency: Cognitive predictors of capacity to consent in Alzheimer's disease using three different legal standards. *Neurology*, 46, 666–672.

Marson, D.C. and Harrell, L. (1999). Executive dysfunction and loss of capacity to consent to medical treatment in patients with Alzheimer's disease. *Seminars in Clinical Neuropsychiatry*, 4(1), 41–49.

Marson, D.C., Hawkins, L., McInturff, B. and Harrell, L.E. (1997). Cognitive models that predict physician judgments of capacity to consent in mild Alzheimer's disease. *Journal of the American Geriatric Society*, 45, 458–464.

Maxmin, K., Cooper, C., Potter, L. and Livingston, G. (2009). Mental capacity to consent to treatment and admission decisions in older adult psychiatric inpatients. *International Journal of Geriatric Psychiatry*, 24, 1367–1375.

Mental Capacity Act 2005. London: HMSO. Available at: www.legislation.gov.uk/ukpga/2005/9/contents

Moye, J. and Marson, D.C. (2007). Assessment of decision-making capacity in older adults: An emerging area of practice and research. *Journal of Gerontology: Psychological Sciences*, 62, 3–11.

Murphy, G. and Clare, I. (2003). Adults' capacity to make legal decisions. In C.C.R. Bull (ed.), *Handbook of Psychology in Legal Contexts* (pp. 31–66). Chichester: Wiley.

Nasreddine, Z.S., Phillips, N.A., Bédirian, V., Charbonneau, S., Whitehead, V., Collin, I., Cummings, J.L. and Chertkow, H. (2005). The Montreal Cognitive Assessment, MoCA: A brief screening tool for mild cognitive impairment. *Journal of the American Geriatrics Society*, 53(4), 695–699.

Nys, G.M., van Zandvoort, M.J., de Kort, P.L., Jansen, B.P., Kappelle, L.J. and de Haan, E.H. (2005). Restrictions of the mini-mental state examination in acute stroke. *Archives of Clinical Neuropsychology*, 20(5), 623–629.

Okonkwo, O., Griffith, H.R., Belue, K., Lanza, S., Zamrini, E.Y., Harrell, L.E., Brockington, J.C., Clark, D., Raman, R. and Marson, D.C. (2007). Medical decision-making capacity in patients with mild cognitive impairment. *Neurology*, 69, 1528–1535.

Robertson, K. and Schmitter-Edgecombe, M. (2015). Self-awareness and traumatic brain injury outcome. *Brain Injury*, 29, 848–858.

Ruck Keene, A., Butler-Cole, V., Allen, N., Lee, A., Kohn, N., Scott, K., Barnes, K. and Edwards, S. (eds.) (2019). *A Brief Guide to Carrying Out Capacity Assessments*. 39 Essex Chambers. Available at: www.39essex.com/mental-capacity-guidance-note-brief-guide-carrying-capacity-assessments

Shallice, T. and Burgess, P.W. (1991). Deficits in strategy application following frontal lobe damage in man. *Brain*, 114, 727–741.

Sullivan, K. (2004). Neuropsychological assessment of mental capacity. *Neuropsychology Review*, 14(3), 131–142.

Toglia, J. and Kirk, U. (2000). Understanding awareness deficits following brain injury. *Neurorehabilitation*, 15, 57–70.

Willner, P., Bailey, R., Parry, R. and Dymond, S. (2010). Evaluation of the ability of people with intellectual disabilities to 'weigh up' information in two tests of financial reasoning. *Journal of Intellectual Disability Research*, 54(4), 380–391.

Chapter 11

Communication in the context of assessing mental capacity

Jane Jolliffe

In this chapter

This chapter covers:

- The functional impact of different communication problems
- Ways to make information more accessible
- Consideration of the amount of information we give
- The use of visual support to aid understanding, weighing up and communication
- What is meant by "all practicable steps" relating to communication
- General practical tips to improve understanding and expression.

The functional impact of communication problems

In this chapter, the term *communication* is used for expression and comprehension. You need to find out about the person's skills and difficulties in both areas to assess capacity. People with communication impairments are described as people with speech, language or communication needs (SLCN). A person who does not share a language with you does not have SLCN, as the communication difficulties may be resolved with the support of an interpreter. Some parts of this section will not be applicable to people whose primary means of communication is signing, whether British Sign Language, or tactile signing. Information on adapting written communication applies to information in some formats, for example, basic Braille.

SLCN occur as a result of many different conditions, some longstanding or developmental and some acquired, for example, stroke, dementia, traumatic brain injury (TBI), learning disability, profound hearing loss and autism. The Royal College of Speech and Language Therapists reports that almost 20% of the population will have a communication difficulty at some point in their lives (Law et al., 2007).

For SLCN associated with some acquired conditions, such as stroke or TBI, skills may improve, so you will need to consider the best time to assess capacity. For other people, their communication skills may deteriorate (for example, people with dementia) or stay almost static (for example, people with a learning disability).

The focus needs to be on the functional impact of a communication problem rather than the diagnostic label, just as the Mental Capacity Act (MCA, 2005) emphasises the need for a functional test of capacity and prohibits assumptions about capacity based on diagnosis.

Simply put, it is essential that you find out about the person's ability to understand:

- Facial expression and tone of voice, for example, a smile
- Gestures and objects, for example, a thumbs up
- Images, for example, a line drawing
- Spoken and written words, for example, words of time, question words
- Spoken and written sentence structure, for example, active voice
- Conversational rules, for example, initiation
- The different functions of communication, for example, requesting information.

This information will allow you to maximise the person's ability to understand the information relevant to the decision and to participate in the assessment.

A person's expressive skills can be classified similarly so you need to find out:

- How the person communicates, for example, gestures, speech, writing
- Whether the person uses any alternative or augmentative communication (AAC)
- Whether the person has a reliable "yes" and "no"
- How easy it is to understand the person's speech
- Whether the person has a stammer
- What kinds of words and sentences the person uses
- Whether the person has a range of communicative functions, for example, to ask as well as answer questions, to describe, to narrate, to reject and protest
- What conversation skills the person has, for example, initiation, turn taking, staying on topic.

In addition to information about the person's communication skills, you should find out about the person's cognition and other skills; for example, does the person have theory of mind, is he able to point or use a pen, and what information is available about his memory, hearing and vision?

Some people with SLCN may have a diagnosis of dyspraxia or dysarthria, both of which affect speech intelligibility. Information about these conditions is available on the Royal College of Speech and Language Therapists' website.

Alternative or Augmentative Communication (AAC)

AAC is anything that replaces or supports spoken and written communication and can be divided into "high-tech" and "low-tech" aids. Low-tech aids use images and symbols and do not rely on technology, for example, an alphabet chart or a communication book. The aid is easy to access and often easy to use for people with cognitive impairments; for example, in a communication book the person points with her finger or eyes to the picture of what she wants. Signing is considered low-tech as it does not need any additional equipment, for example, sign supported English. High-tech aids rely on technology and many are voice output communication aids (VOCA). In some aids, the person's messages are stored on the aid and spoken when the person presses the appropriate button, or the message can be spoken as the person types. Tablets and phones can be turned into high-tech aids. Some aids can be accessed by alternative methods, making them usable for people with physical disabilities, for example, eye-gaze access.

Making information more accessible

If you do not have access to information about the individual's communication skills – for example, following an assessment by a speech and language therapist (SLT) – then the next best solution is to follow rules to make information more accessible to the population of people with SLCN. Some examples of how to do this will follow.

Word choice

Influences on receptive vocabulary

Our receptive vocabulary, the words we understand, is shaped by many influences. Being aware of these factors will help you to use vocabulary more likely to be meaningful to the person.

The most common influences on vocabulary are:

- Age
- Geography – where people live and have lived
- Educational level
- Gender
- Life experiences
- Family background
- Living and learning environments
- Social environment
- Difficulties with learning, for example, specific learning difficulties or a learning disability.

An assessor using words based on this general knowledge about an individual's life would be using population-based vocabulary. In contrast, an assessor using words based on specific knowledge of the person would be using personalised vocabulary. Whilst personalised vocabulary is preferable, there may be many situations where this is not possible, for example, when you have no access to an SLT or when the person will not or cannot engage with an assessment. Either way, the most important point is that you document your rationale and your decision.

Using concrete vocabulary

You should use the most concrete way of explaining something, as many people with SLCN struggle to understand abstract words; for example, describing the time as the length of a favourite programme rather than in hours or minutes. Consistency is important, so the same words should be used throughout an assessment for the same thing; for example, using *new home* rather than swapping from *home* to *accommodation* to *residence* to *place*.

Tips

- When talking about time, use the day or a specific time rather than vague terms like *soon* or relative terms like *tomorrow*.
- Use *first* and *then* rather than *before* and *after*.

Stress

We use stress or emphasis to highlight the most important part of our sentences. The stress is often placed at a point of potential contrast, for example, "What are *your* thoughts about going home?" – that is, your thoughts versus someone else's. Some people with SLCN will not understand the significance of the stress and may respond to a different part of the sentence, for example, telling you about their spouse's thoughts. If you have an awareness of this issue, you will be able to identify when a misunderstanding has occurred and rephrase; for example, "We're talking about you going home; what do you think?"

Abbreviations

Abbreviations are part of everyday communication; however, different abbreviations may mean different things to people depending on their background. For example, *PE* in a hospital setting is *pulmonary embolism* but, in a school, it is *physical education* and in economics it is *performance evaluation*.

> ## Tip
>
> Abbreviations should be avoided unless you have evidence that they are definitely understood by the person, for example, from experience.

Using easy words

If you do not have time to get to know the person, you should use the most common word for something; these are often called "easy" words. This is often the first word that comes to mind when thinking of describing the object, event and so on or the first word you learnt for something. For example: say *cut* rather than *incision*, *belly* rather than *abdomen*, *fire* rather than *inferno*.

> ## Tip
>
> Listen to the person and use the person's own word for something. For example, if a person has started calling pain "an ouch" use *ouch* when talking with them about pain.

> ## Cautions
>
> - Beware of the specialist use of everyday words. For example, "discharge" could be understood as meaning something oozing from a wound instead of leaving hospital.
> - Avoid words or phrases with two or more meanings – working out which meaning is the right one can be difficult for a person with SLCN, for example, "run off" as in drain or "run off" as in run away.

Use of idioms

Idioms are words and phrases with meaning based on everyday use and not in the meaning of the individual words. Idioms are often difficult to understand as the meaning is specific to that grouping of words rather than the meaning of the individual words. For example, "to iron out the bugs" is a saying which has its origin in literally ironing out the bugs in soldiers' uniforms, but has come to mean over time "to sort out glitches"; or "rip off" sometimes means "to cheat", not "to tear off". Some words and phrases have idiomatic or regional usage, for example, "You're twisting my melon", which means "You're confusing me". Many people with SLCN struggle to understand the idioms and will be literal in their understanding of the words. This can lead to confusion and misunderstanding.

Caution

Beware of idioms, especially ones which are more difficult to spot – for example, "cutting down on medication", or "getting on your nerves".

Use of pronouns

Pronouns are words used to replace a previously used noun to reduce repetition – for example, "*John* believes it will be unsafe for you to go home; *he* wants you to move". Working out what the pronoun relates to in a sentence that has been and gone is very difficult. People with SLCN often need the original word repeated to stay on topic. For example: "Last time we talked about your benefits. Now we need to talk about how you spend *them*" will need to be changed to "Now we need to talk about how you spend your *benefits*".

Sentence structure

What is grammar?

Many assessors are uncomfortable with the term *grammar*. However, if you think of grammar as the rules that govern how sentences are put together and the way words change, it is easier to recognise that being aware of grammar is an essential part of making communication meaningful. The information in this section applies to English.

What are the problems for people with SLCN?

People with SLCN will have difficulty understanding some grammatical structures. An assessor should have an awareness of the structures most often misunderstood.

THE PASSIVE

An example of a grammatical rule that is misunderstood by many people with SLCN is the passive voice, in contrast to the active voice. For example, if we use the active voice word order "Bill hit Bob", the order of the words tells us that Bill is the hitter and Bob the "hittee"; in a passive sentence the meaning is the same, but the word order is reversed "Bob was hit by Bill".

WORD ENDINGS

Grammar covers meaning in word endings – for example, the plural "s" (strokes, falls – meaning more than one) and the ending "ed" (work**ed** – meaning in the past). Many people with SLCN will not understand the significance of these subtle changes to words.

LINKING SENTENCES

Grammar covers the rules about linking sentences – for example, with *and*, *if* or *because*. The most difficult type of sentence is the embedded sentence, which is one sentence inside another – for example, "The woman over there, the one wearing the blue trousers, is your physiotherapist". Most people with SLCN will struggle to understand embedded sentences for a variety of reasons. Whenever possible you should simplify and/or split linked and embedded sentences into two or more sentences. For example, "See the woman in the blue trousers?" – wait for the person to look – "She's your physiotherapist".

NEGATIVES

It is essential to be aware of the use of negatives. Negatives are *no*, *not* and its shortened form *n't*, as in "There are **no** beds", "There are **not** any beds" and "There are**n't** any beds". Negative sentences are often misunderstood by people with SLCN as if you had used a positive sentence, which is the exact opposite of what you meant. This example would mean that the person thinks you have said "There are beds". You should try to avoid negatives, particularly *not* and *n't* – for example, by saying what is going to happen rather than what is not: "You are staying in hospital" rather than "You are not going home yet". Alternatively, you could use a word that means the same as the negative version, for example, *unhappy* or *sad* rather than *not happy*. People with SLCN may understand *no* used to indicate the absence of something more easily than *not*; for example, "You have no money" is easier to understand than "You haven't any money".

INFORMATION-CARRYING WORDS

As well as considering the complexity of the grammar we use, we can think about how many information-carrying words (ICW) we use. These are words that have to be understood. For example, if you say "Pass me a blue pen" and there are only blue pens available, then the word *blue* is redundant; however, if there are red and blue pens then the word *blue* has to be understood for you to get the pen you want. In the first scenario, the word *blue* is not an ICW, but in the second scenario it is. Many people with SLCN will have a limit to the number of ICW they are able to process at one time (for example, three words), and you will need to take account of this in your assessment. ICW are sometimes called "key words".

Tips

- Avoid relying on a change of verb tense to identify a past or future event. For example, rather than saying "Remember when you visited your mum?" say "Remember when you visited your mum last Thursday?"
- Use the active voice and avoid the passive voice.
- Use the simplest sentence structure and avoid linking sentences with, for example, *and* or *because* wherever possible.

Giving information

The MCA Code of Practice gives potentially conflicting guidance on the amount of information people should have, stating that people need all the relevant information to make an informed decision, but that you should not give more detail than is needed, as this may confuse them (Department of Constitutional Affairs, 2007, at paragraph 3.9).

You should organise information into themes or topic areas and make sure that the information flows logically from one topic to another. Also, you should ensure that information is related to the immediate decision and not conflate a series of decisions. For example, if a person is deciding about a scan, then she needs to know what a scan will be like and why it has been recommended (for example, to look at a lump), and that treatment will depend on what the scan shows. She would not need to know about all the potential operations and treatments that may follow.

Visual support

What is visual support?

Visual support means adding information through the use of visual means – for example, photographs, drawings, objects and written words. Support applies both to the use of visual materials to support spoken information and also to the support offered to help the person understand and process information from the visual materials. Visual support does not mean just adding images to text but developing and using an accessible resource for the person about her decision.

Advantages of visual support

Some of the advantages of using visual support are:

- The left-to-right sequencing of images can represent events over time.
- Two or more alternatives can be displayed simultaneously.
- The consequences of making a decision one way or another can be illustrated clearly.
- The information is there for the person to revisit at any time.
- Information can be sorted, for example, into lists or pros and cons.
- Images can anchor more complex discussions, for example, different people's points of views and who said what.
- A written script will help you be consistent in the information you give.

Visual support for understanding

The *LBX v K, L and M* [2013] ruling used the term *tangible resources or tools* and highlighted how important they were to aid and improve a person's understanding of the information relevant to the decision. Visual support is often helpful for people with a reasonable level of verbal comprehension, and its use should not be restricted to people with limited verbal comprehension.

Visual support can be used for all of the information or to highlight key information, such as using images for the main topics – for example, in hospital, during the operation, on the ward, back home. Good layout will also help a person to navigate through information – for example, separate pages for each stage.

Visual support may help a person understand a sequence of events more clearly – for example, a timeline from left to right or a photographic journey.

Visual support helps people understand information about a series of events – for example, what happens at the police station when you are accused of a crime or what happens when you go for a hearing test.

Visual support for retaining

Visual support may aid retention, as it provides a permanent resource for the person to revisit or to refer to during discussions. Creating visual support often leads to better organised and more consistent information, which is easier to assimilate. People often retain more information with repetition, and using visual support means that there is a resource to revisit.

An added advantage is that the person has the visual support available when the decision is made, for example, to help him through moving accommodation.

Visual support for weighing up

Visual support can be used to help people sort information into pros and cons, with the pros and cons identified in a meaningful way – for example, thumbs up and down or smiling and frowning faces. A basic pros and cons list is a good starting place for people unused to considering their options, and counting up pros and cons is an accessible way to start considering the decision. Visual support is useful to help a person identify the most important factors in her decision-making – for example, by adding a gold, silver or bronze medal, or a set of rosettes.

Visual support can help a person compare two potential options with differing outcomes so he can more clearly see the consequences of his decision – for example, a comic strip showing a person paying his rent and staying in his home and another showing the person not paying his rent and leaving his home.

Interacting with materials often engages people with SLCN in a way that just talking though a decision does not. Talking Mats ™ is an example of an interactive resource; this system uses three sets of images for topics and options and a scale for the person to convey how she feels about the options – for example, "agree", "disagree", "unsure". Talking Mats ™ uses symbols displayed in a way to suit the person – for example, a mat, a board or a tablet. The system can be adapted in different ways – for example, using photographs or other meaningful images, or having key facts and headings of "true", "false" and "don't know" to find out what a person knows about an issue, such as having diabetes.

Tip

Visual support in the form of thought and speech bubbles offers useful information – for example, on thought processes or the presence of undue influence.

Visual support to aid expression

Visual support can be an aid to expression for people with no or limited speech who can point, nod or shake their heads, do a thumbs up and thumbs down, smile or frown, or direct their gazes. There are many different ways in which visual support can aid expression, such as manipulating images to communicate feelings, for example:

• Turning over options the person disagrees with
• Selecting the options she wants – for example, by pointing

- Ranking options by moving visual support around – for example, his first and second preferences
- Eye pointing to a yes or no image to answer questions.

Many people will be encouraged by an assessor using visual support and give information that they may find difficult to express verbally. For example, if you draw a body, then the person can draw where the PEG tube will go.

Making effective use of visual support

To make effective use of visual support you need to confirm:

- That the person's vision and visual field are sufficient to see the images
- That the person does get information from images.

People who may not get information from images include people with a profound or severe learning disability, autism or visual processing difficulties.

You need to be clear what kinds of images are understood – for example, colour photographs or line drawings. Many people will find colour images the most meaningful. People may also find it more useful to have familiar images used – for example, photographs of their own home rather than a generic home or photographs of specific family members rather than generic photographs of older and younger people.

If visual support will be central to a person's understanding and/or expression, then you should find out what may help or hinder the person getting information from images – for example, busy backgrounds versus lack of background, partially depicted items versus fully depicted items, usual view of items versus unusual views of items.

It is important to understand that some images are abstract; often the less resemblance an image has to the real life equivalent, the more abstract it is. For example, an image of an old fashioned telephone may be unrecognisable to people under 20, and a plus or minus sign may be understood by people who have done maths but not by other people.

Caution

Random use of poorly selected images will not aid a person's understanding and may distract him from the information given to him verbally or in writing.

Good practice in visual support

The following rules will maximise the usefulness of visual support.

IMAGES

- Use colour images as the default.
- Place images on the right, text on the left.
- Use images no smaller than 2.5 cms square as a minimum.
- Use the same image for the same thing throughout the information to maintain consistency.
- Have a contrast between the page colour and the images.
- Avoid background patterns.

TEXT

- Use a sans serif font – for example, Tahoma, Calibri or Arial.
- Use font size 12 or larger.
- Use text aligned to the left with even spaces between words, not justified text.
- Use headers and paragraphs.
- Try to keep sentences to one line.
- Avoid splitting words over two lines.
- Put text in short chunks with plenty of white space around it.
- Highlight important points – for example, in bold, with colour, in boxes or with bullet points.
- Use colour to help people navigate information – for example, green for background information, amber for warning information.
- Avoid underlining.
- Avoid using capital letters to emphasise information.

If the visual support is written, then you need to find out about the reading ability of the person being assessed – for example, reading comprehension and understanding of key words versus full sentences. You need to be aware that some people may read fluently without understanding – for example, people with hyperlexia. In addition, some people have strong preferences about text size and font, and this affects their ability and willingness to try to read.

Tips

- You should keep a copy of all visual support used during the assessment, including any redrafts based on feedback from the person, as it can be used for reassessments and provide evidence of your assessment should the outcome be challenged.
- You should be clear about your rationale for using visual support for that person.

When people cannot use visual support

For people who cannot use visual resources, tactile or object-based resources may be useful to supplement verbal information for some decisions, although more time consuming to develop and make – for example, a 2D or 3D model of the heart which can be felt by the person or a gastrostomy tube stuck to the outside of a person on her stomach. Audio recordings of information may also help people revisit and retain information – for example, a description of what happens during dialysis.

What are all practicable steps?

There are two key elements to fulfilling the communication aspect of the "all practicable steps" requirement of the MCA (2005):

1   Providing a communication-friendly environment
    and
2   Using information about the person's understanding, expression and sensory needs to reduce the impact of specific problems as much as possible OR Using the general rules to help people with SLCN.

What is a communication-friendly environment?

Communication-friendly environments will promote effective communication for most people. The environment should be:

- Familiar
- Quiet
- Free of interruptions
- Free of visual distractions
- Free of background noise in the room – for example, a washing machine
- Free of background noise around the room – for example, doors closing, stairways or lift noise.

A communication-friendly environment will also be a cognition-, or thinking-, friendly environment (see Chapter 9).

The communication should be face-to-face with ideally only two people having the discussion so people can use their one-to-one skills without needing group communication skills. There should be clear roles if more than one person is present, and the roles should be explicitly stated if and when they change – for example, for a scribe.

Sensory needs

Make sure that the person is wearing glasses or a hearing aid if they are required. Take into account any issues with the person's visual field or visual inattention when thinking about the placement of visual materials.

Communication time

You need to think about the person's processing time both for incoming information and for formulating his response. Many people try to help the person with SLCN by rephrasing or prompting too soon, but interrupting can often confuse the person.

Tip

Leave it long enough that you become uncomfortable before rephrasing or promoting a response or count to ten in your head.

For some people any time pressure, however subtle, will affect his ability to focus – for example, impending dinnertime or an afternoon trip, and the assessment will need to be scheduled accordingly.

Phrasing questions

You need to be aware of the kind of questions you are asking and to be sure why you are using a particular kind of question. Examples of question types include:

* Open questions
* Open but focused
* Closed – yes/no
* Closed – either/or
* Closed – multiple choice.

Caution

A question with only two options is called a forced alternative question, and some people with SLCN will always choose the last item in a forced alternative question. For example, when asked "Do you want fish or pie?" the person says "pie", but when asked "Do you want pie or fish?", the person says "fish".

It is advisable to use open questions if possible or start with open questions and narrow down as needed, which is called the funnel technique. For example, you could ask "What changes have you noticed in yourself since your head injury?" as an open question and then ask an open but focused question such as "What physical changes have you noticed since your head injury?" and then focus down further with a closed yes/no question such as "Have you noticed any changes in your walking since your head injury?" if the person does not report difficulties following the open questions. Asking an open but focused question after a lead-in sentence can help the person respond to a topic change and give the necessary information; for example, "We're going to talk about looking after your money. What do you spend your money on every week?"

If you want to verify that a person understands by changing a question to see if there is consistency in her response, it is important that this is done without using a sentence that is difficult to understand. For example, if you want information on a person's understanding of her own skills, you could ask "Can you walk up steps?" and "Do you have trouble walking up steps?" or "Do you get on with your neighbours?" and "Do you fall out with your neighbours?"

Leading questions can make some people respond how they think you want, or expect, them to or in a way that they think will get them what they want. A particular type of leading question is the tagged-on or tag question; for example, "You want to go home, don't you?", "You don't want to go home, do you?" or "You know you will be safer in a residential home, don't you?"

Cautions

- Avoid using any tag questions; for example, "You are always getting into debt, aren't you?"
- Some people with SLCN (for example, related to a developmental delay or learning disability) will only understand specific question words; for example, *what for?* rather than *why?* or *what time?* rather than *when?*.

Tips

- If a person struggles with forced alternatives, try changing the order of the options; for example, "Do you want to stay or move?" and "Do you want to move or stay?"
- Remember it is possible to find out about people's decision-making using a series of well-planned yes/no questions, but it is important that each question is asked from opposing viewpoints to check for understanding or a tendency to answer "yes" to all questions.

- When asking closed yes/no questions, add in some distractor items to check for understanding. For example, when doing a financial capacity assessment with a person who does not have children you could ask, "Do you need to pay for bills? childcare? food? rent?"

General tips to improve communication

Before the assessment

- Find out the level of the person's understanding and expression from an SLT or another staff member who knows him well.
- If a person can only respond yes/no then check the consistency of her responses with a member of staff or ask her some basic questions which you should both know the answers to – for example, "Is your name Gita? Is your name Julie? Are you from London? Are you from Edinburgh?"

Ideally you should do the assessment with someone who is able to communicate well with the person, especially if the person is unknown to you. However, this option is often unavailable and so, if you have little information about a person's communication skills or only a short time to prepare for the assessment, the good practice rules discussed here should be followed.

Tips for promoting understanding

- Talk using a slightly slower pace.
- Use easy words.
- Use KISS – **K**eep **I**t **S**hort and **S**imple, that is, 12 words per sentence or less.
- Give only one piece of information at a time.
- Allow the person plenty of time to absorb the information, which may be over several hours and, therefore, require a second visit.
- Use lead-in statements when you change topic; for example, "Let's talk about your money".
- Encourage people to tell you if they are having difficulties understanding you.
- Be sensitive to clues that people have misunderstood you.
- Use words and sentences you have heard the person use or heard used by the person's other communication partners.
- Use gesture and facial expression to help get you get your message across.
- Use everyday images, for example, those out of a magazine.
- Draw or write to help illustrate your point or to clarify what the person is saying, for example, a timeline of events or a family tree.
- Use mime for concrete concepts if possible.

Tips for promoting expression

- Give the person plenty of time – be patient.
- Be responsive, for example, to the person's facial expression.
- Be aware of your own facial expression and body language.
- Encourage the person to use any means of communication – for example, drawing, gesturing and speaking. Make the conversation feel normal and welcoming.
- Use basic communication aids – for example, picture boards, talkers, pen and paper, self-adhesive notes.
- For people with word-finding difficulties, use prompts to help get the word out (for example, "What is the first sound of the word?") or prompts about function or appearance (for example, "What does it do?", "What does it look like?").
- Use different kinds of questions, for example, forced alternative.
- If you do not understand the speaker, use questions to narrow the topic; for example, "Are you talking about your family?", "Your parents?", "Your mum?". Repeat back what you think the person has said for confirmation.
- Request clarification or repetition – do not pretend to understand when you do not.
- Apologise or explain your lack of understanding – for example, "I'm sorry I misheard you" or "I'm sorry I missed that, please tell me again."
- Reflect information you think you have gained back to the person to check that your understanding is accurate. For example, "Did you say you want to move house?"

Caution

Be careful not to put words into the person's mouth by guessing what key words he is trying to say in case you are wrong but he does not correct you.

Summary

This chapter has covered how to improve communication with people with SLCNs during a capacity assessment. Key points include:

- Find out the level of the person's understanding and expression before the assessment
- If a person can only answer yes/no, then check for consistency in these responses
- Talk at a slower pace

- Use gesture, facial expressions or mime
- Use concrete vocabulary
- Avoid abbreviations
- Use words that the person is used to
- Avoid idioms and pronouns
- Keep sentences short and simple
- Use the active voice
- Avoid negatives
- Organise topics or questions into themes
- Use visual support to aid understanding, retaining, weighing up and expression
- Provide a communication-friendly environment
- Give people time to respond and do not put words into their mouths
- Use different types of questions, such as open, closed – yes/no, and closed – multiple choice
- Change the way you ask a question to check for understanding and consistency
- Avoid leading questions
- Encourage drawing and writing
- Reflect information back to the person to check you have understood correctly.

References

Department for Constitutional Affairs (2007). *Mental Capacity Act 2005: Code of Practice*. London: The Stationery Office. Available at: https://assets.publishing.service.gov.uk/government/uploads/system/uploads/attachment_data/file/497253/Mental-capacity-act-code-of-practice.pdf

Law, J., van de Gaag, A., Hardcastle, B., Beck, J., MacGregor, A. and Plunkett, C. (2007). *Communication Support Needs: A Review of the Literature*. Scottish Executive Social Research. Available at: www.gov.scot/Publications/

Mental Capacity Act 2005. London: HMSO. Available at: www.legislation.gov.uk/ukpga/2005/9/contents

Royal College of Speech and Language Therapists [online]. Available at: www.rcslt.org

Talking Mats. Available at: www.talkingmats.com

Case law

LBX v K, L and M Ruling [2013] EWHC 3230 (Fam)

Montgomery v Lanarkshire Health Board [2015] UKSC 11

Useful websites for further information

Accessible information: http://easy-to-read.eu/european-standards

Accessible information: www.england.nhs.uk/ourwork/accessibleinfo/

Action on Hearing Loss: http://actiononhearingloss.org.uk

British Deaf Association: https://bda.org.uk/

The Communication Trust: https://thecommunicationtrust.org.uk

Royal National Institute for the Blind: www.rnib.org.uk/nb-online/top-tips-communication

The Stroke Association: www.stroke.org.uk

Chapter 12

Using a semi-structured interview to assess capacity

Janice Mackenzie

In this chapter

There are several methods of assessing someone's mental capacity, such as using vignettes or a standard questionnaire measure or having a structured conversation. All of these have their place in different circumstances but, when assessing mental capacity around decisions that have serious consequences (such as a change in accommodation or some medical treatments), one of the most useful and flexible tools to use is a semi-structured interview. The reasons for this are explained below.

Reasons a semi-structured interview can be useful

- Using a similar structure for all your capacity assessments means that you will not forget to ask something or be taken completely off-track by someone who is very talkative or tangential in their speech due to cognitive problems
- In any assessment, it is best practice to write down the questions you ask, as well as the answers. In using a semi-structured interview, the questions are already printed, which will save you time and reduce the impact that writing has on your rapport with the person. (By doing this you are able to show how you elicited the answers from the person being assessed and prove that you did not use leading questions, which is especially useful if your opinion is questioned or you are arguing your case in the Court of Protection.)
- It is a fairer assessment, as you ask similar questions of everybody and are less likely to discriminate
- It is more efficient, as:

  ○ You can pick up the assessment where you left off, if you do the assessment over two or more sessions, without unnecessary repetition
  ○ You do not ask unnecessary questions
  ○ It reduces session preparation time, as you do not need to decide what questions to ask for each individual, although you can tailor the questions to the person and her circumstances

- As it is semi-structured, you can go with the flow of the conversation and come back to earlier questions if they were not covered
- You can leave some questions out altogether if they have already been answered or are not relevant
- You can insert additional questions, if the "flow" of the assessment means this is helpful, and you can write extra information on the back of the sheet
- You are always moving towards the goal in a structured manner
- It is good for inexperienced staff, as various prompts help them to explore areas more deeply and not just take the person's first answer
- It helps staff feel more confident about going into an assessment, as they do not have to think of all the questions to ask
- The structure of the questions helps you to think about how you would ask for other information to reduce the likelihood of using leading questions, which can cause problems for people who are suggestible or who confabulate (when the brain fills in the gaps in the person's memory for him – see Chapter 10), for example, due to executive functioning problems caused by alcohol-related brain damage or traumatic brain injury
- It makes the assessment less of a cognitive effort for the assessor, and so you can pay more attention to what the person is saying and how she is saying it, rather than having to think of what to ask next
- It can be adapted for people at different levels of cognitive, communication and functional ability.

Making and adapting a semi-structured interview

Sometimes it is not appropriate to use a standard semi-structured interview or there may not be one for the specific decision around which capacity is being assessed. In these cases, other questions need to be formulated, but the structure of the semi-structured interview can help you think through what information you need to gain from the person to be able to come to a conclusion about her mental capacity. In my experience, some people argue that it takes too long to complete a semi-structured interview, and they prefer to have a short, unstructured conversation with the person; however, this may not be as robust an assessment and may cause difficulties if it is not obvious whether or not the person has capacity. It can also make completing the relevant documentation more difficult, as you may not have enough evidence to support your findings.

I have developed several semi-structured interviews through clinical experience, but the first one I developed was for a research project to make sure that every participant was asked consistent questions (Mackenzie, Lincoln and Newby, 2008). This was completed before the Mental Capacity Act (MCA, 2005) had been passed, but it was influenced by the Adults with Incapacity (Scotland) Act 2000, which has a similar approach and ethos. I found it so useful during the capacity assessments that I continued to use it clinically and adapted it through use, experience and feedback from other professionals who have used it. It has been distributed through teaching and training and used by numerous professionals in various fields. Over the years it has been developed further to help more inexperienced staff and to take in examples of best practice. The original semi-structured interview in the research project was to assess discharge destination, which often includes the care required on discharge (see www.assessingcapacity.com), and it has been adapted to assess various different questions, such as managing finances (Appendix 5), drinking alcohol (Appendix 8), admission for care and treatment (see www.assessingcapacity. com), treatment decisions, and making or revoking a Lasting Power of Attorney (Appendix 6). It has also been adapted by speech and language therapists to assess decisions around following recommended swallowing guidelines (Appendix 4) and for people who have language difficulties (see www.assessingcapacity.com).

Our research project also compared the impressions of capacity formed by professionals in a multi-disciplinary team (MDT) with formal assessment (Mackenzie, Lincoln and Newby, 2008). Therefore, an MDT questionnaire was also developed to aid uniformity in this structured approach. Following the completion of the study, a slightly adapted version (see www.assessingcapacity.com) was adopted clinically as both the MDT and I found it useful. I have also used it as an interview proforma to gain background information about the person to be assessed from staff when visiting wards as an independent assessor. It was felt that, in conjunction with the semi-structured interview, it maintained a more rigorous approach to capacity assessments. This is important, as the results can potentially remove someone's rights and restrict his personal freedom.

The semi-structured interview is not to replace the legal test of mental capacity or formal documentation produced by organisations, but it can be used to gain insight into the person's thought processes and to help the assessment of the four-part functional legal test (MCA, 2005). It is important to establish before the assessment (using MDT and/or family and friends' knowledge and skills):

- The actual risks and issues surrounding the decision in question
- The relevant information that has been given to the person
- The person's beliefs and values that may impact on decision-making
- Ways that the person's capacity has been enhanced.

The assessment with the person can then be administered taking the following aspects into account:

- Assess the person's insight into his current cognitive and physical problems and situation, starting generally and becoming more specific, prompting if necessary.

- Assess other factors that may be influencing the person's capacity, for example, mood, anxiety, family opinions on the specific decision and possible undue influence of others.
- Directly question the person regarding actual risks and issues to see if he is aware of them and believes them to be related to himself, including what he thinks his family and friends would say about them. This assesses understanding and retention of the relevant issues.
- Assess the person's memory of, and awareness of, safety advice given by professionals.
- Assess his insight into how problems will affect him in different situations, for example, when at home compared to being in hospital.
- Assess the person's risk awareness and problem-solving skills in specific situations by using hypothetical situations that are relevant to him.
- Assess his insight into his needs, how these would be provided for and if he would be safe without help, as well as what he thinks his family and friends would say.
- Assess his ability to take and believe the advice of professionals.
- Assess the person's ability to weigh and use the information by looking at the pros and cons of the alternative options.
- Ask the person which option he would choose and the reasons for his choice, as well as the impact his choice might have on other people and what his family and friends think of his choice.

The whole assessment evaluates the person's ability to communicate his decision. See Chapters 9 and 11 for information on enhancing capacity and ways of adapting the assessment for people with speech and language difficulties. The case study in Box 12.1 illustrates the process of a capacity assessment using a semi-structured interview.

Using vignettes

Standardised vignettes using hypothetical situations can lack the stress, social context, restrictions and consequences that are often attached to real complex decision-making situations (Unsworth, Thomas and Greenwood, 1995) and so the results may not reflect real-life decision-making. Grisso and Appelbaum (1991) found that patients understood information that was relevant to their own illness better than when presented with hypothetical information. Also, when using a vignette in clinical practice, rather than research, the results may not be applicable to the situation unless all of the same details are used. This is because capacity is decision-specific, and the lack of capacity for one decision does not preclude capacity for a different, even if similar, decision (Vellinga et al., 2004). However, situations in which vignettes could be clinically useful are the making of an Advance Decision to Refuse Treatment (ADRT; see Chapter 14) or a Lasting Power of Attorney (LPA; see Chapters 14 and 18), as these would deal with hypothetical situations due to the nature of the documents (Vellinga et al., 2004). It is important to try to make the vignette as close to the person's experience as possible to try to overcome some of the problems mentioned earlier. Vignettes can also be useful to provide some emotional distance from the situation to help the person weigh up the benefits and risks more objectively and, therefore, fully engage in the assessment (see Chapter 25 for an example).

Other interviews

Another example of an interview for assessing capacity is the Aid to Capacity Evaluation (ACE), which is related to medical treatment decisions (Etchells et al., 1999). Although this is based on law in Ontario, Canada, it gives examples of questions that are useful for capacity assessments in the UK. Another Canadian example is the Communication Aid to Capacity Evaluation (CACE), which has been developed for people with communication disorders regarding decisions about discharge destination (Carling-Rowland et al., 2014). Again, aspects of this can be useful when carrying out capacity assessments with people with communication difficulties in the UK.

Box 12.1   Case study of a capacity assessment using a semi-structured interview

The brief was to assess two linked decisions, assessing the ability to manage daily finances and to revoke an existing Lasting Power of Attorney (LPA), which is a legal document that is drawn up to allow someone else to look after a person's property and affairs and/or health and welfare as an "attorney" (similar to a Power of Attorney in Scotland).

Background: Aileen was a 77-year-old lady who had a stroke two years ago, which affected her mobility. She was discharged home from hospital with carer visits, but problems arose when her daughter started providing her with alcohol and spending her money. Aileen had not had problems with alcohol in the past. Aileen reported that she was forced to change her will and transfer her house to her daughter, and the Local Authority raised concerns about Aileen's welfare during this time. Aileen made a new will and successfully applied to the High Court to reverse the transfer of her property. She had a son who lived abroad, and he was not happy with the care

Aileen was receiving at home and so she moved into a Nursing Home (NH). LPAs for Health and Welfare and Property and Affairs were drawn up around this time and registered shortly afterwards by her son's solicitors with her son appointed as attorney. The Council was applying to the Court of Protection to revoke the financial LPA and to appoint their authorised officer to act as the deputy for Aileen's property and affairs.

Information from informants: Aileen owned her own house, and her daughter was living there rent-free. Aileen's income consisted of her state pension and benefits related to disability. She had no insurance policies, shares or savings. Her outgoings consisted of a telephone bill, which was paid from her own account by direct debit, and toiletries brought by her son's friend every week. NHS Continuing Healthcare funded the NH. Staff at the NH thought Aileen was not confused, and her memory was not obviously impaired.

Observations: Some anxiety, good concentration and a variable memory were noted on assessment.

Cognitive assessment: This was carried out to clarify Aileen's cognitive strengths and weaknesses in order to adapt the capacity assessment and enhance her capacity. The assessment found that her strengths were in comprehension and short-term attention; she had some problems with verbal memory and word-finding; and she had significant problems with orientation in time, visual memory, visual perception and use of strategy.

Enhancing capacity: Aileen's capacity was enhanced by providing simplified information, listing all of the options and prompting for pros and cons, providing written information, using repetition, rewording questions and repeated visits.

Assessment of capacity

Insight: Aileen was aware of her physical problems but not of her cognitive problems initially, although her awareness improved during the cognitive assessment. Her previous lack of insight may have been due to her forgetting her problems or not having awareness of the problems due to not being challenged cognitively in the NH.

Other factors: Aileen reported no mental health problems, and she still talked to her daughter, even though she had taken advantage of Aileen.

Income: Aileen was aware of her pension but required a prompt regarding her benefits, and she was not aware of the full amount of her income.

Outgoings: Aileen required a prompt regarding her telephone bill, and she was unaware of how the NH was paid for, but she knew that she had enough money to live on.

Assets: Aileen knew that she owned her house and had no savings but stated that her son could help with bills if required and that Social Services could take value from her house (once it was sold) for the cost of the NH if necessary.

Value of money: Aileen was aware of the cost of everyday products and, when asked what she would do with a gift of £100, she stated that she would save it, as she did not require anything at that point in time.

LPAs: Aileen had limited knowledge about the LPAs but knew that her son had one for her and looked after her money. She reported that her daughter "had been spending it". Aileen required a prompt to report her LPA for health and welfare, and she could not remember being given written information about the LPAs when they were drawn up.

Future wishes: Aileen was happy with the current situation and did not want to look after her finances, although she thought that she could.

Revoking the LPAs: Aileen was unsure how to revoke the LPAs and required help to think through the previous process of drawing them up; however, she was able to think of a solution to her memory problems and could report advantages and disadvantages of the situation.

Current situation: Aileen was aware of the challenge to the LPA by the council and remembered details of the social worker (S/W) who had visited her to discuss this.

Weighing up options: Aileen reported that an advantage of someone looking after her money for her was that she then had no worries, but that a disadvantage was that someone might spend her money. She stated that a S/W could look after money "as last resort" if Aileen revoked the LPAs, but she could see no pros or cons to this versus a family member.

Retaining information: Four days later, Aileen remembered the gist of the discussion and was able to remember a solution to the problem over a shorter period of time.

Outcome of the LPA capacity assessment: In my opinion, Aileen had the capacity to revoke the LPAs at that point in time as she:

- Understood the relevant information in relation to her situation
- Could retain it for long enough to make a decision
- Could weigh up and use the pros and cons to arrive at an informed decision
- Could communicate her decision.

Outcome of the finance capacity assessment: It was not clear whether or not Aileen had the capacity to manage her own finances, as she did not do so at the time of the assessment and she would have had to be supported to try to manage her finances, for example, using cognitive strategies, before it would be possible to state that she was unable to do so due to her memory problems. However, she did not want to do so and was happy with the LPA being in place.

Recommendations: It was recommended that Aileen had access to her own solicitor with the details kept in her bedside drawer and also given to the manager of the NH. In addition, she should be provided with a copy of the written information about LPAs so that she would be able to refresh her memory when required.

References

Adults with Incapacity (Scotland) Act 2000. London: HMSO. Available at: www.legislation.gov.uk/asp/2000/4/contents

Carling-Rowland, A., Black, S., McDonald, L. and Kagan, A. (2014). Increasing access to fair capacity evaluation for discharge decision-making for people with aphasia: A randomised controlled trial. *Aphasiology*, 28(6), 750–765. CACE available at: www.aphasia.ca/wp-content/uploads/2012/11/Communication-Aid-to-Capacity-Evaluation-CACE.pdf

Etchells, E., Darzins, P., Silberfeld, M., Singer, P.A., McKenny, J., Naglie, G., Katz, M., Guyatt, G.H., Molloy, D.W. and Strang, D. (1999). Assessment of patient capacity to consent to treatment. *Journal of General Internal Medicine*, 14(1), 27–34. ACE available at: www.jcb.utoronto.ca/tools/documents/ace.pdf

Grisso, T. and Appelbaum, P.S. (1991). Mentally ill and non-mentally ill patients' abilities to understand informed consent disclosures for medication. *Law and Human Behavior*, 15(4), 377–388.

Mackenzie, J.A., Lincoln, N.B. and Newby, G.J. (2008). Capacity to make a decision about discharge destination after stroke: A pilot study. *Clinical Rehabilitation*, 22, 1116–1126. Available at: www.researchgate.net/publication/23567198_Capacity_to_make_a_decision_about_discharge_destination_after_stroke_A_pilot_study

Mental Capacity Act 2005. London: HMSO. Available at: www.legislation.gov.uk/ukpga/2005/9/contents

Unsworth, C.A., Thomas, S.A. and Greenwood, K.M. (1995). Rehabilitation team decisions on discharge housing for stroke patients. *Archives of Physical Medicine and Rehabilitation*, 76, 331–340.

Vellinga, A., Smit, J.H., van Leeuwen, E., van Tilburg, W. and Jonker, C. (2004). Instruments to assess decision-making capacity: An overview. *International Psychogeriatrics*, 16(4), 397–419.

Part 3

Specific decisions and conditions

Chapter 13

Capacity to consent to medical procedures

Deborah Slater

In this chapter

The law requires professionals to ensure that a person is able to give consent before any form of treatment, investigation or care is given. Consent must be valid and it should be given freely and voluntarily (Royal College of Nursing, 2017). This section will explore what you need to know and the process you need to follow to carry out an assessment of capacity to consent to treatment.

What do you need to do to ensure a person is making an informed decision to consent to a medical procedure?

Just because a person is agreeing to proposed treatment or care, does not mean that he is providing informed consent, especially if he has not been given all of the relevant information. Further, consent has to be given freely without coercion or undue influence. Gaining valid consent before treatment is important as, if this does not happen and the person suffers harm as a result of the treatment, healthcare professionals could be held to account for negligence (Department of Health, 2009).

Providing information prior to the assessment of capacity

You must ensure that the person is provided with all the relevant information she needs and in a format that is appropriate for her, to enable her to make an informed decision.

The person needs to be able to understand, retain, use and weigh up the information in relation to the proposed procedure before communicating her decision (Mental Capacity Act (MCA, 2005) Code of Practice, 2007). Different decisions will require different levels of information (two examples are provided here) and some people may require the information to be adapted (see Chapters 9 and 11 for guidance on this). It is preferable to do the information-giving and the capacity assessment over several sessions but, depending on the urgency of the situation, this may not be possible.

Assessing capacity

It is the role of the clinician to ensure that every person who is undergoing a procedure fully understands:

- What the proposed procedure involves
- Any significant risks of the procedure and/or complications that may occur afterwards
- The pros and cons of having the procedure
- The pros and cons of not having the procedure
- The pros and cons of any reasonable alternatives.

In addition, the person should be informed that he is able to reconsider his decision at any time (Department of Health, 2009).

The person must be able to (MCA Code of Practice, 2007):

- Understand the information in relation to his own circumstances and the wider consequences of his decision (Does the person have a general understanding of what the decision is that he needs to make and why he needs to make it?)
- Have a general understanding of the likely consequences of making or not making this decision
- Retain the information for long enough to make the decision, in the case of one-off treatment decisions, or longer if it is an ongoing decision
- Use the relevant information and weigh up the risks and benefits of the procedure and other options
- Communicate his decision.

Each procedure and treatment will require a different capacity assessment, as mental capacity is decision- and time-specific; however, if the procedures and treatments are similar or linked, then the assessments may be covered in the same session.

Caution

If the person does not have the capacity to make an informed decision, then it is important to check if there is an Advance Decision (Advance Directive in Scotland), Lasting Power of Attorney (LPA) for Health and Welfare, or Court Deputy for Health and Welfare in place for the person before moving to the next step of making a decision.

If there is already a LPA in place, then the relevant person named in that document will be the decision-maker, as with a Court Deputy, or the person may have already made a decision regarding her future health and wellbeing prior to losing her capacity in an Advance Decision to Refuse Treatment (see Chapter 14 for further information).

Case examples

Here are two example scenarios of relatively common decisions in everyday clinical practice regarding capacity for consent.

Scenario 1: Procedure for a person to have a Percutaneous Endoscopic Gastrostomy (PEG) tube insertion (in order to receive food through a tube directly into his stomach)

Sammy had a stroke, resulting in a compromised swallow and an inability to take sufficient food, drink and medications orally. He was losing weight and required regular intravenous fluids. Staff were struggling to ensure that he was taking medications for his medical condition, as he tended to hold them in his mouth for long periods or he spat them out.

Sammy previously had a nasogastric (NG) tube (tube into his stomach via his nose) but he continually removed this, thus further compromising his medical condition and nutritional and hydration needs. Due to these issues, the medical team thought that it was in Sammy's best interests to insert a PEG tube directly into his stomach.

Previously, Sammy had consented to the insertion of the NG tube but, due to his continuous removal of the NG tube and his condition deteriorating, it was felt that a capacity assessment needed to be carried out regarding a PEG tube insertion.

In order to have capacity, Sammy would need to understand:

- The reason the PEG tube needs to be inserted, for example, difficulties with his swallow and his inability to tolerate a NG tube
- The benefits of the PEG tube insertion, for example, how it would improve nutrition and hydration and allow medications to be given, thus optimising his health and wellbeing
- The risks and potential complications of the procedure, including the anaesthetic and risk of infection (This will differ for every person depending on his medical condition and any pre-existing comorbidities.)
- The benefits and risks of not having the PEG tube inserted – removing the potential risks of the procedure versus the likely outcome of a deterioration in his health and, potentially, death.

Tip

Remember that, as this is a one-off decision, the person will only need to retain the information long enough to make the decision at that point in time.

Scenario 2: Surgical removal of a cancerous growth in a person with a traumatic brain injury

Rebecca had sustained a traumatic brain injury in a road traffic collision and had cognitive difficulties as a result. She had been in hospital for a couple of months when she required surgical treatment for the removal of a cancerous growth that had been found. The surgical team needed to assess her capacity to consent to the procedure, which included a general anaesthetic.

Previous attempts to try to explain to Rebecca what would be involved had not been successful, as she kept saying that she did not want to talk about it. Staff who knew her well felt that if the surgeon returned later in the day and spoke to her when she was more alert and more able to engage, then a more representative assessment of her understanding could be undertaken.

The surgeon therefore left information regarding the procedure with Rebecca to read in her own time with support from staff. In addition, the surgeon asked staff to find a quiet room for when he returned later in the day to further discuss the procedure with Rebecca, along with a member of staff who knew Rebecca well providing support.

In order to have capacity Rebecca would need to understand the following:

* The reason for the operation, for example, that the cancerous growth needs to be removed
* The benefits of the removal of the cancerous growth, for example, if the growth was removed then the likelihood of the cancer being removed would be higher and the long-term prognosis may be better, even though she may also require chemotherapy and/or radiotherapy
* The risks and potential complications of the procedure, including the anaesthetic procedure and any complications that may occur (This will differ for every person depending on her medical condition and any pre-existing comorbidities.)
* The benefits and risks of not having the growth removed – removing the potential risks of the surgery versus the potential for the growth to get bigger and for the cancer to spread to other areas of the body, which could shorten her lifespan.

In both scenarios, it is important to remember that ensuring the person has all the relevant information in a format he can understand will enable him to make an informed decision if he has the mental capacity to do so.

Caution

A person who makes an "unwise" decision is not to be assumed to lack the capacity to make that decision, but further assessment may be necessary if the decision is out of character or the person repeatedly makes decisions that put him at significant risk of harm (MCA Code of Practice, 2007).

Tip

Be aware that a person's background and lifestyle may influence her decision-making outcome (see Chapter 5).

An example from case law

In *Montgomery v Lanarkshire Health Board* [2015] a precedent was set regarding the level of information to be given by doctors to patients before they make informed decisions about treatment. The case was about a pregnant diabetic woman who was not advised about a 9–10% risk of shoulder dystocia during vaginal delivery, as the doctor did not routinely advise of this because she thought the risk of a grave problem for the baby was small but, if advised of the risk, then the mother would opt for a caesarean section, which was not in the maternal interest. Unfortunately, the baby was deprived of oxygen during the delivery, due to the extra procedure that had to occur, and ended up with cerebral palsy. The judgment decreed that a person should be able to decide which option to choose and, therefore, the person needs to be given all of the relevant information in order to be able to make an informed decision. The doctor has to make sure that the person is aware of:

* Any material risks, that is if the person is likely to attach significance to the risk
* Reasonable alternative or variant treatments.

It was also noted that:

* The assessment of whether a risk is material cannot be reduced to percentages
* The doctor's advisory role involves dialogue and not bombarding the person with technical information which she cannot reasonably be expected to grasp
* The therapeutic exception should not be abused – that is the doctor should not prevent the person from making a decision that is not in the person's best interests.

This case law example is a marked change to law and replaces the previous "Bolam test" (*Bolam v Friern Hospital Management Committee* [1957]), which asks whether a doctor's conduct would be supported by a responsible body of medical opinion. The Bolam test will no longer apply to the issue of consent, although it will continue to be used more widely in cases involving other alleged acts of negligence.

References

Department for Constitutional Affairs (2007). *Mental Capacity Act 2005: Code of Practice*. London: The Stationery Office. Available at: www.gov.uk/government/uploads/system/uploads/attachment_data/file/497253/Mental-capacity-act-code-of-practice.pdf

Department of Health (2009). *Reference Guide to Consent for Examination or Treatment*. 2nd ed. Available at: www.gov.uk/government/uploads/system/uploads/attachment_data/file/138296/dh_103653__1_.pdf

Mental Capacity Act 2005. London: HMSO. Available at: www.legislation.gov.uk/ukpga/2005/9/contents

Royal College of Nursing (2017). *Principles of Consent: Guidance for Nursing Staff*. Available at: www.rcn.org.uk/professional-development/publications/pub-006047

Case law

Bolam v Friern Hospital Management Committee [1957] 1 WLR 582

Montgomery v Lanarkshire Health Board (Scotland) [2015] UKSC 11

Chapter 14

Advance care planning

Deborah Slater

In this chapter

There are several ways in which someone can plan for her future care, and this chapter will look at these, with specific emphasis on what you need to know and do when someone has made an Advance Decision to Refuse Treatment (sometimes called a Living Will). The differences between this and an Advance Statement of wishes will be explained, as will the roles of people who hold a Lasting Power of Attorney for health and welfare or a personal welfare deputyship.

The Mental Capacity Act (MCA, 2005) provides a framework to enable competent, informed adults, who are capable of understanding the implications of their decisions, to refuse specific medical procedures or treatment in advance, including lifesaving treatment by making an ADRT or appointing an Attorney to make decisions for them (MCA Code of Practice, 2007). In Scotland, an ADRT is known as an Advance Directive and, although it is not currently legally binding in Scotland, it is a clear statement of the person's past wishes and so has to be taken into account when making decisions on her behalf once she has lost the capacity to make that decision (Compassion in Dying, 2014c).

What is an Advance Decision?

An Advance Decision (short for an Advance Decision to Refuse Treatment; ADRT) is a document that is a principle in law and medical practice that allows a person who is aged 18 or over to refuse specific medical treatment for a time in the future when he may lack the capacity to consent to or refuse that particular treatment plan (Department of Health, 2009). A valid and applicable ADRT has the same meaning as a decision made in the present (Department of Health, 2009).

Caution

An Advance Decision must be followed if it is valid and applies to the current circumstances, even if the decision may result in the person's death or serious injury.

An ADRT is legally binding as long as it complies with the MCA (2005), is valid and is relevant to the situation. An ADRT must specify the treatment that the person is refusing in clear detail. Healthcare professionals are protected from liability by the MCA (2005) if they withhold treatment believing an ADRT to be valid and applicable. If healthcare professionals do not follow it, they could face criminal charges or a civil claim; however, if they are not sure of its existence or validity, and they proceed with treatment in the person's best interests, then the MCA (2005) would protect them from liability (Department of Health, 2009). If there is doubt about the validity of an ADRT, then it should be referred to the Court of Protection and life-saving treatment, or treatment to stop a significant decline in the person's condition, can continue to be administered until the Court provides a decision (Department of Health, 2009).

If a member of staff disagrees with the person's decision to refuse life-sustaining treatment due to his beliefs, then that staff member can choose not to treat the person but he must make sure that another member of staff takes over the person's care (NHS Improving Quality, 2014).

Caution

You need to be aware that the person can cancel his decision, or part of it, at any time as long as he has the capacity to do so – this can be done verbally or in writing.

An ADRT does not legally have to be stored anywhere and can be cancelled at any time by being destroyed by the person who made it. It is the responsibility of the person to inform professionals if he changes his mind and wants to cancel his ADRT (Compassion in Dying, 2014a).

If the person has the capacity to make a decision at the time it needs to be made, then the ADRT is not yet applicable; therefore, the person can decide what he would like to do concerning the proposed treatment or procedure (NHS Improving Quality, 2014).

Who can make an Advance Decision?

Any person over the age of 18 can decide if she wants to refuse treatment in the future. People make Advance Decisions in a number of different circumstances, which may include:

- When they are fit and healthy, even if there is no prospect of illness
- In preparation for growing older
- After being informed that they have a specific disease or condition as part of their treatment planning, and
- When they have a chronic physical health or mental health condition that will fluctuate or deteriorate.

Various websites can assist a person to compile an ADRT. The websites offer clear advice and guidelines in how to complete one to ensure validity (Compassion in Dying, 2014a).

There is no set format for a written Advance Decision, as contents will vary depending on a person's situation and wishes, but the following information should be included (NHS Improving Quality, 2014):

- Full details of the person making the ADRT including date of birth and address
- The name and address of the person's GP and whether the GP has a copy of the ADRT
- A clear statement of the decision and treatment the person is refusing and the circumstances in which the decision will apply
- The date the ADRT was written
- The person's signature or the signature of someone the person has asked to sign on her behalf and in her presence
- The signature of the person witnessing the signature.

In the case of a verbal ADRT, again there is no formal format as this will be dependent on the person's situation and wishes. As professionals, you should document a verbal ADRT in the person's healthcare records; this will give a written record that could reduce uncertainty about future decisions. The record should include (NHS Improving Quality, 2014):

- A communication that the decision to refuse treatment should apply if the person lacks the capacity to make the specific treatment decision in the future
- A note of the decision and the treatment that the person wants to refuse and the circumstances in which the decision will apply

- Details of another person who was present when the verbal ADRT was made and the role of that person (healthcare professional/family member)
- Whether that person took part in the decision or is just aware it exists.

ADRTs should be reviewed regularly to take account of changes in the person's condition and new medical procedures (NHS Improving Quality, 2014).

Caution

People are only able to make Advance Decisions to *refuse* treatment, and they have no legal right to *demand* specific treatment (MCA Code of Practice, 2007).

How do you ascertain if the Advance Decision is valid?

It is the responsibility of the person who has made the ADRT to inform healthcare professionals of its existence when it is required, or a family member may do this if the person is too ill.

Some people may request that their ADRT information is documented in their healthcare records. Other people may not want this, but they must find other ways of ensuring healthcare professionals are aware that there is an ADRT in place, informing healthcare professionals where they can find this information when it is required. Some people may carry a card or wear a bracelet or family may inform staff of its existence (MCA Code of Practice, 2007).

An ADRT is valid and applicable if (MCA Code of Practice, 2007):

- The person was aged 18 or over at the time of making it
- The person had the mental capacity to make that decision at that time. (Healthcare professionals should always start from the assumption that the person had the capacity to make the ADRT in the first instance.)
- The person has not done anything that goes against her ADRT, such as having a form of treatment or procedure that she had stipulated she did not want in the ADRT
- The person has not withdrawn her decision
- The person has not transferred the power to make the decision to a solicitor or family member via a Lasting Power of Attorney (LPA).

In addition, when deciding if an ADRT is valid and applicable, it is important to consider if the person would have changed her decision if she had known more about the current circumstances, for example, new treatments with better outcomes (MCA Code of Practice, 2007).

If the Advance Decision is to refuse life-sustaining treatment, then it must:

- Be in writing
- Be signed and witnessed, and
- Clearly state the decision still applies even if the person's life is at risk.

The ADRT may be recorded in healthcare notes and written by someone else, but it must have been witnessed by a third party and signed by all parties. For example, if a person is not able to write the ADRT due to a disability or due to her condition, then a family member or doctor can write it for her, but it must be signed by the person who it applies to and she must have the capacity to make the ADRT. The ADRT must then be signed by the person writing the ADRT and by a third person as a witness (MCA Code of Practice, 2007).

What can an Advance Decision be used for?

An Advance Decision can be used to refuse any medical treatment, including life-sustaining treatment, such as (Compassion in Dying, 2014a):

- Being put on a ventilator if someone cannot breathe on his own
- Being given food or fluids via artificial means, for example, via a drip or a tube through the nose or stomach
- Antibiotics for a life-threatening infection, and
- Cardiopulmonary resuscitation if someone's heart stops (CPR).

What can an Advance Decision not be used for?

An Advance Decision cannot be used to (Compassion in Dying, 2014a):

- Ask for something against the law, such as assistance to end the person's life
- Refuse food and drink by mouth or refuse care that keeps someone clean and comfortable. (These are part of basic care and health professionals have a statutory duty to provide this; however, this does not include force-feeding a person who is refusing food or drink and the BMA advises that "refusals of basic care by patients with capacity should be respected, although it should be continued to be offered" (Department of Health, 2009, at paragraph 1.51).)
- Choose someone else to decide about treatment on his behalf. (This can only be done by making a Lasting Power of Attorney for Health and Welfare.)

- Demand certain treatments. (It is the doctor's role to decide whether treatment is medically appropriate, but it is the person's decision as to whether he accepts the treatment or not.)

Also, if a person uses an ADRT to refuse treatment for "mental disorder", then this may not apply if he is detained under the Mental Health Act (1983) (NHS Improving Quality, 2014).

The interaction between advance decisions and Lasting Power of Attorney or Court-appointed Deputy

If a Lasting Power of Attorney (LPA) for health and welfare is already in place and an ADRT is made afterwards, then the ADRT will override the LPA for the specific decision included in the ADRT. Alternatively, if a valid LPA for health and welfare was made after an ADRT, then this would make the ADRT invalid and the LPA would supersede it, if it includes the same treatment mentioned in the ADRT (NHS Improving Quality, 2014). However, the wishes expressed in the ADRT would have to be taken into account by the Attorney when making a decision in the person's best interests. It is worth noting that an LPA for health and welfare is only valid once the person has lost the capacity to make those decisions, but the LPA would likely be drawn up before this point, while the person still has the capacity to make the LPA. Because a Court-appointed Personal Welfare Deputy is only appointed after someone has lost the capacity to make these decisions, it is unlikely that there would be a circumstance in which an ADRT could be drawn up after the Deputy is in place for that decision. If there is already an ADRT in place, then the Deputy would have to respect it. An Attorney can only refuse life-sustaining treatment if the LPA states it specifically and a Deputy is unable to do this, as this decision must be taken by the Court (MCA Code of Practice, 2007, at paragraph 8.46). (See Chapter 18 for example questions to assess someone's capacity to make or revoke an LPA and Appendix 6 for an example semi-structured interview for this decision. Although these relate to making or revoking an LPA for financial affairs, most of the questions can be adapted to making an LPA for health and welfare.)

The Court of Protection tends to only appoint Personal Welfare Deputies in extreme cases, as the best-interests process can usually be used for health and welfare decisions, or the Court will make one-off decisions. If a Deputy is appointed, then the scope and duration should be as limited as possible (MCA Code of Practice, 2007, at paragraph 8.26). However, serious family disagreements leading to problems with the best-interests process and ongoing issues may require the appointment of a Deputy (MCA Code of Practice, 2007, at paragraph 8.39).

What is an Advance Statement?

It is worth noting that there is another document that professionals may come across called an Advance Statement, which is sometimes called a "Statement of Wishes". An Advance Statement differs from an Advance Decision in that it is a general statement in which the person can express her wishes and preferences in relation to future treatment and care when she does not have the capacity to make these decisions herself (Age UK, 2019).

The Advance Statement allows the person to write down anything that is important to her such as:

* Food preferences
* Spiritual needs/views
* Information about her daily routine
* Any fears she may have around treatment and care
* A preference of where she would like to be cared for, for example, home, residential home or hospital
* Any people or family members she would like to be consulted with on her behalf
* Practical issues.

An Advance Statement is not legally binding; however, it does have legal standing as it must be taken into account when someone is deciding what is in the person's best interests as it states the person's past views, beliefs and values (Compassion in Dying, 2014b).

A person can have both an Advance Statement and an ADRT at the same time (Compassion in Dying, 2014b), as the former is expressing preferences for her health and care and the latter is refusing certain treatments in the future.

An Advance Statement can be given verbally, but it is better if the person writes it down as an enduring record of her preferences, so that people are able to refer to it in the future (Age UK, 2019).

References

Age UK (2019). *Factsheet 72: Advance Decisions, Advance Statements and Living Wills*. Available at: www.ageuk.org.uk/globalassets/age-uk/documents/factsheets/fs72_advance_decisions_advance_statements_and_living_wills_fcs.pdf

Compassion in Dying (2014a). *Advance Decisions (Living Wills)*. Available at: https://compassionindying.org.uk/making-decisions-and-planning-your-care/planning-ahead/advance-decision-living-will

Compassion in Dying (2014b). *Advance Statements*. Available at: https://compassionindying.org.uk/making-decisions-and-planning-your-care/planning-ahead/advance-statements/

Compassion in Dying (2014c). *Understanding Advance Directives—Scotland*. Available at: https://compassionindying.org.uk/wp-content/uploads/2014/11/AD02-Understanding-Advance-Directives-Scotland.pdf

Department for Constitutional Affairs (2007). *Mental Capacity Act 2005: Code of Practice*. London: The Stationery Office. Available at: www.gov.uk/government/uploads/system/uploads/attachment_data/file/497253/Mental-capacity-act-code-of-practice.pdf

Department of Health (2009). *Reference Guide to Consent for Examination or Treatment*. 2nd ed. Available at: www.gov.uk/government/uploads/system/uploads/attachment_data/file/138296/dh_103653__1_.pdf

Mental Capacity Act 2005. London: HMSO. Available at: www.legislation.gov.uk/ukpga/2005/9/contents

Mental Health Act 1983. London: HMSO. Available at: http://www.legislation.gov.uk/ukpga/1983/20/contents

NHS Improving Quality (2014). *Advance Decisions to Refuse Treatment: A Guide for Health and Social Care Professionals*. Available at: http://endoflifecareambitions.org.uk/wp-content/uploads/2016/09/Advance-Decisions.pdf

Useful resources

39 Essex Chambers (2012). *Advance Decisions – getting it right?* Available at: http://www.39essex.com/docs/articles/advance_decisions_paper_ark_december_2012.pdf

Office of the Public Guardian (OPG): www.gov.uk

Chapter 15

Capacity assessment for swallowing disorders and feeding management

Catherine Blakemore

In this chapter

The content of this chapter includes a definition of swallowing disorders and considers how the problem may affect the individual. It summarises assessment and management options for swallowing disorders and feeding. It also discusses ways to support an individual's understanding of relevant information in relation to making an informed decision about swallowing and feeding management and how to assess an individual's mental capacity to make a decision about these issues.

Swallowing disorder and feeding options

The medical term for a swallowing disorder is *dysphagia*. Dysphagia describes any problem that compromises an individual's ability to chew and swallow normal fluid or food, or manage oral or pharyngeal secretions, such as saliva. Dysphagia may be part of a developmental disorder, or an acquired disorder. The causes of dysphagia can vary; it can be due to structural changes (for example, following head and neck surgery), neurological disorder (for example, brain injury, stroke, dementia or cerebral palsy), or functional/non-organic problems (for example, functional neurological syndrome). Understanding the cause will clarify the swallow prognosis, as dysphagia can be temporary, chronic or progressive. This and the individual's wishes will influence management.

There are four stages to the swallow:

1 Oral preparatory phase – requires hand to mouth control, response to the hand/spoon or cup delivering the diet/fluid, and mouth opening and shaping. In this phase increased anticipatory salivation may occur.
2 Oral phase – the bolus is mixed with saliva and broken down through chewing to form a cohesive bolus, then transported to the back of the mouth ready for swallowing.

3   Pharyngeal phase – the vocal folds and false folds close to protect the airway, the larynx elevates and tilts anteriorly, allowing the epiglottis to provide further airway protection as the bolus travels through the pharynx and into the oesophagus (food pipe).
4   Oesophageal phase – the bolus moves into the oesophagus and down to the stomach.

Difficulties in any of the stages of the swallow may result in the bolus penetrating the airway to the level of the vocal folds and potentially passing below this into the trachea and tracking to the lungs. This is known as aspiration. For individuals where cognition or sensation is altered, there may be a risk of silent aspiration, whereby the individual is not aware and does not react or attempt to protect her airway. Choking or asphyxiation is also a potential consequence of dysphagia.

Clinical presentations and consequences of dysphagia include:

- Coughing, choking, wet voice quality
- Weight loss, dehydration, malnutrition
- Chest infections which may be recurrent or aspiration pneumonia
- Repeated need for antibiotic treatment for chest infections
- Admission to hospital
- Reduced quality of life
- Reduced life expectancy
- Death.

It is the role of the Speech and Language Therapist (SLT) to understand the cause of the dysphagia, assess the swallow and consider appropriate management options for eating and drinking for the individual. This may also require input from members of a multi-disciplinary team (MDT), for example, dietitians, nutrition specialist nurses and medics.

Swallow assessments

Bedside swallow assessment – Utilises patient and medical history, clinical presentation, oro-motor assessment and presentation on oral trials. This assessment is not appropriate for patients known to be a high risk of silent aspiration.

Videofluoroscopy (VFS) – X-ray of swallow. This is the gold standard assessment and is helpful in establishing a baseline of the swallow, assessing oral trials, detecting silent aspiration, and reviewing progress in rehabilitation, efficacy of strategies and manoeuvres for swallowing.

Fibreoptic Endoscopic Evaluation of Swallow (FEES) – Camera test of swallow. It can be performed at the bedside for medically unstable or immobile patients. It can detect silent aspiration and provide imaging of secretions. It is helpful in reviewing aspiration risk and progress in rehabilitation, efficacy of strategies and manoeuvres for swallowing.

Possible management options

- Advice regarding oral-pharyngeal secretion management
- Modification of fluid or diet, for example, thickened fluids or puree diet/ Level 4 diet
- Consideration of altered modes of delivery through adapted cups or cutlery
- Advice regarding useful strategies or manoeuvres for swallowing, enabling safer eating and drinking
- Therapy exercises to improve swallow function
- Advice on safest swallowing guidelines. In severe dysphagia it may be appropriate for the person to be placed "nil by mouth" (NBM) and consider alternative methods of feeding (AMF), for example, nasogastric tube (NGT), percutaneous endoscopic gastrostomy (PEG), radiographically inserted gastrostomy (RIG), or percutaneous endoscopic jejunostomy (PEJ)
- Guidance on "risk feeding" decisions, that is, oral feeding guidelines set with the acknowledgement of aspiration risk. Risk feeding may be appropriate for individuals who have the capacity to make this decision, or it may be decided in their best interests for their quality of life in the absence of capacity for this decision.

Alternative Methods of Feeding (AMF)

In severe cases of dysphagia, the risk of aspiration and/or choking may be so great that the safest management option would be to remain nil by mouth and consider alternative methods of feeding (AMF). AMF may be agreed for a short-term period, for example, an NGT, or as a middle- to long-term option, for example, PEG, RIG or PEJ. For some individuals it may be that AMF are required to enable nutrition, hydration and medication needs to be consistently managed, but small amounts of fluid or diet may be possible as therapy or for quality of life.

Acknowledgment has been given to the fact that, although AMF may significantly reduce the risk of aspiration events, thereby reducing the risk to deterioration in health due to aspiration, it does not eliminate the risk fully (The Royal College of Physicians, 2010). The document also acknowledged that in certain circumstances and stages of disease, AMF do not improve quality of life or indeed prolong life. Therefore, the risks and benefits for each individual case can be very different.

Capacity assessment regarding swallowing and feeding decisions

When should capacity regarding feeding be considered?

In an ideal situation, the person will be cognitively able to engage in all aspects of swallow or feeding management and would be able to understand the findings of assessments, management options and consequences and make an informed decision about her care. However, in a large proportion of our caseload there may be reason to question an individual's capacity where there is impairment to mind or brain.

In instances where there is no diagnosed impairment to mind or brain, but an individual appears to struggle with reasoning and understanding of information, it may be appropriate to discuss with the MDT whether mental capacity should be further explored.

Mental capacity assessment is always for a specific decision, and there are many scenarios linked to swallowing and feeding that may require an individual to understand, retain and weigh up information. Examples of swallowing and feeding related decisions may include:

- A decision to not comply with swallowing guidelines, strategy use, adapted cups or cutlery when there is known aspiration risk
- A decision regarding AMF, for example, whether to have NGT or PEG
- A decision regarding risk feeding, for example, oral intake with the acceptance of aspiration and/or choking risk
- A decision to commence with trials of taking food or drink orally for therapeutic benefit or to promote quality of life.

Decision-making: Options and thresholds

A decision may have multiple related options. Before the assessment, the complexity and level of detail of the information relating to each option available should be considered. The threshold for each decision will be different depending on the situation and the complexity. Understanding of the clinical evidence base and the individual's clinical history is helpful in weighting this and relevant case law may provide further guidance. For example, the consequences of aspiration to an individual on the Acute Intensive Care Unit (AICU), who is immobile and ventilator-dependent, may be different to a younger healthy mobile person with no history of clinical signs of deterioration in chest status and would therefore require a more in-depth capacity assessment. (See Table 15.1 for examples of different scenarios.) The identified pros and cons can also be used for the best interests decision discussion if the person does not have capacity to make the decision.

Table 15.1 Examples of different assessment scenarios

Clinical scenario	Decision to be made	Options available	Threshold	Pros	Cons
1. Tara: Post-stroke with severe oral pharyngeal dysphagia. Immobile and frail. High risk of aspiration with any oral intake.	Tara needs to decide whether to have an NGT as a short-term measure.	A) To remain NBM and have an NGT for a short period of 4 weeks initially, with planned review B) To accept the risk of aspiration and continue with oral intake for quality of life	Tara would need to understand the following: She has had a stroke and now has dysphagia Oral intake is very likely to be aspirated causing deterioration in health and chest complications The consequences of aspiration, including pneumonia and possible death The doctors have decided that her ceiling of care is to be ward level only, and she is not deemed fit for resuscitation Swallow may improve with rehabilitation and management can be reviewed in 4 weeks	For option A) Would reduce the risk of aspiration-related health complications May support nutrition and hydration, allowing time for the swallow to recover Would allow time for general recovery and rehab of swallow to take place Reduced risk of aspiration/choking related death For option B) May be preferred option for comfort Least restrictive option There may be improvement to quality of life in the short-term	For option A) Most restrictive option May be uncomfortable Will need regular checking by nurses Assistance with feeding will be needed Aspiration risk is not fully eliminated For option B) Aspiration and choking may be distressing Chest infections and pneumonia may develop May be in hospital for longer May prevent rehabilitation and recovery May result in death

(Continued)

Table 15.1 (Continued)

Clinical scenario	Decision to be made	Options available	Threshold	Pros	Cons
2.Earle: Has cognitive impairment and is a known silent aspirator with normal fluids following a brain injury. Earle has been stable with swallowing guidelines advised by SLT but is keen to have a McDonald's meal with his family. Earle does not believe that he has a swallowing problem because he does not cough when eating and drinking.	Earle needs to decide whether to take normal fluid and normal diet despite known aspiration risk	A) To accept the risk of aspiration and potential consequences of taking normal fluid and diet B) To follow the guidelines set by SLT of Level 2 (mildly thick fluid) using a provale cup and Level 4 (puree diet) (Cichero et al., 2017)	Earle would need to understand the following: He has dysphagia following his brain injury and is a silent aspirator That he will not experience overt difficulties as he has altered sensation and is not aware that fluid and diet is being aspirated That further silent aspiration will cause deterioration in his chest and health and may result in a longer stay in hospital Ongoing aspiration events may result in future readmissions to hospital Aspiration can result in pneumonia and death	For option A) Would allow Earle to eat what he likes and is therefore the least restrictive option Would improve his quality of life in the short-term through increased enjoyment of eating and drinking Would be less restrictive when going out to eat and drink For option B) May reduce the risk of aspiration Will help maintain health through reduced likelihood of chest infection May enable discharge from hospital sooner due to being medically stable Would reduce the risk of readmission or need for medical treatment due to aspiration-induced chest infection/pneumonia Reduced risk of aspiration/ choking related death	For option A) May result in deterioration in chest and health May not be able to eat out with family due to deterioration in health May reduce quality of life in the longer-term due to recurrent chest infections May increase length of time in hospital/readmission to hospital May result pneumonia/death For option B) Most restrictive option Not Earle's preference Would reduce quality of life and enjoyment of eating and drinking Would make eating out with family and friends more difficult

Involvement of the medical team may be important to fully understand the implications of one option versus another, for example, delaying discharge, interrupting rehabilitation, delaying chemotherapy and the possibility of death. Advance care planning can be particularly helpful in instances where an individual is anticipated to deteriorate in health or cognition. It may enable the person to be involved in discussions and decisions about his care while he is well and able which, in turn, may help to optimise his ability to participate in the capacity assessment. Advance care planning decisions, including the level of escalation of medical care in the event of aspiration pneumonia and deterioration in health, should be discussed early and incorporated into the decision-making process, for example, treatment for infection at ward level or in the community only versus escalation to AICU. The "ceiling of care" (the point at which no further escalation of care will take place) for medical management will be dependent on the individual and her circumstances. The person's beliefs and previous wishes should be taken into account if she is found to lack the capacity to make the decision, and any formal legal documentation like an Advance Directive/Advance Decision to Refuse Treatment, or "living will", should be followed.

Many speech and language therapy teams will have their own protocol for risk feeding, which should be led by the principles of mental capacity legislation in terms of assessment and decision-making. In more complex scenarios, it may also be appropriate to seek advice from the care organisation's legal team regarding local policy.

How can capacity be supported? Education and insight-building

It is important to make sure that the person being assessed is given all of the relevant information before the assessment. The most appropriate professionals related to the decision, for example, speech and language therapists, clinical psychologists, nutrition nurses, dietitians or medics, should explore the options available with the person. In instances where the decision is complex, the outcome could be fatal or capacity is unclear, it would be advisable to involve a more experienced professional who is an expert in capacity assessments, for example, a member of the legal department, a clinical neuropsychologist or a senior safeguarding nurse. Assessing with two staff members is good practice in such cases. The way in which the information is presented should also be considered, particularly when the individual has altered sensory, cognitive and/or communication abilities. (See how to support people with communication difficulties in Chapter 11).

Box 15.1   Education and insight-building resources and tools

There are several ways to support an individual with his education and increase his understanding of the information relevant to the decision:

1   Supported conversation using written information, biofeedback during assessments in VFS/FEES and repeated viewings and explanations of his swallow impairment. Reference to aspiration or choking events and the impact on the person's progress in rehabilitation or wellbeing may also be helpful.

2   Anatomical pictures of swallow or apps may help raise understanding of the swallow phases and abnormalities and aspiration – for example, the Dysphagia app produced by Northern Speech Services.

3   Documentation of symptoms the person has experienced when certain fluid or diet trials were assessed may be helpful for individuals with memory impairment or those who lack insight or deny their problems.

4   Knowing a person's timeline of aspiration events, for example, numbers of times she has been admitted to hospital or required antibiotics for chest infection.

5   Expert patient role in education, for example, in the instance of NGT or PEG insertion decision. Providing the opportunity for the person to meet with someone further along in the process who has undergone the procedure may be helpful.

6   Meeting relevant professionals, for example, nutrition nurse or dietitian to help explain what having an NGT or PEG may entail.

7   Semi-structured interview – Having a pre-prepared template of possible questions may be helpful in structuring and recording responses for the capacity assessment. (See the example semi-structured interview created by a specialist speech and language therapist in Appendix 4.) Flexibility is required when using a pre-made questionnaire to ensure that the questions are relevant to the threshold and decision-specific to the individual.

8   Listing pros and cons for each option. A facilitated version may involve a sorting exercise of pre-prepared statements or "true or false" statements.

9   Talking Mats™ may also help people who require more support cognitively or communicatively. Taking pictures of the mats after each discussion would be helpful in keeping a record of an individual's progress with education and rationalising of information.

10   Research cited in Royal College of Physician Guidelines (Royal College of Physicians, 2010) in relation to "oral feeding difficulties and dilemmas" and the evidence base may be helpful for some people.

Instances when capacity for feeding decisions might be reviewed

It is important to consider at the time of forming an opinion on capacity whether there is potential for change in the person's insight, cognition or swallow that would lead to a review of his capacity, or of the swallow guidelines, at a later date.

In cases where there are changes in the swallow, either improvements or deteriorations, a review of the options and the ceiling of care, or the advance care plan, would be required. In addition, another assessment of capacity may be required if the salient factors have changed.

Other examples of when the result of a capacity assessment would need to be reviewed include:

- If a person experienced a choking episode or aspiration event and found it distressing, which in turn led to an increase in her insight and understanding and changes in the way she weighs the pros and cons of the decision
- If an improvement in cognitive abilities (for example, post-brain-injury or post-stroke) is noted, as this may lead to an improvement in decision-making ability due to increased ability to understand, retain and weigh the relevant information
- If a deterioration in cognition (for example, in progressive conditions such as dementia or multiple sclerosis) is noted, as this may lead to an impairment in decision-making ability due to reduced ability to understand, retain and weigh the relevant information
- If a person's swallow function improves and the options for feeding management change, resulting in consideration of other options (e.g., oral intake and PEG weaning).

Box 15.2 Case study example of a complex capacity assessment

Mark was a 47-year-old man with an alcohol-related brain injury and dysphagia. He was seen by SLT and advised to take Level 2 fluids (mildly thick) and Level 5 diet (minced and moist diet), with supervision at mealtimes. Guidelines were informed by bedside swallow assessment, as an instrumental assessment was not possible due to challenging behaviour.

Mark was very vocal and frequently threatened to eat and drink whatever he liked and would ask family to bring in inappropriate food when therapists were present. Physical improvements in rehabilitation meant that there was increased risk of Mark accessing high-risk textures and self-feeding.

Mark was very mistrustful of information given and repeatedly became very aggressive in any discussion about dysphagia and the provided guidelines. He repeatedly reported that he would do what he wanted to do and, on one occasion, threw modified drinks on the floor. Due to this, a capacity assessment was commenced. During the capacity assessment, Mark continued to assert that he had no problems and would do what he liked; however, when left alone, observed behaviour with food and drink was not consistent with Mark's expressed wishes. In these instances, he was observed to be compliant with guidelines.

A carefully controlled trial was arranged in which Mark was given a normal drink and normal food. Mark asked for the consistencies advised by the SLT. Covert observation and monitoring of his behaviour on several controlled occasions enabled the team to agree that he had understood, retained, used and weighed up the relevant information given regarding the risk of non-compliance. It was thought that his beliefs and values around hospitals and people in authority telling him what to do may have influenced his responses on the capacity assessment, even though the reasons for the capacity assessment and the possible outcomes were made very clear to him (for example, that there is a difference between knowing the risks and being willing to take them and not knowing the risks). He was deemed to have capacity to decide about what to eat and drink. The approach to discussions about swallowing was also then modified by the team to help manage challenging behaviour.

Summary

Swallowing and feeding decisions can be complex and have the potential to greatly impact an individual's health, quality of life and life expectancy. It is therefore essential that the individual is given the opportunity to make an informed decision and be supported in the process, through education and insight-building work, and also during the capacity assessment. Key considerations when assessing capacity for swallowing and feeding management decisions are:

- What decision needs to be made?
- Who are the most appropriate professionals to be involved in the process of education, insight-building and assessment of capacity?
- What options are available?
- What would be the impact on health?
- What is the ceiling of care?
- What are the pros and cons for each option?

- What resources or tools will help the individual to understand, retain and weigh up the benefits and risks?
- Does the decision need to be reviewed, for example, in the instance of improvement/deterioration in swallow or cognitive ability?

References

Cichero, J., Lam, P., Steele, C.M., Hanson, B., Chen, J., Dantas, R.O., Duivestein, J., Kayashita, J., Lecko, C., Murray, J., Pillay, M., Riquelme, L., & Stanschus, S. (2017). Development of international terminology and definitions for texture-modified foods and thickened fluids used in dysphagia management: The IDDSI Framework. *Dysphagia*, *32*, 293–314.

Royal College of Physicians (2010). *Oral Feeding Difficulties and Dilemmas: A Guide to Practical Care, Particularly Towards the End of Life*. London: Royal College of Physicians.

Chapter 16

Assessing capacity in relation to a change of residence or accommodation and care needs

Janice Mackenzie

In this chapter

A change of residence or accommodation is possibly the most common reason for a formal capacity assessment. This could be regarding discharge destination from hospital or a change of accommodation within the community. Often, but not always, it is closely linked to a decision about someone's care needs. The level of care someone requires may influence the type of accommodation required, for example, four care calls a day at home versus needing care or supervision 24 hours a day. As these two decisions can be separate, and they can involve different relevant information, they will be dealt with separately here, but with the acknowledgement that there is overlap between the assessments. Often one capacity assessment will cover both decisions, for example, "Can Gladys make a decision about her future care needs (which would affect her discharge destination)?"

Change of residence or accommodation

Providing the relevant information before the assessment

It is important to provide the person with as much information as possible about the options before the capacity assessment. Sometimes it is not possible to give specific details about an option, for example, if one of the options is a care home, then it is not always possible to give information about a specific care home, as the care home would be looked for after the capacity assessment and best interests decision, if required. In this case, it is adequate to provide general information about this setting compared to another setting, for example, sheltered accommodation, and compare the two. Other times, the need for a care home may be obvious, but the person needs to be able to choose between two specific options. In this case, it would be good for the person to be able to visit the specific care homes in order to give her as much information as possible before the assessment.

What is relevant to this decision?

Case law sets guidance relating to the information the person would need to be able to understand, retain, use and weigh to make an informed decision. This can be tailored to individual situations as appropriate (*B v A Local Authority* [2019]). With regards to deciding where to live, the relevant and non-relevant factors detailed below were established in the ruling of *LBX v K, L and M* [2013] (taken from Ruck Keene et al. (2019) and the original legal ruling).

Relevant:

1 What the options are, including information about what these are, what sort of property each one involves and what sort of facilities they have
2 In broad terms, what sort of area the properties are in (and any specific known risks beyond the usual risks faced by people living in an area, if any such specific risks exist)
3 The difference between living somewhere and visiting it
4 What activities he would be able to do if he lived in each place
5 Whether and how the person being assessed would be able to see his family, friends and anyone else important to him, if he lived in each place
6 That he would need to pay money to live there and that he would need to pay bills (although this does not need to be understood in detail and may be dealt with by his appointee)
7 That he has to comply with the relevant lists of "do's and don'ts" relating to the placement, otherwise he will not be able to remain living there
8 Who he would be living with at each placement
9 What sort of care he would receive in each placement in broad terms, in other words, that he would receive similar support in the proposed placement to the support he currently receives, and any differences if he were to live at home
10 That there is a risk that a family member or other contact may not wish to see him if he chooses a place against his family's wishes. (However, the ruling in question added the caution that this should not be presented as a permanent risk with severe consequences for the longer-term relationship between the person and the contact involved. Nevertheless, it would be appropriate to warn him of the risk that he may not get many, or any, visits from his contacts if there are practical problems that would have an impact on visiting, for example, if there are long distances to travel or restricted visiting hours relating to certain placements.)

Not relevant:

1 The cost of the placements
2 The value of money

3   The legal nature of the tenancy agreement or license
4   What his relationship with his family members might be like in 10 or 20 years, if he chose to live independently now. (Any long-lasting social rejection or breakdown in relations would not count as a "reasonably foreseeable consequence" as required by the Mental Capacity Act (MCA, 2005).)

Caution

Although the cost of placements was not deemed relevant in this case, relating to someone with a learning disability deciding about accommodation in the community, you can see that the cost of placements may be relevant in other situations. For example, if I were choosing whether to go into a residential home or pay for extra care in my own home, I would consider cost to be a relevant factor.

Questions to consider when providing information and conducting the capacity assessment

- What are the person's needs relating to her cognitive, physical and emotional wellbeing?
- How do her cognitive, physical and emotional difficulties impact on her functional abilities?
- What other factors might be influencing her decision? For example:
  - Emotional attachment to property and/or area
  - Proximity to family and friends
  - Knowledge of local area
  - Anxiety about moving
  - Low motivation to move
  - Influence of others
  - Financial concerns
  - Potential loss of independence
  - Other conditions that may affect her ability to accept change, for example, being on the autistic spectrum or showing rigidity of thinking/lack of cognitive flexibility due to executive functioning problems
- How did she live before her mental capacity was called into question? (if appropriate)
- Have her needs changed so that the property/area is no longer meeting them?

- Has the property/area changed so that it is no longer meeting her needs?
- What would her ability to cope be like if she were living in each of the options?
- Which option suits her needs most?
- What would happen if her needs were not met? Is she willing to accept the potential consequences?
- What would she do if she came upon a problem due to her needs not being met by the property?
- Can she understand the viewpoint of others in relation to this decision, even if she may not agree?
- Can she weigh up the pros and cons for each option, for example, thinking about the least restrictive option and her emotional needs as well as her physical needs?
- What other accommodation needs and issues should be considered? For example:
  - Accessibility to front door
  - Condition of the accommodation with regards to level of repair, cleanliness and clutter
  - Adaptations already in situ or viability of those recommended
  - Ability to use stairs or room for stairlift, through-floor lift or extension as required
  - Location and size of bathroom or toilet
  - Number and size of rooms accessible to her
  - Ability to accommodate necessary equipment
  - Safety within house/flat, for example, ability to turn off or remove the cooker
  - Local area – safety and proximity to shops, public transport and other community resources
  - Neighbours – ability to help or potential difficulties
  - Family – proximity, ability to help and what input they gave previously.

Also, please see the semi-structured interview for assessing a person's capacity to make a decision about her care needs and discharge destination (based on Mackenzie, Lincoln and Newby, 2008; see www.assessingcapacity.com for the most recent version).

Care needs

As mentioned, a capacity assessment about someone's care needs is often closely linked to accommodation or place of residence, but not always. Sometimes, care provision is recommended to make a person's life easier once he returns home from hospital, or so he can stay in his home, when there is no thought of changing his place of residence. Other examples of situations when these decisions can be separate may include when the person:

- Needs to consent to care or help in his current setting
- Needs to consent to pay for carers to visit (which can sometimes lead on to an assessment regarding capacity to manage his finances)
- Is refusing to let the carers into his home.

Providing the relevant information before the capacity assessment

As with all capacity assessments, you must make sure that the person has been given as much of the relevant information as possible before the assessment. Providing this in written form, in addition to discussions, and using functional tasks to highlight difficulties will help to enhance his capacity (see Chapters 9 and 11). People often remember their abilities in their home environment prior to coming into hospital and assume that they will be functioning at that level again when they return home, even if they are aware that their needs are different whilst in hospital. During a capacity assessment, they may state: "I know I can't walk but I'll be fine once I get home." Sometimes, if the person's abilities have changed, a visit to his previous home environment can help to increase his insight. This can make the relevant information less abstract, and the person can see how he will cope in specific situations in real life, rather than in a simulated environment.

What is relevant to this decision?

With regards to care needs, the relevant and non-relevant factors detailed next were again established in the ruling of *LBX v K, L and M* [2013] (taken from Ruck Keene et al. (2019) and the original legal ruling).

Relevant:

1 What area(s) a person needs support with
2 What sort of support he needs
3 Who will be providing him with support
4 What would happen if he did not have any support or he refused it
5 That carers might not always treat him properly and that he can complain if he is not happy about his care.

Not relevant:

1 How his care will be funded
2 How the overarching arrangements for monitoring and appointing care staff work.

Questions to consider when providing information and conducting the capacity assessment

As you will see, these are similar to those requiring consideration for a change of accommodation or residence but with some different aspects to take into account:

- What are the person's needs relating to his cognitive, physical and emotional wellbeing?
- How do his cognitive, physical and emotional difficulties impact on his functional abilities?
- What other factors might be influencing his decision? For example:
  - Emotional attachment to family and/or carers
  - Anxiety about having carers he does not know
  - Low motivation to look after his own needs
  - Influence of others
  - Financial concerns
  - Potential loss of independence
  - Other conditions that may affect his ability to accept change, for example, being on the autistic spectrum or showing rigidity of thinking/lack of cognitive flexibility due to executive functioning problems
- How did he live before his mental capacity was called into question? (if appropriate)
- Have his care needs changed so that the help he currently receives is no longer meeting his needs?
- Have the carers changed so that they are no longer able to meet his needs, for example, the carers with specialist brain injury knowledge have left the care agency?
- What would his ability to cope be like in each of the different options proposed?
- Which option suits his needs most?
- What would happen if his needs were not met? Is he willing to accept the potential consequences?
- What would he do if he came upon a problem due to his care needs not being met by the care package (or lack of it)?
- Can he understand the viewpoint of others in relation to this decision, even if he does not agree?
- Can he weigh up the pros and cons for each option, for example, thinking about the least restrictive option and his emotional needs as well as his physical needs?
- What other care needs and issues should be considered? For example:
  - Getting in and out of bed
  - Moving around the property

- o   Getting washed and dressed
- o   Toileting and accessing the facilities and/or managing a catheter
- o   Meals and drinks – preparing them and eating or drinking safely
- o   Accessing the community and mobility around it, for example, using public transport and ability to attend appointments
- o   Vulnerability regarding people coming to the door or when out in the community
- o   Finding his way about in the community
- o   Crossing roads safely
- o   Shopping – planning and remembering what to buy, managing to find items in the shop, paying for the shopping, carrying the shopping back to his accommodation and putting it away; or managing online shopping orders and deliveries
- o   Taking medications – remembering to take them, physical abilities to do so independently and consideration of controlled medications and addictive behaviours
- o   Other medical care requirements, for example, managing PEG care or changing dressings.

Also, please see the semi-structured interview for assessing a person's capacity to make a decision about his care needs and discharge destination (based on Mackenzie, Lincoln and Newby, 2008; see www.assessingcapacity.com for the most recent version).

Summary

In case law, making decisions about where to live and about care needs are seen as separate with different relevant information attached to each; however, these decisions can often influence each other. For example, some of the factors the person would need to take into account when deciding where to live include the property and area, the activities and facilities available, access to family and who she would be living with, the rules and basic costs of living there, the care provided and the difference between living there and just visiting. The decision regarding care needs appears to be simpler in some ways but can be more complex in reality if someone does not have insight into his abilities (see Chapters 6 and 22 for more information). When making a decision about his care needs, a person would need to take into account what he needs support with, what this support would look like and who would provide it, what would happen if he did not have this support and that carers might not always treat him well. The level of care required may influence and restrict the options available for accommodation.

References

Mackenzie, J.A., Lincoln, N.B. and Newby, G.J. (2008). Capacity to make a decision about discharge destination after stroke: A pilot study. *Clinical Rehabilitation*, 22, 1116–1126.

Mental Capacity Act 2005. London: HMSO. Available at: www.legislation.gov.uk/ukpga/2005/9/contents

Ruck Keene, A., Butler-Cole, V., Allen, N., Lee, A., Kohn, N., Scott, K., Barnes, K. and Edwards, S. (eds.) (2019). *A Brief Guide to Carrying Out Capacity Assessments*. 39 Essex Chambers. Available at: www.39essex.com/mental-capacity-guidance-note-brief-guide-carrying-capacity-assessments

Case law

B v A Local Authority [2019] EWCA Civ 913

LBX v K, L and M [2013] EWHC 3230

Chapter 17

Assessing capacity to consent to sexual relations

Dan Ratcliff

In this chapter

This chapter discusses the different approaches to assessing capacity to consent to sexual relationships. First, it examines the two-stage test of capacity to consent to sexual relations in civil law (using the Mental Capacity Act, 2005), including the criteria to fulfil the legal test of capacity, as well as considering the need to assess broader considerations in order to inform risk management and where to target education and support. It also addresses the additional issue of assessing capacity to decide on contact with other individuals and explores the considerations in cases where individuals have capacity to consent to sex, but where they are still at risk. The chapter also explores ways to enhance an individual's capacity to consent to sexual relationships. Finally, it examines assessing capacity to consent to sexual relationships under criminal law, with reference to the Sexual Offences Act (2003) and highlights the differences between this approach and that of the approach under civil law.

Introduction

Capacity to consent to sexual relations is an area of assessment that creates a great deal of confusion and anxiety for assessors. This is often for good reason, as the legal judgments in this area have at times lacked clarity and on occasion have appeared contradictory. This is also a highly emotive area of human behaviour that is often impacted upon by legal and policy directives which serve to both promote independence and decision-making and safeguard vulnerable people deemed to be at risk. These two aims are not always easily reconciled.

Assessors must be aware that there are two approaches in assessing capacity to consent to sexual relationships:

1   A civil law test of capacity arising from the framework of the Mental Capacity Act (MCA, 2005) and associated case law. This applies in cases where capacity

to consent to sexual relationships is queried, but a criminal offence is not suspected to have occurred. This will likely cover the majority of situations that arise. Any cases addressed in a civil court. such as the Court of Protection, will require an assessment using this framework. This will be addressed first.

2   A test of capacity arising from the Sexual Offences Act (SOA, 2003). Such a test would be considered if it is thought that a person may have committed a specific offence under this Act. If the police are considering, or are pursuing, a prosecution in a criminal court using this legislation, then this test should be referred to by assessors. More on this can be found at the end of the chapter.

A two-stage process regarding the civil law test of capacity

If there are still concerns about a person's capacity to consent to sexual relations following attempts to support him or her with this decision, it is recommended that you take a two-stage approach to assessment:

Stage 1: Assessing the criteria required to fulfil the legal test of capacity

Over the years there have been a number of legal judgments and positions that have been described as "notoriously tricky" (*London Borough of Southwark* [2016]). Although there still remain some nuanced areas requiring clarification, the Courts (for now) have largely reached a broad consensus on the threshold of understanding for consent to sex (*IM v LM & Others* [2014]; *London Borough of Southwark* [2016]). The threshold for understanding is relatively basic and has been deliberately crafted this way by the Courts in order to avoid unnecessary paternalism (*IM v LM & Others* [2014]).

The level of understanding that a person must demonstrate is as follows:

1) The person must have an understanding of the basic mechanics of sexual intercourse (X City Council v MB, NB and MAB [2006]).

Given the test is specific to the type of sexual act, the exact nature of this understanding will differ depending on circumstances. For example, the nature of a sexual act between a man and a woman will be different from a sexual act between same-sex individuals. The person does not need to have experienced sexual intercourse before, but he must be able to identify the key anatomical features involved (such as penis, vagina) and the way in which they are used (for example, penis entering the vagina). The person does not need to use the proper names for sexual organs (Butler-Cole, 2017).

2) The person must understand, at a basic level, the reasonably foreseeable consequences of sexual intercourse.

This means the possible health risks from sex and the risk of pregnancy (in the context of sex between a man and woman). With regard to health risks, there has been no direction in recent Court judgments to indicate that the person must be able to name specific sexually transmitted diseases or that death may result. Only limited knowledge of sexually transmitted infections is required. The ruling from the judge in the case of *A Local Authority v H* [2012] states, "In my view it should suffice if a person understands that sexual relations may lead to significant ill-health and that those risks can be reduced by precautions like a condom." An understanding of how to use condoms has not been held to be relevant for determining capacity to consent to sex (*LB of Southwark* [2016]).

With regard to pregnancy, it is enough that the person, in relation to heterosexual sex, understands that there is a risk of pregnancy and has a basic understanding of what contraception is (*X City Council v MB & Others* [2006]). She does not have to demonstrate an understanding of the social and emotional consequences of pregnancy (*IM v LM & Others* [2014]) or what is involved in caring for a child (*A Local Authority v A* [2010]). It is unlikely that the risk of pregnancy would need to be understood by a person for whom this was not a realistic outcome, for example, a person in a same-sex relationship, or a woman beyond childbearing age (Butler-Cole, 2017).

3) The person must understand that he has a choice and can refuse.

In terms of consent, the person must also understand that he can change his mind and withdraw consent at any time leading up to and during the act (*A Local Authority v H* [2012]; *LB Tower Hamlets v TB & Ors* [2014]; *LB Southwark v KA* [2016]).

Some individuals are unable to appreciate that they are able to say no, and there are various reasons for this, including the psychological consequences of long-term sexual abuse. Where a person can demonstrate an understanding of her right to say no under assessment conditions, concerns can still be expressed by other people that the person would not be able to say no in the real world. However, the ability of the individual to exercise her capacity to give consent to sex in real-life situations is not relevant for the purpose of determining capacity. Whilst concerns regarding this are legitimate and raise questions for ongoing support and risk management, they are not a reason to conclude the person lacks capacity.

In many other areas, such as property and financial affairs, the Court of Protection readily accepts that if a person is unable to make decisions "on the ground" or "in the moment", for example, due to impulsivity, then he may lack capacity (see Chapter 22). However, in the area of sexual relationships, the Court's position has differed. The Court of Protection has consistently taken the view that problems with decision-making relating to sex on particular occasions is something that must be left to criminal law, after the event (Butler-Cole, 2017).

> ## Caution
>
> The person's sexual partners are not relevant to the question of capacity to consent to sex.

The Courts have so far been clear: the test of capacity in the area of sex is act-specific and not person-specific (*IM v LM & Others* [2014]). The sexual partner and the nature of the relationship between individuals is therefore not relevant. The Courts have been pragmatic in recognising that it would be intrusive for the person and impractical to revisit the issue of capacity every time the person wishes to engage in sexual activity with someone. Explaining to assessors that they must assess capacity in relation to sexual relations without reference to the individual's circumstances or the particular risks she may face from a partner is recognised as difficult (Butler-Cole, 2017).

Furthermore, the test is the same, even if the person is in a long-term monogamous relationship (*CH v A Metropolitan Council* [2017]).

Stage 2: You may have to assess understanding more broadly

If the person has demonstrated capacity to consent to sexual relations or is "borderline" but may have capacity with some additional education, you should ask further questions that go beyond the legal test. This information will help with risk management and knowing where to target further education and support.

The following areas should be considered (Dodd et al., 2015):

- Where it is and is not appropriate to have sex
- Power issues (For example, would you have sex with a person if he offered you money?)
- Issues around age or illegal relationships (For example, at what age can people have sex?)
- Stranger danger (For example, what could happen if you take a lift from someone you have just met?)
- Alcohol and drugs (For example, what can happen if you drink too much?)
- Abuse and exploitation (For example, what can happen if you say yes to sex when you want to say no?)
- Contraception (For example, what can happen if you have sex without using a condom?)
- Grooming/harassment (For example, what can happen if people give you things for sex?)

- False allegations. (For example, what can happen if you do not tell the truth about things you do sexually?)

In addition, there should also be consideration for assessing the person's knowledge of risks relating to using social media. This is becoming one of the most significant areas of risk for sexual harm for vulnerable people, both in terms of becoming victims and possible perpetrators (see Chapter 7).

Additional important questions to consider

What about the weighing-up component of the test of capacity?

The Courts have been generally clear that the weighing up component, whilst not an "irrelevant consideration", is "unlikely to loom large in the evaluation of capacity to consent to sexual relations" (*IM v LM & Others* [2014]). The Courts have recognised that people do not decide to have sex with people on the basis of weighing up complex, abstract or hypothetical information, and they are often guided more by intuition. Consequently, people with a mental impairment or disability should not have to be held to higher standards than non-impaired individuals (*IM v LM & Others* [2014]). Therefore, you should not focus excessively on this area of the functional test.

What about the separate issue of capacity to decide on contact?

Although capacity to consent to sexual relations is treated as act-specific, the issue of capacity in relation to contact with another person *is* treated as person-specific (*IM v LM & Others* [2014]). In the case of *A Local Authority v TZ No2* [2014] a man with a mild learning disability was found to have capacity to consent to sex, but lacked capacity to 1) decide whether or not an individual with whom he may wish to have sexual relations with is safe; and 2) decide on the support required to keep himself safe when having contact with a potential sexual partner. This case exemplifies the absurdity of giving with one hand, by finding that the person has capacity to consent to sex, but taking away with the other, by finding that the person does not have capacity to choose sexual partners without support (Butler-Cole, 2017).

This has implications for the assessment of capacity to consent to sex, especially in cases where the person has multiple partners or is placing himself in risky situations. In such cases, you must consider assessing capacity for contact as well as for sex.

What information is relevant?

In order to have capacity to decide on contact, a person must know who the other person is, in broad terms what the nature of her relationship with him is and what sort of contact she could have with him. The person must also understand the positive and negative aspects of having contact, which will naturally be influenced by the person's own evaluations. Her evaluations will only be irrelevant if they are based on demonstrably false beliefs. For example, if she believed that a person had assaulted her when he had not. The person also needs to know what a family relationship is and that it is in a different category than other categories of contact. However, you must take care not to impose your own values and beliefs about family relationships on the assessment (*LBX v K, L and M* [2013]). Other information relevant to the decision is whether the person with whom contact is being considered has previous criminal convictions or poses a risk to the protected party. If so, there must be a discussion of the potential risk that the person poses and, if such a risk exists, whether the risk should be taken. This may entail looking closely at the reasons for conviction and the protected party's ability to understand the danger posed to himself or others around him (*PC and NC v City of York Council* [2013].

What information is not relevant?

Information that case law has ruled irrelevant to deciding on contact includes abstract concepts such as the nature of friendship and the importance of family ties, the long-term possible effects of contact decisions and risks that are not an issue. Therefore, a consideration of financial abuse or assault when there is no indication of its likelihood would be irrelevant (*LBX v K, L and M* [2013]).

What if someone has capacity to consent to sexual relations but is at risk?

1) The person is acting promiscuously, with the associated risks

There are cases where people willingly and happily engage in sex with multiple partners. Whilst not being directly exploited, they nevertheless may place themselves in risky situations. In cases of vulnerable adults with capacity for sex who display promiscuous behaviour, services supporting them need to focus on how best to minimise the risks with education and support.

If support and education have been tried but there are still doubts about the person's capacity to decide on contact with others, for example, the person continues to place herself at significant risk, then an assessment of capacity should be carried out. This may be relevant in cases where the person's initial approach to individuals to start up a relationship would place them at significant risk, for example, in the case of Mia who has a mild learning disability and an autistic spectrum disorder whose desire for sex is almost compulsive, leading her to engage with men with no appreciation for her safety.

2) The person is being exploited by another individual

In cases where there are concerns that a vulnerable person deemed to have capacity to consent to sexual relations and contact is being exploited by another person or persons, there is the possibility that the High Court can exercise its power under a legal process called *inherent jurisdiction*. The Court can authorise an intervention to protect the individual, providing that it is necessary and proportionate (*Re: F* [1990]). It is important, however, that services are able to demonstrate that they have worked with the person to support him and help him reduce the risks, as far as is practical given the circumstances, and that relevant safeguarding processes have been followed. If there is any doubt about whether sufficient procedural safeguards have been considered or implemented, it is advisable to seek advice from your organisation's safeguarding team or legal department.

Enhancing capacity

It is essential that, where a lack of capacity is found, attempts to enhance a person's ability to consent to sex should be made. (See Chapter 9 for more information on enhancing capacity and Herbert et al., 2019, for specific examples around sex education and other issues.) Furthermore, a Court judgment has made it clear that, where it has been evidenced that further education work regarding the relevant information is required, there should not be undue delay in this taking place. Although no definitive time limit was stipulated, the Court considered that a delay of over a year in providing education was wholly unreasonable (*CH v A Metropolitan Council* [2017]).

Tips

- Some people may use idiosyncratic words to describe body parts, and so you will need to be clear about what the person is actually referring to. If the person uses idiosyncratic words, it is reasonable for you to also adopt these words or phrases during the assessment.
- In cases where a person appears to have a lower level of understanding, it is advisable to use visual materials to support discussion.
- It is generally helpful to start off with open questions, with more specific questions being used if the person's responses are limited. For example,

with regard to consequences of sex, start with a general question such as: "Tell me what can happen if you have sex?" and, if required, follow with more specific questions such as: "Could you become ill/sick/unwell from sex?"

- It is strongly recommended in this area of assessment that you use a structured assessment framework (for example, Dodd et al., 2015) to ensure that all areas have been sufficiently addressed.
- It is advisable to keep up to date with developments in case law. Online resources are available, for example, 39 Essex Chambers.

Assessing capacity to consent to sexual relationships under the Sexual Offences Act 2003 (criminal law)

Issues around capacity to consent to sexual relations within a criminal context are addressed in the Sexual Offences Act (SOA, 2003). The SOA states that person A commits an offence if she knows, or could reasonably be expected to know, that person B, with whom she has had sexual contact, has a mental disorder, and, because of this (or for a reason related to it), that he is likely to be unable to refuse. Person B is considered unable to refuse if he lacks the capacity to choose whether to agree to the sexual act because he lacks sufficient understanding of the nature or reasonably foreseeable consequences of what is being done.

In practice, the test of capacity to consent to sexual relationships under the SOA (2003) is similar to that expected under the MCA (2005). There is, however, a key difference: the test is now person-specific. This means that the assessor, in working out whether a person has capacity to consent to a sexual relationship, should take into account the characteristics of person B and the interaction or relationship dynamics between person A (the alleged offender) and person B in determining whether *at the time of the alleged offence* person B had capacity. It is not enough that the assessor shows that the person demonstrates understanding of the sexual act, its consequences and a rudimentary weighing up under assessment conditions. The assessor then has to answer the question: At the time of the alleged offence(s), was person B able to exercise this understanding and judgment? A range of additional factors can then be considered relevant to person A, person B and the circumstances surrounding the sexual contact. For example, person B may demonstrate a range of characteristics that would undermine his capacity when applying his knowledge and weighing up in real world conditions, such as acquiescence, high levels of suggestibility and reduced cognitive functioning when under pressure or duress (for example, problem-solving, planning and memory). Similarly, there may be factors known about person A, the alleged offender, that may be relevant in determining person B's capacity, such as whether she has a history of aggressive or intimidating behaviour towards person B, or whether she is in a position of power and influence over person B.

Assessors should also be aware that there are other offences under the SOA (2003). For example, the use of inducements, threats or deceptions to obtain sexual activity with a person with a mental disorder is also illegal, as is sexual activity between care workers and people with a mental disorder (Herbert et al., 2019).

References

Butler-Cole, V. (2017). Capacity to consent to sexual relations and the Mental Capacity Act 2005. *Advances in Mental Health and Intellectual Disabilities*, 11(2), 40–46.

Dodd, K., Jones, K., Liddiard, H. and Stroud, J. (2015). *Exploring Sexual and Social Understanding: An Illustrated Pack Designed for Working with People with Learning Disabilities*. Worcestershire: British Institute of Learning Disabilities.

Herbert, C., Joyce, T., Gray, G. and Betteridge, S. (2019). *Capacity to Consent to Sexual Relations*. Leicester: British Psychological Society. Available at: www.bps.org.uk/sites/bps.org.uk/files/Policy/Policy%20-%20Files/Capacity%20to%20consent%20to%20sexual%20relations.pdf

Mental Capacity Act 2005. London: HMSO. Available at: www.legislation.gov.uk/ukpga/2005/9/contents

Sexual Offences Act 2003. London: HMSO. Available at: www.legislation.gov.uk/ukpga/2003/42/contents

Case law

CH v A Metropolitan Council [2017] EWCOP 12

IM v LM & Others [2014] EWCA Civ 37

LB Tower Hamlets v TB & Ors [2014] EWCOP 53

LBX v K, L and M [2013] EWHC 3230

A Local Authority v A [2010] EWHC 1549 (Fam)

A Local Authority v H [2012] EWHC 49 (COP)

A Local Authority v TZ (No 2) [2014] EWHC 973 (COP)

London Borough of Southwark v KA & Ors [2016] EWHC 661 (Fam)

PC and NC v City of York Council [2013] EWCA Civ 478

Re: F (Mental Patient: Sterilisation) [1990] 2 AC 1

X City Council v MB, NB and MAB [2006] EWHC 168 (Fam)

Useful resource

www.39essex.com/resources-and-training/mental-capacity-law

Chapter 18

Assessing capacity to manage financial affairs

Janice Mackenzie and Kate Wilkinson

In this chapter

Managing financial affairs is a vast topic taking in numerous decisions at various levels of difficulty. This chapter covers some of the decisions that require a formal assessment of capacity when someone is having problems managing her financial affairs. It also looks at the capacity to make a Power of Attorney and a will. Finally, it discusses some ideas to help care staff supporting a person with managing an allowance. (See Chapter 12 for a case study of a capacity assessment regarding financial affairs and making a Lasting Power of Attorney.)

Specific decisions

Having the capacity to manage your finances is not a single decision. Rather, it contains lots of different decisions, and thus people may have the capacity to manage some aspects of their finances, but not others. For example, someone may have the capacity to manage his benefits on a day-to-day basis but not have the capacity to manage a large compensation payment of several hundred thousand pounds, as the second task would be more complex than the first. However, as an assessor, you have to be careful that you do not impose a threshold that is higher than would be passed by "the average person on the street". For example, how many of us would know how to invest £500,000 wisely so that we received an income from it? We would likely seek advice from professionals to help us with this decision. This should be the same threshold that is used for someone who has sustained a brain injury in a road traffic collision. (See Chapter 7 for more information on thresholds for capacity.)

When asked to assess someone's capacity to manage his finances, you must clarify what specific question is being asked. For example, is he able to:

- Manage his benefits, or a monthly payment, on a day-to-day basis with regards to budgeting and paying bills?
- Manage outstanding debts, including credit card bills?

- Manage a large compensation payment?
- Manage complex finances which include savings, shares, a pension, and income from a property portfolio?
- Decide to sell or buy a house or another large purchase or investment?

As most assessments around capacity to manage finances involve an ongoing decision – that is, decisions have to be made on an ongoing basis and not just once – it is important to check that the person can carry over understanding and retention of the relevant information in order to weigh and use it in everyday life. However, some decisions, such as making a Lasting Power of Attorney, making a will or selling a house can be one-off decisions and, therefore, the person need only have capacity for as long as it takes to make the decision. Remember that financial decisions can also cover business matters, legal transactions and managing assets.

Cautions

- When assessing a person's capacity for ongoing financial decisions, it is important to make sure that she can understand and remember the information over a longer period of time, rather than just within the capacity assessment session.

    - Tip: Assessing the amount of information remembered between sessions can help to identify problems in this area.

- Highly structured environments and skilled staff who understand brain injuries can help the person appear to have capacity when she does not. Even the process of a capacity assessment can help someone with executive functioning problems structure her thoughts to supply reasonable answers, but she may not be able to use this information to make decisions in real life (ABI and MCA Interest Group, 2014). (See Chapter 22 for more information.)

    - Tip: Taking someone out of her environment to make decisions, for example, to an unfamiliar shop, can highlight these difficulties.

- Although you are required to enhance a person's capacity to manage his finances before the assessment, as with other decisions, the person has to be able to demonstrate managing his finances with limited support during the assessment. For example, you may enhance his capacity by teaching him new skills, explaining decisions in simple language or helping him practice skills that he has difficulty with and think of ways around problems he encounters, but he would then have to be able to

---

put this into practice himself. This is due to the fact that he is unlikely to have continual support when making decisions about money in the community, again, due to it being a series of ongoing decisions. This does not include support for sensory, literacy or physical problems, for example, if someone requires support to access the cash machine or to read a bill.

○ Tip: Assessing people in functional situations with limited input from staff can clarify these issues.

Tips

- It is important to assess the person's ability to manage finances in a functional way as well as asking questions, for example, by giving her some money to see how she manages it. You could start by giving her a small amount of money over a day or a week to see if she spends it as she said she would and look at patterns of behaviour. You could then extend the test period to a month to monitor budgeting ability. In addition, you could ask the person to pay a bill whilst under supervision, go to the bank or post office to withdraw money or check a statement or do some transactions on online banking. This would assess for the discrepancy that can happen, when someone has executive functioning problems or an addiction, between what someone says and what she does (see Chapter 22).
- Reviewing any capacity assessment done while someone is in hospital following discharge is important due to the constraints on the ability to assess someone's capacity to manage his finances whilst in hospital.
- It is important to take into account a person's history when assessing capacity to manage finances and to take a non-judgmental stance, making sure that a lack of capacity is because of the impairment of mind or brain and not due to personal values or a skills deficit, for example:

   ○ What was his view on money previously; was he a spender or a saver?
   ○ Was he generous with his money previously?
   ○ Did he have budgeting skills previously?
   ○ How did he pay bills previously?
   ○ What sort of lifestyle did he have, for example, someone who has never paid a television licence due to an objection to tax or someone who used to "fix" his electricity meter may not think to report these outgoings or see them as important.

Starting the capacity assessment

As with all capacity assessments, before you begin you will need to check that the person has been supported to make her own decisions and that strategies have been employed to enhance her capacity to manage her finances but these have been unsuccessful. (For ways to introduce the capacity assessment and enhance her capacity throughout the assessment process see Chapters 8, 9 and 11.) You will also need to know the relevant information before the assessment session and make sure that the person has also been given, or has access to, this information. The relevant information that the person needs to be able to understand, retain, use and weigh will vary depending on the specific decision. The person can have information written down in front of her, as few of us would be able to remember all of our financial information off the top of our head, but she would need to be able to work out what it means and be able to find the right information herself. Before the capacity assessment, you will need to ask someone other than the person being assessed for details of her financial situation. The informant will need to be aware of the situation and what income and outgoings the person has on a weekly, monthly and yearly basis. (See Appendix 5 for a semi-structured interview template regarding managing financial affairs based on Mackenzie, Lincoln and Newby, 2008.)

Examples of information to be gathered beforehand

Does the person:
- Own or rent her property?
- Pay a mortgage or rent?
- Have loans or debts to repay?
- Have a current account – is this an individual account or joint with someone else?
- Pay bills by Direct Debit or cheque, or pay at the Post Office or using meter cards?
- Use credit or store cards or have a hire purchase arrangement? If so, does she have debts on these accounts or a regular fixed payment sum?
- Have financial dependents?
- Have any other business matters or legal transactions relevant to the decision being assessed?
- Gamble in any form? (for example, online gambling sites, bingo, lottery scratch cards)

How much does she pay for:
- Mortgage/rent?
- Loan/credit card repayments?

- Telephone?
- Gas?
- Electricity?
- Water?
- Council tax?
- Insurance?
- Shopping?
- Other outgoings, for example, television licence, the running costs of a car, regular entertainment or subscriptions?

What sources of income does she have and how much does she receive? For example:

- Employment/sick pay (and when it will end)?
- Benefits – which ones?
- Pensions – both state and private?
- Other income, for example, from rental properties or share dividends?
- Are there any changes in circumstances in the foreseeable future?

Does she have any savings and/or investments, and are any of them in joint names? Consider:

- Savings accounts
- ISAs
- Money stuffed under the mattress
- Shares/dividends
- Insurance policies
- Premium Bonds.

The extent of information that you require to know before commencing the capacity assessment will vary depending on the specific question being asked. For example, it would be useful to find out the level of wealth the person has in personal possessions if she is wishing to make a non-financial gift, but this may not be necessary if you are assessing her capacity to manage her day-to-day finances.

It is important to gain an idea of how the person manages her finances from other people, such as family, friends and staff, and whether they think that she is capable of managing her finances or not. Practical examples are often the best evidence. Also, it is useful to ask what support she has had to manage her finances now and in the past in order to gain a fuller picture of her abilities.

Managing finances on a day-to-day basis

Most people can manage a small amount of money given to them as a daily or weekly allowance, but this is not what is meant by "having the capacity to manage finances on a day-to-day basis". Having control over your daily finances is what most of us do in everyday life. We receive income from some source and then use this money to live by paying bills (including rent or a mortgage), buying food and clothes, and using the rest to entertain ourselves or save towards something that we want.

Caution

Some people are unable to manage their finances, even though they have no impairment of mind or brain, and get into debt; however, we cannot use this as an example of how they lived before and let them continue to do this once they do have an impairment of mind or brain and their capacity to manage their daily finances is being questioned. As vulnerable adults, they need help if they are struggling.

As an assessor, you need to be aware of practical considerations, as well as more abstract concepts regarding finances. It may not be necessary to assess these formally, depending on the level at which the person is functioning, but, if there is any doubt, use props to assess these concepts, such as coins, notes and an example utility bill. It is important for the person to be able to manage these basic concepts before any further assessment of managing finances takes place. For example, you will need to know if the person can:

- Understand and read numbers (this ability can be damaged by a stroke, for example)
- Recognise coins and notes
- Add and subtract small amounts of money to have an idea of how much he is spending and how much change he should get
- Understand how to read and pay a utility bill
- Understand what a bank account is, how it works and the pros and cons of having one
- Understand how to use a cheque book, debit card or credit card, as appropriate, and know the pros and cons of having one
- Explain a bank or credit card statement to you.

The Coins and Costs Test (Willner et al., 2010) was developed to assess basic financial knowledge of people with mild intellectual disabilities. If a person does not have a basic understanding of numbers and/or money, then there is no need to continue with the financial capacity assessment, as it is clear that he would not have the capacity to manage his finances. However, if he has a problem with reading numbers or a utility bill, it may not impact on his capacity to manage his finances, as he could get practical support for this.

Once the basics have been established, you will need to assess more in-depth topics specific to the area of finances that you are assessing. Some examples of areas you may wish to investigate include:

- Whether the person thinks that her cognitive problems would affect her ability to manage her finances and she would need help with this, and the reasons behind these beliefs
- How the person's finances are currently managed and what, if any, help she receives with this (for example, paying bills or using an accountant)
- Whether she received any help managing her finances prior to the changes in her cognition
- Whether she ever got into financial difficulty prior to changes in her cognition
- Her knowledge of her income – sources and amounts – and money available to her (for example, savings) and where this is kept
- Her knowledge of outgoings, such as bills, rent and shopping
- Whether she is in debt, including credit cards, and what her plan is to manage these
- Any history of, and future plans for, large purchases or investments
- What she would do if she did not have enough money one week or month and if her plans would affect other people
- What would happen if she overspent her budget one week or month or if she did this regularly
- Any financial dependents and how financial decisions may impact on them
- Rough value of money and prices of everyday objects
- What she would do if she wanted something that she could not afford
- Plans for an unexpected windfall and reasoning behind this
- Her normal procedure for dealing with bills and what she would do if she could not afford to pay one
- Financial vulnerability – family, friends or strangers asking for money or advising how it should be spent
- The ability to seek advice and consider and act on it when dealing with more complex financial interactions
- What the person thinks the options are for that specific area of finances and the pros and cons of each option

- Which option the person would choose and why and whether this would affect anyone else
- Whether she can consider the views of others about her ability to manage her finances.

The amount of detail that needs to be covered will depend on the complexity of the financial situation of the individual. Other questions may relate to someone's vulnerability, for example (Empowerment Matters, 2014):

- Whether she can remember her PIN and passwords or has to write them down
- Whether anyone else knows her PIN and passwords or gets money out for her
- What she would do if someone did ask for her PIN or password for online banking
- What she would do if she thought that money was missing from her bank account.

Caution

As an assessor, you must remember that people are allowed to make "unwise" decisions. It is common for people to do this with money, especially when emotions are involved, even when they have the capacity to make these decisions.

An "unwise" decision may be the reason that you have been asked to assess a person's capacity to manage his finances, and this can muddy the waters of the assessment. Discovering the reasoning behind the decision can sometimes clarify whether or not someone has the capacity to make the decision. For example, Tomas bought his wife an expensive piece of jewellery when they were struggling financially, but he did so as he thought it may help to save their marriage. This may be misguided, but it does not mean that he is incapable of managing his money, as his priorities may be different from those of other people and this act may reflect his values. It would be important to find out whether he could weigh up the pros and cons of this act whilst holding an overall awareness of their financial situation in mind.

Buying or selling a house

When buying or selling a house, the person may need to have an understanding of the following areas, as well as having an idea of his general finances and the value of money, so that he is aware whether he can afford to buy it or pay the mortgage:

- The reason for the sale or purchase
- Which property he is selling, if he has more than one

- General prices of houses in the area, to make sure that he is not paying too much or selling his house for too little
- A rough idea of fees that will be charged by the estate agent and solicitor, as well as taxes and mortgage fees if relevant, and whether he can afford them
- That the purchase or sale could fall through.

Someone else can manage the interactions with solicitors and estate agents on the person's behalf if he does not want to.

Making a financial gift

The degree of understanding required when making a financial gift varies with the significance of the gift, for example, if the gift is small then the degree of understanding need only be low but, if the gift is the person's only asset, then the degree of understanding is as high as that for making a will (*Re Beaney deceased* [1978]). A person must be aware that she is making a gift, what the gift comprises and who will receive it. She must also be aware of roughly how much money she has and the proportion of her whole wealth that the gift will make up as well as the impact of the gift on her own ability to manage financially and its impact on other people. This is especially relevant when the gift is a large proportion of her assets and may affect the provisions of her will (*Re Beaney deceased* [1978]). For example, if Ruby wants to give a large sum of money to one of her sons, then she needs to be aware of how this will impact on her other two children, including their inheritance.

Making a will: Assessing testamentary capacity

Assessing someone's capacity to make, revoke or change a will is somewhat different from other areas of mental capacity. Unlike some decisions, it is a specific, well-established area of law and the "test" of capacity is based on pre-existing case law, rather than on the Mental Capacity Act (MCA, 2005). Therefore, it may be helpful to start with some legal terminology, as you may come across it when looking into this area:

- *Testamentary capacity* is the legal term used to describe a person's legal and mental ability to make, revoke or alter a valid will.
- The *testator* is the person making the will.

Why assess?

If there is reason to doubt someone's testamentary capacity at the time she wishes to make, change or revoke her will, it is important that a thorough (and well-documented) assessment is carried out. If this is not done, the will may not be valid and may be subject to challenge in the Courts. Conversely, if the testator is wrongly assessed as lacking testamentary capacity, her right to decide whom to leave her estate to when she dies will be lost, an equally undesirable outcome.

Who should assess?

Such an assessment may well end up being examined in the Courts; therefore it is best practice for someone who is experienced and skilled in assessing mental capacity to carry out the assessment. In addition, case law has laid out the recommendation of a "gold standard" of getting a medical opinion on capacity. This is not a legal requirement, rather guidance on best practice (*Raymond Allen James v Karen James & Others* [2018]). However, it is likely that a professional with expertise in complex assessment of capacity, such as a clinical psychologist or social worker, with relevant experience would carry as much weight with the Court.

What is the legal test of testamentary capacity?

As mentioned earlier, the MCA is not used to determine testamentary capacity in England and Wales; rather a separate test is used, which is based on long-standing case law (*Banks v Goodfellow* [1870]).

Banks v Goodfellow [1870] states that, in order to make a valid will, the testator must:

- Understand the nature of making a will and its effects
- Understand the extent of the property of which she is disposing
- Be able to comprehend and appreciate the claims to which she ought to give effect
- Have no disorder of the mind that perverts her sense of right or prevents the exercise of her natural faculties in disposing of her property by will.

In more straightforward language this means she must:

- Understand that when she dies her property and assets will pass to the people she has named in her will
- Understand roughly what she owns in terms of property, money and personal belongings. It is not necessary to fully understand the actual value of assets, for example, property (Jacoby, 2007)
- Know who her family and friends are and the extent of their involvement in her life
- Be aware of who would normally be expected to benefit from a will (for example, relatives and friends) and which members of family or friends may feel

they have a claim to her estate. (She may need to say why she is excluding or including certain people in her will)

- The testator must not have a disorder of the mind or brain that causes her to dispose of her property in a way that is different from if she had no disorder of the mind or brain.

The same case law has determined that the level of understanding required varies depending on the complexity of the particular situation, for example, the will, the assets and the claims on the testator (*Banks v Goodfellow* [1870]).

Common law also states that, for a will to be valid, the person making it must be doing so of his own free will and not be under any undue influence from anyone else. Therefore, this is something you will need to explore in any assessment.

This test is somewhat different than if the MCA were to be applied to this decision. The main difference is that the MCA would require the testator to understand all the information relevant to the decision, including the reasonably foreseeable consequences. Case law only requires that the testator appreciate the claims he ought to recognise in his will and that the will reflects them. For example, case law states that inability to understand the collateral consequences of a will does not make a will invalid (*Simon v Byford* [2014]).

Box 18.1   Examples: What are collateral consequences?

- A person with more than one child who leaves everything to just one child in her will, resulting in feelings of distress and anger in the other children and ruptures in family relationships
- A person who has been married more than once leaving his entire estate to his second wife and making no provision for children from his first marriage
- A person who decides to leave all of her money to a pet cat instead of her daughter, who has looked after her for the last few years of her life.

When the MCA first came into effect, it was not clear which test should be applied to testamentary capacity (that is whether the MCA superseded pre-existing case law). The MCA Code of Practice (2007) states that its own definition of capacity is "in line with the existing common law tests and does not replace them". Further case law then clarified this ambiguity in the case of *Walker v Badmin* [2014], where the Court's judgment was that "the correct and only test" for testamentary capacity is the one outlined in *Banks v Goodfellow* [1870].

This section has focussed on England and Wales; however, the same principles of determining testamentary capacity are adhered to in Scotland, Northern Ireland and the Republic of Ireland. The only significant difference is the age at which an individual can demonstrate testamentary capacity. As in England and Wales, people in Northern Ireland and the Republic of Ireland must be 18 years old to make a valid will. However, in Scotland a person as young as 12 can make a valid will. In England and Wales, the Court of Protection can make a will or amend an existing will for someone who lacks the capacity to do so (MCA Code of Practice, 2007, at paragraph 8.27).

Cautions

- Remember that capacity assessments are decision-specific. Therefore, if someone lacks capacity to manage his finances, this does not necessarily mean he lacks testamentary capacity. Conversely, just because someone has been found to have capacity to manage her finances, it cannot be assumed that she has the capacity to make a valid will.
- People can make decisions about disposing of their estate that other people deem to be unwise, unfair or even unreasonable. This does not mean they lack testamentary capacity.

How to assess

Here are some examples of potential questions to ask as part of an assessment of capacity for making, revoking or changing a will:

- What is a will?
- Why are you making one?
- When does a will come into effect?
- When will the people named in your will be given the things you have said you want them to have?
- Do you have any property? What do you have? How much do think it is worth?
- Do you have any belongings? What are they? How much do think they are worth?
- Do you have any money saved? How much do you have?
- Do you have any money invested anywhere? Can you tell me more about this?
- Tell me a little about your family and friends. Would any of them expect to be named in your will?
- Who do you want to give your things to when you die? Who do you want to have your house/car?

- Why would you choose these people?
- Is there anyone you do not want to leave anything to? Why?
- Do you think anyone would be upset by your choices?
- Has anyone suggested who you should leave your possessions to?
- What do you need to do if you decide you want to cancel or change your will?

If someone wants to revoke or change a will, as well as the questions above, also ask:

- Can you tell me what your current will says? What are the current arrangements?
- How do you want to change your will?
- Why do you want to change your will?
- Has anyone asked you to change it/suggested that you should change it?

Tip

In any assessment, but particularly in a case of changing a will, you need to be sure that the person is making choices of his own free will and is not under any undue influence from a third party.

Making or revoking a power of attorney

Lasting Power of Attorney (LPA) replaces the previous Enduring Power of Attorney (EPA) in England and Wales, although EPAs made before 1st October 2007 continue to be valid. The equivalent document to an LPA in Scotland is called a Power of Attorney (PoA). Due to the similarities, the term *LPA* will be used throughout. The process is slightly different in Northern Ireland.

There are two types of LPA; one relates to health and welfare and the other to property and affairs (finances). One important difference between the two types is when they can be implemented. An LPA for property and affairs can be used when the person still has the capacity to make the decisions but chooses not to. An LPA for health and welfare can only be used once the person has lost the capacity to make these decisions (OPG and OPG (Scotland)). Only LPA for property and affairs will be discussed here, although some of the questions may also be relevant to health and welfare (see Chapter 14).

What is an LPA for property and affairs?

An LPA is a legal document that allows a person over the age of 18 to decide who should manage her finances. She can appoint one or more attorney(s) to manage her money. She can either choose to ask them to do this once she has lost capacity to manage her money or while she still has the capacity to do so, if she would prefer to no longer do it herself. The attorneys have to act in accordance with the Code of Practice of the country's mental capacity law (for example, the Mental Capacity Act (MCA, 2005) in England and Wales) and make decisions in the person's best interests. Once the LPA is drawn up, it has to be registered with the Office of the Public Guardian (OPG or OPG (Scotland)) before it can be used. Once it is registered, it can be used immediately or at some point in the future. It can take up to 10 weeks for this process to occur, which may be problematic in the instance of someone losing capacity suddenly. The OPG and OPG (Scotland) provide advice on LPAs and PoAs on their respective websites.

The person can revoke the LPA at any point, if she has the capacity to do so. In order to do this, she would need to file a deed of revocation with the OPG/OPG (Scotland) and send copies to the attorneys. The Court of Protection (or Sheriff Court in Scotland) can revoke an LPA if the attorneys are not carrying out their duties correctly or not doing so in the person's best interests. This route would have to be taken once the person has lost the capacity to revoke the LPA. An LPA will automatically stop in the following circumstances (OPG):

- In the event of death or bankruptcy of the person or the attorney
- If the attorney is married to the person and the marriage breaks down
- If the attorney lacks the mental capacity to make decisions
- If the attorneys refuse to continue with their duties.

Assessing mental capacity to make an LPA

Solicitors would usually assess a person's capacity to make an LPA, as it is a legal decision and they may be involved in drawing it up; however, following a brain injury, it can be quite complicated to assess and a health professional or social worker may be asked to assess this and sign the relevant form instead. Families often ask for this assessment due to urgent financial matters following a brain injury, but sometimes the person does not have the capacity to make an LPA and the family have to apply for deputyship through the Court of Protection (or guardianship through the Sheriff Court in Scotland), which can be a long and costly process. Due to this, it is advisable for everyone to make an LPA before they lose mental capacity. (See Appendix 6 for a semi-structured interview template regarding making or revoking an LPA, based on Mackenzie, Lincoln and Newby, 2008.)

Tip

It is not necessary to assess a person's capacity to manage his finances before assessing whether he can make an LPA. These are two very different decisions and, as we know, capacity is decision-specific. He could have the capacity to make an LPA but not have the capacity to manage his finances on a day-to-day basis. Nevertheless, he would need to have a general idea of what he is asking the attorney to do – for example, manage his benefits and pay his bills or manage a large compensation claim. This is so he can assess whether or not the attorney is the best person for the job and the related benefits and risks of asking that person to be an attorney.

Caution

An Ordinary Power of Attorney (OPA), or General PoA in Scotland, can be made for temporary situations, such as being abroad or in hospital, while the person retains the capacity to do what the attorney is being asked to do. In this situation, you would need to assess his capacity to manage his finances as well as making an OPA. If the person loses the capacity to manage his finances, then the OPA would no longer be valid and an LPA would be required.

Often, the family have not spoken to the person about the details of an LPA but have suggested to him that it would be a good idea. In this case, it is important to go through an easy-to-read leaflet that describes LPAs and to leave it with him to read and think about before commencing the capacity assessment. Once you are ready to start the assessment, the following are examples of areas that you may want to investigate to help you decide whether or not a person has the capacity to make an LPA. Assess whether the person is aware of:

- Who is currently managing his finances, for example, if he is in hospital, and why this is occurring
- Who will manage his finances on discharge from hospital and if he wants to look after his own money
- What an LPA is, what types there are and what it means if he has one, including the powers it gives to the attorney and when the attorney can use them

- The ability to insert restrictions into the LPA and the reasons why he may want to do this
- Any advice he has been given about LPAs and by whom
- Why he wants to make an LPA
- In what situations he might want to change who the attorney is or revoke the LPA
- How to revoke or change the LPA
- What to do if he thought that the attorneys were spending his money on themselves
- Ways to access his own solicitor (not the same solicitor as the attorney engages)
- Other people's views about his ability to make an LPA
- How he would like his finances to be managed in the future if he did have an LPA
- The benefits and risks of someone else (family member, friend or professional) managing his money, as well as the pros and cons of doing it himself
- Who he would like to be the attorney(s), the reasons for this and if this would affect anyone else
- Any reason that the potential attorney(s) could be untrustworthy
- Any reason that the LPA should not be created
- The fact that the LPA has to be registered with the OPG before it can be used.

Tip

People often cannot consider the possibility that the person they would like to be their attorney could do anything against their best interests and so will say that there are no risks to that person managing their finances. While it is good that they trust the person whom they are asking to be their attorney, they also have to be aware of the small possibility that something might go wrong. In this case, it can be helpful if you make the situation less emotional by depersonalising it slightly using a vignette; for example, "Alec has asked his son to look after his money using an LPA. Could any bad things happen in this situation?" People can usually come up with one or two potential difficulties with this situation which they did not consider when discussing their own situation, due to the emotions involved.

If an assessment of capacity to manage financial affairs is not being carried out at the same time (as this is not necessary but is sometimes requested), then some additional questions about the person's finances would need to be asked. It is important to note that the person need not have as high an understanding of the information as if he were managing his own finances. Examples of questions include:

- What finances would need to be managed by your attorney (who holds the LPA)?
- Do you think you currently:
  - Own your own home? Alone or jointly? How much is it worth at the moment?
  - Have a mortgage/Pay rent?
  - Have enough money coming in to live on?
  - Have any debts (including overdraft or credit cards)? If so, what?
  - Have any savings/investments? If so, what?
  - Have any people who depend on you? Do they have their own income?
- Where do you get your money from each month, and how much is it (sources of income/which benefits are you on)?
- Where do you keep your money (home, bank accounts – any joint accounts)? How much do you have in each?
- What bills do you have each month, and how much are they roughly?
- What other things do you spend money on in a month (outgoings)?
- If you had a bill to pay from your account today, how would you manage it?

Assessing mental capacity to revoke an LPA

If a person's capacity to make an LPA is called into question after the fact, it is not possible to assess her capacity to make the LPA retrospectively as capacity is time-specific. It is possible, however, to assess the person's capacity to revoke the LPA and, assuming that she has the capacity to revoke it and has chosen not to, it must be assumed that she had the capacity to make the LPA in the first place. The earlier assessment regarding making an LPA can also be used in this instance with just a slightly different slant on it, for example, the reason for revoking the LPA and the benefits and risks of revoking the LPA.

It is possible to change or cancel an LPA after it has been registered, if the person has the capacity to do so, by contacting the OPG/OPG (Scotland). If a person is choosing to revoke an LPA, then it would be prudent to assess her capacity to manage her finances at that point in time as, if she is unable to manage her own finances, the LPA may have to be revoked by the Court. It is advisable to seek legal advice about this issue if it arises. If the person wants to remove one attorney, but has one or more other attorneys who can continue, then the assessment of her capacity to manage her finances would not be required; however, she would need to have capacity to decide to remove the attorney.

Appointeeship

If the person only has benefits or a state pension as income, and no savings or capital (including property) other than a small amount to cover one month's outgoings, then an appointeeship may be applied for. This is arranged through the Department for Work and Pensions (DWP), once the person has lost the capacity to manage her finances and does not require going through the Court of Protection. A person would lack capacity to manage her benefits if she was unable to (Livingstone, 2011):

- Understand, retain and weigh up what benefits she may be entitled to, as well as the consequences of not claiming them or not reporting a change which would affect her benefits
- Apply for them and understand methods of payment
- Manage them on a daily basis.

Appointees have to act in the person's best interests, and they have the following responsibilities (Livingstone, 2011, p. 26):

- Completing claim and renewal forms
- Receiving or collecting benefits – these will be in the name of the appointee, but the money must be used for the welfare of the claimant
- Dealing with any correspondence about the benefits
- Reporting any changes in the claimant's circumstances
- Repaying any overpayments of benefit.

Deputyship

A Property and Financial Affairs deputy is appointed by the Court of Protection if a person who does not have capacity to manage his finances does not have an LPA. (The Court can also appoint a Personal Welfare deputy, for health and care decisions, who may or may not be the same person as for financial decisions. See Chapter 14 for more information.) Deputies have similar powers to attorneys, but they cannot make gifts unless the Court has stated that they can (OPG). They have to act in the person's best interests and have to report to the Court every year. More than one deputy can be appointed, and this can be a family member, friend or professional, such as a solicitor.

Supporting people to make decisions

Support should be offered to people with or without the capacity to make a financial decision if they are struggling with some aspect of it. For example, if someone who has the capacity to make a decision appears to be under undue influence to change his will or give away money, he could be offered the support of an advocate (Empowerment Matters, 2014).

Even though someone has an attorney, appointee or deputy, he may be able to make some decisions about how to spend his money, for example, being supported to budget for a limited amount of money per week (Livingstone, 2011) or deciding whether to buy a new coat or presents for his family (Empowerment Matters, 2014). The person's capacity to make these decisions may be assessed on an informal basis by a support worker or carer. "The person can be empowered through putting in place the means for [him] to be involved and as independent as possible – leaving the person to make unwise decisions within safe limits" (Empowerment Matters, 2014, p. 101).

Care staff can help support the person with his money if there is a transparent system in place and there are clear rules regarding how to handle his money. They may also be able to help someone who has the capacity to make decisions around his finances but who has physical, communication or sensory difficulties which affect his ability to action some of the decisions.

When supporting someone to manage a small weekly allowance from an appointee, for example, care staff would need to (Livingstone, 2011):

- Help the person to think about the pros and cons of the decision and other alternative options, for example, waiting to see if the item is in the sale that starts next week
- Help the person think about the other demands on his income, for example, if he will have enough money left for his cigarettes after buying a computer game
- Help the person to budget for big expenses, such as Christmas presents or holiday spending money
- Keep detailed records of all income and expenditure.

Summary

Capacity to manage financial affairs covers many decisions and so you need to be specific about which one you are assessing. Although it may be uncomfortable to talk about money with people, it is necessary to find out the relevant information from an informant before the assessment, so you are aware if the person is conscious of her actual situation. One of the most important aspects of assessing a person's capacity to manage her financial affairs is to ensure that she can put her decisions into action. This means being able to remember information over time and act on the decisions she has discussed with the assessor. This is different from some other one-off decisions and requires more functional assessment. However, there are some one-off decisions in this sphere, such as making an LPA and writing a will. Even though someone has been found to lack capacity to manage his money on a daily basis, he may be able to make day-to-day spending decisions and should be supported to do so.

References

Acquired Brain Injury and Mental Capacity Act Interest Group (2014). *Acquired Brain Injury and Mental Capacity. Recommendations for Action Following the House of Lords Select Committee Post-Legislative Scrutiny Report into the Mental Capacity Act: Making the Abstract Real.* Available at: https://empowermentmatters web.files.wordpress.com/2014/11/making-the-abstract-real.pdf

Department for Constitutional Affairs (2007). *Mental Capacity Act 2005: Code of Practice.* London: The Stationery Office. Available at: https://assets.publishing.service.gov.uk/government/uploads/system/uploads/attachment_data/file/497253/Mental-capacity-act-code-of-practice.pdf

Empowerment Matters (2014). *Making Financial Decisions: Guidance for Assessing, Supporting and Empowering Specific Decision Making.* Available at: https://empowermentmattersweb.files.wordpress.com/2014/09/assessing-capacity-financial-decisions-guidance-final.pdf

Jacoby, R. (2007). How to assess capacity to make a will. *British Medical Journal*, 335, 155–157.

Livingstone, J. (2011). *Guidance on Money Management.* Chesterfield: ARC. Available at: https://arcuk.org.uk/publications/files/2011/09/Guidance-on-Money-Management.pdf

Mackenzie, J.A., Lincoln, N.B. and Newby, G.J. (2008). Capacity to make a decision about discharge destination after stroke: A pilot study. *Clinical Rehabilitation*, 22, 1116–1126.

Mental Capacity Act 2005. London: HMSO. Available at: www.legislation.gov.uk/ukpga/2005/9/contents

Willner, P., Bailey, R., Dymond, S. and Parry, R. (2010). Coins and costs: A simple and rapid assessment of basic financial knowledge. *Journal of Applied Research in Intellectual Disabilities*, 24, 285–289.

Case law

Banks v Goodfellow [1870] LR 5 QB 549
Raymond Allen James v Karen James & Others [2018] EWHC 43
Re Beaney Deceased [1978] 1 WLR 770
Simon v Byford [2014] EWCA Civ 280
Walker v Badmin [2014] EWHC 71

Useful websites

Office of the Public Guardian: www.gov.uk
Office of the Public Guardian (Scotland): www.publicguardian-scotland.gov.uk

Chapter 19

Assessing capacity in relation to signing a tenancy agreement

David Fowler

Who should assess a person's capacity to enter into a tenancy agreement?

Anyone involved with the person can assess her capacity if it is in doubt. However, only certain people can then decide whether it is in the person's best interests to enter into a tenancy agreement if she is deemed to lack capacity. Practically, therefore, it is advisable that the person who would be making the best interests decision about whether to enter into a tenancy contract (if the person is found to lack capacity) also decides whether the person has capacity at that time. Where this is not feasible, the prospective best interests assessor will at least need either oversight of the capacity assessment or to be satisfied that it was of sufficient quality.

Things to consider when assessing capacity

What is the decision to be made?

Be clear about the decisions the person is being asked to make in connection to the tenancy agreement. There may be more than one decision to be made, and it is important to be clear about these when considering the person's decision-making capacity. Relevant information will need to be identified for each decision separately, whilst keeping in mind the interdependent nature of the decision-making process. For example, in the case of *LB Islington v QR* [2014], three separate, but linked decisions were identified:

- Whether to move from a Local Authority property to a supported living environment
- Whether to give up a council tenancy
- Whether to sign a tenancy agreement for supported living.

What information is relevant?

Consider and obtain all the information that might be relevant when deciding whether to sign a tenancy agreement. Anyone undertaking a capacity assessment will, as has been explored in other chapters, need to decide at what level the threshold is set for understanding the information relevant to the decision (see Chapter 7 for further guidance). Key legal matters to clarify and explain to the person being assessed include:

- The person's obligations to pay rent and occupy and maintain the property
- The landlord's obligations to the tenant under contract
- The risk of eviction if the person does not comply with his obligations
- The purpose of, and the terms of, the tenancy
- The rights of the landlord and support staff to enter the property without permission in the case of emergency.

Caution

It is important to be clear about the legal status of the agreement being signed before assessing the person's mental capacity to make the relevant decisions. You need to know whether this is a tenancy agreement or a license to occupy the property. If a person does not have exclusive occupation of his accommodation, then it is likely that he should be asked to sign a license agreement rather than a tenancy agreement. For example, in situations where staff have control over the person, provide personal care and take out rubbish or where there are set visiting hours, it is likely to be a license agreement. The case of *Street v Mountford* [1985] established that for a tenancy to exist three features must be present:

1   Exclusive occupation
2   Rent being paid
3   Occupation for a specific term.

The courts will consider the facts of the proposed arrangements to be more significant in determining the nature of the agreement than the written content of the documents being signed.

Who can sign a tenancy agreement on behalf of a person who lacks capacity?

It is not lawful for someone to make a best interests decision about whether or not to enter into any kind of legal contract, including a tenancy agreement, on behalf of someone else without the appropriate legal power or permission. The people/

roles listed below can lawfully enter into tenancy agreements but only where the scope of their powers specifies this legal authority:

- Someone who has been given Lasting Power of Attorney (LPA) for property and financial affairs whilst the person still had capacity to make this decision and this has been registered with the Office of the Public Guardian (OPG)
- Someone who has been given Enduring Power of Attorney (EPA; pre-October 2007) and this has been registered with the OPG (or Public Guardianship Office pre-2007) following the person's loss of mental capacity
- A Deputy appointed by the Court of Protection to make decisions on the person's behalf
- A person with a specific order to sign conferred by the Court of Protection.

Tips

- If someone already lacks the capacity to manage aspects of her property and affairs, and she has assets and income other than social security benefits, then it is often sensible for someone (a family member, solicitor or Local Authority) to apply to the Court of Protection to be appointed as a Court Deputy.
- If there is no one with the legal authority to enter into a tenancy agreement on behalf of someone who lacks capacity, and the sole purpose of the application is to sign or terminate a tenancy, then an application to the Court of Protection can be made for an order that specifically deals with the tenancy matter.

Caution

- People with appointeeship, acting on behalf of someone who lacks the capacity to manage his benefits and appointed by the Department for Work and Pensions in the UK, do not have the legal authority to sign a tenancy agreement on behalf of another person.
- A tenancy agreement is "voidable" if the person who signs it lacks the mental capacity to understand the decision being made. Should the agreement be "voidable", then the person's compliance does not affect the right to have the agreement cancelled (see *Imperial Loan Co Ltd v Stone* [1892]).

References

Case law

Imperial Loan Co Ltd v Stone [1892] 1 QB 599
LB Islington v QR [2014] EWCOP 26
Street v Mountford [1985] UKHL 4

Chapter 20

The Courtroom

Capacity to litigate, fitness to plead and fitness to be a witness

Karen Dean and Adam Hartrick

In this chapter

The first part of this chapter looks at the assessment of an adult's capacity to litigate using a case study and considers the roles of professionals and the Civil Courts in determining litigation capacity. We also highlight some of the legal issues to be considered in other scenarios, which health and social care professionals may encounter. The second part of the chapter considers an individual's fitness to plead to charges in criminal proceedings. Next, we consider an individual's capacity to give evidence in Court proceedings and provide some practical guidance upon preparing reports and giving oral evidence in both the Civil and Criminal Courts generally. This chapter relates to the law in England and Wales.

The civil courts: Capacity to litigate

Civil courts include the Court of Protection, the County Court, the Family Court and the High Court. The new Court of Protection was established by the Mental Capacity Act 2005 (MCA) and broadly has the same powers as the High Court in this context. The Court of Protection deals with issues relating to an individual's welfare (including medical treatment) in addition to its property and financial decision-making jurisdiction.

Capacity to litigate is an individual's capacity to conduct legal proceedings, which includes bringing a case to Court, defending or responding to a case or appearing in Court as a party to legal proceedings. The capacity to conduct proceedings does not necessarily go hand in hand with the individual's capacity to make decisions regarding his care or medical treatment. Understanding the processes involved in the litigation may require an individual to understand more complex information than the decision that is the subject of the litigation, for example, where he should live. It is primarily for an individual's solicitor to satisfy herself, in compliance with the MCA (2005), that her client, or prospective client, has capacity to give her instructions to conduct Court proceedings; however, health or social care professionals may become involved in this assessment process at the request of the solicitor.

If necessary, solicitors should undertake an assessment of capacity themselves and, if they have any concerns as to the individual's litigation capacity, they should seek an assessment by an appropriate expert. The solicitor will have to consider whether to obtain an opinion from a medical practitioner or whether it may be more relevant to approach another suitably qualified professional, for example, a clinical psychologist, social worker or speech and language therapist. This will depend on the individual's particular condition and the nature of the Court proceedings (*Law Society Practice Note, "Meeting the needs of vulnerable clients"*). On the basis of this expert opinion, and any other relevant information, the solicitor must then decide whether or not the individual has the requisite capacity. Where there are disputes regarding capacity, an application to the Court of Protection can be made to request a declaration about the individual's capacity.

Less commonly, health or social care professionals may be instructed to assess litigation capacity at the request of the Court once proceedings have begun. The Court will consider all of the relevant evidence presented by all parties in the case, including the family's views and any expert opinion from professionals. The Court will have to decide what the background facts are, apply the law to those facts and then make a final decision as to whether or not the individual has litigation capacity.

In either scenario, health and social care practitioners will need to apply the same principles arising from the relevant legal test when reporting to a solicitor or to the Court.

The legal test

The test to be applied to the assessment of litigation capacity in England and Wales is the statutory test set out in the MCA (2005), which has been discussed in detail in previous chapters. In summary, an individual lacks capacity if he is not able to make a decision for himself due to an impairment of, or disturbance in, the functioning of the mind or brain. A person is unable to make a decision for himself for the purposes of the MCA *(section 3)* if he is unable to:

- Understand the information relevant to the decision
- Retain that information
- Use or weigh that information as part of the process of making the decision, or
- Communicate his decision (whether by talking, using sign language or any other means).

The MCA Code of Practice (2007) states that this statutory definition of capacity is in line with the existing common law tests, and the MCA does not replace these. Therefore, the common law principles established prior to the MCA remain relevant and should guide assessors of capacity. The key principles established are as follows:

- "The test to be applied . . . is whether the party to legal proceedings is capable of understanding, with the assistance of such proper explanation from legal advisors and experts in other disciplines as the case may require, the issues on which his consent or decision is likely to be necessary in the course of those proceedings . . . a person should not be held unable to understand the information relevant to a decision if he can understand an explanation of that information in broad terms and simple language." (*Masterman- Lister v Brutton & Co* [2002], at paragraphs 75, 79). In other words, an individual must be able to understand in broad terms, with the help of legal advisors and if necessary other professionals (for example, a health or social care practitioner) the matters which he is likely to have to decide or consent to during the Court proceedings.
- The test is not a narrow one of whether an individual has capacity to take each individual step in the proceedings, but a broad test as to whether she has the capacity to conduct the proceedings as a whole (*Dunhill v Burgin* [2012]).
- The test should also be applied in relation to the particular proceedings in which the individual is involved (*Sheffield City Council v E & Another* [2004]).

Because the MCA presumes someone has capacity unless shown otherwise, the burden of proving someone lacks capacity to litigate is on the party who suggests that the individual lacks capacity.

Section 2 (4) of the Mental Capacity Act states that any question as to whether a person lacks capacity within the meaning of the Act must be decided on the balance of probabilities. In other words, is it more likely than not that the individual lacks capacity? This standard of proof must therefore be applied by the assessor (whether solicitor, healthcare professional or Court) when making a decision about a person's capacity, and when providing an expert opinion regarding this in a report.

Applying the test

The third key principle was established in the case of *Sheffield City Council v E & Another* [2004] and was set out in the judgment at paragraphs 38 and 39 as follows:

The question of capacity to litigate is not something to be determined in the abstract. One has to focus on the particular piece of litigation in relation to which the issue arises. The question is always whether the litigant has capacity to litigate in relation to particular proceedings in which he is involved. . . .

Someone may have the capacity to litigate in a case where the nature of the dispute and the issues are simple, whilst at the same time lacking the capacity to litigate in a case where either the nature of the dispute or the issues are more complex.

Where an individual does lack litigation capacity, she is referred to as a "protected party" within the Court proceedings, and a "litigation friend" must be appointed to conduct the proceedings on her behalf and protect her interests (see Box 20.1 for a case example). This applies to proceedings in the County Court, High Court, Family Court or Court of Protection. If there is no suitable person willing to act as a litigation friend, then the Official Solicitor is usually asked to act as a last resort.

Box 20.1   Capacity to litigate – Case study part 1

Jeff is a 30-year-old patient with a long-standing diagnosis of multiple sclerosis and recurrent admissions to hospital who has been assessed as lacking capacity to make decisions regarding admission to hospital for care and treatment and residence. Jeff is subject to a Deprivation of Liberty Safeguards (DoLS) authorisation for which his brother is the Relevant Person's Representative (see Chapter 28). Jeff wants to return home on discharge, but the hospital disagrees that suitable care can be provided there. Jeff and his brother instruct solicitors who make an application to the Court of Protection to challenge the DoLS authorisation and seek clarification as to capacity regarding these decisions, proposing Jeff's brother act as litigation friend.

The Court decides that the expert evidence of a clinical neuropsychologist and a nursing care consultant is required to assist the Court in determining the issues and gives permission to Jeff and the Hospital Trust to jointly instruct Dr North, an independent Consultant Clinical Neuropsychologist, to:

1)   Report upon the question of Jeff's capacity

   (i) To litigate
   (ii) To make decisions about where he should live
   (iii) To make decisions about the care he should receive and

2)   Report upon the extent to which a residential placement would impact upon his state of health.

For Jeff to have the capacity to conduct proceedings, he would need to understand as much as the ordinary person on the street who has capacity; therefore, he does not need to understand all the details of the law, as these will be explained to him in layman's terms by his legal advisors. However, he would need to be able to understand and retain information and advice relating to the specific Court proceedings and be able to use and weigh this information and advice to make informed decisions about the proceedings and to communicate these.

Some examples of the decisions Jeff may have to make, and the information he would have to understand, include:

- Understanding how the proceedings are going to be funded
- Being able to approve in general terms the information set out in documents served on his behalf in the proceedings, for example, the Statement of facts or grounds which will have supported the application to the Court of Protection
- Understanding the conclusions of the clinical neuropsychologist and care experts; understanding any advice given to him by his solicitor as a result of those conclusions and being able to make a decision as to how to proceed in the case.

When instructed to assess litigation capacity, information regarding the nature of the Court proceedings, or the decisions which may need to be made, should be set out by the instructing solicitor in the letter of instruction. If this information is not provided, then the assessor should seek further information from the instructing solicitor. The assessor may be asked to complete a "Certificate as to capacity to conduct proceedings (Official Solicitor)", which is a standard form published by the office of the Official Solicitor and Public Trustee.

The legal test should also be set out by the instructing solicitor in the letter of instruction but, if any clarification is required as to the test or its application in a particular case, then further information should be sought from the instructing solicitor.

When arriving at a conclusion regarding litigation capacity, the questions to be considered are on balance:

- Is the person more likely than not to have litigation capacity? or
- Is the person more likely than not to lack the capacity to litigate?

Consent and confidentiality

Professionals involved in assessing litigation capacity need to be mindful of their ethical duties towards individuals. This includes their duty of confidentiality when considering disclosure of information and, in the case of health professionals, whether the individual patient consents to the assessment or not. Issues of consent and confidentiality can be complex, and professionals will be assisted by the guidance issued by their respective professional bodies, such as the British Medical Association, the Law Society and the British Psychological Society. Doctors should also be mindful of compliance with guidance issued by the General Medical Council, and nurses of the Nursing and Midwifery Council Code of Practice. In brief terms, where an adult lacks the capacity to consent to examination, unless there is a Lasting Power of Attorney in place which delegates this decision, then a decision has to be made upon the basis of the individual's best interests with reference to the checklist in Section 4 of the MCA. Provided that the individual is compliant, and the assessment is considered to be in her best interests, it will usually be possible for an assessment of capacity to be carried out.

If an individual refuses a capacity assessment, he cannot be forced to undergo this. The consequences of refusal should be carefully explained. For example, if a claim could not be brought to Court by the individual until the Court was satisfied that he had capacity to litigate, this might be sufficient to persuade him. If he persists with a refusal, professionals should note the refusal in the relevant records together with any other evidence which may be relevant to the question of whether or not he has capacity. For example, the individual's actions or behaviour or anything he has said during the course of discussions which may be of significance.

Professionals should always ensure that the Court has granted permission for information to be shared, to assist the assessment, and permission for the assessment to be disclosed to avoid any confidentiality issues arising. In proceedings concerning an individual's capacity, the Court will usually make an Order giving permission, and professionals should always ensure they have seen and read it.

If a report has been prepared as to capacity in the Court of Protection, or in Family Law proceedings, even if the individual whom it concerns has given consent to disclosure of the report for use elsewhere (for example, in a personal injury claim) permission will be required from the original Court to use this information outside of the original proceedings. This is required by the Court of Protection Rules 2007 (rule 91) and the Family Procedure Amendment Rules 2012 (rule 29.12). Disclosure could amount to contempt of Court, which is a criminal offence. Professionals therefore need to satisfy themselves that the necessary permission has been given and, where there is any doubt, they should seek legal advice.

Box 20.2   Capacity to litigate – Case study part 2

The Court grants permission to Dr North to see Jeff for the purposes of assessment and permission to Jeff's legal representatives to disclose to Dr North the papers in the case and Jeff's medical records. The Court orders

> a date by which Dr North is to send the report to Jeff's solicitors and a date by which Dr North is to answer any questions posed by the parties.
>
> Jeff's legal fees are funded by the Legal Aid Agency, who refuses to authorise Dr North's fees.
>
> The parties approach Dr South, employed by another Hospital Trust, to produce a report under Section 49 of the Mental Capacity Act. Dr South receives a letter of instruction from the parties but cannot see any reference to her name in the Order.

In the scenario in Box 20.2, Dr South should seek assurance that an Order has been made by the Court giving her permission to assess Jeff and permission to disclose her report to Jeff's legal representatives.

The criminal courts: Fitness to plead

One of the most important issues that may need to be determined in any given case is whether an accused is fit to plead to the charge, or charges, against him. To be fit to plead, the accused must have capacity and the ability to fairly participate in his own trial. For example, the accused may be able to deny the allegation yet be unable to undergo the entire trial process. Therefore, it is important to be aware of any impairment or disturbance in mind or brain caused by, for example, permanent or temporary mental illness, brain injury, learning disability or communication disorder, which results in the accused being vulnerable and unable to fairly participate. For context, an individual who does not speak English would be unfit to plead; however, this can be addressed through the use of an interpreter.

Whether an individual is fit to plead is a matter that is now determined by a Judge, who will require psychiatric and/or psychological expert evidence to make that decision. It is a determination that can only be made after examining expert evidence. If an accused is not fit to plead, and a trial would be inherently unfair, then a Jury hearing will take place to determine whether or not the accused committed the offences alleged against her. For example, if the accused is charged with murder, did she commit the act which resulted in the death? If the accused is found by a Jury to be responsible for the act or omission, then the Court is able to dispose of the matter by way of a hospital order, a supervision order or an absolute discharge. Similar disposals are available in relation to those found not guilty of an offence by reason of insanity, but that is a different consideration to whether or not an accused is fit to plead to charges laid against her and to participate fairly in the criminal trial process.

The legal test

It is vitally important that mental health professionals asked to give expert opinion on the question of fitness to plead have a clear understanding of the relevant legal test. The first point to note is that in relation to fitness to plead, the question being asked relates to the accused's state of mental health or disability as at the time of trial, and not his state of mental health or disability at the time of the alleged offence.

The test the Judge will apply in determining fitness to plead was originally laid down almost 200 years ago by Baron Alderson in the case of *R v Pritchard* (1836). This case concerned an accused who was unable to speak or hear. The Court determined there were three broad matters upon which evidence was required:

- Whether the accused wilfully chose not to speak as opposed to being unable to as a result of a disability (burden of proof upon the prosecution)
- Whether he could plead to the charge or not, and
- Whether he was of sufficient intellect to comprehend the course of proceedings in the trial so as to "make a proper defence" – which was said to include the ability to challenge any of the jurors to whom he may object and to comprehend the details of the evidence.

In broad terms, this test has been affirmed over the years, but the modern reference point is the 2003 Appeal Court decision in the case of *R v M (John)*. In that case the Appeal Court approved Baron Alderson's legal test derived for fitness to plead, which can be distilled to six matters in respect of which an accused must be capable of doing in order to be regarded as fit to plead to charges laid against him, and tried on them. The accused must be able to do all of the following:

- Understand the charges
- Decide whether to plead guilty or not
- Exercise his right to challenge jurors
- Instruct solicitors and Counsel
- Follow the course of proceedings
- Give evidence in his own defence.

Further guidance is provided in *R v Marcantonio and R v Chitolie* [2016] (at paragraph 7):

> The Court is required to undertake an assessment of the defendant's capabilities in the context of the particular proceedings . . . have regard to what the legal process will involve and what demands it will make on the defendant. It should be addressed . . . in the context of the particular case. The degree of complexity of different legal proceedings may vary considerably. Thus the

court should consider, for example, the nature and complexity of the issues arising in the particular proceedings, the likely duration of the proceedings and the number of parties.

It is for the Judge to determine whether the legal test is satisfied. To do this, the Judge must have appropriate expert evidence from two medical practitioners, one of whom must be approved under the Mental Health Act and would therefore usually involve the instruction of a Consultant Forensic Psychiatrist. However, it should be noted that the expert must have knowledge of the field. A Consultant Forensic Psychiatrist may have the expertise regarding mental illness, yet not have sufficient expertise in relation to learning disability or cognitive impairment. In such cases, further reports are obtained from a Psychologist within the appropriate discipline.

It is essential, therefore, that any appropriate expert who is asked to consider a potential Defendant's fitness to plead considers all six matters listed and gives an opinion on each matter within the report that she writes, having interviewed the individual concerned. If a Psychiatrist consulted considers neuropsychological assessment would inform her opinion, then that recommendation should be made within the report. If neuropsychological assessment is undertaken, then the Psychiatrist should be given a further opportunity to consider her opinion in the light of those test results.

Scope for reform

Fitness to plead is a complicated and sometimes contentious topic. It must, of course, be remembered that the accused in *R v Pritchard* (1836) was unable to speak or hear but otherwise of sound mind.

The Law Commission's Report: Unfitness to Plead (Volume 1) was published on 13 January 2016. The report concluded that the Pritchard legal test ignores multifactorial aspects of mental illness and conditions which impact upon ability, for example, delusions. Instead, undue reliance is placed upon intellectual ability. When do delusions prohibit rational decision-making process and what aspects of the evidence will the jury rely upon?

The Law Commission's proposals encompass a single test which prioritises effective participation creating "a test in keeping with the modern court process . . . [which] would accommodate advances in psychiatric and psychological thinking . . . [and] more appropriately identify those who are unable to engage with the trial process" (p. 11). This new test would explicitly incorporate decision-making capacity, taking into account all assistance available to the defendant.

It does not appear that there are any firm proposals for changes to the law currently, notwithstanding the Law Commission's consideration of the issue.

Until reform takes place, the current position on fitness to plead is, as summed up by Lord Justice Toulson: "psychiatric understanding and the law in relation to mentally ill defendants do not always sit together comfortably" (*R v Murray* [2008], at paragraph 5).

Capacity to give evidence in Court

The question of capacity to give evidence in Court is different from fitness to plead. The question of capacity to give evidence looks at whether an individual can understand and answer questions about what has happened, not whether or not she has the capacity to plead guilty or not guilty or the ability to participate in a criminal trial to determine charges against her.

The individual must have the capacity to understand the oath that has to be sworn to speak the truth. The starting point is that all individuals are able to be a witness, whatever their age, unless they cannot understand the questions asked or cannot answer the questions in a way which can be understood with assistance by special measures, for example, communication aids, if required. If a witness's capacity to give sworn evidence is challenged, the party wanting to call the witness must prove, on the balance of probabilities, that the individual has capacity. It will be determined from the outset, by questioning of the witness by the Judge, and expert evidence, as discussed earlier, would probably be required if there was a serious challenge to an important witness's ability to give evidence.

Writing the report

Issues to address in the report regarding fitness to plead

The starting points are the six matters listed earlier, but these issues also need to be addressed by the expert professional as appropriate:

- Has the accused sufficient cognitive abilities to understand the charges and offer a response to them? Can he decide for himself whether to plead guilty or not?
- Is the accused able to give instructions to a lawyer both in relation to the facts alleged and the evidence available? Is the accused likely to be able to follow evidence given in Court and give instructions on evidence given by others as the trial proceeds?
- Is the accused able to listen to and follow the evidence? Does he understand what is said and able to respond if something is said with which he does not agree?
- Is the accused able to give evidence in his own defence if he wishes? This would entail understanding questions asked orally, the ability to apply his mind to answering and conveying intelligibly the answers he wishes to give.

Note there is no requirement for what the accused says to be reliable, plausible or inherently believable. It is not for the expert to give an opinion on what the accused says about the allegations against her. It is for the Judge to determine fact and the jury to determine guilt.

During the trial process, when evidence is given by others about the accused, the accused needs to simply understand what is being said, communicate intelligibly with her lawyers about it and put forward any comments she has so that they can be communicated to the Court. It is not necessary that any comments made are valid or helpful either to her own case or her representatives. However, it is important that the accused can comment on whatever she wishes during the course of the trial.

It is important to identify any adjustments to the trial process, which could reasonably be made, that would enable the accused to be regarded as fit to plead and stand trial. This could include, for example, sitting next to his solicitor throughout the trial to help with taking notes and noting down the accused's comments as evidence is given, rather than relying upon him to remember points raised over a period of time.

In order to accomplish this, the expert will need to understand and have detail available to her of all of the charges that the accused is required to answer and go through them all with him.

Guidance and mandatory contents of the report

In terms of writing the report regarding fitness to plead, the expert must comply with the guidance relating to content set out at section 19.4 Criminal Procedure (Amendment) Rules 2015 as amended. The expert's role is to help the court by providing objective opinion on matters within his expertise. In this situation, the expertise required relates to an individual's capacity to stand trial by reference to the legal test set out above.

For expert evidence within civil courts, including both the Court of Protection and the High Court, an expert must be independent, as in criminal courts. Permission of the Court must also be obtained by the parties before instructing expert evidence. The expert has an overriding duty to assist the Court upon matters which are within his expertise. The expert must not seek to determine disputed factual issues but provide an expert opinion on questions posed that are within his expertise. The rules on admissibility of evidence are more flexible within civil courts than they are in criminal courts. In particular, the MCA is silent upon the evidential requirements which need to be satisfied before a Judge can determine an application within the Court of Protection, but very often expert evidence is called upon.

The following should be set out in the expert reports and is applicable to both criminal and civil cases:

1 Qualifications and experience to establish credibility and relevant expertise
2 Reference to and copies of any literature or other source material relied upon
3 A summary of her understanding of the facts of the matter which are relevant to the expert's opinion
4 Confirmation of any consultations

5   Confirmation of what testing has been undertaken with appropriate explanations in lay terms
6   An expressed opinion on the questions asked
7   If applicable, the range of opinion on any particular matter, giving reasons for the expert's own opinion
8   An explanation of any qualifications to the opinion given
9   A summary of the conclusions reached
10   Standard declarations as to the duties of an expert to the Court and truth as to the contents.

The report should be typed, single sided and double spaced with numbered paragraphs and headings with the cover of the report including details of the Court, case number and parties' details. It is important to be objective and avoid being selective.

Giving evidence in Court

If called to give evidence in any court, always take your report and source materials to Court with you. Be honest, direct and balanced; listen carefully to the question asked and, if it is not clear or you do not understand it, say so and do not guess or speculate, unless specifically directed to do so by the Judge. Avoid getting into a confrontational situation with any of the Advocates.

Organise your thoughts and verify and clarify your involvement and contact, for example, how many times did you meet the person and in what contexts?

Tips

- Re-read your report and reference materials.
- Form key points you want to bring out.
- Stay within your expertise.
- Start with the basics and then expand where relevant.
- Remember the Judge is a lawyer, not a medical practitioner.
- Consider there will be varying levels of understanding within the Court room.
- Not everyone may have read your report in detail.
- Repeat what your report says; do not be afraid of repetition if it is relevant and appropriate.
- Consider forms of address (Sir, Your Honour etc.) and direct your answers to the Judge.
- Consider which type of oath you would like to swear.
- Listen to the question and in answering it be concise.

Summary

- Legal representatives need to satisfy themselves that their clients have the capacity to become a party to proceedings in the Civil Courts.
- Health professionals may be asked to assess litigation capacity.
- The standard of proof to be applied is the balance of probabilities.
- The Court of Protection can make a declaration about litigation capacity where there are disputes.
- The statutory test set out in the Mental Capacity Act is applicable, and the common law principles established prior to the Act remain relevant to guide assessors.
- Whether an individual is fit to plead in criminal proceedings is determined by a Judge, following consideration of psychiatric and/or psychological expert evidence.
- The key question is the accused's state of mental disability as at the time of Trial, not at the time of the alleged offence.
- The question of capacity to give evidence in both the Civil and Criminal Courts relates to an individual's understanding of the oath to speak the truth and her ability to understand and answer the questions.

References

Court of Protection Rules 2007, No. 1744 (L.12)

Criminal Procedure (Amendment) Rules 2015, part 19.4 (as amended by Criminal Procedure (Amendment) Rules 2018 (2018 No. 132 (L.2) s.9)

Department for Constitutional Affairs (2007). *Mental Capacity Act 2005: Code of Practice.* London: The Stationery Office. Available at: https://assets.publishing.service.gov.uk/government/uploads/system/uploads/attachment_data/file/497253/Mental-capacity-act-code-of-practice.pdf

Family Procedure Amendment Rules 2012, No. 679 (L.3)

Law Commission (2016). *Unfitness to Plead: Volume 1: Report* (Law Com No. 364).

Law Society Practice Note (2015). *Meeting the Needs of Vulnerable Clients*, 2 July.

Mental Capacity Act 2005. London: HMSO. Available at: www.legislation.gov.uk/ukpga/2005/9/contents

Official Solicitor and Public Trustee (2007). *Certificate as to Capacity to Conduct Proceedings (Official Solicitor).* Available at: https://assets.publishing.service.gov.uk/government/uploads/system/uploads/attachment_data/file/582243/capacity-to-conduct-proceedings-certificate.pdf

Case law

Dunhill v Burgin [2012] EWCA Civ 397

Masterman-Lister v Brutton & Co [2002] EWCA Civ 1889

R v M (John) [2003] EWCA Crim 3452

R v Marcantonio and R v Chitolie [2016] EWCA Crim 14

R v Murray [2008] EWCA Crim 1792

R v Pritchard (1836) 173 E.R. 135

Sheffield City Council v E & Another [2004] EWHC 2808 (Fam)

Professional guidance

British Medical Association: www.bma.org.uk/advice/employment/ethics

British Psychological Society: www.bps.org.uk/news-and-policy/bps-code-ethics-and-conduct; www.bps.org.uk/news-and-policy/practice-guidelines

General Medical Council: www.gmc-uk.org/ethical-guidance/ethical-guidance-for-doctors/consent; www.gmc-uk.org/ethical-guidance/ethical-guidance-for-doctors/confidentiality

The Law Society: www.lawsociety.org.uk/

Nursing and Midwifery Council: www.nmc.org.uk/standards/code/

Solicitor's Regulation Authority: www.sra.org.uk/Solicitors/code-of-conduct/rule4a

Useful resource

Ruck Keene, A. (2015). *Assessment of Mental Capacity: A Practical Guide for Doctors and Lawyers*. 4th ed. London: The British Medical Association and the Law Society.

Chapter 21

Assessing the mental capacity of people living with dementia
Getting practice right

Ian Leonard

In this chapter

The potential impact of dementia on decision-making capacity is explored, predominantly through the use of clinical case descriptions. Tips on best practice and how to avoid the more common errors made in this area are also discussed.

Setting the scene

When a person develops dementia, she will usually have experienced many decades of autonomous decision-making. During that time, she will have made many decisions, some of which others have considered unwise, uncharacteristic or indeed perverse. From taking a luxury cruise rather than paying off a credit card debt to moving in with the boyfriend she met last week or resigning from a boring job, she may have given many of those decisions little conscious thought, relying on "gut feelings".

Her right to make such decisions may rarely have been questioned previously, but the onset of dementia often changes that. Dependent on the person's circumstances, illness factors and the stance taken by others involved, there may be a shift from the presumption of capacity to the need for an assessment or even an unjustified presumption of a general lack of decision-making capacity.

Although some people lose confidence for decision-making in areas of retained capacity and are keen to hand over responsibilities to others, most are not. Others doubting their judgment can bring the first, unwelcome sense of friends or family starting to try to take independence away from a person who finds her memory sometimes failing. The scale of the issue is increasing due to an aging population and increasing recognition of both dementia and its potential to impact on decision-making capacity.

Transition between decision-making capacity and lack of it

A high proportion of people with dementia have a gradual, slow progression, as in the case of Rose (see Box 21.1). There is usually a period of time within which they retain capacity to put arrangements in place to influence their future situation, even if this has not been done prior to the onset of dementia. Some potential actions require the person to be aware of specific information about the necessary arrangements, for example, to ensure Advance Decisions/Directives and Lasting Powers of Attorney will be valid.

Box 21.1   Capacity to consent to assessment within the context of emerging dementia – Case study

Rose was a 73-year-old widow who was an infrequent attender at her doctor's surgery and had generally refused screening appointments and vaccinations. Two years ago, she fell and fractured her femur. The hospital discharge letter noted mild memory problems during the acute admission, but she was not seen by her GP after this. She reluctantly attended a GP appointment with her daughter, who described Rose's worsening memory impairment, including times when she became lost in the area where she had lived for 30 years, mild weight loss and increasing disputes with family members. Rose was angry about her daughter's description, insisting there was nothing wrong. When she scored poorly on a brief cognitive assessment, she stated it was because she was upset at being made to see a doctor. She refused to consider referral for further assessment on the grounds that there was nothing to assess.

Her GP thought that Rose did not understand the changes to her abilities and was failing to retain memories of the events that concerned her family. Attempts to discuss and improve that understanding were rejected by Rose, who walked out of the consultation. The GP's opinion was that, whilst Rose probably lacked capacity to decide whether to accept a referral to the local Memory Assessment Service, the strength of her disagreement meant that it would not be in her best interests to pursue a referral at that point. Her distressed daughter followed Rose from the consultation.

Four months later, Rose was again brought by her daughter to an appointment, though obviously again attending under pressure. She now acknowledged occasional lapses of memory but insisted these were normal for people her age and that she wanted no interference from anyone. Her daughter reported Rose had experienced problems paying for shopping after losing her bank card and was no longer cooking or eating reliably. There had been a small fire in her kitchen the previous week and her daughter had documented a further 5kg weight loss from the last appointment. The GP concluded that Rose's safety was at increasing risk from her memory problems, and this now outweighed the possible distress of a specialist assessment. Despite Rose's continued resistance, her GP, documenting Rose's continuing lack of capacity to decide on whether to be assessed, made a referral in Rose's best interests. She was careful to include this explanation in the referral letter so that if, as seemed likely, Rose rejected an initial contact from Memory Assessment Services, this lack of capacity would be taken into account in the service response.

The change in decision-making after a diagnosis of dementia is not from the starting point of a fully reasoned approach to all decisions, as few people attempt to engage with their world in that way. Rather, there is an inability to identify when a reasoned-through approach may be appropriate and to then be able to implement that approach, either independently or with assistance. It is a requirement that capacity assessments promote a person's capacity (see Box 21.2). Though there are points beyond which all approaches will be ineffective because of the severity of a person's dementia, interventions will at least improve the person's involvement in decisions. If this is not by enabling retention of capacity on a specific issue, then it can be by facilitating the expression of wishes and feelings that are relevant and assisting the person to influence decisions made on his behalf as much as possible. There are also common mistakes in applying the Mental Capacity Act (MCA, 2005) and its Code of Practice (2007) that must be avoided (see Box 21.3).

Box 21.2 Tips for approaching a capacity assessment with someone who has dementia

- Approach a capacity assessment as a test of your ability to analyse and, if necessary, promote decision-making capacity, not of the ability of the person with dementia to demonstrate it.
- Use principles of good communication for people with dementia – resolve any sensory impairments, minimize distractions, use unambiguous language and non-verbal prompts and be alert to lowered spans of attention. (See Chapters 9 and 11 and also "Communication and language" at www.alzheimers.org.uk.)

- Recognise that if you cannot describe the salient, relevant information for the decision, you cannot (other than for someone with an extremely severe impairment) form an opinion on the person's capacity to make that decision. (See Chapter 7 for relevant information.)
- Ensure any information required to improve understanding is provided in the most accessible way for the person. Provide relevant, salient information only – greater amounts of information may reduce overall understanding.
- Discuss issues through open, structured questions avoiding unnecessary complexity.
- Be prepared for assessments of important issues to be a process spread over time (see Chapter 9).

Box 21.3   Common pitfalls when assessing the capacity of someone who has dementia

- Failing to do a capacity assessment – interpreting a person's perceived lack of objection as agreement, and thinking that this means a capacity assessment, and potential best interests process (or equivalent), is not required, despite there being grounds to question capacity.
- Failing to do a capacity assessment – a person's objections resulting in progression to the best-interests process (or equivalent) in a way that ignores the possibility of "valid" refusal, especially if it is seen as an unwise decision.
- Completing a capacity assessment but failing to describe how the nature and/or degree of mental impairment causes the lack of capacity (the causative nexus). (See Chapter 2.)
- Overstating a situation, for example, stating that a person has "no awareness" or "no understanding" when he has a mild degree of impairment and can have some relevant discussion. (This can lead to adverse consequences ranging from colleagues' discomfort to a legal challenge.)
- Documenting clear deficits in one or more criteria of the legal test but concluding that the person "has capacity" as he does express a preference. (See Chapter 2.)
- Over-relying on a single short interview to give a definitive answer.
- Failing to clarify the salient, relevant information required for the decision leading to capacity for the specific decision not being addressed or setting too high a threshold for the "broad" understanding that is required. (See Chapter 7.)

Effects of dementia on decision-making in practice

Changes to brain function in dementia can affect both cognition and emotional responses. Cognition is a complicated concept involving attention, memory and executive function (Hodges, 2018) that can be impaired by a wide variety of changes at multiple brain locations. Overall severity of dementia, unless at the extremes of the range, is a poor guide to decision-making capacity. The pattern and degree of an individual's cognitive changes are of greater importance. Specific elements of the functional test of mental capacity in the MCA (understand, retain, use and weigh, communicate) cannot be mapped directly on to well-defined single cognitive domain; a pragmatic approach to linking impairments and capacity is required. Memory impairment most obviously affects the retention of information but is also relevant to understanding and the using and weighing of information. Executive function is relevant to understanding, but also the using and weighing of information and includes the ability to integrate emotional factors into decision-making where relevant. See Chapter 10 for a more thorough discussion of the impact of cognitive difficulties (in a range of conditions) on capacity.

Although cognitive change is common to all dementias, there are differences in the typical pattern of deficits apparent depending on the underlying causation (Ames, O'Brien and Burns, 2017; Hodges, 2018). This affects the cognitive components of decision-making in different ways:

- **Alzheimer's Disease:** Memory impairment and language deficits are usually the most prominent symptoms. People are more likely to retain capacity for decisions that involve mainly historical salient information than ones where recent information is most relevant. (See Box 21.4 for an example of such a capacity assessment.)
- **Vascular Dementia:** Impairment is often patchy, with a number of cognitive domains affected; problems with attention, information processing and executive functioning are frequently found, whereas an ability to express views is often retained. (See Box 21.5 for an example of such a capacity assessment.)
- **Frontotemporal Dementia:** A lack of interest in decision-making is an early feature and, though executive functions are affected, memory deficits also commonly occur.
- **Lewy Body Dementia/Parkinson's Disease Dementia:** Impaired executive function is prominent along with deficits in attention. Hallucinations and/or delusions are also relatively frequent. (See Box 21.6 for an example of such a capacity assessment.)

Box 21.4   Capacity to make a Health and Welfare Lasting Power of Attorney in the context of Alzheimer's Disease – Case study

Kathleen was a 72-year-old lady with increasing problems with her memory. Assessment led to a diagnosis of Alzheimer's Disease and treatment with donepezil, a cholinesterase inhibitor, which brought improved interest in her daily activities but no significant improvement in her ability to recall information. At a post-diagnostic meeting, the possibility of making a Lasting Power of Attorney (LPA) was raised.

Kathleen did not have significant financial assets and rented her flat. State benefits were her only income and her only child, Susan, already managed these as an appointee. It was agreed an LPA for Property and Financial affairs would not be of additional benefit. Kathleen became increasingly anxious when it was explained, contrary to what she had previously believed, that Susan would not automatically be able to make decisions for her regarding her health and welfare if she could not do so herself.

Kathleen blamed doctors for her husband's death 20 years ago, convinced that the risks of an operation had not been explained to him properly. Neither did she trust other professionals, complaining that social workers had tried to take Susan away 50 years ago. She insisted that it should be her daughter who made decisions on her behalf and any other arrangement was "stupid".

When Kathleen's capacity to make an LPA for Health and Welfare was assessed two weeks later, she could not recall any previous conversation on the issue, nor whom it might have been with. She found it hard to credit that doctors, social workers or other professionals would be able to make decisions for her if she could not do so herself and insisted that this should fall to Susan, her only relative. She could think of no one else she trusted to make such decisions and, when told she would be able to change her mind whilst she had the capacity to do so, she became cross saying "I know my mind. I want Susan in charge, not you lot". An attempt to reassure her that she did not have to change her mind elicited the response of "I'm not an idiot, you know".

When the issue of life-sustaining treatment was explained, and that this required a separate signature, Kathleen demanded to sign immediately saying that she did not want doctors deciding if she should be "turned off" or not.

Conclusion

Although Kathleen's memory problems were clear, she showed a broad understanding of the issues which, in her personal situation, were relatively simple. Her decision was consistent with long-term attitudes, and she had a very limited range of potential attorneys. She retained the information long enough to use and weigh this, with an emotional aspect being part of the process but not to the exclusion of practical considerations. The high weight she gave to her daughter and not professionals taking decisions on her behalf was grounded in her own life experiences. Kathleen communicated a consistent decision that she wanted to give authority to her daughter for decisions on any issues in which she lacked capacity. Therefore, she demonstrated capacity to make an LPA for Health and Welfare.

Box 21.5   Capacity to make decisions on residence for the purpose of receiving care in the context of Vascular Dementia – Case study

Brian, a 79-year-old man, had moved into residential care four months previously, after a hospital admission due to the latest in a series of a strokes. These had produced a stepwise cognitive impairment with memory difficulties, poor concentration and problems processing information being most apparent. At discharge from hospital, he was judged to lack capacity to decide about the move. He fell repeatedly, taking no advice about walking safely. He was muddled and aggressively demanding of his son and carers, insisting that he had recovered and should be allowed to return to live at home, where his son also lived. His son disclosed to the Social Worker involved that he was relieved Brian would not be going home after years of friction. This included repeated physical assaults on his son, which were worse during periods of intermittent heavy drinking. Brian's daughter, who lived over 200 miles away, visiting monthly, supported her brother's view of the situation. Brian was found to be unable to understand important aspects of his impaired function and unable to use and weigh salient information to understand the foreseeable consequences of a return home in contrast to remaining in care. A Deprivation of Liberty Safeguards (DoLS) Authorisation was granted for six months.

During his time at the care home, Brian's mobility improved, as did his ability to care for himself. He still needed assistance to dress and shower, but actively requested it and showed some gratitude to carers. His conversation reflected a more detailed understanding of what he could and could not do safely for himself. His son visited daily and Brian made clear his wish to return home. His son explained that he wanted him home but was unable to take him there because "the Social Worker said so". Brian's independent Relevant Person's Representative (see Chapter 28 on deprivation of liberty) brought a challenge to the authorisation on the grounds that Brian had capacity to decide where to reside and, even if he was still found to lack capacity, the deprivation in place was not in his best interests.

The psychiatrist who was asked to reassess Brian's capacity declined to do so on the grounds that Brian was not being given salient, relevant information about his son's actual views. Brian's son did not want Brian to be told of his reluctance to have him home, saying it would simply worsen their relationship further to no one's benefit. He was persuaded that his view was a key piece of information that his father was entitled to be told about, given its role in preventing his return home. Brian was upset and saddened by the information, but gave the view that, if that was his son's wish, he was willing to remain in the care home rather than to return home "unwanted". Assessment found this to be a decision Brian made with capacity about the options practically available to him.

In addition, each individual may have significant fluctuations in her cognitive abilities. This can be an inherent part of dementia (Vascular and Lewy Body Dementias particularly) or due to super-imposed acute confusional states (delirium) of which infections and medication are common causes. Urinary and chest infections may not give rise to major physical symptoms but still cause a worsened mental state. Medications commonly found to increase cognitive impairment in people with dementia are opioids (prescribed for pain) and a wide variety of drugs with anticholinergic effects (ones for urinary incontinence, depression and allergies are important to consider).

Any improvement in capacity may only be apparent some weeks after an underlying cause is treated. Urgent decisions will still need to be taken on a person's behalf if he lacks capacity due to a temporary cause. Where decisions are non-urgent, and spurious urgency for the convenience of others must be guarded against, optimising a person with dementia's physical health can be crucial in restoring decision-making capacity.

Box 21.6   Capacity to manage financial affairs in the context of Lewy Body Dementia – Case study

David was a 68-year-old director of a family-run firm with a multi-million-pound turnover, which he ran alongside his three younger siblings. There had been various disputes over several decades about how best to manage the business, but their disagreements had always been resolved between them eventually. David had always been the most cautious of the family. After he had impulsively made two particularly disadvantageous deals and become erratic in his attendance at the office, the Finance Director and Company Secretary met with him. They were very concerned about his decision-making and persuaded him to consult his GP with work-related stress, although he was reluctant to do so.

The GP was surprised by David's fragmented account of events and a new tremor of his hands. This led to a private appointment with a Neurologist who arranged neuropsychological testing as well as brain scans. Although his scores on standardised testing were only slightly below the average range, the assessment concluded that there had been a moderate decline in executive function and a mild decline in memory for new information. A brain scan strongly suggested reduced activity of dopaminergic systems. His wife reported that he made uncharacteristic social gaffes and had been intermittently very suspicious for the last 18 months. He repeatedly told her that he had seen their children nearby, even though she knew this was not possible as they had busy lives many miles away and they denied having been in the area. She also noted that he had experienced a number of falls.

A likely diagnosis of Lewy Body Dementia was discussed with David, who reacted angrily, declaring it all to be related to the stress caused by the recent business problems. He stated that he was having to stay out of the office more to monitor his wife, who he suspected of having an affair, but that this was also allowing him time to recoup the business losses through online poker and investing the capital from cashing in his large private pension. He acknowledged these plans were not going well, but they needed more time to work. He then said that he had no more wish for discussion but was going to sell his part of the business to his siblings and retire with immediate effect.

Conclusion

Whilst David's ability to retain information remained relatively good, and could be promoted by using written accounts, his understanding of his situation and ability to use and weigh information were significantly impaired. This meant that he lacked capacity to manage his property and financial affairs at that time, including any decision to sell his share of the business.

Summary

This chapter emphasizes the importance of changes in decision-making capacity to a person living with dementia and the ways in which this, or its effects, can potentially be reduced. It also illustrates the interaction of different components of cognitive change and decisions to be made in individual circumstances. A particular cognitive change can only produce a loss of decision-making capacity when combined with an individual's specific situation.

References

Ames, D., O'Brien, J.T. and Burns, A. (eds.) (2017). *Dementia*. 5th ed. Boca Raton, FL: CRC Press.

Department for Constitutional Affairs (2007). *Mental Capacity Act 2005: Code of Practice*. London: The Stationery Office. Available at: https://assets.publishing.service.gov.uk/government/uploads/system/uploads/attachment_data/file/497253/Mental-capacity-act-code-of-practice.pdf

Hodges, J.R. (2018). *Cognitive Assessment for Clinicians*. 3rd ed. Oxford: Oxford University Press.

Mental Capacity Act 2005. London: HMSO. Available at: www.legislation.gov.uk/ukpga/2005/9/contents

Part 4

Complex situations

Chapter 22

What to do when someone says one thing, but does another

Capacity to make a decision and put it into practice

Victoria Teggart and Kate Dimmock

In this chapter

This chapter will explore the difficulties raised when a client's behaviour and actions are inconsistent with the intentions and plans he discusses during an interview-based capacity assessment. It will consider how an "impairment of mind or brain" can affect a person's ability to act upon her intentions in the moment and how behaviour may not always be guided by reasoning. Detailed case examples will illustrate how it may be necessary to extend a capacity assessment beyond the interview format to incorporate behavioural observations and reports of everyday actions in order to fully understand decision-making capacity.

A discrepancy between stated decision and behaviour "in the moment"

Imagine these scenarios:

- You have completed an assessment with Michael, a client with a traumatic brain injury (TBI), regarding his capacity to make decisions about day-to-day money management. At the interview, Michael was able to discuss financial priorities, such as paying rent and bills, and buying food before non-essential items. He was also able to tell you the pros and cons of not following such a plan. You judged that he had capacity in this matter and control of his financial affairs was passed back to him. Two months later Michael's social worker contacts you to report that he is in arrears for his rent and utilities and has spent his money purchasing a job lot of novelty T-shirts that he plans to resell on an Internet auction site for a profit.
- You assessed whether Constance, a retired nurse with diabetes and a diagnosis of dementia, had capacity to make decisions regarding her healthcare needs. Specifically, you focused upon whether she was able to recognise potential signs of poor health, for example, leg ulcers due to diabetes, and if she knew how to act on these appropriately. Constance was able to list a range of potentially

harmful symptoms and in each case gave a good account of the appropriate course of action that she would follow, including making an appointment with her GP or calling an ambulance in an emergency. She was able to state the risks of not seeking medical attention for these symptoms. A month later, she is admitted to hospital with severe leg ulcers. The medical opinion suggests that these had been present and getting worse for at least three weeks. There is no indication that Constance contacted her doctor or any other medical professional during that time.

So how can you start to understand these differences between stated intentions and actions? Do you just assume that the person changed his mind and is merely making an "unwise" decision, or might these actions be a sign that capacity is still in doubt and he may need help in these areas?

Why might people say one thing and do another?

There are a number of possible explanations for why a person may say one thing in a capacity interview and later follow a different course of action:

1   The person changed her mind about the decision she had made. This may have been related to a change in her circumstances or learning new information related to the situation.
2   The person may have stated during the interview what he believed the assessor wanted to hear or stated an opinion that he felt would get him to his preferred outcome in the most efficient way. An example might be agreeing to have carers visit him at home after discharge, when he has already planned to turn them away.
3   The person may have fully intended to follow through on her stated course of action but has acted differently due to pressure or coercion from others.
4   The impairment of mind or brain that led to capacity being questioned in the first place has affected the person in a way that makes him unable to follow through on his stated course of action or unable to make a reasoned and informed decision at the point when it needs to be made.

Caution

Do not assume that someone who acts against her previously stated plans has simply changed her mind. Ask yourself:

- Has the impairment of mind or brain affected her behaviour and ability to follow through on her plans?
- Is she acting against her own wishes due to pressure from other people?

How impairments of mind or brain can affect behaviour

The Mental Capacity Act (MCA, 2005) is not specific about the causes of the impairment of mind or brain, and this could refer to "a disability, condition or trauma" (MCA Code of Practice, 2007, p. 42). Therefore, a wide range of conditions could be considered to potentially cause an impairment of mind or brain, which in turn can result in impairments in cognitive functions that affect a person's ability to understand, remember, reason and communicate – the abilities assessed in the functional test of capacity.

However, changes can also be seen in cognitive abilities that affect how much control a person has over her actions. These are often referred to as the "neurobehavioural symptoms" of a condition (Worthington, Wood and McMillan, 2016). Such difficulties are most likely, but not exclusively, seen in conditions such as acquired brain injury (caused by stroke, encephalitis, hypoxia, traumatic brain injury or alcohol-related brain damage) and dementia (for example, Alzheimer's disease or vascular dementia). Table 22.1 outlines some of the commonly observed neurobehavioral symptoms that may impact upon a person's ability to carry out his stated intentions.

Some of these aspects of behaviour, such as reduced awareness, may become apparent during an interview-based capacity assessment. However, some neurobehavioural changes can occur in the absence of deficits in understanding, remembering and reasoning that would impact on the person's performance on the functional test of capacity.

Table 22.1 Neurobehavioural symptoms

Symptom	Presentation
Poor Initiation	Inability to translate intentions into actions (Oddy, Worthington and Francis, 2009), loss of "get up and go"
Perseveration	Difficulty in stopping actions, speech or thoughts (Johnstone and Stonnington, 2001) – gets stuck on one way of doing things and is unable to switch to a more effective response
Reduced self-awareness and insight	Poor understanding of own strengths and difficulties, and how these may impact on functional tasks (Klonoff, 2010)
Poor emotional regulation	Difficulty managing the intensity of an emotional response (Rushby, De Sousa and McDonald, 2012)
Impulsivity	Failure to look ahead and anticipate consequences of actions – acting without thinking (Evans, 2009)
Confabulation	Unintentional, inaccurate recollection of information (Johnstone and Stonnington, 2001)

Assessing capacity to make a decision and put it into practice: The influence of neurobehavioural symptoms

When considering the potential influence of neurobehavioural symptoms on capacity, it is important to bear in mind the nature of the decision to be made. One-off decisions such as discharge destination from hospital may be less vulnerable to influence by some of the symptoms listed. In contrast, many situations involve ongoing decisions, in which the individual is repeatedly required to make a decision at the time that action is required, for example, making choices about how to spend money or deciding how care needs will be met. This highlights the need to try and assess whether the individual can make an informed decision, not just within the context of a somewhat detached capacity interview, but also at the point these decisions actually need to be made and acted upon.

So how do you decide if actions that contradict the individual's expressed intentions represent a change of heart or are due to the neurobehavioural symptoms of his condition? This requires a flexible approach to capacity assessment, taking account not just of what the individual says within an interview, but also what he does in real-life situations. This information can be obtained by talking to those that know him well about past behaviour or by directly observing current behaviour. If there is a difference between what he says he will do and what he actually does or has done, then you will need to look more closely at his capacity. In order to decide whether this means he lacks capacity, you must decide if this discrepancy is directly related to the impairment of mind or brain that the individual has been diagnosed with (the causative nexus).

The following case studies illustrate situations in which behaviour did not match stated intentions and preferences. Each is followed by a detailed discussion of the assessment strategy used to consider whether the individual lacked capacity for the decision in question. The scenarios and assessment strategies are applicable to behavioural changes resulting from any impairment of mind or brain.

Box 22.1   Case study 1 – From managing money well to being in debt

Amira was a 26-year-old woman with a diagnosis of autism and learning disability. She lived with her parents until the age of 18 then moved to a shared supported placement for young people with additional needs. At the age of 24, Amira stated that she wanted to try living by herself. Her capacity to make this decision was assessed by her social worker, Tom, and she was found to have capacity. She was aware of the areas in which she needed support and was happy to accept input from support workers in her own home. Her capacity to make decisions about her finances was also assessed. It was decided that Amira was able to make decisions about day-to-day spending, including buying essentials such as food, and paying bills. Based on the capacity assessment, the social worker believed that she had the capacity to manage her benefits.

In the first year of living alone, Amira appeared to manage her money well. She always had food in the house and was able to do activities whenever she wanted. In the second year, however, her support worker started to become concerned about her general wellbeing. She lost a lot of weight, was wearing clothes that were old and becoming worn and had recently forgotten her mother's birthday. The support worker noticed that her fridge was nearly empty a lot of the time, and Amira did not offer her a cup of tea as she always had previously. The support worker was concerned and contacted the social worker.

Understanding Amira's behaviour (Box 22.1)

When Tom first approached Amira, she denied any problems and said that she had enough money to manage on. However, Tom was still concerned and decided to investigate further. He first asked the support worker if there had been any changes in other aspects of her functional abilities, such as personal care. The support worker reported that everything else appeared to be the same; Amira was generally well presented, apart from her old clothes, the flat was always clean and tidy and she managed to get herself to appointments on time as always. Tom also contacted Amira's parents, who told him that over the last few months she had seemed a bit more distant and had also asked them for extra money on a few occasions. When they asked her what she needed this for, she said that food had got much more expensive, and she did not have enough to manage on now.

Based on this information, Tom did not think that there had been any overall changes in Amira's ability levels and therefore did not think it was likely that her money management skills had changed. He decided to spend more time with Amira trying to understand what was happening. After a while, she was able to tell him that she had met a young woman who lived in the building. At first, the woman was very friendly, and they spent time in each other's flats. Amira enjoyed having a friend nearby and was happy to buy the woman a bottle of wine the first time she asked, because her friend did not have as much money as she did. However, the friend asked more often for alcohol, then cigarettes and started to be threatening when Amira said she could not afford it. Amira said the woman threatened to tell the landlord that she was a drug dealer if she refused and said she would "hurt her" if she told anyone. Amira said that she was scared to lose her flat and so she decided to keep buying alcohol for the woman. She was aware that she was not eating properly herself but decided this was the price she had to pay to keep her flat and to keep herself safe. She stated that she was scared and did not know what else she could do, but that she did not really want to see this woman anymore.

Based on this conversation, Tom considered that Amira had capacity to make this decision about how to spend her money, as she was aware of the potential benefits and risks. Therefore, he was not able to take any action under the Mental Capacity Act (2005) and best interests process. However, he did feel justified in starting safeguarding procedures under the Care Act (2014), which allows for actions to be taken to protect adults with care or support needs who are at risk of abuse or neglect.

Box 22.2   Case study 2 – Not doing what you say you want to

Desmond was a 56-year-old man with a history of depression and excessive alcohol use. He suffered a stroke four years ago. During his hospital admission, concerns were raised regarding his ability to meet his own care needs and his capacity to make a decision regarding discharge destination and care needs on discharge. However, he left the ward against medical advice and returned to live at his home alone. A year later, his sister raised concerns with Social Services. His home was in a state of disrepair, with no floor upstairs, an unsafe staircase and no working central heating. He owed thousands of pounds to the utilities companies, and his gas had been cut off. The care team considered that he needed high levels of support in order to maintain his own safety and welfare. His capacity was assessed, and he was deemed not to have capacity to decide where he should live or how his care needs should be met. Desmond was therefore moved to a residential home.

At the residential home, Desmond demonstrated that he was able to wash and dress himself reasonably well. He went out alone and frequently came back drunk. Throughout his time there, Desmond consistently expressed his wish to return to live at home. He was able to state that there would have to be a lot of work done on his house to make it habitable and said that he would ask his friends to help him with this. During another capacity assessment, he was judged to have capacity to decide where he should live and was recorded to have made "an unwise decision". He was not placed under Deprivation of Liberty Safeguards (DoLS), and there were no restrictions placed on his movements.

Two years later, Desmond remained in the residential home. He continued to maintain that he wanted to go home but had not taken any steps in relation to the DIY needed to make his house safe. In fact, he had not visited his house in that time. He was deemed to be "unmotivated", and it was documented that he did not want to spend his money on the repairs and outstanding bills.

Understanding Desmond's behaviour (Box 22.2)

In order to understand the reasons behind Desmond's behaviour, neuropsychological assessment was completed. In terms of cognitive functioning, this highlighted severe deficits in learning new information, language, attention, planning and problem-solving. Observations during interview and assessments also highlighted verbal disinhibition, poor recall of previous conversations, and a tendency to confabulate. An example of the latter was stating that he had recently visited a dentist to get new dentures, when he was not even registered with a dentist and did not have any false teeth.

From the assessment, it was concluded that these cognitive problems were likely to impact upon both his decision-making and his ability to follow through on any such decisions. A detailed capacity assessment was therefore undertaken which explored the following:

*   Desmond's ability to understand the extent of the work required in his house
*   His ability to make a plan of action and decide upon the first steps that needed to be taken
*   His ability to act on his plans for taking the first steps
*   Desmond's understanding of his support needs.

During the initial capacity interview, it was apparent that Desmond was not aware of the extent of the work required to make his house habitable. However, with support, he was able to make a list of reasonable first steps to be taken between then and the next meeting. These included getting new keys for his house; getting the front door fixed, which he said his friend John would do; and buying carpets and a bed, which he said he would ask his support worker to help with.

At the second interview, Desmond had not taken any steps towards his goals. When asked about this, he initially stated that his support worker had not done anything about it, and also said that his friend John was away on a cruise. He acknowledged that he had not given his support worker any money in order to make the required purchases. During this interview, Desmond presented as frustrated and challenging, and mostly blamed others for the lack of progress on his house. He also stated that he had new keys for the house but, when asked, was unable to find them on his key ring.

Desmond also frequently stated that he did not need any help or support with everyday living or in making repairs on his house. When asked about his plans at the second interview, he frequently responded, "I'll get it done."

In Desmond's case it was formulated that his failure to take action regarding returning home was due to a combination of poor initiation, planning, cognitive flexibility and reduced insight, complicated by confabulation and inability to keep going with behaviour intended to achieve a goal (goal-directed behaviour). These cognitive and behavioural impairments were likely to be consequences of both the stroke and alcohol-related brain damage.

Based on this assessment, it was concluded that Desmond did not have capacity to make the decision to return to his previous property, as he was unable to understand the amount of work needed and was also unable to plan or implement any of the work. Supporting Desmond was complicated by the fact that he was unwilling to let anybody help him with the house renovations and he still had control over his own finances. An outcome of this assessment was the recommendation that an assessment of financial capacity was also completed.

Box 22.3   Case Study 3 – Saying one thing and doing another

Alice was a 53-year-old woman in an inpatient neurorehabilitation unit who had suffered a subarachnoid haemorrhage (a bleed in the brain) and hydrocephalus (excessive fluid on the brain). This had resulted in significant mobility difficulties and a poor swallow.

She had been assessed by a speech and language therapist as requiring a soft diet, because of the potential risk of choking, and had been told this directly. She had, however, been observed to pick up a piece of toast that was within reach and try to eat it. Also, she would accept unsafe food items if offered them by other people.

Despite the physical impact of the injury on Alice's speech, she was able to articulate herself well in conversation and had previously expressed an understanding of the risks surrounding her swallow. This resulted in her actions being seen as "behavioural" by staff on the unit – that is, she was choosing to go against recommendations and "doing it on purpose".

A mental capacity assessment was requested in order to clarify whether she could make an informed decision to eat foods deemed unsafe for her.

Understanding Alice's behaviour (Box 22.3)

In terms of the functional test of capacity:

1   Alice was able to understand the information provided to her regarding her swallow and recognise the risks involved.
2   She demonstrated that she could retain the guidance from staff regarding her swallow and was consistent across sessions when discussing this information.
3   She could weigh up the information in terms of discussing the pros and cons of a decision with some support.
4   She had no difficulty communicating her decision regarding eating following discussion and was consistent with this decision.

Alice consistently stated that she did not wish, nor intend, to eat unsafe foods, as she was aware of the risks to her health. Based on the assessment outlined earlier, it appeared that she had capacity to make this decision. However, it was known from those working with Alice that she had eaten unsafe foods in the past despite her apparent awareness and understanding of the risks. Was this a demonstration of Alice saying what she thought staff wanted to hear during the capacity interview or was she simply changing her mind and making an unwise decision? Alternatively, had the brain injury resulted in any of the neurobehavioural symptoms outlined in Table 22.1, which could be influencing her ability to act in accordance with her decision in the moment?

Informal observation of Alice highlighted other examples of her having the ability to understand and discuss plans and recommendations with the rehabilitation team but not put this into practice, for example, during physiotherapy sessions. Collation of information about her behaviour strongly indicated a tendency to be impulsive or to act without fully thinking through the consequences of her actions.

A cognitive assessment suggested relatively preserved intellectual function, alongside poor attention and deficits in areas of executive function as follows:

- Confabulation on memory tasks
- Inability to maintain her attention for longer than a few minutes
- Very poor planning ability
- Inability to inhibit an automatic action or response despite being able to say immediately afterwards that it was wrong.

She was also observed to be very impulsive throughout the assessment, for example, rushing to answer questions before they were finished.

Much of Alice's cognitive and behavioural difficulties appeared to stem from a general problem of impulsivity. There were several examples of neurobehavioural changes resulting in impulsive or poorly planned behaviour. This added weight to the idea that her behaviour was a result of the brain injury rather than due to her making an unwise decision. It was therefore predicted that Alice would not be able to consistently inhibit her impulsive actions around food in the future and keep herself safe.

Based on the information gathered from a range of sources, the opinion was reached that Alice did not have the capacity to make a decision regarding eating foods deemed unsafe for her. While she could weigh up the information in a discussion, she was not able to use this information to guide her decision-making in the moment (at the point of picking up unsafe foods). In addition, she could not independently pause to reflect on the consequences of her actions.

Caution

It is important to note that the presence of neurobehavioural symptoms does not necessarily mean that someone lacks the capacity to make a decision. For example, if a person is aware that his impulsivity increases his risk of falling and he agrees to restrictions being put in place to reduce this risk, then he may still have the capacity to make a decision about his care needs.

The importance of gathering additional information on behaviour as part of your capacity assessment

Comprehensive information-gathering is key in such cases where interviews can be misleading. The NICE guidelines (2018) suggest supplementing your interview with "real-world observation of the person's functioning and decision-making ability" to gain a holistic view of the person's abilities (p. 23). With the case of Alice, the assessor had the benefit of working on the rehabilitation unit and so had wider day-to-day examples of Alice's behaviour to build into the formulation. With Desmond, the assessor gathered information regarding his actions from other professionals dating back over the lengthy period that he had been supported by mental health services, then used this to formulate an understanding of his behaviour over the longer term. For Amira, the social worker spoke to the support worker and family in order to think about the best way forward.

Whilst pen and paper assessments of cognitive functioning may play a part in these types of assessment, it is important to remember that these may not always match with the person's everyday behaviour (Manchester, Priestly and Jackson, 2004). Some behavioural changes may not be evident on formal cognitive testing or during an interview-style assessment of capacity and results from these processes must be considered alongside wider evidence from those working or living with the individual (George and Gilbert, 2018). Evidence from a number of sources, including assessing how an individual will act by setting tasks or "experiments" in the real world, can provide valuable information. Using a joint approach to assessing capacity through these means with other members of the multi-disciplinary team is recommended. (See Chapter 6 for more information on assessing risk factors.)

The need to consider actions as well as words is highlighted in the MCA Code of Practice (2007), which states, "There may be cause for concern if somebody:

- repeatedly makes unwise decisions that put them at significant risk of harm or exploitation or
- makes a particular unwise decision that is obviously irrational or out of character.

These things do not necessarily mean that somebody lacks capacity. But there might be need for further investigation, taking into account the person's past decisions and choices" (p. 25).

As there are no gold standard psychometric tests for identifying the relevant neurobehavioural symptoms, their presence can only be inferred from clinical judgment based on careful observations of patterns of behaviour. The cases discussed in this chapter highlight the importance of understanding the influence that behavioural changes related to neurological, developmental or mental health conditions can have on capacity assessments.

Tip

People can misunderstand the causes of other people's behaviour. Listen out for labels given to people's behaviour that might indicate the presence of neurobehavioural symptoms, for example:

- "He's not telling the truth, just saying what we want to hear" could be a sign of confabulation
- "She keeps changing her mind" or "He's so impatient" could be a sign of impulsivity or problems with inhibiting a response
- "She just can't be bothered" could be a sign of poor initiation or variable motivation
- "He gives up easily" could be a sign of poor task or goal maintenance.

Establishing whether a person can act upon a decision at the time action is required

These cases also emphasise the need to consider an individual's ability to act upon her decision at the time when action needs to be taken. There are some differences in terms of how explicitly this is stated in the various capacity acts covering the UK and Republic of Ireland.

- The Adults with Incapacity Act (2000) for Scotland states that "incapable" includes being incapable of acting on decisions.
- The Mental Capacity Act (2005) for England and Wales does not specifically make reference to the person's ability to act upon his decisions. However, it is high-lighted that a person must be able to use the information relevant to the decision.
- The Assisted Decision-Making (Capacity) Act (2015) for the Republic of Ireland (ROI) highlights that decision-making capacity "is the ability to understand, at the time that a decision is to be made, the nature and consequences of the decision to be made by him or her in the context of the available choices at that time."
- The Mental Capacity Act (2016) for Northern Ireland (NI) does not reference acting upon a decision but does state a person must be able "to use and weigh that information as part of the process of making the decision."

Although the England and Wales, NI and ROI Acts do not specifically mention ability to act on a decision, they all indicate that the person must be able to use relevant information as part of the decision-making process. As highlighted in this chapter, many decisions need to be made in the moment, and sometimes repeatedly. Therefore, when assessing capacity, it is important to establish that a person is *using the relevant information at the time that she needs to act upon her decision* and demonstrate, as far as possible, that cognitive or neurobehavioural symptoms are not interfering with decision-making in the moment.

Summary

This chapter explores difficulties raised when an individual's behaviour and actions are inconsistent with the intentions and plans he discussed during a capacity assessment. Take-home points include:

- A capacity assessment must include assessment of whether an individual can make an informed decision at the point it needs to be acted upon and put the decision into practice.
- There could be a number of reasons why a person may say one thing and do another, for example, she may have changed her mind or be under pressure from someone else. Alternatively, she may have an impairment of mind or brain, which results in neurobehavioural symptoms that are not always obvious in an interview-based capacity assessment. These symptoms may impact her ability to do what she said she would.
- As there are no gold standard tests for identifying neurobehavioural symptoms, information needs to be gathered from a range of sources, paying attention to the labels that individuals acquire, which might be signs of these symptoms.

References

Adults with Incapacity (Scotland) Act 2000. London: HMSO.

Assisted Decision-Making (Capacity) Act 2015

The Care Act 2014. London: HMSO and TSO.

Department for Constitutional Affairs (2007). *The Mental Capacity Act Code of Practice*. London: The Stationery Office.

Evans, J.J. (2009). Rehabilitation of executive function: An overview. In M. Oddy and A. Worthington (eds.), *The Rehabilitation of Executive Disorders: A Guide to Theory and Practice*. Oxford: Oxford University Press.

George, M. and Gilbert, S. (2018). Mental Capacity Act (2005) assessments: Why everyone needs to know about the frontal lobe paradox. *The Neuropsychologist*, 5, 59–66.

Johnstone, B. and Stonnington, H.H. (eds.) (2001). *The Rehabilitation of Neuropsychological Disorders: A Practical Guide for Rehabilitation Professionals*. Philadelphia, PA: Psychology Press.

Klonoff, P.S. (2010). *Psychotherapy After Brain Injury: Principles and Techniques*. New York: Guilford Press.

Manchester, D., Priestly, N. and Jackson, H. (2004). The assessment of executive functions: Coming out of the office. *Brain Injury*, 18(11).

Mental Capacity Act 2005. London: HMSO.

Mental Capacity Act (Northern Ireland) 2016. London: HMSO.

National Institute for Health and Care Excellence (2018). *Decision-Making and Mental Capacity* (NG108). Available at: www.nice.org.uk/guidance/ng108

Oddy, M., Worthington, A. and Francis, E. (2009). Motivational disorders following brain injury. In M. Oddy and A. Worthington (eds.), *The Rehabilitation of Executive Disorders: A Guide to Theory and Practice*. Oxford: Oxford University Press.

Rushby, J., De Sousa, A. and McDonald, S. (2012). Changes in emotional empathy, affective responsivity, and behavior following severe traumatic brain injury. *Journal of Clinical and Experimental Neuropsychology*, 34(6), 606–623.

Worthington, A., Wood, R.L. and McMillan, T.M. (2016). Perspective on neurobehavioural disability over the past four decades. In R.L.L. Wood and T.M. McMillan (eds.), *Neurobehavioural Disability and Social Handicap After Traumatic Brain Injury* (2nd ed.). Hove: Psychology Press.

Chapter 23

Assessment of mental capacity to make high-risk decisions

Chris Martin and Janice Mackenzie

In this chapter

Many decisions we have to make in life are complex, but some decisions are both complex and have high-risk consequences. This is especially pertinent after an impairment of mind or brain, when a person may lack the capacity to make a decision. The Mental Capacity Act (MCA, 2005) recognises that people are able to make unwise decisions in areas where they have capacity and that their capacity cannot be questioned just because they have made an unwise decision, even if there are high-risk consequences.

This chapter will highlight key issues in the assessment of capacity for highly complex, risky and life-shortening decisions. Professionals who may be well placed to assess capacity in these decision areas, and who have experience in these types of assessment, may include clinical neuropsychologists, clinical psychologists, consultant psychiatrists, speech and language therapists and social workers.

A thoughtful, yet practical, approach is recommended along with a framework to help ensure the person's values and professional's reactions are taken into account in order to help ensure a fair, careful, detailed, accurate and supportive assessment. The Best Interests chapter (see Chapter 29) will also be helpful to refer to in relation to issues that arise in this chapter.

Examples of high-risk decisions

- Samira has an impaired swallowing ability. She is not following swallowing guidelines and is eating food that is not recommended for her. There is a risk to her health, and possibly her life, from choking and aspiration.
- Jerome is reducing his food intake to such an extent that he is consuming insufficient calories and there is a risk of serious physical harm or death from starvation.

- Mae wants to try recreational drugs with her friends against medical advice.
- Brigid is refusing to take medications and not complying with a medication regimen that is reducing a significant risk to her health.
- Mohammed wants to walk and impulsively tries to get out of his wheelchair several times a day, but he has had repeated falls and injuries due to this.
- John is returning to drinking alcohol in amounts over the recommended limit. This is against medical advice, as there is a risk of serious physical harm or death.

Box 23.1 sets out some important points to remember when conducting capacity assessments of high-risk issues. In addition, it can be a challenge to clarify the extent to which a person is able to be fully aware of her medical needs (Gaviria, Pliskin and Kney, 2011). It is important to consider that some individuals can be more impaired, and less capable to make decisions, than they appear, especially when more subtle cognitive problems are not taken into account (Gaviria, Pliskin and Kney, 2011). However, the assessor should try to remedy these where possible, and it is vital that individuals have all of the relevant information (Raymont et al., 2004), in a format that is understandable to them, before the capacity assessment.

Box 23.1   Points to remember

- Assessment of capacity to make a high-risk decision can be cognitively demanding work for the person and the assessor.
- It is often emotionally demanding work for the person, the assessor, the person's family and the treating healthcare team.
- It involves working with issues of life and death, serious harm, autonomy, personal choice and freedom and existential factors and issues.
- Using frameworks to guide the assessment and taking a methodical and evidence-based approach where possible are key aspects of the work.
- Consider the extent formal cognitive assessment may contribute to the capacity assessment.
- These complex assessments will often require several sessions and sufficient time needs to be allowed.
- Clear, fair, well-explained, sensitive and supportive assessments are essential.

What are the differences between capacity assessments for high-risk decisions and lower-risk decisions?

1) There is a higher level of risk to the person and there could be a larger impact of the decision on others

For example:

- High level of family distress if a person dies due to making a high-risk decision
- Impact on family, care needs and quality of life if a person deteriorates, cognitively or physically, as a result of making a high-risk decision
- Impact on capacity to make other decisions if a person's cognition deteriorates as a result of making a high-risk decision.

Caution

If there will be a significant negative impact on herself or others, this does not mean that the person lacks capacity (as unwise decisions are accounted for in the MCA), but it would require a more comprehensive capacity assessment. The Mental Health Act may need to be referred to in situations where a person's mental health is a key factor in the risk to self or others.

---

2) It increases the likelihood of potential legal follow-up or the need for other follow-up procedures

For example:

- Coroner's Court investigation if a person dies when receiving care following making a high-risk decision
- Potential for legal action from the person's family if the person deteriorates after making a high-risk decision.

Caution

Potential legal follow-up would not affect the way that a capacity assessment in this area is carried out (although, as always, the assessment needs to be done carefully and methodically and be clearly recorded) but it is another potential difference relevant to capacity assessments regarding high-risk decisions.

---

3)   There is an increased likelihood that capacity cases involving a high-risk decision will go to the Court of Protection

- This is due to the potential for differences of opinion within teams, between families and professionals, and across services.
- Cases being taken to the Court of Protection can put added pressure on professionals, although it is important to remember that the outcome of a capacity assessment is always just *your opinion*.

The alternative working hypotheses approach

There are two possibilities after an acquired brain injury has caused an impairment of the mind or brain:

1   Some people will have retained the capacity to make a high-risk decision, in John's case (see Box 23.2) to choose to drink alcohol to a damaging level for his health (including leading to serious harm or death).
2   Some people will have lost capacity in this regard.

Box 23.2   Case study regarding high-risk decisions – John

John is a 60-year-old man who has had a stroke and wishes to return to drinking alcohol in amounts over the recommended limit, against medical advice. He has some balance problems since his stroke but few other physical difficulties. However, he has experienced cognitive changes post-stroke, including attention difficulties, reduced speed of processing and executive functioning problems (problem-solving and planning difficulties), and there was some evidence of memory problems prior to the stroke. John has been drinking over the recommended limit for 20 years, and this may have been a factor in the stroke occurring (as it affected his blood pressure). Prior to the stroke, John had been advised by his doctor to stop drinking, as his liver function was impaired.

Clearly this is a potentially high-risk decision to make due to increased likelihood of another stroke, further cognitive decline, or other health problems. What questions may be important to ask to assess John's capacity to make this decision?

A key consideration is:

Has there been a change in John's capacity to decide to return to drinking over the recommended limit following the stroke?

The following section discusses what factors can differentiate these two groups – when someone might have capacity and when someone might not have capacity in this regard. It also proposes a framework that can be used to guide the process.

A step-by-step process

Professionals may worry when their work and the procedures they followed are likely to be investigated. However, following due procedure with reference to capacity law in the country where you work, including clear documentation, is a key aspect of the assessment and often helps to reduce team worries about potential future scrutiny. The following framework can be a useful guide to help:

1 Clarify the specific decision in question.
2 Establish what information is relevant to the decision and the level at which the person is required to understand it.
3 Explore the available options.
4 Assess the benefits and risks involved in each option.
5 Use this information to prepare key questions.
6 Reflect on the ethics of the case and issues raised, preferably in professional supervision.
7 Consider the person's current and previous beliefs, views and values.
8 Reflect on your personal reactions to the case as a professional, preferably in supervision.
9 Introduce the assessment to the person, the multi-disciplinary team (MDT), and family members.
10 Carry out multiple assessment sessions and use supported decision-making approaches to enhance capacity.
11 Feed the results and conclusions of the assessment back to the person and family, as appropriate, and to relevant members of the healthcare team or other services.

These steps will be discussed in further detail here.

The process in detail

1) Clarify the specific decision in question

For example:

- Does Brigid have capacity to decide to refuse to take medications?
- Does Mohammed have capacity to decide on the need for supervision and restraint (a seatbelt on his wheelchair) in the context of repeated falls and injuries while attempting to walk?
- Does John have capacity to decide to return to alcohol use?

2)   Establish what information is relevant to the decision and the level at which the person is required to understand it

For example, in order to demonstrate capacity to decide to return to alcohol use, John would need to show some understanding of:

- The reasons he drinks alcohol and the benefits he gets from it
- The potential risks of drinking alcohol with regards to health, emotional, financial and psychosocial factors
- His problem controlling alcohol intake and others' views on this
- Ways to stop drinking or ways to reduce the harm when doing so
- The fact that he has experienced a brain injury and has problems with his thinking skills as a result
- The difference in continuing to drink alcohol following a brain injury, for example, reduced tolerance to alcohol and reduced seizure threshold
- The pros and cons of continuing to drink alcohol versus limiting his intake versus abstinence.

However, he would not need to understand, for example, *how* alcohol increases the likelihood of seizures after a brain injury to demonstrate capacity with regard to this decision, as many people without an impairment of the mind or brain would not have an understanding of this. (See Appendix 7 for an example of a threshold of understanding for returning to drink alcohol following a brain injury or alcohol-related brain damage (ARBD). See Appendix 8 for an example of a semi-structured interview to aid assessment for this decision.)

Provide the required information to the person as part of the process of supporting decision-making and helping the person make an informed decision. It is better if this is done over several sessions by professionals that the person trusts.

3)   Explore the available options

In John's case, potential options that could be discussed may include:

- John returning to his previous consumption of alcohol over the recommended limit
- John drinking a reduced amount of alcohol
- John abstaining from alcohol completely, which could include strategies such as:
  - John drinking non-alcoholic beverages, for example, non-alcoholic beer
  - John replacing his previous consumption of alcohol with another activity or coping strategy, for example, mindfulness or relaxation, a new hobby or visits to friends or family.

4) Assess the benefits and risks involved in each option

It is important to think of the benefits of each option for the person, as well as the risks, to maintain a balanced viewpoint. It is useful to reflect on this before the assessment, as well as asking the person during the interview. Examples of questions to ask yourself:

- Why does the person want to do this?
- What benefit does she get from it?

When assessing risks, define the risk, identify the consequences and rate the level of impact (see Box 23.3) and the likelihood of it occurring. What is the specific risk? For example:

- Risk of death
- Risk of serious damage to physical or mental health
- Risk of significantly reduced life span
- Risk of further cognitive impairment
- Risk of harm to others
- Risk of financial problems, such as getting into debt or not having enough money to live on
- Risk of resultant high distress, reduced independence and/or quality of life and potential damage to relationships due to above factors.

Consider primary risks, for example, in this case, increased cognitive impairment, and secondary risks, for example, increased distress, decreased functional activity and autonomy or damaged relationships as a result of the primary risk (see Box 23.4).

Box 23.3   Risk Assessment

Rating	Level of impact	Potential consequences
5	Severe	Potentially fatal
4	Significant	Risk of significant damage to self or others (for example, permanently damaged organs from chronic alcohol excess, permanent significant cognitive problems), irreparably damaged relationships (for example, romantic relationship break-ups, loss of friendships), high levels of isolation (for example, rejection/ separation from family), risk of capacity being affected in other areas, significantly reduced independence, risk of severe financial problems, risk of severe depression/anxiety

Rating	Level of impact	Potential consequences
3	Moderate	Risk of higher levels of distress (for example, moderate depression/anxiety, moderately affected self-esteem), damaged relationships (for example, less support from friends and family due to affected relationships), illness requiring hospital admission but not permanent damage, moderate long-term cognitive problems
2	Minor	Strained relationships (for example, increased stress in relationships), mild depression/anxiety, illness requiring medical treatment, temporary cognitive impairment
1	Negligible	Mild discomfort, risk of mild distress

Impact

Likelihood	Negligible	Minor	Moderate	Significant	Severe
Very Likely	Moderate	High	Extreme	Extreme	Extreme
Likely	Moderate	High	High	Extreme	Extreme
Possible	Low	Moderate	High	High	Extreme
Unlikely	Low	Moderate	Moderate	High	High
Very Unlikely	Low	Low	Low	Moderate	Moderate

Figure 23.1 Risk Matrix – Calculating the overall level of risk

How likely is it that these risks will happen? This can be a very difficult question to answer, but it is vital that it is considered. A Risk Matrix combines the potential impact, or consequences, of the risk with the likelihood that it will happen to calculate the overall level of risk (see Figure 23.1).

Box 23.4   Case study – John continued

If John returns to heavy drinking, there is an increased risk of him having another stroke. He had previously been given medical advice to stop drinking due to physical health problems and so returning to drinking will increase his risk of these underlying difficulties. In addition, it would likely increase his risk of falls, due to balance problems since the stroke, and, therefore, the possibility of further brain injuries. John has experienced post-stroke cognitive impairment, and there was some evidence that alcohol excess may have caused some memory problems prior to the stroke. Therefore, returning to drinking alcohol could lead to further alcohol-related cognitive impairment.

Before the capacity assessment, it would be important to investigate whether previous alcohol intake was leading to environmental risks, such as leaving the oven or hob on when cooking after consuming alcohol and resultant fire risks. Also, explore whether or not John was getting into conflict with others due to alcohol, or getting into debt, and if he is currently getting into conflict with others post-stroke without alcohol. For example, is there a risk to others from his behaviour that could be exacerbated by alcohol? On the other hand, John's mental health would need to be considered, as drinking may help his anxiety in the short-term, due to it being his long-term coping strategy. It may also be intrinsically linked to his relationships and social life.

From the information discussed thus far it appears that, if John returns to drinking excessively, a significant outcome, such as significant damage to his health, is very likely and a severe outcome (death) is possible.

5)   Use this information to prepare key questions

Key questions will investigate the person's understanding of the risks, his plans, his reasoning with regard to the decision and his ability to consider and weigh up alternative courses of action. (See Boxes 23.5 and 23.6 for some example questions.)

Box 23.5   Examples of questions in relation to the potential decision

What are your plans?

How often do you plan to do (this decision)?

What is your thinking behind planning to do (this decision)?

What are the benefits of (this decision)?

What are the risks of these plans (in general)?

What problems can (this decision) cause?

Has it caused you any problems in the past?

How do you intend to manage these problems?

What are the risks of these plans for you now?

How does (your ABI/neurological condition) affect your plans?

How could (this decision) affect your thinking skills/physical health/mental health?

How could (this decision) affect your relationships with other people?

How could (this decision) affect your finances?

Does (this decision) affect your ability to make safe decisions?

How would you know if (this decision) was becoming a problem?

Would you stop/reduce/change (this decision) if it became a problem? How would you do this?

Who could help you if (this decision) became a problem?

What would be the best possible outcome/consequence of (this decision)?

What would be the worst possible outcome/consequence of (this decision)?

What other options are there? What are the benefits and risks/problems of those options?

What will you choose to do?

Box 23.6   Case study – Questions for John

Think about how you can predict that someone is planning to drink to a damaging level. Aspects that are important, for example, include asking questions about his intentions and considering if this seems credible in context, and asking others who know him well how much alcohol they think he will consume. This is a way of checking John's reported plans against the predictions of someone who knows him well.

Asking the person about some reasons behind his drinking is important. For example, is it to help him socialise? For enjoyment? For relaxation? As a release? To forget a loss?

Do you plan to drink alcohol in the future? What other options are there?

What are the risks of drinking alcohol in general?

What problems can alcohol cause?

Has drinking alcohol caused you any problems in the past?

If John does plan to return to drinking over the recommended limit:

How much alcohol will you drink in a week?
Why do you plan to drink alcohol?
What do you see as the benefits of drinking alcohol?
What are the problems with drinking alcohol?
What are the risks of drinking alcohol for you now, following your stroke?
How could alcohol affect your thinking skills?
How could alcohol affect your physical health/mental health?
Could you have a seizure if you drink alcohol after your brain injury?
Will alcohol affect the way your medications (give examples) work?
How could alcohol affect your relationships with others?
How would returning to drinking alcohol affect your finances?
Does drinking alcohol affect your ability to make safe decisions?
How would you know if you were drinking too much?
Would you stop or reduce your drinking if it was causing problems?
How would you do this? Have you got any help or support to do this?
Have you got any strategies to keep you safer when you are drinking?
What are the benefits and risks/problems of not drinking alcohol?
What are the benefits and risks/problems of drinking a limited amount of
    alcohol?

6) Reflect on the ethics of the case and issues raised

It is important to ensure that we are not being overprotective, for example, questioning a person's capacity just because she wants to make an unwise decision or being more restrictive than necessary if someone does not have the capacity to make the decision. There is a balance between being professionally cautious and being over-cautious and completely risk-averse. Positive risk-taking, whilst trying to manage the risks, is sometimes the best compromise for the person and professionals. It is useful to reflect on these issues in your professional supervision sessions.

Caution

Case law has placed an emphasis on the importance of emotional wellbeing, even if this means that there will be potential risks to the person's physical wellbeing: "Physical health and safety can sometimes be bought at too high a

> price in happiness and emotional welfare. The emphasis must be on sensible risk appraisal, not striving to avoid all risk whatever the price, but instead seeking a proper balance and being willing to tolerate manageable or acceptable risks as the price appropriately to be paid in order to achieve some other good – in particular to achieve the vital good of the elderly or vulnerable person's happiness. What good is making someone safer if it merely makes them miserable?" (*Local Authority X v MM & Another* [2007], at paragraph 120).

The results of a capacity assessment, when the person is found to lack capacity, can lead to decisions that affect her level of independence, choice and self-determination. Effectively, when using the MCA (2005), society gives services (specifically the best interests decision-maker) the power to make the decision on the person's behalf, after consultation with the person, family and other services as appropriate. Understandably, the person may not feel the service has the right to make a decision that she does not want (see Box 23.7). This should be approached clearly and compassionately.

Box 23.7   Case study – John continued

It is likely, from reviewing the available evidence from appropriate sources, that John's capacity to return to drinking alcohol has changed following the stroke, due to his new difficulties with attention and executive functioning. From conversations with him, it appears that his ability to understand and weigh up the potential consequences and risks has decreased.

If John was found not to have the capacity to decide to return to drinking over the recommended limit, the best interests decision may be that he would need to stop drinking. However, John may not agree with this, and he may feel angry and upset. He may feel it is his right to be able to drink as much as he wants, as he was able to prior to the stroke.

---

7)   *Consider the person's current and previous beliefs, views and values in relation to the decision*

For example:

- Was Brigid previously reluctant to take medications due to the belief that they are likely to have side effects that are not good for her body? Or is this a change in behaviour following the impairment?

- Has Mohammed always been someone to challenge himself physically and take risks to achieve more?
- Has heavy alcohol consumption been a conscious choice and longstanding part of John's life? Has he experienced, or is he experiencing, alcohol dependency? What is important to him in life?

Exploring John's case further

What are John's community cultural views regarding alcohol and drinking to excess? For example, does he feel a cultural pressure not to drink due to his religion? Or does he feel a social pressure to drink?

Questions to elicit this:
- What have other people advised you about alcohol?
- What are your family's and friends' views about you drinking alcohol?
- How do your family and friends react if you say that you are not going to have a drink?

8) Reflect on your personal reactions to the case as a professional

In this way, you can prevent your reactions unconsciously influencing the capacity assessment process. It is important to examine and discuss these areas in supervision so that you are able to approach the assessment with an open mind. The questions below might help this process.

Examples of reflective questions to ask yourself, relating to "John"

- What are your general views on alcohol?
- What are your views on people drinking to a damaging level in general?
- What are your cultural and/or religious views about this?
- What are current societal views about drinking to excess at this stage of history in the West?
- How are these different for different age groups/communities/demographic groups?
- Do you think that a person has the right to harm himself with his behaviour if it is not hurting others?
- How can we, and do we, know when we are being overprotective?
- Can someone who is drinking or planning to drink to excess at a level where it is seriously damaging to his health be in optimal mental health?

Some awareness of answers to these questions is necessary to make sure that you acknowledge value judgments and that they are "in their rightful place", that is, not centre-stage and not the key factor in a decision about someone's capacity to make a specific high-risk decision.

9) Introduce the capacity assessment to the person, the MDT and family members

In John's case, this involves explaining to him about the assessment of capacity to choose to drink alcohol post-stroke and why this assessment is necessary. It also involves encouraging him to take part in it, which includes developing a reasonable working alliance where possible and clearly explaining the rationale and possible results of the assessment. It is important to help the person be on board with the process where possible. This can be experienced as more empowering and can feel more respectful for the person, as he is able to put across his point of view.

This stage includes sensitively getting relevant views from family and friends, as appropriate.

10) Carry out multiple assessment sessions and use supported decision-making approaches to enhance capacity

A semi-structured interview approach is recommended in order to form a flexible plan for the sessions (see Appendix 8 for an example). Before the assessment, ensure that the person has been given the relevant information in a suitable way. Supported decision-making approaches can also be used during the assessment, including using written summaries of key information, process diagrams, decision trees and breaks as appropriate and ensuring that you give the person sufficient time to process the information. Consideration of how much material to cover in each assessment session is required, according to the person's cognitive and emotional needs. Some people process the information given between sessions, but multiple sessions also allow for repeated questioning on some areas and allow people to demonstrate "carry over" of information, which is important for an ongoing decision, such as drinking alcohol. (See Chapters 10 and 11 for more information.)

Consider the following questions:

- To what extent does the person understand the risks and the likelihood of the risks occurring and how can this be enhanced?
- Can the person think of ways to reduce the risks and is it likely that he will employ them? (Practical assessments can help clarify this for both the person and professionals, for example, taking him into a pub and seeing how he reacts. See Chapters 6 and 22 for more information.)

- Can the person be supported to understand and remember the pros and cons of the different options?
- Is the person able to weigh up the pros and cons incorporating the risks of the decision? (For example, "I am aware there is an increased risk of a further stroke and further health problems if I return to drinking alcohol, but it is a risk I'm willing to take because I enjoy drinking alcohol and it is an important part of my social life"; or "From these recent conversations with the team, I'm more aware of the increased risk of another stroke if I return to drinking alcohol and so I have decided to substantially cut down my alcohol intake but I intend to drink a small amount for enjoyment and relaxation and so I accept a level of risk.") (See Box 23.8.)

Caution

The idea that an alcoholic cannot be expected to use and weigh the relevant information before having a drink was dismissed by the Court of Appeal: "The decisions which RB wishes to make require a process of using and weighing up relevant information. On the basis of the expert evidence and of the district judge's findings of fact, RB is not capable of carrying out that mental process. The difficulties which RB has in using or weighing information and making consequent decisions accord closely with the situation described in paragraphs 4.21 and 4.22 of the Code of Practice. RB is unable to appreciate and weigh up the risks which he will run if he resumes his former way of life and goes out on drinking bouts. Therefore, applying MCA section 3(1) (c), RB does not have capacity to make this decision" (*RB v Brighton and Hove Council* [2014], at paragraph 70).

Further reflection on complexities in the assessment process, once it is complete, and compassionate contemplation of the person's perspective and experience, may provide further learning opportunities for the assessor and the MDT.

Box 23.8   Case study – John continued

John is no longer able to understand and weigh up the pros and cons of drinking to excess due to the effects of the stroke.

Examples illustrating this are:

- John is not able to pay attention to medical information in order to help him understand the likelihood of the risks that apply to him. Also, he lacks insight into his own situation and denies that some of the information relates to him. Although John is supported with key written information and a decision tree, this does not enhance his capacity for this decision.

- Also, John presents with disinhibition and impulsivity and, when taken to the pub, he showed that he was unable to stop himself from ordering a whisky, although he had said that he would have a soft drink. Afterwards, he was disappointed in himself, as he had wanted to prove that he could manage to go into a pub without drinking alcohol. This affects his capacity as it prevents him effectively weighing up a decision in the moment that it has to be made. Instead, he jumped to an impulsive response that was due to habit and was not reasoned through using the additional knowledge he now has.

- John is only able to highlight positives to drinking and no potential negatives or risks, for example, "I enjoy drinking, and it is a way I socialise with people."

- John was not able to highlight even some basic problems of returning to drinking excessively, such as "If I drink too much, it is not good for my health, and there is a risk it could cause further health problems."

When the person is provided with a written summary of the relevant information, it is often illuminating to discover how much the person believes, and takes on board, the potential problems and risks associated with the decision.

11) Feed the results and conclusions of the assessment back to the person and family, as appropriate, and to relevant members of the healthcare team or other services

A challenge with the assessment process is to ensure the assessment is sufficiently detailed, as supportive as possible, and manageable within current healthcare timeframes and caseload pressures. (See Box 23.9 for potential pitfalls in capacity assessments.) However, time must be allocated for discussing the results of the assessment, and the next steps in the process, with the person and her family, if appropriate, as well as with other professionals and services involved. It is advisable to prepare the key pieces of information in a written summary for the person beforehand and feed the information back in a clear and compassionate manner, being sensitive to the person's and family's reactions. People, and their families, can be understandably upset and high distress may be evident when the conclusion of a capacity assessment does not fit with their view. Several feedback sessions may be more appropriate to allow the person and her family time to process the information and generate questions that can be discussed in a future session. Feedback should be structured to fit each individual situation.

Box 23.9   Potential pitfalls in capacity assessments

- Being overprotective
- Treating the person, or her views, without respect
- Failing to take a compassionate approach (A good rule is to think "Which aspects of an assessment would be important to me if my capacity was being questioned in an area? How would I like the assessor to approach the assessment?")
- Not doing a capacity assessment, as the person does not agree with the alternative option
- Letting the person do as she likes despite the risk, without carrying out a capacity assessment, as you do not want to "cause a fuss" by challenging her capacity or because you feel that she has the right to make her own decisions
- Not having a clear and defined question in mind when assessing capacity
- Not being clear about potential outcomes of the assessment or not sharing this with the person
- Not planning and setting aside enough time for the assessment, feedback and report writing
- Being too anxious to carry out a careful assessment due to potential challenges and pressures
- Doing too brief or insufficient an assessment when the consequences can be serious
- Avoiding asking a necessary question if it is difficult or uncomfortable
- "Going it alone" and not getting other services involved in the process and discussions

    o   Tip: Discuss issues with the MDT, social services, family if appropriate, and other involved services to get a sense of the key issues relevant to the assessment to help form your questions

- Not getting supervision and seeking a second view or opinion on your assessment

  - Tip: Get advice from senior and knowledgeable colleagues before and after the assessment.

When and how to escalate a decision to the Court of Protection

Most capacity assessments, and the subsequent best interest decisions, will not require a referral to the Court of Protection (CoP) and this is not automatically required just because a decision has serious consequences. Some examples of this include:

1   If a person with a disturbance of mind or brain intended to drink to excessive levels against medical advice yet clearly had the capacity to do so
2   If someone with a swallowing problem wanted to eat food against advice, but lacked the capacity to make this decision, and the subsequent best interests decision, agreed by all involved, was that it is in her best interests for her to be allowed to eat the food as "risk feeding" to improve her quality of life.

During the capacity assessment process regarding decisions that may result in serious consequences, it is helpful to ask yourself the question: "Is this a decision that may need to go to the Court of Protection?" Discuss this issue with the MDT and other services, as appropriate. This question may arise early in the process or later during the course of the assessment or during the best interests process.

If there is a disagreement about what is in the person's best interests, then the case must be referred to the CoP (preferably after discussion with your legal team) if other avenues, such as mediation or a disputes resolution procedure, have not worked. This could also occur if it is thought that other people, for example, the person's family or professionals, may not be acting in the person's best interests. Discuss issues that arise with appropriate relevant services, such as the MDT, social services and local safeguarding teams.

If it was unclear, or there were disagreements between professionals, about whether or not a person had the capacity to make a decision, then this could be an appropriate referral to the CoP. A referral to the CoP may also be required if the family disagrees with the outcome of a capacity assessment after a second opinion.

Some situations *must* be referred to the CoP (MCA Code of Practice, 2007), such as:

- A proposal to withdraw artificial nutrition and hydration from a person in a permanent vegetative state (PVS) if there is disagreement (see Appendix 13)
- A proposal for a person who lacks capacity to consent to donate an organ
- When it is unclear whether a serious medical treatment is in the person's best interests.

Enforcing best interests decisions can be difficult if the person does not agree with the outcome, and often it will involve a deprivation of her liberty. These cases may also need to be referred to the CoP, including cases involving a deprivation of liberty in the community. (See Chapter 28 for more information.)

Caution

It has been argued that the best interests process cannot be used to deprive someone with alcohol problems of his liberty in order to stop him drinking after a brain injury; however, in a 2014 case, the Judge disagreed: "In the present case deprivation of liberty is necessary in order to protect RB from seriously injuring himself. That must be in his best interests" (*RB v Brighton and Hove Council* [2014], at paragraph 83).

Tips

- When considering what is in a person's best interests regarding returning to alcohol use (which could also be applied to other high-risk decisions), case law suggests factors to take into account: "I have to bear in mind how near to the borderline of capacity DM is; the nearer the line the more weight may be attached to his wishes and feelings. I must also pay regard to the strength and consistency of the views which he has expressed about being able to drink, together with the possible adverse impact on him (anger, disappointment, frustration etc) of knowing that his wishes and feelings have not been allowed to prevail" (*DM v Y City Council* [2017], at paragraph 21).
- The Judge weighed up the different aspects of the decision and came to the conclusion that "although by moving he would be fulfilling his stated

wish, he would be losing much else of real value to his quality of life" (*DM vY City Council* [2017], at paragraph 28). This concludes that stated wishes are not the only factor to consider when debating what is in the person's best interests, and observations of a person's life and choices, that may not be explicitly stated, are also important.

Summary

The assessment of mental capacity for high-risk decisions is a complex and challenging area. There can be serious consequences of the decision, and there is an increased likelihood of legal intervention, including referral of cases to the Court of Protection (CoP), which can increase staff anxiety. However, in other regards, it does not differ greatly from other capacity assessments, and the approach described can help provide a framework and structure to the process.

It is important to remember that someone's capacity to make a high-risk decision that she used to make regularly may change after an impairment in, or disturbance of, the mind or brain. Therefore, an assessment may be required to ascertain if she has the capacity to make a decision to return to her previous high-risk lifestyle. Sufficient time must be allocated to capacity assessments that can have serious consequences. Finally, there are certain situations in which the case should be referred to the CoP, usually when there is disagreement between interested parties regarding the outcome of the capacity assessment or what is in the person's best interests, or where a deprivation of liberty is being proposed and the person is contesting it. (See Chapters 27, 28 and 29 for more information.)

References

Department for Constitutional Affairs (2007). *Mental Capacity Act 2005: Code of Practice*. London: The Stationery Office. Available at: https://assets.publishing.service.gov.uk/government/uploads/system/uploads/attachment_data/file/497253/Mental-capacity-act-code-of-practice.pdf

Gaviria, M., Pliskin, N. and Kney, A. (2011). Cognitive impairment in patients with advanced heart failure and its implications on decision-making capacity. *Congestive Heart Failure*, 17(4), 175–179.

Mental Capacity Act 2005. London: HMSO. Available at: www.legislation.gov.uk/ukpga/2005/9/contents

Raymont, V., Bingley, W., Buchanan, A., David, A.S., Hayward, P., Wessely, S. and Hotopf, M. (2004). Prevalence of mental incapacity in medical inpatients and associated risk factors: Cross-sectional study. *Lancet*, 364, 1421–1427.

Case law

DM vY City Council [2017] EWCOP 13

Local Authority X v MM &Another [2007] EWHC 2003

RB v Brighton and Hove Council [2014] EWCA Civ 561

Chapter 24

Assessing mental capacity when the decision needs to be made urgently

Janice Mackenzie

In this chapter

As has been highlighted previously, it is good practice to take your time gathering the relevant information from various sources, consulting with staff and family who know the person well, checking to see if there is an attorney or deputy, enhancing the person's capacity, and doing the capacity assessment over more than one session. However, sometimes it is not possible to do all of these things as thoroughly as you might like due to time limitations. This chapter will outline the main points from the Mental Capacity Act (MCA, 2005) regarding urgent situations and provide some ideas for clinical practice.

Assessing mental capacity in urgent situations

The MCA Code of Practice (2007) states that if the situation is urgent or an emergency, for example, if someone needs an emergency surgical procedure, "the only practical and appropriate steps might be to keep a person informed of what is happening and why" (at paragraph 2.9) and that "urgent decisions will have to be made and immediate action taken in the person's best interests" (at paragraph 3.6). You need to adapt your capacity assessment to the time that you have available, whilst trying to take all possible steps to enhance someone's capacity, help the person make his own decision and do the best assessment that you can. In urgent situations, it is likely that the person will only need to remember the information for as long as is required to make the decision as it will probably be a one-off decision, such as medical treatment, rather than an ongoing decision (or a series of ongoing decisions) such as care needs or finances. The Code of Practice (2007) is clear that the "reasonable" steps that have to be taken to determine whether or not someone has the capacity to make the decision at that point in time will be different in emergency situations to those in non-urgent cases (at paragraph 6.35).

Caution

This is not an excuse for a quick assessment because you are busy or the capacity assessment has not been started in a timely manner and the time for a decision is approaching. If the decision is not urgent, then you need to make time to do a thorough assessment, within reason. You have to remember that someone's rights and liberties are at stake and that your assessment could take these away or, alternatively, that a vulnerable adult could be put at risk due to the outcome of your assessment. This is a significant responsibility, and so the assessment should not be rushed or taken lightly.

Protection from liability when providing urgent treatment or care

If there is reasonable belief that the person lacks capacity to make the decision in question, Section 5 of the MCA (2005) provides "protection from liability so that [carers and professionals] can act in connection with the person's care or treatment . . . as long as it is in the person's best interests" (Code of Practice, at paragraphs 6.3 and 6.4). This includes carrying out necessary medical procedures or therapies and providing care in an emergency. To be protected from liability, you must follow the statutory principles of the MCA (2005), take reasonable steps to assess whether or not the person has capacity to make the decision at that point in time and have "reasonable grounds for believing that the action is in the best interests of the person who lacks capacity" (Code of Practice, at paragraph 6.28). These actions should be documented clearly, and you must show that you have considered all relevant circumstances and applied the best interests checklist (see Chapter 29). Staff should use their usual clinical and professional judgment to decide what treatment or care will be offered (Code of Practice, at paragraph 6.33).

It is likely that, in most cases, it would be in the person's best interests to treat him in an emergency without delay, as long as an advance decision to refuse treatment is not in place (see Chapter 14 for more information). Section 5 does not protect professionals if they have been negligent, but protection is granted if the professional was not aware of the advance decision or "was not satisfied that the advance decision was valid and applies in the current circumstances" (Code of Practice, at paragraph 6.38). Section 6 of the MCA (2005) clarifies that Section 5 does not provide protection from liability "where there is inappropriate use of restraint or where a person who lacks capacity is deprived of their liberty" (Code of Practice, at paragraph 6.39). These issues are covered by the Deprivation of Liberty Safeguards/Liberty Protection Safeguards (see Chapter 28).

The Adults with Incapacity (Scotland) Act (2000) states that practitioners can treat people in an emergency under the common law authority. Practitioners would be expected to follow normal procedures for assessing someone's capacity to make the decision and deciding on the course of action if the person lacks capacity as much as is possible in the circumstances.

Tips

If you work in a setting in which urgent (rather than emergency) decisions need to be made regularly, then it might be prudent to develop resources so that they are ready whenever they are required. Ideas include:

• Creating a list of all the relevant information for each common decision you come across.
• Printing the list in easy-read form so that the person can have a copy, to reduce the potential impact of problems with memory and attention.
• Creating a decision tree containing the common options and possible outcomes for each decision to help people think these through quickly. (See Chapter 9.)
• Saving the relevant information list and decision tree on a computer so that they can be amended for each individual by deleting or adding information depending on her situation.
• Making your own semi-structured interview so that you have an efficient way of assessing whether or not the person understands the relevant information and why the decision needs to be made, can remember it long enough to make the decision and can weigh up the different options and use this information to make and communicate an informed decision. (This also helps to ensure that similar standards are being used to assess mental capacity across the team.)

Summary

The MCA (2005) states that practitioners should follow the normal route of assessing capacity and deciding on the course of action as much as possible, but that they will be protected from liability if they act in the person's best interests in emergency circumstances, with some exceptions. The Adults with Incapacity (Scotland) Act (2000) follows a similar process with regard to urgent medical treatment.

(See www.assessingcapacity.com for a best interests process decision tree which includes urgent decisions.)

References

Adults with Incapacity (Scotland) Act 2000. London: HMSO. Available at: www.legislation.gov.uk/asp/2000/4/contents

Department for Constitutional Affairs (2007). *Mental Capacity Act 2005: Code of Practice*. London: The Stationery Office. Available at: https://assets.publishing.service.gov.uk/government/uploads/system/uploads/attachment_data/file/497253/Mental-capacity-act-code-of-practice.pdf

Mental Capacity Act 2005. London: HMSO. Available at: www.legislation.gov.uk/ukpga/2005/9/contents

Chapter 25

Mental capacity assessment

What to do when someone is refusing to engage or is ambivalent

Janice Mackenzie

In this chapter

Some of the most difficult situations arise when someone does not want to complete a capacity assessment or is ambivalent about the assessment or outcome. Although there is some guidance about this in the Mental Capacity Act (MCA, 2005) Code of Practice (2007), it is only through clinical experience that you start to build up ideas of what to do when this happens. Some ideas about how to handle these situations are discussed here.

What do you do when someone does not want to complete a capacity assessment?

There may be many reasons why someone does not want to engage in an assessment of her mental capacity. Assessors need to keep in mind that the mental capacity laws were introduced to empower and protect vulnerable people, and so the assessment should also empower the person and not make her feel threatened or evoke negative emotions. Unfortunately, we do have to be intrusive to a degree in order to ask the right questions and do a capacity assessment that is fit for purpose, but hopefully this will come across as interest in her point of view rather than the assessor being "nosey" or judgmental. (See Box 25.1 for some ideas to increase someone's engagement in the capacity assessment. Also see Chapters 8 and 9.)

Box 25.1   Some general tips to aid engagement in the process

- Provide the relevant information before the assessment — why the decision has arisen, all of the viable options available to the person and the timescale for making the decision.

- Introduce the purpose and process of the capacity assessment and its possible outcomes before the formal capacity assessment session.
- All assessors to meet the person beforehand to become familiar with her and so that she feels more comfortable with them.
- The assessor who has a better relationship with the person to lead the assessment in cases where the person may be difficult to assess.
- Start the capacity assessment informally, through conversations, at first so that the person has started to think about the issues before the formal capacity assessment, as this may feel less threatening.
- Feed back the results of any cognitive and functional assessments before the capacity assessment to increase the person's insight into her difficulties.

It is important to find out why the person does not want to take part in the capacity assessment and see if it can be resolved. Depending on the reason, the approach you take may differ – see some ideas here. Unfortunately, these techniques usually take a little time and sometimes require the help of other team members and the family or friends of the person being assessed; however, if it helps her feel more comfortable with the capacity process, then it is worth taking your time over.

The person does not understand the reason for the assessment

At the start of the assessment session, introduce the capacity assessment and explain the reason you are doing it and the possible outcomes in a supportive manner (see Chapter 8). This step could be enhanced by creating an information sheet in an easy-read format. Encourage her to put across her point of view so that you, as the assessor, can see both sides of the story. Use the techniques mentioned in Chapters 9 and 11 to try to aid her understanding. Also, explain the consequences of not carrying out a capacity assessment, for example, taking longer to get out of hospital (Code of Practice, 2007, at paragraph 4.57).

The person does not like or trust the assessor

If possible, change the assessor to someone that the person knows, likes and trusts. You could help the other professional with the assessment by providing a list of questions that you would like answered or doing a joint assessment if that is acceptable to the person being assessed. If it is not possible to engage another assessor, then have some "getting to know you" sessions before approaching the capacity assessment again. Asking a friend, relative or advocate to sit in on the assessment may also help, especially if they understand why the assessment has to take place; but be careful that they do not influence the answers and information provided by the person.

The person does not like authority figures or "the system" and therefore does not want "interference" in her life, especially if found not to have the capacity to make the decision in question

This is the most difficult scenario to overcome. Sometimes a professional that she trusts can persuade her to talk about the relevant issues, but this may have to be done in an unstructured, informal manner, for example, while going for a walk, to reduce the "confrontational" nature of a formal assessment. However, it is important that the person is aware that the assessment is taking place and that the quality of the assessment is not compromised. Trying to find some common ground, such as a shared interest or experience may help to make you appear "more human" to the person and less part of the "system". Trying to get a friend or relative to persuade her to take part may also help.

The person is in denial and/or unwilling to admit his difficulties

Often the person will disagree with what the staff and professionals say about his abilities. This may be due to him not being willing to admit his difficulties, in which case you could try to reassure him and persuade him to explore these issues with you.

Tips

- Give concrete examples of times when he has had problems to show that you are aware of the difficulties that he is experiencing, and then it may be easier for him to agree with these than say them himself.
- Do a joint assessment with the member of staff who has been assessing the functional difficulties, as then the person is not able to deny that it happened, although he may still come up with excuses for why it happened.
- Some therapeutic work with a clinical psychologist can reduce the denial and help the person accept his difficulties without it being a threat to his notion of self.
- Friends and relatives who are willing to discuss with the person examples of difficulties he is experiencing can be useful, as it is often more difficult for him to dismiss these than the examples professionals and staff raise.

Further questioning can also tease apart the problem to see if it is a lack of insight into his difficulties – which is likely to result in the capacity assessment finding that he does not have the capacity to make the decision – or psychological denial, a form of psychological defence, which could be discussed further and may result in the person having the capacity to make the decision. (See Chapters 9 and 10 for further information on insight and denial.) An example of such questioning is in Box 25.2.

Box 25.2 An example of questioning to distinguish problems with insight from denial of problems

Assessor: Do you have any difficulties walking? (Amit is hoisted for transfers and uses a self-propelled wheelchair.)

Amit: I use my wheelchair to get about.

Assessor: How do you get from your bed to the wheelchair?

Amit: I just get in it myself.

Assessor: Do you have any help to transfer from the bed to your wheelchair?

Amit: No, I just stand up and then sit in my wheelchair.

Assessor: Did you do that just now when the nursing staff were getting you into your wheelchair for your session with me?

Amit: No, they hoist me. I don't know why. I think it's just to cover their backs, but I can do it on my own. I'll do it on my own when I get home, so I won't need any carers.

Assessor: Have you been practising transferring into your wheelchair with the Physio?

Amit: No, they won't do it either, but I know I can do it.

Assessor: Would you mind showing me how you would do it in the gym just now?

Amit: No, I don't want to fall.

If the line of questioning in Box 25.2 were continued further, Amit would likely backtrack and state that there is no risk of him falling, but he just does not want to do it at the moment. He may then start to get agitated and verbally aggressive and want to terminate the session. Sometimes, it is better to leave it once you have your notion that he does have some awareness of his problems and then continue on a different track or complete the assessment on a different day so as not to damage your rapport. If Amit lacked insight into his problems, he probably would have agreed to show the assessor how he transfers. If this was done in a controlled way, then this demonstration might increase his insight, as he would find that he could not do what he thought he could.

People who are in denial are more likely to argue with you than people who lack insight and, therefore, the latter group tend not to refuse to participate in a capacity assessment. The latter group are often completely unaware of the situation, and therefore reports of their problems come as a shock to them. They are unable to generalise this information to another situation, for example, transferring in hospital versus transferring at home or transferring from the bed versus transferring from the toilet. They are also likely to forget what you told them, as it does not fit with their view of the world, and, later in the same session, may tell you that they are able to do the task that you told them earlier they are unable to. People in denial, however, tend to have a small inkling that there is something not quite right, but this thought may not yet be conscious. Their minds try to supress it to preserve their self-esteem by thinking up reasons for why something may have happened that meant that it was not their fault. Of course, a lack of insight and some denial can co-exist, but they usually relate to different difficulties. Rehabilitation and strategies to try to increase people's insight into their problems are discussed in Chapters 6 and 9.

The person is worried that if he reports difficulties, then he will not be allowed to do what he wants

Often the person will not say this overtly, but you pick up a sense of it by his response to the options being discussed. Reassure him that you are not trying to trick him and that you are trying to make the process as transparent as possible after you have explained in your introduction the reasons why you are doing the assessment and what might happen afterwards. One way to help people feel safe to discuss difficulties is to say something along the lines of: "It is better if you know the risks and are willing to take them than if you don't know what the risks are. I would like to know if you are aware of what the possible risks are of (the option the person has chosen) and any difficulties that you think might occur."

You could add: "If you know what the risks are and you are willing to take them then you can make your own decision, even if the staff or your family might not agree with it. However, if you are not aware of the risks, then it could be danger-ous for us to let you make your own choice (assuming that they are choosing the risky option) and we would need to have a meeting to discuss which option is in your best interests. We would have all of the people involved in your care at the meeting, including you and your family/friends, the nursing staff and therapists and the social worker. We would take your views and what is important to you into consideration before making the decision."

In addition, you could reassure him that, even if you find that he does not have the capacity to make this decision, it does not mean that the outcome or option he wants will not come to pass, as the best interests process has to take into account his emotional wellbeing as well as his physical wellbeing (see Chapter 29).

The person is worried that if she says positive things about an option other than the one she wants, then she will be made to accept it

This is common, even in people who have been willing participants up until this point. Even if you explain that you have to consider all of the possible options to see if she can weigh up the good and not-so-good things about them and that, just because she says that there are good things about, for example, a residential home, does not mean that you are going to "put her" in one, people sometimes go wide-eyed when the oft-dreaded words "residential home" are mentioned. Reassurance can help at times but, at other times, people can be unable or unwilling to be flexible and think about any option other than the one they want. In this situation, it can help to provide some emotional distance by saying: "What if it wasn't about you, but about someone like you, someone in the same position as you? Would there be any good things about a residential home for that person?"

This often arises when assessing someone's ability to make a Lasting Power of Attorney. The person will be insistent that there are no negative points to her relative looking after her money for her, even if you point out that some people may spend some of the money on themselves. At this point, the person often becomes indignant and refuses to believe that her relative would ever do anything like that, as she trusts them. A more emotionally removed perspective can be taken when viewing someone else's family: "Imagine that Mabel is in the same situation that you are in and she wants her daughter to look after her money for her. Do you think that there is any chance that her daughter could spend some of Mabel's money on herself?"

This often solves the problem and she is able to admit that Mabel's daughter could indeed steal her money.

What if the person still refuses to participate in the assessment?

It goes without saying that you cannot force someone to undergo a capacity assessment, and threatening someone into doing one is unacceptable. The Mental Health Act (1983) can only be employed when there are serious concerns about someone's mental health, and it would be rare that it could be employed when someone refuses a capacity assessment.

If the person lacks the capacity to consent to the capacity assessment, then the assessment can usually take place if "the person does not object to the assessment, and it is in their best interests" (Code of Practice, at paragraph 4.58). This may need to be on an informal basis. Remember that the outcome of a capacity assessment is based on the balance of probabilities and so, if it is clear that the person is unable to understand, retain, use and weigh up the relevant information and communicate his decision, it is sufficient to use the information that you have managed to gather, even if you have not completed a thorough assessment (see Box 25.3 for an example of this). In such a situation you would still need to be able to provide evidence from your discussions and/or observations to support your conclusions. It should also be noted that this approach might also bring up ethical issues (see Chapter 31).

Box 25.3   Case study regarding a truncated capacity assessment

Jin was a 26-year-old man who had communication and cognitive problems following a traumatic brain injury a year prior to the assessment. His wife was starting to struggle financially after using up her savings and required access to his accounts to help pay the mortgage and bills for their family. She had been advised to wait to see if Jin regained capacity to manage his finances before applying for deputyship, but this had not happened. Jin wanted to make a Lasting Power of Attorney (LPA) to allow his wife to manage his finances, and so the clinical neuropsychologist and speech and language therapist began education around this. Jin required this information to be repeated during the capacity assessment itself due to memory problems. After five sessions of assessment, Jin became ill and then started to refuse sessions, possibly due to low mood, and it was not possible to continue with the assessment for several weeks. However, the education and questions had been repeated several times, and the assessment was being continued to see if it would enhance his capacity. It was decided that, on the balance of probabilities, he did not have the capacity to decide to make an LPA at that point in time. It was advised that this was revisited at a later date or, if matters had to be dealt with more urgently, that an application to the Court of Protection was made for deputyship.

If none of the strategies detailed above work then the case may have to be taken to the Court of Protection, as only the Court can finally decide if someone does or does not have the capacity to make a decision. However, this would be very rare as usually someone can be persuaded to put across his point of view with some encouragement.

What do you do when someone is indecisive or ambivalent?

If someone is ambivalent about taking part in the capacity assessment, then some of these ideas could be employed to help her engagement. On occasion, a person can agree with everything you have said and can appear to be showing that she has the capacity to make the decision, but then another member of staff states that she has told them something completely different. Sometimes, the person consistently says one thing to you and something different to someone else, for example, family members. If you are satisfied that this is not due to memory problems, what do you do?

Tips

- Try to have a meeting with both the person and the other staff member or family member to discuss this change of, or difference in, opinion.
- Approach it in an open-minded and non-judgmental way, as you did with your assessment, to ensure that the person feels supported and able to discuss her real feelings and opinions.
- If possible, pick neutral ground so that the person is not swayed by her surroundings, for example, at a medical centre instead of in the residential home where she is staying for respite or her own home.
- Check that the person can consistently express her opinion about things she likes and dislikes, for example, by showing photographs of two options such as Brussels sprouts and ice cream or a spider and a cat.
- Help her to think through the pros and cons for each of the options again.
- Try not to influence her either way. This can be hard to do, as sometimes we subtly highlight issues or bring her attention to benefits unconsciously, so we need to be aware of our behaviour in these situations. You may need to help the other staff or family member with this process before the meeting starts, as they may be less aware of their biases than you are. It can be useful to have a discussion with the other staff or family member to find out what their priority is and see if there is any hidden agenda.
- Accept whatever the final decision is, even if it is not the one that the person came to whilst in discussion with you. This does not reflect badly on you or your practice, and so do not take it personally.

> **Caution**
>
> It is important to repeat the assessment with the other staff or family member present on another occasion to assess for consistency following the change of heart.

If the person is unable to come to a consistent decision after the joint meeting or is easily influenced by other people, then it may mean that he does not have the capacity to make the decision.

It may be that he cannot hold issues in mind unless they are placed in front of him and so, when he is with you, he realises the importance of the care he receives from staff but, when he is with family members, he realises the importance of not disrupting the family home with carers coming in four times a day. Holding both of these ideas in his head at once and weighing them up could be difficult for him. Asking within the capacity assessment what other people's views are and what he thinks of them could help to bring this issue to light earlier.

If it is a one-off decision, then the person could be supported to think through these issues using written or pictorial information by an independent person who is not invested in any of the options and who would not be the best interests decision-maker. If it is an ongoing decision, or a series of ongoing decisions, such as care needs or finances, then he may not have the capacity to make the decision(s) due to his suggestibility and inability to hold in mind all of the relevant information in order to weigh it up and use it every time it is required.

Summary

People may sometimes refuse to take part in a capacity assessment or may appear to be saying different things to different people. A clear introduction to the capacity assessment and time spent building rapport are the two most important aspects of engaging someone in the process. Sometimes it is necessary for the assessment to be done on an informal basis by a professional the person likes. Involving other staff members and family or friends can also help resolve issues of engagement or situations in which the person has made contradictory statements.

References

Department for Constitutional Affairs (2007). *Mental Capacity Act 2005: Code of Practice*. London: The Stationery Office. Available at: https://assets.publishing.service.gov.uk/government/uploads/system/uploads/attachment_data/file/497253/Mental-capacity-act-code-of-practice.pdf

Mental Health Act 1983. London: HMSO. Available at: www.legislation.gov.uk/ukpga/1983/20/contents

Chapter 26

Changes in capacity over time and in different situations

Kate Wilkinson

In this chapter

Mental capacity is not always stable, as it can change over time or in different situations. Someone who has capacity to make a certain decision at a specific time can lose it at a later date and, by the same token, someone found to lack capacity might regain it later on. Potential mechanisms by which capacity might change include a deteriorating or improving underlying condition or a temporary or fluctuating underlying condition impacting on decision-making.

A deteriorating underlying condition impacting on decision-making

Sometimes the impairment of mind or brain can be of a deteriorating nature, for example, degenerative conditions such as Alzheimer's disease or vascular dementia or cognitive problems associated with multiple sclerosis (MS) or Parkinson's disease. As the person's underlying condition deteriorates, this can have a negative impact on his ability to make decisions; therefore, he may lose capacity to make some decisions.

Box 26.1   Case study regarding deteriorating cognition

Ranjit was a 43-year-old man who had been diagnosed with primary progressive MS four years previously. This was associated with marked physical and cognitive problems, which were getting worse. As his condition progressed, he began struggling to cope at home even with carer support (he lived alone in a two-storey house), and there were concerns that he was at risk. Therefore, one year ago his social worker proposed he move to an adapted, ground floor supported-living flat. Ranjit expressed a firm wish to stay living in his house, which his care team felt was unwise given the risk his physical and cognitive problems posed. After attempting to support Ranjit to make this decision, the social worker had concerns that he may lack capacity, and so she carried out an assessment of his capacity to decide where to live. It was found, at that time, that Ranjit did have capacity to make this decision and so stayed living at home.

A year later, Ranjit suffered a bad fall at home and was admitted to hospital and transferred to a rehabilitation unit for several weeks in an attempt to improve his physical and functional abilities. When discussing discharge planning with Ranjit, the prospect of discharge to a supported-living flat was brought up again. Ranjit expressed the same desire to remain living at home. The team thought that Ranjit's cognitive abilities had deteriorated over the past year and the risks had increased. Discussions with him had raised further concerns regarding his capacity to make decisions about where to live, therefore his capacity was re-assessed. He was found to lack capacity to make this decision due to the impact of his deteriorating cognition on his decision-making ability. Subsequently, a best interests meeting was held and, after weighing up the benefits and risks of the different options, a decision was made for him to move to a supported-living flat, with which Ranjit reluctantly agreed.

Tip

In cases where deterioration in capacity is possible or even likely, it is good practice to try and support a person to make any one-off decisions (for example, making a Lasting Power of Attorney, making a will or deciding where to live) or involve him in advance care planning as early as possible when he is most likely to still have capacity.

In relation to ongoing decisions (for example, whether to accept care or managing daily finances), you must remember that it is possible that a person who has had a capacity assessment and been found to have capacity to make a specific decision previously may lose capacity to make this decision over time. Things that might indicate a change in decision-making abilities, and the need for a re-assessment, are changes in behaviour or decision-making with associated risk (for example, impulsive spending when he has previously managed budgets well, or beginning to refuse carer visits when he previously agreed to them).

Capacity to make one-off decisions may also need to be re-assessed, especially if the person's circumstances have changed (see Box 26.1 for an example).

Tip

It is good practice when writing your record of the capacity assessment to state that it is possible the person may lose capacity to make this decision in the future and, therefore, capacity may need to be re-assessed at a further date, either if the nature of the decision changes (for example, a change in risk) or the person's decision-making ability deteriorates.

Caution

People with deteriorating cognitive abilities retain the right to change their minds about what they want, and you should not assume this means they have lost capacity. However, in such circumstances, and especially when the person might be at risk, it is appropriate to re-assess capacity to rule this out.

An improving underlying condition impacting on decision-making

Some conditions that commonly affect decision-making ability also have the potential to improve over time (for example, traumatic brain injury, stroke, hypoxic brain injury, encephalitis, the removal of a brain tumour or a mental health condition improving due to new medication). As recovery happens, the person may regain capacity to make certain decisions.

Box 26.2   Case study regarding improving cognition

Jenny was a 53-year-old woman who sustained a traumatic brain injury aged 26 in a road traffic accident. As a result of her injuries, she received a significant financial compensation pay-out. In the immediate months and years following her brain injury, Jenny presented with impaired attention, memory and executive functioning ability, as well as impulsive behaviour. Concerns were raised about her ability to manage her finances and, after an assessment, Jenny was found to lack capacity to manage her finances, and her parents were awarded Deputyship for property and affairs.

Jenny now felt capable of managing her finances and making decisions about property, and tensions were emerging between her and her parents regarding her monthly allowance, which was relatively limited. Jenny had managed her monthly budget successfully for a number of years and was becoming increasingly frustrated with having to ask permission to pay for more significant purchases (such as holidays or redecorating the house), as her allowance only covered basic living costs. She requested a formal re-assessment of her capacity to manage her finances through her solicitor, in light of markedly reduced impulsivity over the years and improved financial management abilities. She hoped to be discharged from the Court of Protection.

A reassessment of capacity by a clinical neuropsychologist found she now had capacity to make everyday financial decisions as well as decisions concerning larger financial sums, such as selling or buying property or making decisions regarding the financial settlement from her personal injury claim.

Caution

Do not forget that people can regain capacity. It is important to revisit capacity in conditions that can reasonably be expected to improve. Remember, capacity is time-specific and, if a person's decision-making abilities have improved, it would be unethical to allow a capacity assessment from a time when she was less able to impact on her right to make her own decisions.

Tip

As with deteriorating conditions, it is good practice when writing your record of the capacity assessment to state that it is possible the person may regain capacity to make this decision in the future and, therefore, capacity may need to be re-assessed at a further date.

A fluctuating or temporary impairment of mind or brain that leads to temporary loss of capacity or fluctuating capacity

The two previous examples detailed capacity changing in one direction over time (either improving or deteriorating). However, sometimes capacity to make a specific decision is lost temporarily or fluctuates (comes and goes) due to a temporary or fluctuating underlying condition.

Temporary conditions which are likely to resolve

Some conditions that can lead to lack of capacity are temporary and can be treated or are likely to spontaneously resolve. Some of these include:

- Intoxication through alcohol or illicit drugs
- Impact of temporarily prescribed medications, for example, strong painkillers, benzodiazepines, or anything with a sedative effect
- Serious infection, for example, a urinary tract infection (UTI)
- Other medical conditions that commonly impact on cognition (for example, liver dysfunction)
- Extreme emotional distress or depression.

Caution

The factors detailed here can all have a more significant impact on the decision-making ability of people with pre-existing cognitive difficulties, for example, those caused by dementia or acquired brain injury.

Fluctuating conditions that impact on capacity

Some conditions that impact on decision-making are less easy to resolve and can cause capacity to fluctuate. Examples of these include:

- Dementia, where a person's level of alertness, confusion, cognitive abilities and thus capacity, changes throughout the day. (For example, "sundowning": when someone's cognitive abilities decline towards evening. In some cases, such as those with Lewy bodies dementia, these factors can sometimes fluctuate hourly.)
- The impact of regular, daily medications that can affect capacity throughout the day. (For example, strong painkillers, benzodiazepines, or anything with a sedative effect.) Capacity may fluctuate in line with timings of medication,

either improving after the medication due to a reduction in pain or agitation or reducing due to sedative effects of the medication

- Cognitive problems associated with Parkinson's disease can improve immediately after medication is taken at various times throughout the day
- Extreme anxiety states that can fluctuate throughout the day, or change from day to day, or week to week, or that change depending upon the situation
- Mental health difficulties that fluctuate over weeks and months, such as psychosis or bipolar disorder, which may also depend on medications being taken.

Tip

In cases of fluctuating capacity, it is good practice to include people in advance care planning or support them to make a formal Advance Decision to Refuse Treatment (ADRT; see Chapter 14 for further guidance on these issues).

Box 26.3 Case study regarding fluctuating capacity

Maud was a 56-year-old woman who had sustained a hypoxic brain injury five months previously after untreated pneumonia caused a respiratory arrest, followed by a cardiac arrest.

She was being treated in an inpatient neuro-rehabilitation unit. As a result of the hypoxia, she had suffered neurological damage, which impacted on her mobility and ability to carry out familiar functional tasks (such as washing and dressing, self-care and domestic tasks). Maud's cognition had also been significantly affected, and a cognitive assessment indicated difficulties with memory, attention, executive functioning and reduced information processing speed. She was also experiencing very high levels of anxiety, as the brain injury impacted on her ability to regulate her emotions and level of arousal and, therefore, she could become overwhelmed easily and found it much harder to calm down. Maud was receiving therapy from a clinical neuropsychologist for support with this.

The multidisciplinary team (MDT) developed concerns about Maud's ability to make a decision about whether to remain on the ward or to self-discharge and so asked the clinical neuropsychologist to carry out a capacity assessment relating to this. The reason for the MDTs concerns related to the fact that sometimes Maud was happy to be on the ward and keen to engage in rehabilitation and "get better" but, at other times, she was determined she wanted to go home immediately. This was contrary to the advice of the MDT, as her house was not accessible, her care needs could not be met there and she was unable to be left alone due to safety concerns.

After gathering some information from the team, it became apparent that the times when Maud wanted to go home and could not be reassured were the times when she had very high levels of anxiety and was feeling panicked. Often these episodes were triggered by breathing difficulties.

Maud had been given a lot of information relevant to the decision repeatedly, and in a format she could understand, prior to the assessment by both the clinical neuropsychologist and the occupational therapist (OT) working with her. The OT and clinical neuropsychologist then undertook a joint assessment of her capacity to make a decision about whether to remain in hospital for rehabilitation or to self-discharge. Two assessments at different time points were planned due to the fluctuating nature of her decision-making and levels of arousal and anxiety.

During the first assessment session, Maud was having a "good day". She was feeling calm and the outcome was that, with support, Maud was able to make a decision whether or not to stay in hospital for treatment at that point in time. Her decision, at that time, was that she wished to remain.

The second assessment, two days later, was somewhat different. Maud was having what she described as a "bad day" and had repeatedly requested to go home from the ward. She reiterated this insistence during the assessment. Her presentation was markedly different, demonstrating high anxiety and levels of physical arousal. Her ability to reason was also very different, and she was unable to use and weigh the relevant information due to the extreme anxiety and heightened physiological arousal she was experiencing as a consequence of her brain injury. She was deemed to lack capacity to make a decision about being accommodated in hospital for treatment at that time and, therefore, was persuaded to stay.

The outcome of the assessment was that, most of the time, Maud had capacity to decide to stay in hospital and, in those times when her ability to use and weigh relevant information was intact, she wanted to stay. However, at times of high anxiety and arousal, she was unable to use and weigh information and just wanted to "escape" and had, therefore, temporarily lost capacity to make this decision. Often, she could be persuaded to stay and assisted to calm down and reduce her levels of arousal with breathing exercises. Staff members felt justified in persuading her to stay, as this was her wish when she had capacity. The team decided not to apply for a Deprivation of Liberty Safeguards (DoLS) authorisation, as the majority of time she had capacity and this would have been overly restrictive most of the time. However, after discussion with Maud, it was written in her care plan that, if staff could not persuade her to stay or help her to feel calmer, a capacity assessment should be repeated at the time she wanted to leave and an emergency DoLS applied for, in her best interests, if it was found that she lacked capacity.

Tips

- If the person has to make a one-off decision, and the lack of capacity is temporary or fluctuating, then the decision should be delayed until capacity is regained (MCA Code of Practice, 2007).
- If the decision is ongoing (making the same or similar decision(s) repeatedly, for example, accepting care, managing finances or managing a health condition) and the lack of capacity is fluctuating then a broad view of the "material time" of the decision must be taken. That is, if there are only very limited periods in the day that the person has capacity and the rest of the time she lacks capacity (she lacks capacity more often than not), then overall she effectively lacks capacity to make this decision (Ruck Keene et al., 2019).
- In cases of fluctuating capacity, it is important to time the assessment appropriately around the time of day when it is known the person functions best and around medication times, in order to minimise the negative (or maximise the positive) impact these have on capacity (see Chapter 9).

Cautions

- Cases of fluctuating capacity highlight how important it is to carry out multiple assessments at different times in order to form an opinion on capacity, rather than just relying on a one-off assessment. This should be done routinely, as often the fact that capacity is fluctuating is not always apparent until more than one assessment is undertaken.
- If you deem a person to lack capacity overall to make ongoing decisions due to fluctuating capacity, you must regularly monitor her capacity to ensure the balance has not swung to her having capacity more often than not (Ruck Keene et al., 2019).

Summary

Capacity is not necessarily stable and can change over time, either due to a deteriorating, improving or fluctuating underlying condition impacting on decision-making. It can also change depending on the situation. If the assessment is regarding a one-off decision, and the lack of capacity is temporary or fluctuating, then the decision should be delayed until capacity is regained. Where it is likely that capacity might change, it is good practice to keep capacity under review and re-assess when appropriate. Finally, in cases of fluctuating capacity, or in cases concerning a deteriorating condition where capacity is likely to be lost at some point, it is good practice to involve the person in advance care planning while she still has capacity.

References

Department for Constitutional Affairs (2007). *Mental Capacity Act 2005: Code of Practice*. London: The Stationery Office.

Ruck Keene, A., Butler-Cole, V., Allen, N., Lee, A., Kohn, N., Scott, K., Barnes, K. and Edwards, S. (2019). *A Brief Guide to Carrying Out Capacity Assessments*. London: 39 Essex Chambers. Available at: www.39essex.com/mental-capacity-guidance-note-brief-guide-carrying-capacity-assessments/

Involving friends, family and other professionals in the assessment of mental capacity and the best interests process and dealing with any potential conflict

Stephen Mullin

In this chapter

This chapter will consider ways of including the family and friends of a person whose capacity is being assessed, as well as other professionals with working him, in the assessment of mental capacity and the best interests process. The chapter will also consider how to manage some difficult issues that can arise when working with others in the assessment of mental capacity.

Involving others

Why should we aim to involve family, friends and other professionals in the assessment of mental capacity?

When undertaking an assessment of mental capacity, the Mental Capacity Act (MCA, 2005) states that it is essential that the conclusion reached is based upon the individual's ability to:

- Understand information relevant to the decision
- Remember relevant information for long enough to participate in the assessment
- Use and weigh up information relevant to the decision
- Communicate his decision to others.

The assessment's conclusion must be based upon evidence that the person does or does not have all of the above abilities in relation to the decision in question and, if not, that it is because of an impairment in, or disturbance of, the mind or brain. It cannot be based upon the views, wishes or beliefs of others, including those of close family members.

The MCA Code of Practice (2007) states that "all practicable steps" must be taken to help a person to make a decision before an assessment of capacity is considered. In order to be able to take reasonable steps to help the person, it is necessary to have an understanding of her abilities, difficulties or support needs, such as any sensory or cognitive difficulties, preferred communication method, current pain or fatigue, or the best time of day for her (see Chapters 9 and 11 for further details). It can therefore be very useful to speak to family, friends and other professionals prior to directly assessing the individual's capacity. One example of consulting other professionals who have worked with the person before is asking a speech and language therapist how best to communicate with the person, either by modifying speech (such as by using shorter sentences, checking for understanding) or by using other methods of communication (such as using pictures). A clinical neuropsychologist may be able to advise about memory, attention, executive functioning and other cognitive issues. It is often good practice to undertake an assessment jointly with another professional who knows about a client's communication needs or cognitive difficulties.

Why should we aim to involve family, friends and other professionals in the best interests process?

It is essential that all appropriate and involved parties be given the opportunity to contribute to best interests meetings, if the person is found to lack capacity to make the decision (the best interests process is discussed in more detail in Chapter 29). Best interests meetings bring together all those involved in the decision-making process and provide an opportunity to discuss views, concerns, hopes and preferences in an open way.

Principles for consideration when involving others in the assessment of capacity and best interests process

The Mental Capacity Act (2005) sets out five principles that should be borne in mind when applying the Act (see Chapter 2 for more detail). In addition to the five key legal principles, when deciding whether and how to involve others it is suggested that the following additional practical and ethical principles be considered.

Consent

If you already have consent from the individual to talk to family members, and other people that the person knows, as part of your clinical work, for example, during rehabilitation, then it is unlikely you would need to ask for specific consent to discuss capacity issues with them. In addition, if you are providing clinical input as part of a multidisciplinary team, then speaking to your colleagues from other disciplines is included in a person's consent to be treated. Therefore, it is not necessary to gain additional consent to discuss capacity issues within the team.

However, if you are not already involved with the significant others of the individual or professionals providing support, then you will need to gain informed consent to involve others in your capacity assessment. If the person is unable to give informed consent, then a decision to seek the involvement of others can be made if it is in the person's best interests (MCA Code of Practice, 2007).

The avoidance of harm

We have a duty to work to reduce, or ideally avoid, any harm to a person due to be assessed (The British Psychological Society, 2018). Harm may occur, through the unintentional disclosure of confidential or personal information to others or through the discussion of excessively upsetting or distressing ideas. Harm may also potentially be caused by including people in meetings who are perceived to have caused the person harm in the past, for example, including a family member that the person has alleged has abused her in the past. If the risk of harm of assessment cannot avoided, then it should be considered whether it could be postponed or not undertaken. Any anticipated harm arising from an assessment should be discussed with the person before undertaking an assessment. We will discuss ways of managing such difficult situations here.

Proportionality

If there is a possible risk of harm arising from an assessment, it may not be appropriate to continue with an assessment. The decision of whether or not to proceed should be based upon the "Principle of Proportionality" (McBride, 1999; Reid, 2007). This is that any harm, which may occur from an assessment, should be less than any risks associated with not completing the assessment.

Timeliness

Thorough assessments take time; however, delaying the outcome of an assessment may lead to harm (for example, if the assessment is of capacity to have a medical procedure). It is important to balance the need for obtaining detailed information from others against the time required to obtain it. Our aim should be to undertake an assessment that is detailed enough to be accurate and helpful, but which can be completed quickly enough to avoid unnecessary delay with coming to a conclusion.

Relevance

When seeking information relevant to the assessment of capacity or determination of best interests, it is essential to seek only information that is likely to be relevant to the issue in question. Obtaining unnecessary information may be unavoidable in some situations but runs the risk of both delaying the decision-making process and obtaining or sharing sensitive or highly personal information. For example, if considering an individual's best interests regarding future accommodation after an acquired brain injury, it would not typically be necessary to seek information about a previous divorce many years in the past.

Practicality

It is reasonable to involve only those who are practically able to participate. For example, it may not be reasonable to delay a best interests meeting for an extended period to permit a specific individual to attend, unless his participation is felt to be crucial; in which case, it may be more practical to use teleconferencing or gain information from him beforehand. There is no fixed guidance as to what a reasonable delay may be, as this will depend upon the circumstances of the specific decision in question. In some cases where the decision is not urgent, it may be reasonable to wait for a significant period of time, but in cases where there is risk associated with delay, this may not be possible. In all cases, it is recommended that the decision regarding whether to proceed with an assessment or meeting or to delay it must be taken based upon the risks or benefits to the person being assessed and not the wishes of others. For example, if a person's mother is out of the country for two weeks, and she is required to provide some of the relevant information about the person's finances, it may be reasonable to delay an assessment of capacity to manage finances, but it would not be reasonable to delay an assessment of capacity to leave hospital against medical advice.

Confidentiality

People who may lack the capacity to make a decision still have the right to keep their affairs private. It would not be ethical to share information with people who do not need to know it. It is always necessary to balance the possible harm due to loss of privacy against other possible causes of harm that could be reduced by sharing relevant information. For example, if considering an individual's best interests regarding future accommodation, it would not typically be appropriate to discuss information about an individual's previous sexual relationships. However, this may be appropriate in some cases, for example, if considering shared housing with people who may be vulnerable. It may be appropriate to share limited information about a person's previous relationships if such information may reduce a potential risk to the person or others.

Truthfulness

While it may not be acceptable to share all information with all the people involved in the decision-making process, it is not acceptable to be untruthful. For example, if collecting information relevant to a sensitive medical or personal issue, it is often acceptable to inform a person being interviewed that the purpose of the discussion is to inform an assessment of capacity, without being able to divulge the specific nature of the question under consideration, but it would not be acceptable to be misleading regarding the reason for the interview. It is acceptable to tell a person that you are unable to answer a specific question, but it is not acceptable to provide a misleading or knowingly inaccurate answer.

Examples of how these principles can be applied are given in Box 27.1.

Box 27.1 Examples of the principles in action

Ada has recently had a stroke and wishes to make a will stating what she would like to be done with her property and savings in the event of her death. She is undergoing an assessment of her capacity to make this decision.

Q1. When assessing Ada's capacity to make a will, would it be reasonable to speak to her family and ask them to confirm the family tree?
• It would be entirely reasonable, as the identity of individuals who might reasonably expect to be included in the will is one of the central questions of the assessment.

Q2. Would it be reasonable to ask Ada's family and friends how close Ada's relationship is with her gardener?
• It is possible that this is appropriate if Ada is choosing to leave money to her gardener in her will, particularly if there are concerns around undue influence or financial exploitation. However, caution should be exercised over the possibility of motivations based on secondary gain (for example, family members who stand to inherit more if the gardener is not included in the will).

Q3. Would it be reasonable to ask Ada's family how she previously managed her money and what she chose to spend money on?
• In this situation, how Ada previously managed her money is not likely to be of direct relevance. It would, however, be relevant to know if Ada was prone to impulsive action or to frequently changing her mind and so some information about Ada's current behaviour with regard to her finances may well be relevant. However, it is possible for a person to have the capacity to make a will while not having the capacity to manage her finances.

Who should or should not be included in capacity assessments and best interests decisions?

When thinking about who to include, it is important to establish if the person to be assessed has given Lasting Power of Attorney (LPA) to somebody else, and this has been registered, or if he has a Deputy appointed by the Court of Protection. If either of these is in place, then it is essential to check if they refer to the kind of decision to be taken. Deputies or Attorneys will have the ability to make decisions on the person's behalf for either property and financial matters or health and welfare issues (or in some cases, both). There is not usually any need to undertake an assessment of capacity if the person has an LPA in place, and wishes to use it, or has a Deputy who covers the decision in question. Exceptions to this (when it would be necessary to assess capacity) include:

- Assessing whether a person who has previously made an LPA now lacks capacity to make a decision and requires the LPA to be activated
- If a person who has a Deputy or LPA in place wishes to challenge this and make changes to or stop the arrangement.

In cases where a person does not have a Deputy or an LPA in place, members of the following groups should be consulted if appropriate and practical to do so (MCA Code of Practice, 2007, section 5.49):

- Any family, friends or professional carers who are actively engaged in providing care for the person
- Any healthcare professionals who are providing treatment to the person in an area of relevance to the decision in question
- Other close relatives
- Other close friends
- Anyone who takes an interest in the person's welfare.

As can be seen, this can include a potentially broad range of people, who may have very different relationships with the person.

People who provide practical care for an individual should be consulted if appropriate and practical to do so, as they are likely to have information about how best to work with the person. However, there is no "hierarchy of relationships" to consider when deciding who to include or not to include. Clearly some people will know the person much better than others, but everyone has a unique network of relationships, and it is neither possible nor appropriate to attempt to determine if some individuals' views should be given more weight than others.

Caution should be exercised when considering including people if it is reasonable to believe that they may not have the person's best interests in mind, or if there is a potential conflict of interest (MCA Code of Practice, 2007, Section 5.67). For example, if a carer or relative is suspected to have abused an individual or to be financially exploiting them or if she may directly benefit financially from one of the potential outcomes of a best interests decision (and if this outcome is not clearly in the best interests of the person in question). Professional discretion should be used when deciding whether to interview such people as part of the capacity assessment process, and any information gathered should be treated with caution. Consideration should be given to these issues when deciding whether or not to invite such people to participate in a best interests meeting and advice should be sought from local safeguarding services.

Caution

Remember, in cases of suspected or proven abuse or criminal behaviour, support should always be sought from the appropriate authorities, whether it is NHS safeguarding services, social care, or the police.

Independent Mental Capacity Advocates (IMCAs)

The MCA Code of Practice (2007) states that an IMCA should be appointed when an individual has no close family members or friends to represent him or if there are family members or friends who can take part in a best interests meeting, but there is significant disagreement between them regarding what is in the person's best interests, or a clear conflict of interest. The role of an IMCA is to get to know the person being assessed, to support her through the best interests process and to speak on her behalf.

Managing potential conflict or disagreement

Although it is best practice, involving a number of different people in the assessment and best interests process may also increase the chance of conflict or disagreement.

Managing potential conflict or disagreement in the assessment of capacity

When collecting information from different people, potential conflict can be avoided by speaking with people individually, rather than in a large group. This has the benefit of allowing people to speak freely and express their views. The potential cost of this approach is the time that it requires. Where there is disagreement between sources, it must be remembered that it is not the job of the assessor to decide which view is correct, but rather to have a practical idea of how best to support the person being assessed. Where there is doubt how best to support somebody, it is generally better to provide extra support that is not required than to provide too little support.

When the results of an assessment of capacity are challenged by another professional or by a significant other, such as a member of a person's family, it is advisable to be able to clearly show how the assessment was undertaken, what steps were taken to support the person being assessed and what evidence the conclusion was based upon. This should include questions asked and answers given in the person's own words. (See Chapter 3 for details on how to record assessments.) You should sit down with those involved and discuss things in a collaborative way. If the disagreement leads to conflict, then it is wise to use active listening and de-escalation skills and ensure the person feels heard, even if you do not agree.

Where these steps do not resolve the conflict, a second, independent opinion should be sought, ultimately with a referral to the Court of Protection if this does not resolve the disagreement. The process for disagreements about treatment options in Scotland is different, but the Court of Sessions would be the ultimate decision-maker.

Managing conflict or disagreement between participants in a best interests meeting

The best interests meeting is an opportunity for all those involved to present their views about what may be in the person's best interests and why. Everyone should listen to, consider and discuss the different range of options in order to reach agreement about which possible course of action to take (Joyce, 2008).

Disagreement about the best way to proceed is common. The issues being discussed are often very sensitive or emotive and feelings may run high and, therefore, at times, disagreement may turn into conflict if a participant behaves unreasonably towards others. Sometimes, it may be necessary to hold more than one meeting with different participants in each or, if one person who has been invited feels unable to sit in a room with another participant then he can give written information about his views beforehand, to be read out in the meeting. (Chapter 29 has detailed advice on how to hold and chair best interest meetings, as well as ways to resolve conflict.)

Summary

- When assessing capacity or working to find out what is in somebody's best interests, it is good practice to draw upon as many different sources of information and perspectives as practical to do so.

- Speaking to others who know the person well before beginning an assessment may help the assessor to support him and maximise his capacity. When speaking with others, it is essential to bear in mind at all times the importance of reduction of potential harm and maintaining the individual's right to privacy and to being treated with decency and respect.
- When involving others in the best interests process, there is no hierarchy regarding who should be invited to participate; anyone providing direct care or taking an interest in the person's welfare may contribute. However, in circumstances of suspected abuse or a conflict of interests, caution should be exercised regarding whether or not to involve someone. Advice should be sought from local safeguarding authorities.
- In situations where there are no family members or significant others who can contribute to the process, or there is conflict between interested parties, it is recommended that an Independent Mental Capacity Advocate (IMCA) be involved.
- Disagreement and conflict can occur during both the assessment and best interests process, especially when inviting a diverse range of views. Active attempts to resolve any such conflict should be made, which will involve relying on thorough documentation, good active listening skills and ability to maintain a good rapport with all involved.
- In some cases, a second opinion on assessment or referral to the Court of Protection may be needed to resolve disagreement.

References

The British Psychological Society (2018). *Code of Ethics and Conduct*. Leicester: The British Psychological Society.

Department for Constitutional Affairs (2007). *Mental Capacity Act 2005: Code of Practice*. London: The Stationery Office.

Joyce, T. (2008). *Best Interests: Guidance on Determining the Best Interests of Adults Who Lack the Capacity to Make a Decision for Themselves*. London: British Psychological Society.

McBride, J. (1999). Proportionaility and the European convention on human rights. In E. Ellis (ed.), *The Principle of Proportionality in the Laws of Europe* (pp. 23–35). London: Hart Publishing.

Mental Capacity Act 2005. London: HMSO.

Reid, A. (2007). *A Practitioner's Guide to the European Convention on Human Rights*. 3rd ed. London: Thompson.

Part 5

Issues related to the Mental Capacity Act (2005)

Chapter 28

Capacity assessment, deprivation of liberty and the Liberty Protection Safeguards

David Fowler

In this chapter

This chapter applies aspects of practice described in previous chapters to the particular challenges presented by capacity assessments in the context of decisions
relating to deprivation of liberty. It will draw on case law, legislative guidance and
my own personal perspective as a Best Interests Assessor under the previous Deprivation of Liberty Safeguards regime, to provide tips and techniques for professionals involved in this work.

Deprivation of liberty

Article 5 of the European Convention on Human Rights (1953) is intended to prevent the arbitrary deprivation of a person's liberty by the state. There are, however,
some exceptions to this. The most relevant for health and care staff is the "lawful
detention of persons of unsound mind". Each member state is required to have its
own processes and legislation in place to ensure that the deprivation of people of
"unsound" mind is undertaken lawfully.

In 2004, the European Court of Human Rights (ECHR) ruled that the application of common law principles within the UK represented a potential breach
of people's Article 5 rights in a landmark case – *HL v UK* (often referred to as
the "Bournewood" case) (*HL v UK* [2004]). As a result of this, England and Wales
introduced the Deprivation of Liberty Safeguards (DoLS) in 2009, which were
incorporated into the Mental Capacity Act (MCA) by an amendment in the Mental
Health Act (2007). The intention was that it would provide robust legal safeguards
for people who it was felt needed to be deprived of their liberty for care and treatment in hospitals or care homes but who did not meet the criteria for detention
under the Mental Health Act (MHA, 1983).

In 2014, a Supreme Court ruling in the cases of *P & Q v Surrey County Council*
[2014] and *Cheshire West and Chester Council v P* [2014] (the "Cheshire West" ruling)

provided greater clarity concerning the meaning of the concept of *deprivation of liberty*. Any person who is under continuous supervision and control and not free to leave might be deprived of his liberty if he is unable to consent to his care and treatment and where his circumstances are imputable to (because of) the state. It was also made clear that people receiving services might be deprived of their liberty in settings other than care homes or hospitals, for example, their own homes or supported living schemes. In such instances, commissioners of services would be required to apply to the Court of Protection for an order approving the deprivation of the person's liberty (as opposed to a DoLS application) (*P and Q v Surrey County Council* [2014]; *Cheshire West and Chester Council v P* [2014]).

Deprivation of Liberty Safeguards

The terminology of DoLS described hospitals and care homes as "Managing Authorities" and Local Authorities (who authorised DoLS applications) as "Supervisory Bodies". To address some of the criticisms of the ECHR, a DoLS application could only be authorised for a maximum of twelve months. Further, once an application had been authorised, the person ("Relevant Person") had to have independent advocacy in place, albeit these individuals – known as the "Relevant Person's Representative" – were either family members or friends. However, in circumstances where it was not possible to select a family member or friend, a paid representative, often an Independent Mental Capacity Advocate (IMCA), was appointed (DoLS Code of Practice, 2008).

As part of the application process for DoLS, Supervisory Bodies were required to commission a minimum of two independent, specially trained, professionals to assess whether the person met the criteria for DoLS. These individuals were Independent DoLS Best Interests Assessors (BIAs) (social workers, nurses, clinical psychologists or occupational therapists who have undertaken an additional period of study) and DoLS Mental Health Assessors (MHAs) (Section 12 approved doctors – doctors who are trained and qualified in the use of the Mental Health Act and who have undertaken additional study with regard to DoLS). The criteria against which they assessed applications were (DoLS Code of Practice, 2008):

- Is the person deprived of his/her liberty?
- Does the person lack the capacity to consent to be deprived of his/her liberty for the purpose of receiving care or treatment?
- Is the person over 18?
- Would the deprivation of liberty conflict with the wishes of a Lasting Power of Attorney (LPA), Court appointed Deputy or Advance Decision to Refuse Treatment?

- Does the person have a mental disorder as defined by the Mental Health Act 1983?
- Does the person meet the criteria for detention under the Mental Health Act 1983?

Similar factors had to be considered by care commissioners for people in the community where they believed people receiving services might be being deprived of their liberty.

A capacity assessment to decide whether the person was able to consent to her care or treatment arrangements (including proposed restrictions) must have been undertaken before authorisation for a person's deprivation of liberty was sought. A second assessment was then undertaken, either by a BIA/MHA for people in care homes or hospitals (DoLS) or by the Court in community cases, as part of the process of deciding whether the person's deprivation of liberty was lawful.

Liberty Protection Safeguards

The Cheshire West ruling led to a significant increase in applications for DoLS authorisations and contributed to a demand for change. As a result, the Mental Capacity (Amendment) Act (2019) replaced the previous Deprivation of Liberty Safeguards regime with the Liberty Protection Safeguards (LPS) and sought to address some of the perceived shortfalls.

Key features of the LPS (Spencer-Lane, 2019):

- It does not define "deprivation of liberty", so this continues to be based in case law, such as the Cheshire West ruling and European Court of Human Rights decisions.
- It can be used in settings other than care homes and hospitals including supported living arrangements, private and domestic settings, day centres and transport arrangements.
- It applies to people aged 16 and over, in line with the MCA.
- The following agencies, described as "Responsible Bodies" (changed from "Supervisory Bodies" under DoLS), can authorise arrangements resulting in a deprivation of liberty:
  - The "hospital manager" for arrangements in a NHS hospital
  - The "responsible Local Authority" (England) or local health board (Wales) for arrangements in an independent hospital
  - The relevant clinical commissioning group (England) or local health board (Wales) for arrangements provided through NHS continuing health care
  - The "responsible Local Authority" for any other arrangements

- Under LPS, a responsible body may authorise arrangements if the following authorisation conditions are met:

  1 The person lacks capacity to consent to the arrangements – this is the LPS capacity assessment
  2 The person has a mental disorder within the meaning of Section 1(2) of the Mental Health Act (1983)
  3 The arrangements are:

     - Necessary to prevent harm to the person
     - Proportionate in relation to the likelihood and seriousness of harm to the person

- A programme of regular reviews must be included in the arrangements and an authorisation can be renewed after the initial 12-month period, following consultation, for another 12 months and then renewed again after this, if conditions have not changed and are expected to stay stable, for up to three years
- The interface with the MHA is similar to that of the DoLS (see Chapter 30).

The responsible body can rely on previous assessments for the first two criteria of the "authorisation conditions", but certain steps have to be undertaken before the arrangements can be authorised (Spencer-Lane, 2019):

- Key individuals have been consulted in order to ascertain the person's wishes or feelings, unless it is not practicable or appropriate to do so
- An appropriate person (family member or friend who the person agrees to and who has agreed to be appointed) or IMCA has been appointed. (The appropriate person is entitled to support from an IMCA.)
- A pre-authorisation review has been completed.

The pre-authorisation review

This review can be completed by either an approved mental capacity professional (AMCP; similar to the Best Interests Assessor position in DoLS), or some other health or care professional.

The pre-authorisation review must be undertaken by an AMCP if (Spencer-Lane, 2019):

- The person does not wish to reside in, or receive care or treatment at, a particular place
- The arrangements provide for care or treatment in an independent hospital
- The responsible body refers the case to an AMCP and it is accepted.

Alternatively, if the person is aged 18 or over, and the arrangements would be carried out in a care home, the responsible body can decide whether it or the care home manager should undertake the assessments (Spencer-Lane, 2019).

During the pre-authorisation review, an AMCP is required to (Spencer-Lane, 2019):

- Speak to the person
- Consult the appropriate relevant people (who are interested in the person's care or welfare) when possible
- Review the information
- Decide whether the "authorisation conditions" have been satisfied.

Those reviewers who are not an AMCP need to (Spencer-Lane, 2019):

- Review the information
- Decide if it is reasonable for the responsible body to conclude that the "authorisation conditions" have been satisfied.

How can you prepare effectively for a capacity assessment?

Before undertaking a capacity assessment regarding deprivation of liberty, it is helpful to:

- Explain to professionals the rationale behind the process, allow time for them to think about their practice and help them to provide a fuller account of any restrictive care practices being employed.
- As part of your information-gathering, make sure you take into account any previous capacity assessments concerning related issues or consult with the professionals who have completed them. Where they exist, they can give a clearer sense of the person's care needs and any functional deficits resulting from cognitive impairments.
- You will also need to gather information about the current accommodation, care, treatment, related restrictions and alternatives before your assessment and clarify the extent to which the person has been provided with this information. It is this information that will inform the "relevant factors" that will form the basis of your assessment.

Be clear about the decision to be made

You are asking the person to decide not only where he should live or how he should be looked after, but also whether to be subject to specific restrictions and to be deprived of his liberty in order to receive care or treatment.

The DoLS Code of Practice framed the question as "whether to be accommodated in the relevant hospital or care home for the purpose of being provided with care or treatment" (Ministry of Justice, 2008). However, this description of the decision was criticised in the Law Commission review of DoLS for not getting "at the heart of Article 5" (Law Commission, 2017), as it is not solely the accommodation or placement that gives rise to someone being deprived of her liberty but rather, the restrictions – the elements of supervision, control and lack of freedom to leave (*Cheshire West and Chester Council v P* [2014]). Under LPS, the question is now framed as "whether to consent to the arrangements that would lead to a deprivation of liberty", which covers these elements.

Identify the relevant information

You will need to use your judgment in each particular situation to decide what the relevant factors are (see Chapter 7 for further guidance on determining these) and then present them to the individual in a manner tailor-made to enhance his understanding of the information (see Chapters 9 and 11). Key words in the MCA Code of Practice (2007) are *enable*, *encourage* and *help*.

Chapter 3 in this book has already highlighted the general relevant information identified in the MCA Code of Practice (2007); this includes:

- The nature of the decision
- The reason why the decision is needed
- The likely effects of deciding one way or another or of making no decision at all.

In the specific context of LPS, the following may be a helpful additional checklist, with the information needing to be understood by the person in broad terms:

- The nature of where she is residing, for example, care home or hospital
- Why she is there – specifically a broad understanding of her care and treatment needs, for example, the person is in hospital to receive rehabilitation for a brain injury
- The nature of his care or treatment arrangements (the restrictions being employed) and of other, less restrictive arrangements that may be available. (For example, this might include the person having to seek permission to leave and where not doing so might lead to specific steps being taken to return him.)
- The foreseeable consequences, both positive and negative, of the options available. (Remember, the consequences of remaining subject to a regime that deprives the person of his liberty are unlikely to be exclusively positive.)

(See Appendix 1 for a case example.)

Tip

Look around you and observe your surroundings and the actions of the carers. The mind-sets of care staff and the content of care plans are often focused on care and treatment. Care staff may not have considered the question of restraint, other than in the most general terms, such as "the front door is locked". The complex nature of deprivation of liberty often means that care or treatment providers do not realise that the *nature* of the restrictions (and not the purpose) are central to the question of whether someone is deprived of her liberty. This means that they do not always recognise or record the exact nature of restrictive practices. Further, it is possible to become accustomed to repressive practices when working within institutions and no longer see them for what they are.

Caution

It is important that you do not make assumptions about a person's ability to understand information before giving her an opportunity to engage with the key factors relevant to the decision. Only after a person has had the facts presented to her in the most accessible format, having taken account of any barriers to communication, can a fair assessment be made.

How can you successfully assess capacity in the context of a deprivation of liberty?

If you are the care or treatment provider considering whether an LPS application is necessary, try to match the expertise of the assessor to the needs of the person; for example, someone with an acquired brain injury who has subtle cognitive problems may need a more experienced assessor than someone who has significant cognitive problems, as the outcome may be "borderline". If you then go on to apply for the authorisation, make sure that you explain the LPS process to the person and her family. This will give them an opportunity to process the information and prepare any questions they may have before the pre-authorisation review.

Sometimes, family members may misunderstand the reasons for making an application and the scope of the LPS authorisation itself. It is helpful to consider possible factors that may lead to this situation. These could include:

• Existing conflicts of interest concerning, for example, finance, property or tenancies

- Lack of communication resulting from, for example, long-term family grievances, geographical distances or intergenerational differences of perspective
- Anxiety and high emotion generated by distress and empathy for the deprived person's situation
- An inability to comprehend the complexity of the law.

Tips

I have found the following to be useful strategies to address these difficulties:

- The provision of easy-to-read guides for families and friends explaining DoLS; the Office of the Public Guardian, charities and local authorities have published these on the Internet. (New ones relating to LPS will become available once it has been implemented.)
- Meeting families and friends face-to-face.
- Taking time to listen to histories, stories and experiences that might not always be directly relevant to the assessment itself.
- Considering whether information might be more acceptable to a family if it comes from a professional whom they already know and respect.

If the person has nobody else who is willing or able to be consulted, make sure that an IMCA has been instructed. It is useful to work closely in partnership with the person, advocate and staff throughout the assessment process. It is important not to overlook asking the person the key question: "Do you believe the restrictions in place/being deprived of your liberty/the current arrangements (that we have discussed) are necessary for the provision of your care/treatment?" Although there is a need to ask the question directly, you must be flexible in your use of language so that the particular person can understand the question in his specific environment. (See www.assessingcapacity.com for an example of a semi-structured interview that can be used as a guide for an assessment of capacity for this decision.)

Caution

It is important that you do not conflate the two parts of the capacity assessment (the "two stage test"). Just because someone has an "impairment or disturbance in the functioning of her mind or brain" does not mean she necessarily lacks capacity to make the decision. Determining whether the person has such an impairment is important but only in the context of the wider test for capacity laid out in the Mental Capacity Act (2005), which also requires an assessment of whether the person's impairment means that she is unable to understand, retain, use and weigh the relevant factors (the causative nexus). Assessments are only legitimate when this specific test is applied (see Chapter 2).

Myth-busting

Myth 1: It would be wrong to support the person as this would distort the assessment outcome.

- If you are used to identifying cognitive problems using a range of cognitive tests, such as tests of orientation or memory, it is possible to fall into the trap of thinking that these tests represent the entirety of the capacity assessment rather than elements in the overall assessment of a person's decision-making ability.
- Thus, it is important to remember that the person needs to be given all possible assistance to make the relevant decision. Tests may reveal cognitive deficits, but the assessor needs to consider how the difficulties identified may be overcome in order to assist the person to make the relevant decision.
- Perhaps the key is to regard the assessment as a decision-making partnership that may or may not be successful, rather than one of inquisitor and subject where the subject passes or fails an interrogation. As the person has been deprived of his liberty, the parallels to prisoners and their captors may be uncomfortable but illuminating.

Tip

If there are barriers to communication that are not feasible for you to overcome within the time the decision needs to be made, then you can propose a brief authorisation with a condition attached that, for example, an assessment and advice from a speech and language therapist is sought before the assessment is completed.

Caution

In order to understand and weigh up the relevant information, the person needs to have some insight into his difficulties and how they may impact upon him if he is not subject to the restrictions in place. In addition, it is important to be aware of the "frontal lobe paradox" (George and Gilbert, 2018), as some people with brain injuries are able to tell you what they should do but are unable to put it into practice, to use the relevant information in other words, due to executive functioning difficulties (see Chapter 22 for more information).

Respecting the person

Consider how the person you are assessing understands her own world; try and see things from her point of view. Understanding her lived experience, including potential feelings of oppression and helplessness, will help you to work in partnership with her.

Within my experience as a Best Interests Assessor under DoLS and Social Worker, people who are subject to restrictive care practices and who are believed to lack the capacity to consent to their care arrangements are often perceived as different and can be subject to discrimination and treated less favourably. It is helpful to remain aware of the power imbalance that always exists in the relationship between an assessor and the person being assessed and try to reduce this as much as possible. For example, it is not just the person completing the capacity assessment or the care providers who should consider whether restraints are necessary and proportionate but, most importantly, the person being deprived of her liberty herself. A good approach is to treat the assessment as a consultation where the relevant person and the assessor share their concerns and knowledge. This will help the person to view the process through the prism of supported decision-making and thus generate a relationship based in respect.

Caution

Be careful not to rely too heavily on uncritical considerations of case records and the views of other professionals. In my experience, daily records can sometimes provide a skewed perspective of the person as a result of either positive or negative attributions based on either his resistance or compliance with his care or treatment. If you listen to the person's own words, take note of his non-verbal communication and engage with his family, friends and community it will help you to formulate an understanding of his personality, values, preferences and beliefs.

Myth-busting

Myth 2: A capacity assessment in the context of a deprivation of liberty is exclusively about whether the person is able to understand the harms he might come to should he not be subject to the proposed restrictions.

When discussing the question of physical risks with other professionals, family and friends it is quite possible to feel overwhelmed by the emotions of others and even intimidated by threats of being held personally responsible should their fears prove justified. It is understandable that you would want to protect a vulnerable person and it is easy to regard giving choices about personal safety to vulnerable people with impaired cognition as naïve or uncaring. However, the individual's right to liberty, security and privacy is at the centre of all considerations. It is important to understand the person's views and feelings about the positive consequences of *not* being deprived of his liberty, whilst also encouraging him to weigh these against any potential negative consequences that may occur in that situation.

Dealing with disagreement

If your decision about the person's capacity conflicts with the views of others, you will need strategies to acknowledge the differing perspectives and to move forward. Involving the relevant care team in the assessment process or making a joint visit with another professional may allow you to have face-to-face discussions where evidence can be shared and misunderstandings avoided. Any assessment is best seen as a collaborative process where all parties involved feel listened to and respected. Often decisions about capacity are finely balanced and the key is to be able to demonstrate to all concerned your thought processes and your careful consideration of all the available evidence. However, in some circumstances it might not be possible to reach a consensus. The Code of Practice for the Mental Capacity Act is clear that disagreement should be resolved informally wherever possible. This could include seeking a second opinion or assistance from a mediator. Ultimately, where disagreement cannot be resolved, it might be necessary for the case to be taken to the Court of Protection. (See Chapter 27 for more information.)

Summary

This chapter has discussed applying the practical structures described in previous chapters to the particular challenges presented by issues of deprivation of liberty. It has also explored some tips and techniques based in law, official guidance and my own professional experience. In order to provide the person with the salient factors that she needs to make her decision, you need clarity about the restrictions that constitute the deprivation of liberty as well as an understanding of the relevant accommodation, care and treatment. The practicable steps within these settings that will enable people to make decisions about their own freedom have been considered. In order to make a decision, the person must be provided with sufficient relevant information and assisted to make sense of this. Your skills in collaborating, supporting, sharing and negotiating form the basis for successful practice in assessing capacity about whether to be deprived of liberty and form the basis for safeguarding people who may lack capacity to consent to their own confinement.

Key points

- The decision that needs to be made concerns not just accommodation, care and treatment but also the restrictions that create the confinement.
- You will need to use your judgment in each particular situation to decide what the relevant factors are, and then present them to the individual in a manner tailor-made to enhance his understanding of the situation.
- The individual's rights to liberty, security and privacy is your central concern.
- Collaborate with others (for example, family members, friends, health and social care professionals) and consider all points of view.
- Provide a written record of the assessment and make sure you are clear in explaining how you came to your decision and your reasoning behind it, including examples of the discussion you had with the person and evidence gathered from other sources.

References

Department for Constitutional Affairs (2007). *Mental Capacity Act 2005: Code of Practice*. London: The Stationery Office. Available at: https://assets.publishing.service.gov.uk/government/uploads/system/uploads/attachment_data/file/497253/Mental-capacity-act-code-of-practice.pdf

European Convention on Human Rights 1953. Strasbourg: Council of Europe. Available at: www.echr.coe.int/Documents/Convention_ENG.pdf

George, M. and Gilbert, S. (2018). Mental Capacity Act (2005) assessments: Why everyone needs to know about the frontal lobe paradox. *The Neuropsychologist*, 5, 59–66.

Law Commission (2017). *Mental Capacity and Deprivation of Liberty* (Law Com No. 372).

Mental Capacity Act 2005. London: HMSO. Available at: www.legislation.gov.uk/ukpga/2005/9/contents

Mental Capacity (Amendment) Act 2019. London: HMSO. Available at: www.legislation.gov.uk/ukpga/2019/18/enacted

Mental Health Act 1983. London: HMSO. Available at: www.legislation.gov.uk/ukpga/1983/20/contents

Mental Health Act 2007. London: HMSO. Available at: www.legislation.gov.uk/ukpga/2007/12/contents

Ministry of Justice (2008). *Mental Capacity Act 2005 Deprivation of Liberty Safeguards: Code of Practice to Supplement the Main Mental Capacity Act 2005 Code of Practice*. London: TSO. Available at: www.cqc.org.uk/sites/default/files/Deprivation%20of%20liberty%20safeguards%20code%20of%20practice.pdf

Spencer-Lane, T. (2019). How the law on authorising deprivation of liberty will change. In *Community Care*. Available at: www.communitycare.co.uk/2019/04/26/law-authorising-deprivation-liberty-will-change/

Case law

Cheshire West and Chester Council v P [2014] UKSC 19, MHLO 16
HL v UK 45508/99 [2004] ECHR 471
P and Q v Surrey County Council [2014] UKSC 19

Chapter 29

Best interests decisions

Dan Ratcliff, Emma Fowler and Jane Jolliffe

In this chapter

The Mental Capacity Act 2005 (MCA) for England and Wales requires that, if a person lacks the capacity to make a decision, a decision has to be made for the person that is in his best interests. Making a best interests decision is an important process that needs to be followed once someone is found to lack mental capacity and is a fundamental requirement of the Act. Scotland, The Republic of Ireland and other countries have different legislative requirements, which guide how decisions are made for people who lack capacity to make the decision themselves, but Northern Ireland has a similar best interests principle. Within the context of the MCA, this chapter will help identify factors that need to be considered when working out what is in a person's best interests. Guidance will also be given on who should be consulted and how best to elicit the person's wishes and how to keep them at the centre of the best interest's decision-making process. This chapter is not a re-statement of the MCA and its supporting Code of Practice, rather it is an overview of how these frameworks can be applied in practice. You are strongly advised to consult the MCA Code of Practice (2007) in addition to this chapter, especially where references to it are made.

What are best interests?

The term *best interests* is not defined by the MCA, but the Code of Practice outlines a number of factors that must be considered in any best interests decision (DCA, 2007, Section 5.13). This is known as the best interests checklist (see Box 29.1).

> ### Box 29.1 Best interests checklist (Mental Capacity Act Code of Practice, 2007, Section 5.13)
>
> - Working out what is in someone's best interests cannot be based simply on someone's age, appearance, condition or behaviour.

- All relevant circumstances should be considered when working out someone's best interests.
- Every effort should be made to encourage and enable the person who lacks capacity to take part in making the decision.
- If there is a chance that the person will regain the capacity to make a particular decision, then it may be possible to put off the decision until later if it is not urgent.
- Special considerations apply to decisions about life-sustaining treatment:

  o The fundamental rule is that anyone who is making this decision must not be motivated by a desire to bring about the person's death.

- The person's past and present wishes and feelings, beliefs and values should be taken into account.
- The views of other people who are close to the person who lacks capacity should be considered, as well as the views of an attorney or deputy.

Although not all of the points in the best interests checklist will be relevant for every decision, they should still be considered and then disregarded if found not to be relevant.

To fully understand what is meant by "best interests", it is helpful to examine some of the common misconceptions about the legal concept of best interests. For instance, why we sometimes mix up best interests with other notions such as medical best interests and how we might use this knowledge to improve our practice (Dunn, Clare and Holland, 2010).

Myth-busting

Myth 1: Ultimately it is views of family members or friends that determine the decision

This misconception is closely linked to other false beliefs about the best interests principle, such as: "the decision taken should prioritise the person's physical wellbeing" or "we should always select the least restrictive option when making a best interests decision".

This misunderstanding typically arises when people involved believe it is their legal right to make decisions, such as when a group of professionals decide what is in someone's best interests without consulting with the person or her family.

The issue here is one of emphasis. The MCA does not discount considerations of physical safety, the opinions of family members or the least restrictive option, but instead requires a holistic approach to decision-making where every relevant factor is equally weighed against the others (DCA, 2007, Section 5.38). Nonetheless, there is a noticeable trend across case law in which greater emphasis is being given to identifying the wishes and feelings of the person and an indication that there needs to be a compelling justification for departing from them. Such principles are reflected more broadly in the UN Convention on the Rights of Persons with Disabilities (Article 12(4)) and were included in the proposed amendments to the MCA put forward by the Law Commission in 2017; however, they were not included in the Mental Capacity (Amendment) Act (2019), which is specifically about Liberty Protection Safeguards.

The expectation that we take a holistic view when making best interests decisions requires us to consider a broad range of factors that will likely go substantially beyond the views of family or friends. Case law has been clear that we must consider *where relevant*, welfare, medical, social, psychological, and emotional factors (*James v Aintree University Hospitals NHS Foundation Trust* [2013]). This applies equally to medical best interests, for example, when a woman was refusing a caesarean section due to a needle phobia, the Court also considered the emotional and welfare consequences to the mother of the possible loss of her child (*F v West Berkshire Health Authority* [1989]).

Depending on the circumstances of the case, there may be a significant variation in the amount and nature of the information considered. In urgent situations there may not be the time to review all possible factors.

Myth-busting

Myth 2: People who lack capacity are entitled to whatever is deemed to be in their best interests

---

The relationship between resource allocation and best interests has been a complex and much contested area. However, a recent Supreme Court judgment has offered some clarity, signalling that it is not the role of the decision-maker to consider options, within the decision-making process, that would not be available to a person with capacity making the same decision. Instead, decision-makers should select from a range of genuinely available options. This includes options that are believed to be forthcoming within the decision-making time frame (*N v A CCG* [2017]; *A County Council v MB* [2010]).

The question of what is genuinely available, however, can sometimes be perplexing in practice. It can be easy for best interests decision-makers to mentally "screen out" options based on prior experience. For example, if decision-makers are aware that specific types of care packages are rarely approved, often on the basis of cost, then these options might not be acknowledged, discussed or considered as part of the decision-making process. Whilst this is understandable, it is not good practice. Even where an option might be difficult to obtain or be challenged by others, if it is potentially available and is relevant to the decision, it has to be considered and weighed against other options.

Funding panels or budget holders often have a different responsibility that involves, for example, the fair allocation of public money. These professionals have to justify their decisions based on the requirements of their role and any relevant legislative or policy obligations. Best interests decision-makers have to justify *their decisions* based on the legislative obligations. To try and anticipate the decisions of others and adjust the best interests decision accordingly could prevent the best interests decision-maker from discharging her duty appropriately.

Who is the decision-maker?

Myth-busting

Myth 3: The decision should be a consensus made by the whole group

The MCA Code of Practice acknowledges that there might be "times when a joint decision is made by a number of people" (DCA, 2007, Section 5.11). However, this approach is not always either optimal or appropriate. Some circumstances require the identification of a decision-maker who will ultimately decide on the best course of action and take responsibility for that decision. Broadly, the person who would be carrying out a best interests decision is the person who should act as the decision-maker in instances where joint or multi-disciplinary decisions are not feasible or appropriate. For example, decisions relating to nursing care should be taken by a nurse and those relating to medical treatment should be made by a doctor. Similarly, some health, care or financial decisions would be made by a person holding a Lasting Power of Attorney (LPA) or a Deputy appointed by the Court of Protection, if they come under the scope of their legal authority (DCA, 2007, Section 5.8). Individual decision-makers are still required to follow the best interests decision-making process (even Attorneys and Deputies) and show that they have, for example, taken into account the views of the person, the views of others involved with the person and considered the least restrictive option. It just means that *they, alone, make the final decision* about how to proceed. Others, of course, can disagree or challenge the decision if they are unsatisfied with it and there is a section about disagreement later in the chapter. It is worth noting that an Independent Mental Capacity Advocate (IMCA), if involved, is *never* the decision-maker and responsibility for resolving a best interests issue should not be given to them.

Beyond these prescribed roles, it can be beneficial to identify a decision-maker that can effectively lead and implement a best interests decision. This does not need to be the same person who undertook the capacity assessment, but the decision-maker should be satisfied of the quality of a preceding capacity assessment before he undertakes the task of working out what might be in the person's best interests through the process detailed below.

Establishing the person's values, beliefs and feelings about the decision

Understanding the person: Consultation and other information sources

For a best interests decision to be valid it must reflect the person. To do this, the decision should take account of the person's expressed wishes, beliefs, values, feelings, priorities and past history. This information may be gained from a variety of sources. The MCA Code of Practice specifies that the decision-maker has a duty to consult other people close to the person who lacks capacity and to take into account the following people's views, if practical and appropriate to do so (DCA, 2007, Section 5.49):

- Anyone the person has previously named as someone they want to be consulted
- Anyone involved in caring for the person
- Anyone interested in the person's welfare (for example, family carers, other close relatives, or an advocate already working with the person)
- An attorney appointed by the person under a Lasting Power of Attorney
- A deputy appointed for that person by the Court of Protection.

In addition, it would be good practice to consult anyone who is interested in caring for the person, for example, if her care needs have changed.

The decision-maker should always remember to ask the person who lacks capacity about who knows them best and who is important to them and to document this clearly. She should ensure that no key individual is excluded based on other people's views of who is important. Where, however, an identified individual is likely to have little relevant knowledge of the person to sufficiently add anything substantial to the best interests decision, information-gathering resources may be better focused elsewhere. For example, is it appropriate to spend a lot of time tracing relatives, where it is clear that they have had little or no contact with the person? However, if a significant other such as a spouse or close friend is not consulted and it is practicable to do so, there must be clear reasons documented for why this has not taken place. These reasons must also be defensible, as they may be challenged, possibly in the Court of Protection.

Similarly, the scope of consultation will be narrower in decisions that have to be taken quickly. For example, when someone is brought to hospital by the police and medical staff believe it is important for the person to be assessed by a mental health professional, they might have to decide whether to prevent him leaving the hospital for a short period until this has taken place. Alternatively, a paramedic providing assistance at home to someone experiencing cognition problems resulting from diabetic hypoglycaemia might only have a short time to decide whether it is in the best interests of the person to go to hospital for treatment.

There are four key pieces of information that will be required from those consulted:

1   What is their relationship with the person who lacks capacity?
2   How long have they known them?
3   What do they think is in the person's best interests?
4   Can they give information on the person's past and present wishes, feelings, beliefs and values?

When consulting relevant people, it is important that the decision-maker does not allow point three and point four to become confused. The wishes and opinions of the person may be very different from what the person being consulted thinks is in the person's best interests.

Information sources to help understand a person's wishes and preferences can be varied and could include photo albums, video footage, affiliation or memberships of groups, and objects or possessions that reflect the person's interests. It is important to remember that the person's views may not have been elicited in response to a discussion about the current decision; the views may have been expressed in the past. The views could have been expressed verbally, in writing or through actions. For example, if a person visited her mother every weekend, this action could inform a best interests decision about whether to support her to visit her mother. For people with limited verbal skills, the decision-maker may need to ask questions about their habits and behaviours and likes and dislikes to find out more about their wishes and preferences. Some detective work may be required.

Beliefs can be religious, spiritual and non-spiritual, such as political beliefs. For example, when planning a funeral for someone, information about his spiritual life is essential. Friends and family may be able to provide this information but, if not, it would be important to consult the person's spiritual advisor, for example, his priest or imam. Similarly, informants should be found who can describe and evidence the values by which the person lived her life. For example, the person may have been very family orientated and, therefore, this would have an important bearing on the location of accommodation in relation to family travelling to visit.

Supporting the person to express her opinions about the decision

It is essential that, wherever possible, an appropriate person communicates with the person who lacks capacity about the current decision. An appropriate person must be able to communicate effectively with the person and understand the decision. Opinions expressed by the person during the best interests process should be considered alongside information gained about the person's opinions, wishes and values during the capacity assessment itself. The method(s) of communication must meet the person's communication and information needs, for example, use of easy read materials or signing. It is also advisable that the conversations held with the person to gain his views and opinions are fully documented, which would ideally involve recording verbatim the questions asked and the answers given.

All practicable steps to ensure participation in decision-making should be made. For example:

•   Visual support
•   Lead-in statements to mark a change of topic
•   Several short conversations over time rather than one long one conversation. (See Chapters 9 and 11 for further examples.)

For some people, repeated conversations about a decision mean they no longer wish to talk about it. This disengagement may make it difficult to find out their views. An alternative approach is to spend time talking with the person about her preferences generally, for example, in accommodation, holidays or co-tenants. This often leads to a rich discussion about the person's likes, dislikes, experiences and feelings. This information should be presented at the best interests meeting and inform the discussion of the benefits and problems of the options under discussion. For example, if a person says he likes gardening, hates dogs and never wants to share a bedroom then this would have a bearing on an option to move to a home with a paved yard, a dog and a shared bedroom.

For a person who has never been able to advocate for himself, such as a person with a severe or profound learning disability, information about his responses and reactions is invaluable. For example, a person may have shied away from smokers, so this would have a bearing on a decision about co-tenants or communal living, or a person's documented enjoyment of being on a swing could inform the purchase of an adult swing.

People should be involved in discussions about the importance of the anticipated risks and benefits of different options in any way possible. This may mean asking a person to rank the benefits and risks in order of importance. For example, awarding a gold, silver and bronze medal or any other system that is meaningful to the person.

What about "unsound" opinions?

Sometimes the views and opinions of the person might be, in our view, unsound or based on misinformation. For example, where a person refuses care as she believes it will cost much more than it actually will, or she does not believe that she would be well looked after. Alternatively, a person may believe that there is no possibility that his health will improve if he accepts a prescribed course of treatment or he might believe that a health problem will be solved by "God" and, therefore, not require any other intervention. In such circumstances the following considerations are worth being mindful of:

- Be careful not to confuse questions of capacity with issues of "wishes, views and beliefs" at best interests stage. We know, by virtue of the fact we are making a best interests decision, that the person lacks capacity to make that decision at that time and so, therefore, some of her views might reflect a lack of understanding. Nevertheless, the requirement to consider those views is not conditional on them being rational or sound. We might decide to allocate less weight to some views or wishes but we are still required to have strong justifications for deviating from those views.
- Reflect, honestly, on whether the assessment of the "validity or rationality" of someone's views are based on objective principles or on personal bias. Are those views and opinions flying-in-the-face of facts or outside conventional religious beliefs or are they just grounded in belief systems that we do not share? Consider if further information, for example, a visit to a care home or a discussion with a religious leader, will help the person to have a more balanced view of the situation.
- For further information on the differing types of beliefs, refer to the section "Values and Belief Systems" in Chapter 5.

Is the current decision consistent with past decisions made by the person?

It is important that the outcome of the decision should be consistent with the history of the person's decision-making on related topics when he had capacity, if possible. For example, a best interests decision to go on a cruise to the Caribbean for a person and her carer would be inconsistent with the person's previous decisions if she had always chosen camping holidays in Wales and dislikes change. Whereas, a best interests decision may be made to give someone tastes of food, even though there is a possibility that it may lead to a chest infection, because he was previously a food critic and enjoying food was a large part of his life. (See Box 29.2 for tips on establishing values, beliefs and feelings). In cases where the proposed decision would be in conflict with the person's expressed wishes, and attempts to resolve the disagreement have failed, it would be essential to get legal advice and consider an application to the Court of Protection. (See the later section on managing disagreement.)

Box 29.2 Tips to help establish the person's values, beliefs and feelings about the decision

- Identify at the earliest opportunity who could provide the information you need.
- If possible, always ask the person if there is anyone he would like to be consulted.
- Ensure you differentiate between information provided by the person and information provided by other people.
- When consulting with others, explore how they have reached a view on the person's wishes or beliefs, for example, "What makes you think Person X would say that/want that", or "Has she ever said anything or done anything to reflect this belief?"
- Always ensure that all *practicable steps* (including methods of communication) have been taken to ensure that the person has been supported to express her own wishes and opinions.

How should factors be balanced and weighed up?

Once the relevant factors have been identified, they need to be structured in a way that evidences a systematic approach to their consideration and weighing up. Often, criticisms that can be levelled at a best interests process are less to do with the actual decision and more to do with a failure to evidence clearly the thought processes and reasoning behind the decision reached.

When making a best interests decision, the following must be considered:

1   What are the benefits/advantages and risks/burdens for each option being considered? Consider these in the following areas (Joyce, 2008):

- Physical/medical
- Welfare: This reflects the person's quality of life and wellbeing. Examples include financial considerations, housing, activity and stimulation, and social or family contact
- Psychological/emotional

2   The likelihood of those benefits and risks occurring
3   The relative importance of these for the person.

Weighing up the risks and benefits, and establishing the relative importance for the person, is often the most difficult part of the best interests process. There are a number of ways of doing this. Essentially, there needs to be an indication in some visual form of the amount of weight (or importance for the person) that is being applied to each benefit or burden. This can be done in a variety of ways. As an example:

- Normal font or = next to the factor represents equal weight
- *Italics* or - next to the factor represents less than equal weight
- **Bold** or + next to the factor represents significant weight (Allen, 2017).

The weight assigned to each factor will depend on the circumstances of each case. However, recent case law (for example, *James v Aintree University Hospitals NHS Foundation Trust* [2013]) has provided increasing emphasis on the importance of the person's own views and wishes, indicating that sufficient weight must be given to them when balancing all the factors. As a general rule, a person's wishes should be given significant weight. Furthermore, if the decision made departs from the person's wishes then there must be strong justification for this. Sometimes there may be many risks but only one benefit, but this benefit may have "magnetic importance" (*Re: M, ITW & Others* [2009]) in making the best interests decision. In other words, this one factor outweighs all other factors.

When applying weightings, it is always helpful to think "knowing what I know about the person, how important would he consider this factor to be?" For example, it may be more important for the person to keep in contact with a friend, or even a pet, than a family relative who she has had little or no contact with during her life.

When documenting the likelihood of benefits and risks occurring, the following guidance may help:

Likelihood refers to the chance that something might happen. Likelihood can be:

Rare – the risk is not expected to occur
Unlikely – the risk is unlikely to occur
Possible – the risk may occur occasionally
Likely – it is likely that the risk will occur
Certain – the risk is almost certain to occur

Please see Appendix 9 for an example of a completed balance sheet which refers to a decision about care and accommodation for an adult with a significant learning disability, mental health issues, poorly managed diabetes and associated physical health problems.

Mitigating the risks and having a back-up plan

Once a decision has been reached, it is important that a plan for mitigating or reducing the risks associated with the course of action is considered. It is likely that the broad strategies for this can be identified as part of making a best interests decision and that the day-to-day detail of how this will be delivered forms part of the ongoing care plan. For example, if the person objected to moving to residential care and yet, on balance, it was decided that it was still in his best interests to move to residential care, then there could be risks to the person's emotional and psychological wellbeing in moving. To mitigate these risks, it might be appropriate to encourage the person to make choices within that decision that could help him to feel more in control and more comfortable with his move. For instance, he might be able to choose where he moves to, who provides his care, how his room is decorated, and the day on which he moves.

Furthermore, if there is the possibility that the chosen course of action may fail in the short-term (for example, if the person returns home and the care arrangements break down) then there needs to be a response that does not result in poorly thought through decisions. Specifying a back-up plan may help avoid this and, if relevant, it should be clearly documented as part of the best interests decision.

What about disagreement?

Decision-makers aim to make decisions that are supported by everyone involved in the person's life. However, a consensus in itself might not be in the person's best interests. Disagreement is sometimes unavoidable, and it is important that decision-makers respond to it, and resolve it, appropriately. The MCA Code of Practice (2007, Section 5.68) recommends the following in cases where there are disputes:

* Involve an advocate to act on behalf of the person who lacks capacity to make the decision
* Get a second opinion
* Hold a formal or informal best interests case conference
* Attempt some form of mediation
* Pursue a complaint through the organisation's formal procedures.

More broadly, other policies or legislation might be utilised, including advocacy afforded under the Care Act where the decision relates to ongoing care needs.

Working with Attorneys who hold an LPA or Court Deputies in situations where they are acting as decision-makers can also present challenges. Difficulties can be averted when professionals position themselves as allies in the process; providing resources, support and advice where needed in the service of reaching the best outcome for the person.

Examples of inappropriate responses to disagreement could include the use of Liberty Protection Safeguards (LPS) to impose a best interests decision on someone who is actively rejecting the outcome or, the contrary response, of deferring implementation of a decision indefinitely in circumstances where professionals are unsure about how to proceed.

Ultimately, entrenched objection should be resolved by the Court of Protection and statutory bodies have an active duty to progress cases to the Court in these circumstances.

Holding a best interests meeting

A formal best interests meeting is not required for every decision in the life of a person who lacks capacity to make the decisions. It is, however, good practice to hold a best interests meeting for decisions that are complex, have a significant impact on the person or where there are differing opinions or disagreement from practitioners and/or carers. Examples of such decisions include:

* Where to live
* What care services a person should receive at home
* What care services a person should receive outside of the home, for example, day service
* Who the person should have contact with
* Having some serious medical treatment (some medical treatments can only be granted by the Court of Protection).

A detailed review of how to organise and manage a best interests meeting falls outside the scope of this chapter (please see Joyce (2008) for additional guidance). However, the following are some points of guidance to consider.

Being clear about the purpose of the meeting

The nature of the decision needs to be clear and, if there is more than one decision to be addressed in a single meeting, they need to be listed separately to avoid confusion.

Preparing prior to the meeting

Prior to the meeting, all of the participants need to be made aware of its purpose and the need to come with all of the relevant information. Also, the Chair and decision-maker need to be identified. In some cases, a decision may be taken to not include someone in the formal meeting if this would result in strong emotions or significant conflict that would hinder the ability to either obtain useful information or promote helpful discussion. However, if it is decided not to invite someone to a best interests meeting, particularly if they may be significant in the person's life, there needs to be a clear and defensible rationale for not inviting them. If it is not possible for all identified people to attend, then their views should ideally be sought prior and then formally presented at the meeting. Ideally, these opinions should be provided in written form (for example, letter or email) by the person/s consulted but absent from the meeting, although this will not always be possible.

Introducing the meeting

At the start of the meeting, the Chair needs to:

1   Specify the decision/s for discussion, clarify that the decision is one that can be made under the MCA and name the decision-maker.
2   Be clear that the options available to the person are the same as those that would be available to someone with capacity.
3   Confirm that the person has been found to lack capacity.
4   Confirm that all reasonable efforts have been made to enable the person to make the decision/s for themselves.

It is helpful to have a clearly set out agenda at the start of the meeting that explains the process. Please see Appendix 10 for an example of a best interests meeting agenda, adapted from the British Psychological Society guidance on determining best interests (Joyce, 2008).

Sharing information in the meeting

Participants should be given the opportunity to consider the feelings, wishes and beliefs of the person and other information about the benefits and risks of the differing options being discussed. It is very easy for best interests meetings to become an uncoordinated expression of people's opinions and views. It is the Chair's responsibility to ensure that time is managed effectively, so that people share their views without anyone dominating the discussion or the focus on the specific decision being lost.

Discussing the benefits and risks of each decision-making option being considered

Once the information and people's opinions have been gathered, it is important to list the options that are available and to address the benefits and risks associated with each option. It may be helpful to write these down on a flip chart or other form of record-keeping using the structure and weighting procedures outlined earlier in the chapter so that everyone can see the information. Occasionally, people may object to some of the options being discussed; for example, if the family strongly feel that the person cannot return home but that is the person's wish or the person does not want to go into a care home. Explaining that all relevant options need to be discussed and considered before a decision is made usually helps people understand the process.

Summarising the information and making a decision

It is helpful if, towards the end, the Chair summarises the key points of discussion and asks each person present what option he/she would choose and the reasons for his/her choice. This can help everyone feel heard and can reduce future disagreements. It can also help the decision-maker to reach a decision and feel supported in doing so. It is essential, particularly if the decision is complex, there are disagreements, or if misunderstandings have developed during the course of the meeting, that the Chair allocates enough time for this. The participants need to decide what *on the balance of probability*, is the best decision for the person and the group should try to reach a consensus if there is not a specified decision-maker. If there is not enough information to reach a decision, or further work could be done to enhance the person's skills or clarify the options, then another meeting should be arranged (Joyce, 2008).

Summary

The best interests process must not be regarded as a procedural 'after-thought' to the issue of mental capacity. In reality, this is one of the most fundamental parts of the decision-making process for people lacking mental capacity and the decision-maker may well feel a weight of responsibility in making a potentially life-changing decision. However, his confidence in the outcome, will be increased if the following key points are followed:

- All options which would be available to a person *with* capacity are considered.
- The person is kept at the centre of the process and her wishes reflected.
- Sufficient consultation with others takes place.
- A balance sheet approach is used for considering all relevant options.
- The relevant weighting of factors is documented.
- All practicable steps to ensure participation of the person in the best interests process is made.
- Particularly strong weighting is given to the person's own wishes and views.
- Consideration is given regarding how to mitigate risks associated with the decision.

- Attempts are made to resolve disagreements.
- It is recognised that the level of information-gathering, and the resolution of disagreements, will be dependent on the time available to make the decision.

References

Allen, N. (2017). *Mental Capacity Act 2005*. Unpublished presentation.

Department for Constitutional Affairs (2007). *Mental Capacity Act 2005: Code of Practice*. London: The Stationery Office. Available at: https://assets.publishing.service.gov.uk/government/uploads/system/uploads/attachment_data/file/497253/Mental-capacity-act-code-of-practice.pdf

Dunn, M.C., Clare, I.C.H. and Holland, A.J. (2010). Living 'a life like ours': Support workers' accounts of substitute decision-making in residential care homes for adults with intellectual disabilities. *Journal of Intellectual Disability Research*, 54(2), 144–160. doi:10.1111/j.1365-2788.2009.01228.x.

Joyce, T. (2008). *Best Interests: Guidance on Determining the Best Interests of Adults Who Lack the Capacity to Make a Decision for Themselves*. London: British Psychological Society.

Law Commission (2017). *Law Commission Amendments to the MCA* [online]. Available at: www.lawcom.gov.uk/project/mental-capacity-and-deprivation-of-liberty/

Mental Capacity (Amendment) Act 2019. London: HMSO. Available at: www.legislation.gov.uk/ukpga/2019/18/enacted

United Nations (2017). *Convention on the Rights of Persons with Disabilities* [online]. Available at: www.un.org/development/desa/disabilities/convention-on-the-rights-of-persons-with-disabilities.html

Case law

A County Council v MB [2010] EWHC 2508

F v West Berkshire Health Authority [1989] 2 All ER 545

James v Aintree University Hospitals NHS Foundation Trust [2013] UKSC 67

N v A CCG & Others [2017] UKSC 22

Re: M, ITW & Others [2009] EWHC 2525 (Fam)

Chapter 30

The Mental Capacity Act's interaction with other legislation

Ian Leonard

In this chapter

This chapter reflects on key areas of other legislation, such as the Mental Health Act, Human Rights Act and Sexual Offences Act, as they interact with the application of the Mental Capacity Act. It provides practical clinical examples illustrating how different pieces of legislation must be combined and describes the tension that is sometimes created by the different underlying values that underpin them. It does not attempt to cover the very wide range of possible situations professionals may meet and practitioners should refer to the relevant legislation and Codes of Practice.

Which interactions are key in clinical practice?

It is inevitable that there are situations where various Acts have implications that must be combined into a single course of action. Their different underlying assumptions, related guidance and legal precedents can lead to considerable complexity in their practical application. After an Act takes effect, consideration of specific instances in Court leads to additional case law that affects how the legislation is subsequently applied. Some legislation proves very difficult to implement effectively in practice and so is replaced relatively quickly. The Mental Health Act (2007) amendment that introduced Deprivation of Liberty Safeguards (DoLS) authorisations, which were only put into practice for the first time in 2009, being replaced by Liberty Protection Safeguards (LPS) in the Mental Capacity (Amendment) Act (2019) is an example of this.

Multiple Acts of Parliament affect what is legal in different situations. This applies to healthcare provision just as it does to employment, buying products or driving a car. The Mental Capacity Act 2005 (MCA) and its 2019 amendment have important areas of interaction with the Mental Health Act 1983, amended in 2007 (MHA), the Human Rights Act 1998 (HRA) and the Sexual Offences Act 2003 (SOA). Codes of Practice and case law indicate when some aspects of the overlapping implications require consideration but applying the Acts in individual situations remains a clinical judgment.

Interactions between the Mental Capacity Act and the Mental Health Act

Different values

Although the values reflected in both the MCA and MHA have wide support, they are not identical values and there is an inherent tension between the different aims. The MHA's guiding principles include "Decisions about care and treatment should be appropriate to the patient, with clear therapeutic aims, promote recovery and should be performed to current national guidelines and/or current, available best practice guidelines" and "Where decisions are taken which are contradictory to views expressed, professionals should explain the reasons for this" (Mental Health Act, 1983; Code of Practice, 2015, p. 22). The MCA Code of Practice states that "The Act is intended to be enabling and supportive of people who lack capacity, not restricting or controlling of their lives" (Mental Capacity Act, 2005; Code of Practice, 2007, p. 19). Both involve an element of paternalism, through their removal under specified, but different, criteria of a person's right to make their own decisions. It is also noteworthy that the MCA is only applicable from the age of 16, whereas the MHA applies to everyone, including children.

An individual's decision-making significantly harming their own mental health is one situation where the presumption of capacity is called into question. An assessment of capacity may be required to clarify intervention planning and the need for applying the MCA or MHA. If someone is found to have capacity, using the MCA guidelines, then treatment may be imposed only through the MHA, though whether it should be will often be contentious.

The relevant information that needs to be understood by the person (and therefore provided by the professional proposing a treatment) in determining their capacity can also be open to differing interpretations. For many years the information deemed relevant by professionals was the relevant standard, legitimized by reference to the "Bolam test" (*Bolam v Friern Hospital Management Committee* [1957]), provided it withstood a logical analysis of risks and benefits as developed in the case of *Bolitho v City and Hackney Health Authority* [1997], but this is no longer sufficient. More recent case law emphasizes that it is not purely a matter for professional expertise, but involves dialogue between a patient and the professional involved that reflects the values of both (see, for example, *Duce v Worcestershire Acute NHS Trust* [2018]; *Kennedy v Frankel* [2019]). Chapter 13 provides more information on this subject.

Within the UK, arrangements vary with respect to compulsory treatment of mental disorder. Scotland has separate legislation for those who lack decision-making capacity (the Adults with Incapacity (Scotland) Act 2000) and the compulsory management of some mental disorders (The Mental Health (Care and Treatment) (Scotland) Act 2003). Northern Ireland has relatively new (2016) combined legislation based on capacity which provides a unified framework but does not abolish clinical dilemmas. Many elements of the legislation are similar to the MCA in England and Wales, but within the definition of "unable to make a decision" there is an added requirement for the person to be able to "appreciate the relevance" of information, in addition to using and weighing it to make a decision.

MHA exceptions to standard MCA consent requirements

The MHA alters the standard consent requirements in relation to treatments given under the MHA and some treatments to non-detained patients. The regulations are summarized here, but for detailed guidance the MHA Code of Practice (2015) should be consulted. Treatment for mental disorder of most detained patients, with those on short-term holding orders the main exception, are regulated by the MHA and not the MCA. Treatment must be "appropriate", which relates to both the evidence base for the treatment prescribed and an individual's wishes and feelings. The powers of an attorney to make decisions on matters of health and welfare are modified, but not abolished, when a person is detained under the MHA.

Two forms of treatment (neurosurgery for mental disorder and surgical implantation of hormones to reduce male sex drive) require consent, plus agreement that the treatment is appropriate and the patient has capacity from a Second Opinion Appointed Doctor (SOAD) and two additional capacity assessors (all appointed by the Care Quality Commission). This applies whether or not the person is detained under the MHA. For these treatments specified in regulations under the MHA, there is no means of giving them to a patient who lacks the capacity to consent.

Electro-convulsive therapy (ECT) and medication given as part of that treatment has its own safeguards (see Box 30.1) in adult patients subject to the MHA and all under 18-year-olds. Although psychiatrists regard ECT as a proven treatment for severe depression (and in some other limited circumstances), the necessity for repeated general anaesthetics during a course brings its own risks and significant numbers of patients report cognitive adverse effects following ECT. Research studies have reached different conclusions on whether ECT causes cognitive problems. Methodological challenges include non-blinded assessment, 'memory' being a complex set of functions, varied administration techniques and interaction with the adverse cognitive effects of underlying mood disorder. Some studies do not find it to cause significant problems, as measured on standardised cognitive assessments, in the long term (for example, Kirov et al., 2016). Others have found significant autobiographical memory impairment and slowed reaction time six months after ECT, with bilateral electrode placement causing greater adverse effect (Sackeim et al., 2007).

Box 30.1   Specific additional safeguards in relation to electro-convulsive therapy

- An assessment by an independent Second Opinion Appointed Doctor (SOAD) for under 18-year-olds (whether detained under the MHA or not) is mandatory. Agreement that treatment is appropriate is a necessary condition for treatment to go ahead, even if the individual is found to be consenting to treatment.
- When an adult patient is detained under the MHA and found to have capacity to consent this must be certified on a statutory form, either by the Responsible Clinician or a SOAD.
- A valid advance decision (see Chapter 14) to refuse ECT (or the decision of a suitably authorized attorney/deputy or the Court of Protection) cannot be overridden.
- When a patient is found to lack capacity, and there is no valid advance decision that precludes ECT, it can only be commenced after either a SOAD assessment confirms it is appropriate or the Responsible Clinician formally documents that ECT is immediately necessary to save the patient's life or prevent a serious deterioration of his condition, with the added requirement that it does not have unfavourable physical or psychological consequences that cannot be reversed (Section 62 MHA).
- If life is at immediate risk and the validity of an advance decision is in doubt, ECT can be given whilst those two circumstances remain current. Urgent steps to resolve the issue regarding the validity of the advance decision would be required.

Patients detained and prescribed medication for mental disorder for longer than three months, or subject to a Community Treatment Order after discharge from hospital, must either have their capacity to consent and their agreement certified on a statutory form by the Responsible Clinician, or the treatment supported by a SOAD. Otherwise it cannot be given, though temporary arrangements are possible pending a SOAD assessment.

Clinical practice

The MHA is only to be used when less restrictive options are either inappropriate or unavailable and only applies to the treatment of mental disorder.

The doctors and Approved Mental Health Professional assessing whether or not to detain an individual under the MHA must consider the less restrictive option of the person consenting to a hospital admission that the assessor thinks necessary. If the person retains capacity but declines admission this can be overridden by MHA detention, though this is unusual and would then most often relate to risk to others.

It is preferable for treatments and interventions to be based on common law consent or best interests, where capacity is absent, whenever possible. The principal area of practice that cannot be managed in either way, and must be managed under the MHA, is treatment for mental disorder to which an individual objects during admission to a place (usually hospital) registered to admit patients under the MHA. This applies whether or not the person has capacity to consent to the proposed treatment. It means that the same treatment for an individual may have different legal requirements in different settings (see Box 30.2 for a case study illustrating this).

Box 30.2 Changing mental health and changing treatment authority

Paul is in his early sixties. He sees himself as retired, but when mentally well he is able to work as a volunteer at a foodbank where his physical strength is especially valued. He enjoys spending time with his family and walking with a local group. Throughout the last 40 years he has had episodes of being unwell, described by doctors as schizo-affective disorder, when his mood becomes unstable and he develops the belief that he has gained special powers, such as telepathy, due to which the government tries to recruit him for their security agencies. These episodes have greatly disrupted Paul's relationships and work in the past and he is keen to avoid any more episodes.

When well, he understands the reasons he is prescribed an antipsychotic (olanzapine) to reduce the risk of relapse and sees the adverse effects he experiences, for which he is prescribed a further medication (procyclidine), as worth tolerating. He is also prescribed one further medication (omeprazole) to prevent the recurrence of stomach ulceration. His General Practitioner prescribes the medications, Paul consents to take them and under common law this is valid.

When Paul last relapsed, at a time of family stress, the Community Mental Health Team tried to support him at home. He agreed to an increased dose of olanzapine but did not take it regularly. As his delusions intensified, he lost his previous understanding of his medication, believing that olanzapine had simply suppressed his special powers and the others were no longer necessary. This constituted a loss of capacity to consent to medication. Continued prescribing then relied on a best interests assessment under the MCA. That analysis of best interests had to include Paul's likely degree of adherence to the prescribed medication.

Despite support, Paul's health continued to worsen and, after multiple arguments with a neighbour that he accused of trying to recruit him for MI5, he was detained in hospital under the MHA.

On admission to hospital, though there was no change in his mental state, the basis for continuing his olanzapine (treatment for mental disorder) and procyclidine (necessary to facilitate treatment with olanzapine) changed to the MHA under which his Responsible Clinician continued to prescribe it. Omeprazole, for physical health reasons, was continued with a best interests MCA justification. During the first few weeks of his admission he also had anti-anxiety medication prescribed under MHA provisions.

After three months on the ward, Paul had improved greatly, was spending time at home on leave and back on the same combination of medication that had previously kept him well for some years. The MHA required that either his Responsible Clinician state that he had capacity to consent to his medication for mental disorder or that his capacity and the treatment must be reviewed by a Second Opinion Appointed Doctor. He was found to have capacity to consent to all prescribed medication. Olanzapine and procyclidine remained regulated by MHA provisions and his omeprazole to common law consent.

Prior to Paul's discharge two weeks later, use of a Community Treatment Order was considered but not thought necessary. Back at home, and no longer subject to MHA legislation, the use of all Paul's medication reverted to that of consent under common law.

Interactions between the Mental Capacity (Amendment) Act – the Liberty Protection Safeguards – and the Mental Health Act

The Liberty Protection Safeguards (LPS), and their predecessor Deprivation of Liberty Safeguards (DoLS), evolved from the recognition that a defined legal process, including a right to appeal, was required in relation to individuals who may have their liberty deprived but were not subject to other legislation such as the Mental Health Act or criminal sanctions.

Although each piece of legislation is concerned with the circumstances in which a person with mental disorder (and for DoLS and LPS as a consequence also lack relevant decision-making capacity) can be deprived of their liberty, the purpose of that deprivation differs. In the MHA, it is a narrow focus on the treatment of mental disorder, in DoLS it is best interests and in LPS the prevention of harm to the individual. The MHA can only authorize a deprivation of liberty in hospital, whereas DoLS relates to hospital and care home settings and LPS is not restricted to any particular type of setting.

These aspects of the different legislations mean that, for some individual circumstances, the decision as to which framework is applicable, or whether both are required simultaneously, may not be straightforward. The former is illustrated by a person in hospital where treatment is both for a physical disorder and its mental manifestations such as delirium. The latter is illustrated by a person who remains detained under the MHA but is temporarily located outside the detaining hospital in circumstances that constitute a deprivation of liberty.

Interactions between the Mental Capacity Act, the Human Rights Act and the Deprivation of Liberty Safeguards/Liberty Protection Safeguards

As consideration of human rights implications has informed capacity and mental health legislation over many decades, it is unsurprising that the way capacity legislation has been framed influences the application of the Human Rights Act.

The HRA articles most relevant to DoLS and LPS are Articles 5 (right to liberty) and 8 (right to private and family life, home and correspondence); unlike Article 2 (right to life), neither are absolute rights. The right to liberty is limited by both detention after a criminal conviction and under the MHA. The right to private and family life is termed a qualified right. This means that they can be restricted in certain circumstances, such as to protect the rights of others or on health grounds (for an individual or the public).

Other than by arrest, depriving a person of his liberty requires as a necessary, but not sufficient, condition that he is of unsound mind, usually framed as having a mental disorder. Such detention under mental capacity legislation has clear parallels with detention under the MHA. When a person is deprived of his liberty, the way in which his private and family life is affected and whether the justification for the deprivation is sufficient become relevant considerations.

The implication of legislation allowing a person who lacks the relevant decision-making capacity to be deprived of her liberty is that it is sometimes in that person's best interests to have her qualified human rights restricted in her overall best interests, as judged by a substitute decision-maker. Though the specific test is different, the provision for compulsory mental health treatment under the MHA allows for a similar objective, in line with providing an entitlement to mental health care and treatment when an individual's own health would otherwise prevent him from accessing this.

The UK is one of the countries signed up to the United Nations Convention on the Rights of Persons with Disabilities (CRPD). This rejects any form of long-term disability as a reason for a deprivation of liberty and requires supported rather than substitute decision-making arrangements. For example, arrangements regularly made with respect to residence and care of individuals with intellectual disability or dementia are very clearly in contravention of these requirements. Many current UK health and social care practices (under both MCA and MHA) cannot be reconciled with the CRPD. Importantly the CRPD does not address how decisions made with support, that are inconsistent (either over time or with other people's reality), should be carried out. It also does not address how issues should be dealt with, in the case of a severely affected individual, when no approach seems able to discern a relevant, reliable expression of preferences.

Interactions between the Mental Capacity Act and the Sexual Offences Act

In general, the MCA and SOA can be seen as having separate functions. The MCA provides the framework within which someone's capacity to make a decision to engage in sexual activity with others can be assessed. The related aspect of the SOA is concerned with whether an offence, a sexual act without consent, occurred in the past. In practice, the information required to be understood by the individual may be more specifically defined in relation to a past act with an identified person and a lack of understanding is not the only way in which mental disorder can lead to a person being unable to make an autonomous decision on the matter.

Key information to be understood in general (and able to be retained, then used and weighed in the context of a specific relationship at a future time) includes the mechanics of the act, that there are health risks involved (particularly the acquisition of sexually transmitted and sexually transmissible infections) and (where relevant) that sex between a man and a woman may result in the woman becoming pregnant. In addition, that any specific proposed sexual act can be agreed to or refused is an important part of relevant understanding.

The combined effects of the Acts can have profound impacts. It is possible to be married but that a sexual relationship would be for one partner to commit an offence as the other has been assessed to lack the capacity to have sex with anyone (*CH v A Metropolitan Council* [2017]). Capacity to consent to a sexual relationship would normally be a part of capacity to marry but there is no routine test and subsequent development of, or increase in, mental impairment may lead to a loss of previous capacity. Under that circumstance, a local authority then has a duty of care to safeguard the person lacking capacity (*IM v LM & Others* [2014]), but also, where possible, promote their capacity to create the circumstances under which the person can enter into a sexual relationship. The Courts may assess capacity to consent to future sexual relations in general terms, but have not considered the suitability of any particular person as a sexual partner. This is an area where significant case law development may be expected. Issues of capacity to decide on contact with others, with a separate set of salient, relevant information to be understood, retained, used and weighed may further complicate an individual's specific circumstances. (See Chapter 17 for more detail and advice on how to assess capacity to consent to sexual relations.)

Other areas of interest

Wills

There remain in existence valid wills created before the implementation of the MCA on which the Act's contents have no bearing. How the MCA affects the current application of the long-established test of testamentary capacity found in *Banks v Goodfellow* [1870] is reflected by ongoing case law, though the MCA Code of Practice is clear that the common law test is not simply replaced. There are some clear differences, for example, regarding burden of proof rather than a presumption of capacity, but both approaches require the information relevant to the circumstances of the individual proposing to make a will to be determined. Where a person lacks testamentary capacity, an MCA based best interests approach to the creation of a statutory will has been used – though not without difficulty. (See Chapter 18 for more detail on assessing testamentary capacity.)

Contracts

The overall capacity to manage financial affairs is an explicit part of the MCA and yet the issues relating to individual contracts a person may enter in to are also affected by other areas of law. One issue taken account of is whether the other party to a contract did, or should have, realised that a person lacked capacity to enter into the contract at the time. In addition, agreements to buy "necessaries", the nature of which are determined by individual circumstances but may include items of food and clothing, are enforceable on reasonable terms even if the person lacks capacity to make the purchase. (See Chapter 18 for more detail on assessing capacity to manage finances.)

Summary

This chapter emphasizes how the MCA cannot be seen in isolation by describing key areas of interaction with other legislation. It provides clinical examples of the interface and sources of further reading. Although the MCA is wide-ranging in its application there are important exceptions when other legislation either takes precedence or modifies how the MCA is applied. The relationship between capacity legislation and other areas of law varies in different countries.

References

Adults with Incapacity (Scotland) Act 2000. London: The Stationery Office.

Department for Constitutional Affairs (2007). *Mental Capacity Act 2005: Code of Practice*. London: The Stationery Office. Available at: https://assets.publishing.service.gov.uk/government/uploads/system/uploads/attachment_data/file/497253/Mental-capacity-act-code-of-practice.pdf

Department of Health and Social Care (2015). *Mental Health Act 1983: Code of Practice*. London: The Stationery Office. Available at: https://assets.publishing.service.gov.uk/government/uploads/system/uploads/attachment_data/file/435512/MHA_Code_of_Practice.PDF

Human Rights Act 1998. London: HMSO. Available at: www.legislation.gov.uk/ukpga/1998/42/contents

Kirov, G.G., Owen, L., Ballard, H., Leighton, A., Hannigan, K., Llewellyn, D., Escott-Price, V. and Atkins, M. (2016). Evaluation of cumulative cognitive deficits from electroconvulsive therapy. *The British Journal of Psychiatry*, 208(3), 266–270.

Mental Capacity Act 2005. London: HMSO. Available at: www.legislation.gov.uk/ukpga/2005/9/contents

Mental Capacity (Amendment) Act 2019. London: HMSO. Available at: www.legislation.gov.uk/ukpga/2019/18/enacted

Mental Health Act 1983. London: HMSO. Available at: www.legislation.gov.uk/ukpga/1983/20/contents

Mental Health Act 2007. London: HMSO. Available at: www.legislation.gov.uk/ukpga/2007/12/contents

The Mental Health (Care and Treatment) (Scotland) Act 2003. London: The Stationery Office.

Sackeim, H.A., Prudic, J., Fuller, R., Keilp, J., Lavori, P.W. and Olfson, M. (2007). The cognitive effects of electroconvulsive therapy in community settings. *Neuropsychopharmacology*, 32, 244–254.

Sexual Offences Act 2003. London: HMSO. Available at: www.legislation.gov.uk/ukpga/2003/42/contents

United Nations (2006). *Convention on the Rights of Persons with Disabilities*. New York: United Nations. Available at: www.un.org/disabilities/documents/convention/convoptprot-e.pdf

Case law

Banks v Goodfellow [1870] LR 5 QB549
Bolam v Friern Hospital Management Committee [1957] 1 WLR 583
Bolitho v City and Hackney Health Authority [1997] UKHL 46
CH v A Metropolitan Council [2017] EWCOP 12
Duce v Worcestershire Acute NHS Trust [2018] EWCA Civ 1307
IM v LM & Others [2014] EWCA 37
Kennedy v Frankel [2019] EWHC 106 (QB)

Part 6

Additional considerations

Chapter 31

Ethical issues in capacity assessments and their outcomes

Janice Mackenzie

In this chapter

Assessing people's mental capacity, and potentially making decisions for them, raises strong feelings in professionals that can be linked to their own ethical code and how they view the rights of others. Ethical issues can arise at each point of the process:

- Supporting someone to make his own decisions
- Questioning someone's capacity to make a decision
- Assessing his capacity to make the decision
- Deciding that someone does or does not have the capacity to make the decision
- Making a decision for someone who does not have the capacity to make it himself.

Supported decision-making

Professionals need to make sure that they take "all practicable steps" (Mental Capacity Act (MCA, 2005), section 1(3)) when supporting someone to make his own decisions, but it is sometimes difficult to know when you have achieved this or if you should keep trying other ideas (see Chapter 9 for more information). If the decision needs to be made in a certain timeframe, then this can restrict the amount of support you can provide and you can feel satisfied that you tried your best in the time available (see Chapter 24). However, if there is no timescale then deciding when to stop supporting the person to make his own decisions and to move onto questioning and assessing someone's capacity can sometimes be a quandary. It is likely that this will be resolved by the resources available within your service with a consideration of what is reasonable. The MCA Code of Practice suggests considering what is "possible and appropriate" (2007, at paragraph 3.4) in the individual circumstances.

Questioning and assessing capacity

Some people worry about putting someone through a capacity assessment and try not to question someone's right to make the decision himself, for example, when someone has a strong desire to return home on discharge from hospital. When carrying out a capacity assessment, some people try very hard to avoid finding that someone does not have capacity to make a decision. There may be a number of reasons for these approaches, for example, not wanting to take away someone's independence or right to make the decision, not wanting to be in disagreement with the person or his family, or thinking about all of the work that is involved if the person is found not to have capacity. It is often people who do not have a lot of experience assessing mental capacity and applying the relevant law to the outcome of the assessment who feel like this. We do need to be careful when we question someone's capacity and to follow the relevant law, for example, not basing it on diagnosis or because someone is disagreeing with the proposed plan or making an "unwise" decision. Also, we need to provide emotional support and information to the person during the capacity assessment process, as it can be distressing for the person to have his capacity questioned, especially if he disagrees with the reasoning behind it (NICE, 2018).

Once you have questioned the person's capacity, and the steps to support him to enhance his capacity to make the decision have not been successful, then you have a duty to carry out a capacity assessment that is fit for purpose, taking into consideration the person's dignity (NICE, 2018). You also need to make sure that you are the best person to carry out the capacity assessment, thinking about experience and training as well as possible conflicts of interest, for example, if you are likely to benefit from the person having or not having capacity or if you know the person on a personal basis. If possible, capacity assessments should be "in the context of a trusting and collaborative relationship" (NICE, 2018, p. 20). If you come to the conclusion that you are not the best person, you must allow someone more suited to the role to carry out the assessment.

Tip

It is useful to remember why mental capacity laws were introduced. They were to:

- Empower people who might otherwise have had decisions made on their behalf without them being asked their opinion
- Put into statute what had been happening in common law for years, in

order to include safeguards and checks
- Protect vulnerable people from abuse and from making harmful decisions when they do not have the capacity to do so
- Provide a framework for making a decision on behalf of someone else who lacked the capacity to make the decision for himself.

Cautions

- As assessors, we must not fall into "noble cause corruption" (the idea of using unethical methods to attain desirable goals that appear to be for the greater good) but approach the assessment and best interests process with an open mind and a non-judgmental stance.
- We must not have an end in mind when we start this process, for example, the preferred outcome for the client or service, but see where it takes us and not be afraid to change our mind later if the evidence is persuasive.
- We must feel confident to state our opinion, even if it causes discomfort or upset, and not feel the need to change our opinion when pressured by others.

Carrying out an assessment of mental capacity need not have negative connotations. It often gives someone the space and time to discuss his point of view, which he may not have had otherwise, or sometimes to show that he has regained capacity if it was previously found that he lacked capacity to make a decision. An assessment of capacity should be a collaborative investigation of issues which, when done well in the right circumstances, will feel like a conversation and, therefore, not too stressful for the person being assessed. It is important to remember that someone does not have to *prove* that he has the capacity to make a decision; the assumption is always that he does have capacity until proved otherwise. However, if someone is found to lack capacity to make a decision then it is assumed that he will continue to lack capacity until this is shown otherwise. Most assessors approach the assessment wanting the best for the person, whether that means that he can make his own decision or that a decision will have to be made for him taking all aspects of his welfare into account.

Tip

Gathering all the relevant information and asking the person's point of view can also lead assessors to have a better understanding of the whole situation and be more empathic in their approach, rather than thinking that someone is being "difficult". This can also lead to people whose capacity has been questioned following informal discussions or due to their diagnosis (something that mental capacity legislation was specifically designed to avoid) being able to make their own decisions, even if they are unwise, as long as they are found to have capacity when assessed.

Substitute decision-making

Finding that someone does not have the capacity to make a decision also need not have negative connotations, as it does not necessarily mean that the person cannot have what she wants. If someone is unable to make a decision by herself then the decision can be made for her by people who are aware of the relevant information and her views and wishes. In England and Wales, decision-making must be in the person's "best interests" and takes place through the best interests process (see Chapter 29). It often includes the person and her family and friends, as well as professionals and staff involved in her care. Safeguards are in place to ensure that the least restrictive option that is in the person's best interests is selected and that the person's emotional and physical wellbeing are taken into account. The least restrictive option must be considered but it does not have to be selected if it is not in the person's best interests (see Box 31.1 for an example of this).

Sometimes this does mean that the person has to do something that she does not want to do, for example, move into a residential home, but often the family and friends of the person are in agreement that this is in her best interests when she would be unable to cope at home with support. Other times, it is found that a more "risky" and less restrictive option is in the person's best interests, and then it is the responsibility of services to try to manage that risk effectively. For example, if someone is likely to become very depressed in a residential home but is at significant risk of falls at home, it may be decided that it is in her best interests to return home anyway, due to weighing up the emotional impact of keeping her physically safe (see Chapter 23 for more information). Sometimes the person finds the best interests process supportive and helpful, especially when she hears her views and beliefs being taken into account. This is not always the case though and some people find listening to all of their difficulties distressing or, if they do not have insight into their problems, they may get irritated by the proceedings. Whether or not someone should attend the full meeting should be carefully considered (see Chapter 29) but, either way, the person should be kept at the heart of the proceedings, for example, by having a photo of her on the agenda or an empty chair to represent her in the meeting if she is not present (BPS, in press).

Box 31.1 Case study regarding the least restrictive option

Yasmin is a 49-year-old woman who has had a stroke that has resulted in cognitive and mobility problems. She has been found not to have the capacity to make a decision about her care needs on discharge from hospital. Yasmin lives with her husband and is very attached to her home. She does not like the idea of living in a residential home with people who are a lot older than her. She would like to go home without carers, as she does not think that she will need care at home. In the best interests meeting, the least restrictive option was identified as Yasmin going home without carer visits and only support from her husband. Although moving to a residential home was not something that Yasmin or her husband would agree to, this option was also considered, as it was an available option that would meet some of her needs, although the most restrictive. The third option that was considered was for Yasmin to go home with four care calls per day and support from her husband. A balance sheet approach was used to look at the pros and cons of the three options.

Home with no care calls may have been the least restrictive option, and Yasmin's choice, however, this was found not to be in her best interests as she would not be able to get to the toilet or make meals during the day when her husband was at work. It would also put strain on her husband in the mornings and evenings, which might damage their relationship. Moving to a residential home would meet Yasmin's physical needs but would be more restrictive than was necessary and would affect her mental health and possibly her relationship with her husband. It was agreed that the least restrictive option that would meet Yasmin's physical, psychological and welfare needs would be to go home with four care calls per day.

Human rights and equality and diversity issues

Due to the Human Rights Act (1998), public bodies such as the NHS and Social Services have to uphold our human rights. Examples of how these can be applied to the mental capacity process are below (BIHR, 2016):

- Article 2: Right to life, for example, thinking carefully about withdrawing treatment or sustenance that may lead to death

- Article 5: Right to liberty and security, for example, thinking carefully about restrictions on someone's liberty and applying for DoLS/LPS if necessary
- Article 8: Right to respect for private and family life, for example, maintaining confidentiality of documents, involving the person in decisions about her life and, when thinking about what is in the person's best interests, promoting family time and not intruding on people's privacy with technology, such as video cameras in bedrooms.

Public bodies must also make sure that people are not subjected to "inhuman or degrading treatment" (Article 3), such as abuse or neglect, or discrimination regarding the rights set out in the legislation (Article 14), for example, due to a physical or mental health problem or a lack of capacity. Throughout the capacity process, it is important to take the person's human rights into account, especially when making decisions on behalf of someone who lacks capacity or in relation to deprivation of liberty (see Chapters 28 and 30). If there is any doubt or disagreement regarding these issues, then it may be necessary to refer the case to the Court of Protection (see Chapter 27).

> **Caution**
>
> Sometimes, while respecting someone's human rights, issues of safety and risk can be overlooked, for example, in the case of self-neglect. People are allowed to make unwise decisions and they have the right to privacy, but they also have the right to life, and this must be paramount. The right to privacy is not an absolute right and can be overridden if there is a good reason to do so, for example, risk to health or public safety concerns (SCIE, 2018). If a vulnerable person is struggling to cope, then this should be investigated and support offered, including involving the local safeguarding team if appropriate. If there is any question about the person's capacity to make decisions about his care needs, this should be assessed, as the self-neglect may be due to issues other than a lifestyle choice, for example, problems with initiating activity in acquired brain injury or severe depression.

As in all aspects of health and wellbeing, issues of equality and diversity should be at the forefront of your mind during mental capacity processes and you should follow your organisation's policies and procedures, which are based on the relevant laws. Awareness of these issues will ensure that each person is treated fairly and receives individualised assessments and interventions according to his needs and based on his "specific circumstances . . . relevant history and presenting difficulties" (BPS, 2019, p. 22).

Summary

Due to the nature of assessing someone's capacity and potentially taking away her right to make a decision about her own life, numerous ethical issues arise. It is important to try to do your best for the person being assessed by following the relevant mental capacity law in your country, approaching the assessment and substitute decision-making process with an open, non-judgmental stance and keeping in mind:

- Issues of autonomy
- Potential conflicts of interest
- Human rights
- Equality and diversity issues
- The reasons that the law was originally implemented.

References

The British Institute of Human Rights (2016). *Mental Health, Mental Capacity: My Human Rights*. London: The British Institute of Human Rights. Available at: www.bihr.org.uk/care-and-support-resources

British Psychological Society (2019). *What Makes a Good Assessment of Capacity?* Professional Practice Board and Mental Capacity Advisory Group. Leicester: British Psychological Society. Available at: www.bps.org.uk/sites/bps.org.uk/files/Policy/Policy%20-%20Files/What%20makes%20a%20good%20assessment%20of%20capacity.pdf

British Psychological Society (in press). *Best Interests Guidance*. Professional Practice Board and Mental Capacity Advisory Group. Leicester: British Psychological Society.

Department for Constitutional Affairs (2007). *Mental Capacity Act 2005: Code of Practice*. London: The Stationery Office. Available at: https://assets.publishing.service.gov.uk/government/uploads/system/uploads/attachment_data/file/497253/Mental-capacity-act-code-of-practice.pdf

Human Rights Act 1998. London: HMSO. Available at: www.legislation.gov.uk/ukpga/1998/42/contents

Mental Capacity Act 2005. London: HMSO. Available at: www.legislation.gov.uk/ukpga/2005/9/contents

National Institute for Health and Care Excellence (2018). *Decision-Making and Mental Capacity* (NG108). Available at: www.nice.org.uk/guidance/ng108

Social Care Institute for Excellence (2018). *Self-Neglect*. Available at: www.scie.org.uk/self-neglect

Chapter 32

Assessing capacity for the Court or as an independent practitioner

Ian Leonard

In this chapter

Some practitioners are required to assess capacity formally as a routine part of their job. For others, it may come up less often, but is expected in the execution of their role, particularly if they work with potentially vulnerable populations. They may also be asked to provide independent opinions as part of their role or, when they have acquired a certain amount of skill and experience, they may choose to carry out capacity assessments in independent practice. You might be asked to provide an independent second opinion on a disputed or uncertain capacity assessment, or to be an expert witness for the Court of Protection. Other requests, for example, assessing someone's capacity to make a will, may come from a solicitor. This chapter provides tips on how to ensure your practice in these areas has a sound basis and notes some specific situations that are common in independent practice.

Ensuring a sound basis for assessments

This requires steps to promote your own competence and confidence when working independently, the establishment of your own governance arrangements and clarity over the steps to be taken for individual assessments as an independent practitioner.

Professional competence

The key priority is to ensure that you have the professional competence to address the issues (see Box 32.1).

Box 32.1 Capacity assessment outside clinical situations – Aspects required to help ensure competence

- Knowledge and experience of the disorder(s) that may be impairing capacity

- Familiarity with the process of capacity assessment
- Sound understanding of the law in relation to the relevant decision, although an encyclopaedic knowledge of case law is not necessary
- Awareness of the information that has been judged important for particular types of decision. Relevant court decisions are discussed in Chapter 7 and on a range of websites with links to further resources (for example, www.39essex.com)
- Awareness of how legal precedent remains in current application, for example, 19th century case law concerning testamentary capacity (*Banks v Goodfellow* [1870]), see Chapter 18
- Clarity about the breadth, but also limits, of the expertise you can justifiably claim
- Reference to specialised texts on particular decisions (Frost, Lawson and Jacoby, 2015) or practice settings (Rix, 2011) may assist
- Use of discussion with an experienced colleague and attendance at a relevant training course are invaluable to improve confidence as well as knowledge.

Governance

When assessments are not being carried out on behalf of an organisation, for example, when you assume the role of an independent expert witness, you have sole responsibility for the system within which information is recorded, the opinion itself and contractual arrangements (see Box 32.2). The required actions are not difficult for practitioners who have worked in robust clinical services but do require putting in place. This is just as important when practicing independently as in your "day job".

Box 32.2 Tips on getting governance right for independent assessments

- You must comply with data protection law concerning security, confidentiality, retention and subject access as the assessment record will constitute sensitive, personal data (UK General Data Protection Regulation from May 2018, www.ico.org.uk). Ensuring physical files are kept locked away and computer files are encrypted reduces the risk of breaching legal requirements.
- Register with the Information Commissioner's Office if assessment information is stored on a computer.

- Clarify professional indemnity for this area of practice.
- Consider any potential for conflicts of interest (for example, if you have personal or family connections to the person being assessed) or potential impact on the therapeutic relationship if you see the individual clinically as well.
- Provide contractual information in advance, including charges but also stating that payment cannot be contingent on the outcome of assessment.
- Do your own administration or use secretarial support – with the additional responsibility to manage those arrangements.

Client matters

Each individual assessment requires the establishment of the authority for you to carry it out and to communicate the outcome. Generally, this amounts to the consent of the person to be assessed, whether or not she is the person commissioning the assessment from you. The person should understand who you are, the purpose of the assessment and how you will do it and communicate your opinion, as well as to whom that will be.

Appropriate consent would necessarily include the authorisation of your access to any important information of which the person's understanding is to be assessed in determining the relevant decision-making capacity. If the person lacks capacity to consent to the assessment, then proceeding with it would require a best interests decision or an attorney or judicial authorisation.

Any assessment must include measures to promote decision-making capacity. This may include repeat discussion, return when further information will be available, deferment until hearing aid batteries have been replaced or a re-visit at an alternative time of day (see Chapter 9). Convenience of assessors is not directly relevant, though there is a balance to be achieved regarding the necessary robustness of an assessment and the resources used to complete it, including the cost to the client.

In non-clinical settings, it is of particular importance to define the relevant, salient information for the individual concerned in relation to a decision. In clinical situations, it will often be a combination of your knowledge of a clinical topic and information available in the healthcare record from other professionals and the person and/or family. Outside that setting you may need information from different sources before an assessment can be undertaken properly, yet you may not have authority to access clinical records that would be freely available to you in a clinical situation. The time taken to gather this information may take longer than you would assume. Once identified, that same information must be available to the person being assessed in a suitably clear format.

Working with solicitors

Solicitors are able to make their own assessments of capacity but, when a client is elderly, unwell or the solicitor is uncertain whether the person has capacity, a referral may be made. An assessment may also be requested when the solicitor thinks the client has capacity, but circumstances suggest this might be retrospectively challenged by those disadvantaged by the decision being made (see Box 32.3 for an example).

Box 32.3 Assessment of testamentary capacity – Case study

Margaret was an 82-year-old widow, diagnosed as having vascular dementia, with two sons and a stepdaughter, all of whom had children of their own. She lived alone with support from her youngest son and stepdaughter but became estranged from her eldest son five years earlier. She contacted a solicitor expressing a wish to write a new will, disinheriting her eldest son. She had a previous will, from 10 years ago written after her husband's death, dividing her estate equally between her three children. She was clear that assets should only be passed down one generation at a time. The solicitor requested a formal assessment of her testamentary capacity.

Margaret accurately described her close family and was also clear that no-one else could expect to be left anything in her will. When discussing the potential make-up of her estate, Margaret included two homes – the bungalow she currently lived in and the family home in which the children had been raised – as well as an approximate value for her savings. Her stepdaughter advised that Margaret's eldest son owned the previous family home, having bought it from his parents 25 years previously. Margaret angrily denied this had ever happened, claimed she should be paid rent and refused to discuss why she no longer saw her eldest son. At interview, she also had some word-finding difficulties and disorientation, reflected in an Abbreviated Mental Test Score of 4/10.

Margaret understood the nature of a will and also who could be seen as having potential claim upon her. She had a significantly flawed understanding of the extent of her property, which impacted on her understanding of the effect of her proposed will, and this could not be corrected by providing further information. Her refusal to discuss details meant that the possibility that her decisions were affected by delusional beliefs about her son could not be clarified further. At this point, Margaret lacked testamentary capacity and could not make a valid new will, so the one from 10 years earlier remained in place.

It is important to ensure a shared understanding of responsibilities. How key background information will be acquired, who will make appointment arrangements, the timescale for report delivery and charging details should all be covered. Ideally a formal Letter of Instruction will contain these but is not strictly essential (see Chapter 20 for a solicitor's point of view).

Court-related assessments

Most health professionals understandably try to minimise their Court involvement but, for some issues, the Courts rely on relevant expertise to enable them to function well. You may be the right person to assist as a professional witness, because of direct involvement with a patient, or an expert witness, due to your knowledge and experience. There are also times when Courts will request NHS Trusts, as public bodies, to provide reports by a suitably qualified professional.

In these circumstances, you should have a detailed explanation of what your report must contain. It may come from a Letter of Instruction or Court Order. The usefulness of your report will depend on a close reading of what is asked. It is important to include the evidence on which you base your opinion, how that evidence has led to your opinion and a clear expression of that opinion. Where relevant, you will also need to qualify your views by reference to information that was unobtainable or comment on the degree of certainty with which you think your opinion is stated. You must remember that it is the Court's function to determine matters; yours is to contribute to a just outcome. It is important to include the relevant declarations and statement of truth that confirm your awareness of and compliance with the rules applicable to the particular Court to which the report is addressed. The Rules and Practice Directions for the Court of Protection were updated in 2017.

If you are required to appear in Court as a witness, having written a good report will be the best preparation. Your awareness of its strengths and weaknesses is also an asset. It is useful to have examples of the questions you have asked and the answers given verbatim, so that you can provide evidence for your opinion. Although you are not on home territory, you are in a professional setting and can expect to be treated with courtesy, though your opinions are there to be tested. Questions may or may not be about whether your view is in a particular sense 'correct'. Its implications or how the opinion fits in to the Court reaching its decisions could be the focus.

Professional obligations

If, in the course of an independent assessment, you become aware of information that justifies action in relation to concerns regarding Adult Safeguarding, Mental Health Act assessment, deprivation of liberty or similar issues, then your wider professional responsibilities remain active. How to act will be situation-specific but the appropriate way to manage any risks identified has to be considered.

Summary

Extending the scope of capacity assessment into independent practice can be professionally rewarding provided it is built on robust foundations. This chapter provides advice on issues to address in establishing a sound framework to practice within and illustrates the type of practice that is then opened up.

References

Frost, M., Lawson, S. and Jacoby, R. (2015). *Testamentary Capacity*. Oxford: Oxford University Press.
Rix, K. (2011). *Expert Psychiatric Evidence*. London: The Royal College of Psychiatrists.
The Rules and Practice Directions for the Court of Protection (2017). Available at: www.judiciary.gov.uk/publications/court-of-protection-amendment-rules-2017-2/

Case law

Banks v Goodfellow [1870] LR 5 QB549

Chapter 33

Teaching and training capacity assessors

Emma Fowler and Janice Mackenzie

In this chapter

A few years ago, along with professionals from a range of backgrounds, we were involved in developing, piloting and evaluating a training programme in Manchester that was designed to improve the confidence and skills of qualified practitioners in relation to the assessment of capacity. The course was entitled "Capacity Assessing in Practice".

This chapter will present an overview of the training, the rationale behind it, and the evaluation of the pilot course. The training produced significant improvements in practice during the pilot study and self-reports showed that this was an ongoing trend over the five years that the course was provided. In addition, the training has been rewarding and enjoyable to develop and deliver. Due to this, we thought that it may be useful to share suggestions and tools that might support you to develop similar training in your service, organisation or local area.

Why was the training required?

Capacity assessors require a working knowledge of the law and robust skills to apply this knowledge across a range of situations. Basic information about the Mental Capacity Act (MCA, 2005) is provided as a standard part of mandatory training for most, if not all, health and social care professionals; however, little information is provided about how to practically assess capacity to meet the standards set by the law. Professionals in Manchester reported feeling a lack of confidence when applying knowledge gained in basic training to assessing capacity in practice. Further, an investigation into the quality of capacity assessments carried out by this group found room for improvement. Consequently, a small project team, consisting of a training officer and experienced health and social care professionals, was established. The brief was to develop practice-based, practical training for qualified professionals across three statutory services. In order to ensure informed support from senior staff and organisational leads, the project plan was presented to, and approved by, the local Adult Safeguarding Board Executive.

Methods

What was the plan?

Our team firstly identified the training objectives and content. Beyond this, we defined who would participate in the pilot course (qualified social workers), who would contribute to the delivery of the programme and how the training would be evaluated. Decisions were based on the data collected from participant and multi-disciplinary team (MDT) questionnaires pre-training which looked at competencies reflecting good practice and development needs.

We hypothesised, based on the existing literature and our own experiences, that improvements in practical abilities and skills, as well as enhanced confidence, would result in the most significant improvements in the quality of capacity assessments undertaken and recorded, resulting in better outcomes for clients and patients.

Who took part?

Fourteen social workers participated in the training (nine women and five men). We selected a pilot group exclusively from this professional background as it is most commonly social workers who are required to undertake the more complex decisions about accommodation or care, including discharge decisions. This approach also made the group more comparable, which helped reduce possible variability in the results. For reasons of convenience, and to reduce the likelihood of people dropping out of the study, participants were self-selecting (see Tables 33.1 and 33.2 for a summary of the background and experience of participants).

Table 33.1 Composition of the group: Social work field

	Hospital	Community	Later-life mental health
N	8	4	2
%	57.1	28.6	14.3

Table 33.2 Composition of the group: Years of social work experience

	Less than two years	3–5 years	More than five years
N	3	5	6
%	21.4	35.7	42.9

How did we evaluate the training and identify any return on investment?

OUR QUESTIONNAIRE FOR PARTICIPANTS

Participants were asked to complete a questionnaire comprising ten questions, both before and after training, to capture information related to practice issues that the project team hypothesised would predict the quality of assessments. For example, one of the questions asked; "How confident are you in undertaking capacity assessments?" Most questions were closed and either measured on a Likert scale or were multiple choice (see Appendix 11 for a full list of questions).

Participants were asked to complete the questionnaire online and, to reduce the likelihood of response bias, for example, responding in a way that might be perceived as "socially desirable", questionnaires were completed anonymously. To ensure that the questionnaire was comprehensible and user-friendly, it was piloted with two professionals unconnected to the training project. Their suggestions were incorporated, which included some changes to grammar but not to the wording of questions.

OUR QUESTIONNAIRE FOR MULTI-DISCIPLINARY TEAMS

A questionnaire comprising seventeen closed questions, measured on a Likert scale, was administered across five wards and over two different sites by a member of the project team; either to the MDT on a ward or to the Ward Manager (one stroke and four care of the elderly). This was administered before and after the training to capture change from a third-party perspective to see if it fitted with any results from the capacity audits or participant interview.

COURSE EVALUATION FORM

An evaluation form was completed by participants after the end of the course. Participants were asked to report on the quality of the training content, the relevance of the content to their work and their confidence in applying the new knowledge. Examples of questions were:

- "Rate the standard and relevance of the training materials" (on a four point scale)
- "I could relate most of the examples and exercises to my work"
- "I am confident I can apply new knowledge/skills to my work".

AUDIT OF CAPACITY ASSESSMENTS CARRIED OUT PRE- AND POST-TRAINING

Participants were asked to submit a list of four assessments from the five-month period preceding the training and a similar list for the five-month period after completion of the course. A member of the project team randomly selected two from each participants' list in order to reduce the potential for self-selecting bias. A group of experienced professionals audited the anonymised assessments against the Manchester City Council (MCC) mental capacity audit tool (based on the BPS mental capacity audit tool (2010)). Auditors were asked to determine whether each individual section of the person's capacity assessment met the audit criteria.

To lessen the likelihood of bias, and to protect the privacy of assessors and clients, the auditors were blind to the time-point of the assessment (pre- or post-training) and the identity of assessors. Three sets of assessments were inter-rated by members of the training project team to check for test-retest reliability.

POST-TRAINING SEMI-STRUCTURED INTERVIEW

Eleven participants were available to be interviewed about their thoughts on the training five months after completing the course (see Appendix 12 for a copy of the semi-structured interview). Results from the interviews complemented quantitative measures and provided additional thoughts, feelings and perceptions from the participants not captured elsewhere.

What did the training involve?

A holistic approach to assessing capacity was taken resulting in five core themes shaping the training. These were cognition, effective communication, psychosocial influences, risk factors and legal aspects of capacity. The training was delivered by five professionals who were experienced in either undertaking complex capacity assessments or in auditing them and who had a keen interest in the work. Trainers were drawn from a range of backgrounds: social care, psychology, occupational therapy and speech and language therapy. All the trainers had been part of the project development group and had supported the implementation of the evaluation strategy.

The participants received a course workbook that included:

- Scenarios incorporating case law
- Anonymised capacity assessments to be audited by participants
- Copies of PowerPoint presentations
- Case studies to discuss
- Cognitive assessment tasks to be undertaken during the course to demonstrate what patients experience when being assessed
- A semi-structured interview (relating to discharge decisions)
- An MDT questionnaire.

The latter two resources were developed and published by a member of the training pool (Mackenzie, Lincoln and Newby, 2008) but could be used by participants in their everyday work.

Time was allocated for reflection, discussion and the identification of environmental barriers to good quality capacity assessments. (See www.assessingcapacity.com for an example lesson plan.)

How did we analyse the data?

Whilst the participant group was of an optimal size for this type of training, it was not a sample of sufficient size to conduct a statistical analysis. Instead, we analysed our quantitative data by combining results, comparing the differences between pre- and post-test results and identifying themes. Qualitative data was coded using thematic analysis, which was supported and supervised by a post-doctoral researcher in the Manchester Learning Disability Partnership.

Ethics

Our training plan, including intended measures and analysis strategy, was discussed with the MCC governance lead who provided guidance and support to ensure that our project complied with legal and ethical requirements. The final plan was reviewed and approved by each participating statutory agency and by the Adult Safeguarding Board in Manchester.

Results

Of the fourteen professionals who attended the training, nine provided a full set of pre- and post-training capacity assessments for audit (with an additional one set provided pre-training), eleven participated in the five-month post-training interviews and seven completed both the pre- and post-training online surveys.

Significant improvements in practice

Three participants had at least one of their pre-training assessments judged to be "inadequate" overall by the auditors; however, 100% of the assessments submitted after the training course were judged to be "adequate" overall. This shows that there was an improvement in the quality of the assessments following training.

Of the eighteen assessments submitted after the training, eleven were praised by auditors and/or inter-raters as being of a notably good standard in their comments. This contrasted with pre-training assessments, which either contained no comments or comments that focussed on constructive criticism. Conclusions of auditors corresponded closely with those inter-rating the assessments with 92% agreement. The lack of agreement on the other 8%, which constituted one out of 12 assessments, may have been due to poor documentation as the second rater noted that the assessment appeared to be adequate but that the documentation was not up to standard.

Approximately half of those who attended the course had utilised either the semi-structured interview and/or the MDT questionnaire that were presented on the course, possibly leading to a more structured approach to assessment. Two out of 18 assessments completed after the training concluded that the person *had* capacity, whereas none of the pre-training assessments had reached this conclusion. This could be linked to an increase in the quality of information provided during the assessment, which was noted by the auditors in the post-training assessments. Data from both questionnaires and semi-structured interviews indicated that every participant had used a broader range of techniques and skills to enhance capacity following the training.

Whilst learners who completed the survey listed fewer development needs and higher levels of confidence assessing capacity following the training, interviews suggested that learner confidence in other decision domains (for example, managing finances) was still low or reduced. This suggests that assessors like to be provided with ideas for questions to ask and the salient information that the person has to be aware of for specific decisions. This information can be found elsewhere in this book.

Feedback from MDT questionnaires reported significant improvement in some areas of colleagues' practice in relation to capacity. Possibly due to the more complex nature of stroke, as compared to dementia, the stroke MDT had reported a very negative experience of colleagues' practice prior to training. This ward showed the biggest improvements following completion of the training particularly in relation to consulting ward staff and in participant's knowledge of cognition and its potential impact on capacity. Other wards also reported improvements in communication and consultation as well as a perceived improved awareness of general concepts such as the "time specific" nature of capacity.

Participants reported experiencing a range of barriers to implementing new learning, including no access to supervision and significant time pressures. However, the reported general feeling was of increased confidence in their knowledge and skills, which had resulted in an increased willingness to try new techniques or to advocate for clients whenever possible.

> I think much more about the environment when I'm assessing capacity now –
> as well as allaying the person's fears by being honest about why I'm there.
>
> (Participant 5)

Analysing an anonymised assessment helped me to reflect on my work. I've tried to structure my assessments better since the training and include more evidence and less opinion.

(Participant 3)

The executive functioning bit was good, as were the tips on how to probe more when you get yes/no answers — it has all helped my assessments. It's clear that sometimes you just can't fully assess on the first interview.

(Participant 9)

Outcomes for the people being assessed

Participants described being able to provide people with a better experience, for example, with a better explanation of the purpose of the assessment or improved communication methods, which facilitated a more robust assessment.

Participants cited these developments in their practice as an explanation for improved outcomes. For example, five participants reported that they had decided that people had capacity more frequently (in two cases for the first time) following an assessment since completing the training. Others provided examples of good practice through joint work with families and professionals to enhance the quality and accuracy of assessments.

It is noteworthy that three participants reported improved outcomes at the "best interests" stage in instances where people had been deemed to lack capacity, even though this was not covered in the training.

[The training] made me think about best interests decisions as well — for example, how often the decision made carries the same or more restrictions than what was already happening. I have recently worked with someone with dementia who lacked capacity but wanted to stay in the community. I decided that, with support, this was in his best interests, partly because I'd taken more time in the capacity assessment to explore his views and opinions. I'm not sure I would have made the same decision if I hadn't had the training.

(Participant 9)

Positive evaluation of the training

All learners reported that the course had been of a high standard and most stated that it had met their development needs in this area or had improved their confidence in undertaking assessments.

I thought the training was excellent and really useful. I was lacking confidence and I feel that my confidence in completing assessments has really improved.

(Participant 4)

The course really helped unpick some of the complexities of assessing. The bit on psychosocial factors really helped with this. The whole course was concise and addressed my concerns. All the information was very practical and the shared contribution from trainers across different agencies made it for me.

(Participant 7)

Barriers to practice

Several barriers to practice were reported during a group exercise during the training. These included time pressures, organisational issues and a lack of clarity of professional roles. Different templates were being used across Manchester to record capacity assessments. Participants reported that these were often not fit for purpose being "laborious and repetitive" and "too wordy" with some lacking in free-text boxes. Appropriate and timely access to specialists when needed was reported as one of the biggest systemic barriers to completing effective assessments:

It can be so difficult in the community compared with hospital settings – it's hard to do a full assessment, partly because you can't get medical information to support the assessment. For example, I struggle to engage later-life psychiatrists and CPNs often don't want to get involved.

(Participant 7)

Operational processes between health and social care were also cited as a barrier. An ongoing priority to integrate services at a nationwide level might improve these issues but reported problems arising from different policies and procedures, separate budgets, competing agendas and limited access to client/patient notes is likely to be a significant challenge to overcome.

Discussion

The development and evaluation of a training course that provided professionals with a holistic approach to assessing capacity was an innovative and exciting advance in the thinking around capacity assessments in Manchester. Our results indicate that the training had been valuable, both in improving participant confidence and in producing better assessments, resulting in enhanced outcomes and experiences for clients. We were surprised and encouraged by some of the improvements demonstrated following the training. Examples included support provided to clients by participants negating the need for a formal assessment and the increase in conclusions that the client had capacity for the decision in question, as a result of a more in-depth assessment. These improvements, combined with the questionnaire data, show that both skills and confidence in assessment outcomes had risen. The differences in outcomes following the training were notable and our inclusion of qualitative methods provided us with valuable insights and feedback that indicated that the training was the main reason for the improvements.

Life beyond the pilot course: Successes and practice development

Following the completion of the training, we made several recommendations that led to significant change. One important example was the development and implementation of a citywide capacity template for Manchester, which was adopted by all relevant organisations. An updated audit tool was also developed (based on the BPS mental capacity audit tool (2010)) that has been successfully used within professional management and peer supervision to evaluate practice.

We continued to measure pre- and post-training levels of confidence, skills and knowledge through online surveys and evaluation sheets. Aggregation of data spanning 2014–2016 indicated that:

- 78% of participants experienced increased confidence following training (with no one reporting they were "not confident" after training).
- The number of people supporting decision-making on every assessment increased from 24% to 82%.

The type of support offered also appeared to change following training, with significantly more participants using, for instance, communication aids and environmental modifications (for example, seeing someone in a quiet room) to take account of cognitive concerns.

The course was described as "an essential part of professional development" by the Adult Safeguarding Board. Word of mouth endorsements from participants meant that demand for additional courses occurred quickly and there was a significant waiting list of professionals who wanted to access the training over the years that it was provided, having been made available to healthcare professions as well as Social Services.

Acknowledgements

Manchester City Council (MCC), Manchester Foundation Trust (MFT), Greater Manchester Mental Health Trust (GMMH) and Pennine Acute Hospitals NHS Trust (PAT) for supporting the pilot study.

Dr Melanie Chapman (MFT) for support and supervision regarding data analysis.

References

British Psychological Society (2010). *Audit Tool for Mental Capacity Assessments*. Professional Practice Board and Social Care Institute for Excellence. Leicester: British Psychological Society.

Mackenzie, J.A., Lincoln, N.B. and Newby, G.J. (2008). Capacity to make a decision about discharge destination after stroke: A pilot study. *Clinical Rehabilitation*, 22, 1116–1126.

Mental Capacity Act 2005. London: HMSO. Available at: www.legislation.gov.uk/ukpga/2005/9/contents

Appendices

Capacity to make a decision regarding admission to the Intermediate Neuro-Rehabilitation Unit for care and treatment

Threshold of understanding

Case study

Ibrahim has been admitted to the Intermediate Neuro-Rehabilitation Unit following a traumatic brain injury. As it is a locked ward and nursing staff are constantly around, the doctor needs to do an assessment of his capacity to make a decision about being admitted for care and treatment to see if a Liberty Protection Safeguards (LPS) application is required. She uses the following guidelines to help her structure her assessment.

What Ibrahim will need to understand in order to make an informed decision:

1   Ibrahim needs to understand:

   a)   Roughly where he is (for example, "in hospital" – he does not need to know the name)

   b)   Why he is in hospital (for example, "help to get back to normal and to learn to do things for myself again")
         This addresses why the decision needs to be made.
         It does not matter if he is unsure of the cause of his problems.

2   Ibrahim needs to understand:

   a)   What the proposed care and treatment will be in general terms (for example, hoist transfers, assistance with washing and dressing, physio sessions)

   b)   Why he needs this care and treatment (for example, "because I can't walk")

c)   The good things/benefits of this care and treatment (for exam-ple, "I will get the care I need; physio will hopefully help me get back on my feet and I will be safe in hospital")

d)   Potential downsides and general risks of this care and treat-ment (for example, "I won't be at home with my family, there's not much to do between sessions, I have to share a room with other people and the food is horrible so my mood might not be very good")

e)   The good things/benefits if he did not receive this care and treatment and left hospital (for example, "I'd be in my own house with my family so I could do what I liked and not have people watching me all of the time")

f)   The potential downsides and general risks if he did not receive this care and treatment and left hospital (for example, "I wouldn't be able to wash or dress myself and couldn't get out of bed without help. If I had a fall, then I might end up back in hospital. I wouldn't get as much physio so I might not get better as quickly.")

g)   His care needs on discharge and how these realistically would be met if he wants to leave hospital (for example, not saying that his family will do it all when they all work full-time).

3   Ibrahim needs to understand:

a)   The restrictions that are inherent in the environment (for example, locked doors, nursing staff keeping a note of where he is)

b)   The restrictions that he might be subject to personally due to the care and treatment provided (for example, 1:1 supervision when eating, accompanied visits off the ward)

c)   The positive and negative consequences of the restrictions (for example, "I know that the restrictions are to keep me safe but I'm not being allowed off the ward by myself and someone is always there when I'm eating").

Remembering the relevant information:

•   Ongoing decisions such as admission for care and treatment require the person to be able to retain the relevant information over time, not just in the short assessment period, so that he can use the information in the next week or month.

- This requires carryover between assessment sessions (it is always better to do more than one assessment session for this reason and for others, such as slow processing speed, unless it is obvious that the person does or does not have the capacity to make the decision).
- For example, if Ibrahim needs to stay in hospital for treatment and rehabilitation, and he would be at risk if he self-discharged, then he needs to be able to remember this for the whole of the admission and not just for 10 minutes with prompting during the assessment.

Dr Janice Mackenzie, Consultant Clinical Neuropsychologist
With thanks to David Fowler (Independent Social Worker
and Best Interests Assessor for DoLS) and Emma Fowler
(Specialist Safeguarding Trainer and Trainee Clinical Psychologist)

A list of possible strategies to try to overcome common cognitive difficulties and other factors that can negatively impact capacity

Memory

- Write down information for the person and encourage her to do the same.
- Use pictures and photos to help engage visual memory.
- Use repetition to help the person learn.
- Help the person learn her strengths and weaknesses in functional tasks, which might be remembered more clearly than a discussion.
- Do work to help retrograde amnesia (e.g., use photo albums, stories from family and friends, emails, diaries).
- Encourage the use of aids for prospective memory (e.g., reminders on phone, diary, calendar, notice board).

Attention

- Reduce distractions in the environment by turning off the TV and removing pets.
- Simplify and chunk information.
- Use visual and verbal information.
- Allow the person to make notes.
- Ask short questions.
- Only ask one question at a time.
- If there is more than one assessor, choose one to ask the questions and the other can ask supplementary questions at the end (rather than swapping between assessors).
- Have short sessions.
- Have breaks during the assessment.

Executive functioning

- Practice problem-solving and planning strategies on functional tasks.
- Visit familiar environments to reduce the abstract nature of the information given.
- Use decision trees to help the person follow through choices to their consequences.

- Use multiple-choice answers or lists for the person to pick from.
- Help to provide lists of pros and cons for the person to consider and weigh up.
- Ask another question or clarify what the person has just said if he is repeating (perseverating on) an answer.
- Check any facts that the person tells you after the session and have another session to clarify things afterwards if you think he may be confabulating.
- Encourage him to stop and think before answering questions if he is showing signs of disinhibition.
- Give gentle feedback when something is inappropriate.
- Allow him to rethink his answers and think around the subject, including consequences, if answers are given impulsively.
- Start an answer for someone who has trouble with initiation (e.g., "What are you having difficulties with at the moment?" (no answer) "You are having difficulties with . . .").
- Ask closed questions if someone has problems with initiation but remember to reverse them (see Chapter 11).
- Gently bring someone back to the point if he goes off on a tangent by repeating the question or repeating what he was saying (e.g., "So you were saying that you were having difficulties with showering. Is there anything else you have difficulties with?").
- Allow some storytelling to build rapport but also keep in mind your time limits and the strain repeated assessment sessions may have on the person if you are unable to keep him on task.

Speed of information processing

- Speak more slowly.
- Allow time for the person to process and answer questions.
- Allow the person to ask questions.
- Do repeated assessments.

Orientation

- Use an orientation board or clock with the date on it and bring her attention to it every day or several times a day if the person has a condition that may improve.
- Do a timeline or information booklet about her life with photos in it and go through this with her.

Insight/denial

- Allow "supported failure" on functional tasks.
- Give feedback on functional tasks.

- Encourage self-monitoring on functional tasks.
- Prompt the person to change her behaviour when she has noticed something going wrong.
- Help her think through the possible options for her behaviour and their consequences.
- Ask her to rate how she thinks she will manage a task before the task and then evaluate her performance after the task and discuss any difference in scores.
- Provide reminders of previous difficulties and how she overcame them, or the help required to do so, during the capacity assessment.
- Use evidence to gently challenge the person's view (e.g., showing someone the CT scan of her brain if she claims that she has not had a brain injury).
- Ask the person and someone who knows her well to rate her behaviour and abilities and discuss any differences and why these may have arisen.
- Arrange, or do, therapy for issues around self-esteem and self-image to make these concepts more flexible for the person and possibly reduce levels of denial.

Effort

- Discuss the reasons for the assessment and the possible outcomes.
- Ask the person what he is worried about and try to reassure him, if possible.
- Help him think about the pros and cons of doing the assessment and putting across his point of view versus not doing it.
- Try to reduce pain or fatigue if possible or see him on a "good day" if not.

Appendix 3

List of potential activities someone needs support with

An example of a written list of potential activities a person needs support with, presented to the person with significant cognitive and physical difficulties as part of the capacity assessment. The decision was whether or not to accept formal support from social care. The items in italics are distractor items (things the person does not need help with). Note: they were not in italics in the list presented to the person, rather this is to highlight them to the reader.

Put a tick (✓) next to the things that you think you need help with

- Managing money
- Taking a shower
- *Painting*
- Tidying the house
- Preparing meals
- *Getting dressed*
- Vacuuming
- *Making snacks*
- Remembering your appointments
- Remembering to eat regularly
- *Washing clothes*
- Catching the bus
- Helping you take your children out of the house for trips
- *Making hot drinks*
- Helping you organise things better
- *Looking after your pets*
- Reminding you to re-order prescriptions for your supplement drinks
- Responding to letters that arrive in the post
- *Going to the pub with your mates*
- Fixing things in the house
- Getting to hospital appointments

Semi-structured interview regarding capacity to make a decision about swallowing

Mary Salmon, Speech and Language Therapist

The questions have been divided into broad categories in relation to the decision-making process. The MCA Code of Practice (2007) stipulates that even if a patient fails the "understanding" aspect, the functional assessment of capacity should still be completed in full to consider **all** the aspects of the patient's decision-making abilities (understand, retain, use and weigh and communicate) and this will also inform the best interests decision. Not all questions need to be asked; it should be used as a guide as the assessor feels appropriate. The assessor should ensure that relevant information has been provided before they ask questions about it (e.g., that the person has already been told what aspiration means (even if that is by another professional).)

This section considers a patient's **understanding** *of their swallowing needs and it can also be used to check their ability to* **retain** *information regarding their swallow.*

What do you know about your swallow?
Are you eating and drinking at the moment?
Do you have any thickener in your drinks/modified diet?
Do you know why that is?
Do you know what has caused your swallowing difficulty?
Have you had any chest infections recently? (If so, how did they make you feel?)
Have you choked at all whilst eating? (If so, what happened? How did you clear it?)
Does eating and drinking make you cough? (If so, how often?)
Do you know what aspiration is?
What can aspiration lead to?
What can a chest infection lead to?
What are the symptoms of a chest infection/pneumonia?
What could a chest infection/pneumonia lead to? (Could you survive it? Could it kill you? Could it make you feel better or worse?)
What are the signs of aspiration that we look for when you're eating or drinking?
Does coughing whilst eating/drinking mean anything?

*This section considers a patient's ability to **use and weigh up** the information about their swallow to support their decision-making.*

>   What are the *benefits* of eating or drinking?
>   What are the *risks* of eating or drinking?
>   Do you believe that you are at risk? (How likely do you think it is?)
>   Do those benefits outweigh the risk of developing a chest infection and/or pneumonia?
>   Do you believe that you are at risk of developing a chest infection and/or pneumonia if you have normal food and fluids? (i.e., how likely do you think it is?)
>   Given your current physical health, how do you think a chest infection would affect you at the moment?
>   Suppose you start eating and drinking again and it gave you a chest infection? Would that affect your decision about eating/drinking?
>   If you got a chest infection which meant that you would need to stay in hospital for longer, would that affect your decision?
>   How about if you went home, got a chest infection from eating and drinking and had to be readmitted to hospital. Would that affect your decision?

This section requires us to identify the patient's decision in this case. If you deem the person to lack capacity overall, the information obtained here will be a useful indicator of the patient's views at the best interests stage.

Given everything you know about your swallow, what is your decision about what diet/fluids you intend to have?

Risks of eating/drinking _____	Benefits of eating/drinking _____

Reference

Department for Constitutional Affairs (2007). *Mental Capacity Act 2005: Code of Practice*. London: The Stationery Office. Available at: https://assets.publishing.service.gov.uk/government/uploads/system/uploads/attachment_data/file/497253/Mental-capacity-act-code-of-practice.pdf

Appendix 5

Semi-structured interview to assess capacity for managing financial affairs/property[1]

Assessment of Capacity to Manage own Financial Affairs/Property: a semi-structured interview
(Developed by Dr Janice Mackenzie, Consultant Clinical Neuropsychologist, and Dr June Robson, Consultant Clinical Neuropsychologist)

Name: _____ **Date:** _____ **Time:** _____

Informant..................... **Relationship to client ....**

Specific question relating to finances (e.g., benefits, sale of house etc.): ....

From Informant, nature and extent of this person's finance/property:

Outgoings (amounts)	Income (amounts)	
House/flat:	Employment/sick pay:	
Loans/debts (inc. credit cards):	End date of sick pay:	
Bill payment method:	Pensions: state	private
Other outgoings:	Benefits:	
Telephone	Other income:	
Gas	Current account own:	
Electricity	Current account joint:	
Water	Savings/ISA (joint?):	
Council tax	Insurance policies:	
Insurance	Shares/Premium bonds:	
Shopping	Any changes in circumstance:	
Other (what?)	Financial dependents:	
	Other business matters or	
	legal transactions:	

Did the person have problems managing his/her financial affairs before the brain injury?

What support does the person receive managing his/her financial affairs now?

Reasons informants believe the person to be able/not able to manage his/her financial affairs at this point in time (including practical evidence, e.g., bank statements, gambling debts, etc.):

1

2

3

4

If necessary, check:

1   Note recognition £5   £10   £20
2   Coin recognition: 1p   2p   5p   10p   20p   50p   £1
3   Adding: "How much is there?" (looking at coins presented)
4   Subtraction:

    a   If you had £1 and spent 75p, how much would you have left?
    b   If you had £5 and spent £2.40, how much would you have left?

5   Understanding of a utility bill:

    a   What period does the bill cover?
    b   How much do you owe?
    c   When do you have to pay by?
    d   How much have you already paid/did you pay last time?
    e   Has VAT been added to the bill? If so, how much?
    f   How much gas/electricity/water have you used during this period?
    g   How can you pay your bill? (all methods)
    h   How would you ask a question about the bill?

6   Understanding of a bank account/cheque book/debit card/credit card:

    a   Do you have one?
    b   What is it used for?
    c   Can you explain your bank/credit card statement to me?
    d   What are the pros and cons (including risks) of having one?

Interview

(As this interview is semi-structured, the following questions are provided to give an impression of an assessment of capacity to manage finances and may be used as a guide for each individual capacity assessment. The wording and order may change according to the level of comprehension and verbal output the person is capable of, the specific problems the person has, the question to be answered and the flow of the interview. The person does not need to answer all of these questions correctly to have capacity to make this decision – think about the salient points of the relevant information and use your clinical judgment to come to a conclusion.)

1 How long have you had difficulties due to (stroke, head injury, brain condition)?

2 Where do you live at present?

3 How do you manage day-to-day now? What happens on an ordinary day?

4 Have you noticed <u>any</u> changes in yourself since your stroke / head injury / brain condition?

5 Have you noticed any <u>physical</u> changes in yourself since your stroke / head injury / brain condition? (prompts: legs, walking, arms, vision)

6 Have you noticed any changes in your <u>memory/attention/word-finding/ planning abilities</u> since your stroke / head injury / brain condition?

7 Have you noticed any changes in your <u>mood/worrying</u> since your stroke / head injury/brain condition?

8 Question further on any difficulties not reported by the person that were reported by health professionals or informant and if he/she requires help from others at the moment due to them. (Including questions to assess whether or not the person <u>believes</u> that he/she has these problems.)

9 Do you think that your (cognitive problems/other issues) would affect your ability to look after your own money? Why/why not?

10 Do you think you need help at present managing any aspect of your finances? Why/why not?

11 What happens at present about managing your money and paying your bills? (What sort of help do you get and from whom?)

12 How did you manage your money before your stroke /head injury/brain condition? Did you receive help?

13 Did you ever get into financial problems before your stroke /head injury/ brain condition? (What happened? OR How did you manage not to?)

14 Where do you get your money from each month and how much is it (sources of income/which benefits are you on)?

15 Where do you keep your money (home, bank accounts – any joint accounts)? How much do you have in each?

16 What bills do you have each month and how much are they roughly?

17 What other things do you spend money on in a month (outgoings)?

18 What major purchases have you made recently? Are you planning on making any major purchases in the near future?

19 If you are short of money one week/month, how do you decide what to spend the money on? Do these choices affect anyone else?

20 What would you do if you overspent your budget one week/month? What would happen if you did this every month?

21 Do you think you currently:

    i   Own your own home? Alone or jointly? How much is it worth at the moment?

    ii   Have a mortgage/Pay rent?

    iii   Have enough money coming in to live on?

    iv   Have any debts (including overdraft or credit cards)? If so, what is your plan to manage them?

    v   Have any savings/investments – if so, what?

    vi   Have any people who depend on you? Do they have their own income?

22 Just so I have an idea if you know roughly how much things cost now:

About how much does a pint of milk cost?
A loaf of bread?
A pint of beer in a pub?
A litre of petrol? (or bus ticket to town, if not a driver)
An average house in the area you live?
(Add other items relevant to the person, e.g., 20 cigarettes, haircut, a coat etc)

23 What would you do if you wanted something (e.g., a holiday) but did not have enough money for it?

24 If someone gave you a hundred pounds to spend on yourself, what might you do with it? (Prompt the person to account for the full £100 if necessary.) Why would you choose to do this?

25   What do you usually do when a bill arrives?

26   What might you do if a bill arrived that you couldn't pay (including nursing home fees)? What would happen if you couldn't pay the bill?

27   Have your family or friends ever asked you for money or advised you on how to spend your money?

28   What would you do if someone asked you for a large amount of money? (Different scenarios e.g., partner, children, friend, neighbour, acquaintance, someone who came to your door talking about an investment scheme?) Why?

29   When might you need to seek help with your finances? Who would you ask and why? (Or what advice was given and what do you think of it – pros and cons?)

30   What choice must be made? What are the options?

31   What are the positive/good things *and* negative/bad things/problems/risks of having someone else (family member/friend/professional) manage your money instead of you doing it yourself?

	Pros	Cons
Option 1: Manage your own money		
Option 2:		
Option 3:		

32   What would you choose to do? Why? Would this affect anyone else?

33   If we were to decide that you couldn't manage your own money at present, because of (problems reported by informants), would you believe us? Why/ why not?

Decision

Can the person:

1	Understand the relevant information in relation to his/her own circumstances?	YES/NO
2	Retain the relevant information?	YES/NO
3	Use and weigh up the relevant information to arrive at an informed choice?	YES/NO
4	Communicate that choice?	YES/NO

Does the person have the capacity to make a decision about managing financial affairs in relation to (specific question) . . . . at this point in time?

YES/NO

Signed:

Designation:

Note

1   Adapted from semi-structured interview published in: JA Mackenzie, NB Lincoln & GJ Newby. Capacity to make a decision about discharge destination after stroke: a pilot study. *Clin Rehabil* 2008 22: 1116–1126.

Semi-structured interview to assess capacity for making or revoking a Lasting Power of Attorney[1]

Assessment of Capacity to Make or Revoke a Lasting Power of Attorney (Property and Affairs) – a semi-structured interview

(Developed by Dr Janice Mackenzie, Consultant Clinical Neuropsychologist, and Dr June Robson, Consultant Clinical Neuropsychologist)

Name: _____ **Date:** _____ **Time:** _____

Informant .... **Relationship to client** ....

From Informant, nature and extent of this person's finances/property:

Outgoings (amounts)
House/flat:
Loans/debts (inc. credit cards):
Bill payment method:
Other outgoings:
  Telephone
  Gas
  Electricity
  Water
  Council tax
  Insurance
  Shopping
  Other (what?)

Income (amounts)
Employment/sick pay:
End date of sick pay:
Pensions: state   private
Benefits:
Other income:
Current account own:
Current account joint:
Savings/ISA (joint?):
Insurance policies:
Shares/Premium bonds:
Any changes in circumstance:
Financial dependents:
Other business matters or
          legal transactions:

Information from informants regarding person's ability to make or revoke an LPA:

1

2

3

4

Interview – Questions in addition to assessment to manage financial affairs specific to LPA

(As this interview is semi-structured, the following questions are provided to give an impression of an assessment of capacity to make or revoke an LPA and will be used as a guide for each individual capacity assessment. The wording and order may change according to the level of comprehension and verbal output the person is capable of, the specific problems the person has and the flow of the interview. The person does not need to answer all of these questions correctly to have capacity to make this decision – think about the salient points of the relevant information and use your clinical judgment to come to a conclusion.)

1   Who is looking after your money now? Why?

2   Are you happy with that situation?

3   (If inpatient) Who will look after your money on discharge? Why?

4   Do you want to look after your own money? Why?

5   Do you know what a Lasting Power of Attorney (LPA) is? Are there different types?

6   Have you been given any advice about making/revoking an LPA? Who by?

7 Why do you want to make/revoke an LPA?

8 What will happen if you have an LPA? What powers does it give to the attorney? When can they use the powers? (e.g., immediately; if you don't want to look after your money anymore; if you lose the ability to look after your money?)

9 Are you going to add any restrictions to what the attorney can do? If so, why?

10 In what sort of situation would you want to revoke/cancel an LPA?

11 What would you do if you found out that your attorney was spending your money on themselves?

12 What would you do if you changed your mind about who you wanted as an attorney?

13 How would you go about revoking/cancelling an LPA?

14 Do you have access to your own solicitor?

15 If you do make an LPA, how would you like your money/finances to be looked after in the future?

16 If we were to decide that you couldn't make or revoke an LPA at present, because of (problems reported by informants), would you believe us?

17 What are the positive/good things *and* negative/bad things/problems/risks of having someone else (family member/friend/professional) manage your money instead of you doing it yourself?

	Pros	Cons
Option 1: Manage money yourself		
Option 2: Family member or friend manages money		
Option 3: Professional (solicitor or specialised company) manages money		

18   Who would you like to be your attorney(s)? Why? Would this affect anyone else?

19   Is there any reason to think that they could be untrustworthy?

20   Is there any reason that the LPA should not be created?

21   Are you aware that the LPA has to be registered with the Office of the Public Guardian before it can be used?

Decision

Can the person:

1   Understand the relevant information in relation to his/her own
    circumstances?   YES/NO
2   Retain the relevant information?   YES/NO
3   Use and weigh up the relevant information to arrive at an informed
    choice?   YES/NO
4   Communicate that choice?   YES/NO

Does the person have the capacity to make a decision about making or revoking an LPA at this point in time?

YES/NO

Signed:
Designation:

Additional questions if an assessment of capacity to manage finances is not being carried out at the same time

1   What finances would need to be managed by your attorney (who holds the LPA)?

2   Do you think you currently:

   (i)   Own your own home? Alone or jointly? How much is it worth at the moment?

   (ii)   Have a mortgage/Pay rent?

   (iii) Have enough money coming in to live on?

   (iv)   Have any debts (including overdraft or credit cards)? If so, what?

   (v)   Have any savings/investments? If so, what?

   (vi)   Have any people who depend on you? Do they have their own income?

3   Where do you get your money from each month and how much is it (sources of income/which benefits are you on)?

4   Where do you keep your money (home, bank accounts – any joint accounts)? How much do you have in each?

5   What bills do you have each month and how much are they roughly?

6   What other things do you spend money on in a month (outgoings)?

7   If you had a bill to pay from your account today, how would you manage it?

Note

1 Adapted from semi-structured interview published in: JA Mackenzie, NB Lincoln & GJ Newby. Capacity to make a decision about discharge destination after stroke: a pilot study. *Clin Rehabil* 2008 22: 1116–1126.

An example threshold of understanding for drinking alcohol after a brain injury or alcohol-related brain damage

- These ideas can be used as part of a comprehensive capacity assessment in this area and should not be used in isolation.
- In addition, they should be expanded or contracted according to the person's situation, as not all aspects will be relevant to everyone, but it is also very difficult to cover all of the possible areas that might be relevant to an individual here.

The information that is relevant to the assessment of whether a person has the capacity to drink alcohol following a brain injury or alcohol-related brain damage is whether the person can understand:

- Some of the potential risks of drinking alcohol. For example:
  - Possible impairments in judgment (e.g., increased impulsivity and risk-taking behaviours)
  - Increased vulnerability (e.g., losing bank card, being mugged)
  - Possible problems with physical coordination which could increase the risk of falling and other injuries
  - Increased risk of health problems (e.g., liver disease, high blood pressure, heart disease, cancer, diabetes)
  - Possible negative interactions with prescribed medications – reducing the effect of some (e.g., anti-epileptic and anti-depressant medication) and increasing the effect of others which can be fatal (e.g., anti-anxiety and pain medication)
  - Increased risk of damage to relationships and how his/her choice affects other people
  - Negative effect on finances
  - Possible impact on levels of depression and anxiety

- His/her problem controlling alcohol intake and others' views on this (if appropriate)
- Ways to stop drinking (e.g., not going to the pub and not having alcohol in the house) or ways to reduce the harm when doing so (e.g., eating beforehand and interspersing a soft drink with an alcoholic one)
- That he/she has experienced a brain injury or alcohol-related brain damage (ARBD) and has some problems with his/her memory/thinking skills as a result
- That his/her health and/or memory could improve if he/she stops drinking
- Some aspects of the difference in continuing to drink alcohol following a brain injury or ARBD. For example:
  - Reduced tolerance to alcohol due to the brain injury and, therefore, the effects may be felt more quickly
  - Worsening of cognitive problems (e.g., memory and flexible thinking) short-term when drinking alcohol and the possibility of permanent long-term problems with cognition
  - Impairing recovery of the brain from the initial injury (if relevant)
  - Increased risk of further brain injury/damage and, therefore, increased impairments
  - Reduced seizure threshold (making it more likely that he/she will have a seizure)

- The benefits and risks/problems of continuing to drink alcohol versus limiting his/her intake versus abstinence.

Semi-structured interview for assessing capacity to drink alcohol after a brain injury or alcohol-related brain damage[1]

Assessment of capacity to make a decision about drinking alcohol after a brain injury or alcohol-related brain damage – a semi-structured interview
(Developed by Dr Janice Mackenzie, Consultant Clinical Neuropsychologist)

Name: _____ Date: _____ Time: _____

Reasons believed to be at risk when drinking alcohol after a brain injury or alcohol-related brain damage (ARBD) (from family, friends and professionals):

1

2

3

4

5

Interview

(These questions can be used as a guide for each individual capacity assessment. The wording and order may be changed according to the level of comprehension and verbal output the person is capable of, the specific problems the person has and the flow of the interview. The person does not need to answer all the questions correctly to have capacity to make this decision – think about the salient points of the relevant information and use your clinical judgment to come to a conclusion.)

1 How long have you been in hospital now?

2 Do you know why you are in hospital?

3 (If relevant) Did you. . . (reason for brain injury, e.g., have a fall/stroke/get assaulted)?

4 Had you been drinking at the time?
(Provide the information if necessary and note reaction)

5 (If relevant) Have you had a brain injury due to the (fall/assault)?
(Provide the information if necessary and note reaction)

6 Have you noticed any difficulties since your brain injury/since you have been in hospital? (e.g., walking/balance, washing/dressing, vision, memory, thinking skills, mood, anxiety?)

7 Have you had any other injuries in the past when you have been drinking?
(Provide the information if necessary and note reaction)

8 Have you had any other problems due to alcohol in the past? (e.g., losing things, problems with your relationships, being mugged, running out of money for food and rent etc.)

9 (Before you came into hospital) How much alcohol did you drink in a day (or week?)

10 (Before you came into hospital) Did you drink every day?

11 What do you like to drink?

12 Do you drink at home or in a pub? Do you meet friends when you are drinking?

13   Would you say that you have a problem with alcohol?

14   (If no. . .) Have you ever had a problem with alcohol?

15   Are you able to control your alcohol intake?

16   Have you ever been told by your family, a friend or a doctor to cut down your alcohol intake? If so, why?

17   Does drinking alcohol affect your health?

18   Does alcohol affect your ability to make safe decisions?

19   Do you feel low in mood or anxious when you are drinking or when you stop drinking?

20   How do you think alcohol will affect you now? Is that different to before your brain injury/stroke/illness?

21   (If relevant) Could you have a seizure if you drink alcohol after your brain injury?

22   Will alcohol affect the way your medications (give examples) work?

23   (If relevant) Could your memory/thinking skills get worse if you continue to drink alcohol?

24   (If relevant) Could your health/memory improve if you stop drinking alcohol?

25   When you leave hospital, will you still want to drink alcohol?

26   (If no. . .) Have you got any strategies to help you not to drink alcohol?

27   Do you think there would be any problems if you did start to drink alcohol again?

28   How would you know if it was becoming a problem? What would you do then?

29   Do you have any help, support or strategies that would keep you safer if you are drinking?

30   If the staff here said that they thought that you would be at risk of. . . (reasons provided by family/friends/professionals, e.g., further injuries/problems with your mental/physical health) if you returned to drinking when you get out of hospital, would you believe them? If not, why not?

31   What are the positive/good things *and* negative/not so good things/risks/ problems of drinking alcohol (unlimited or reduced amount) vs not drinking alcohol for you?

	Pros	Cons
Option 1: Drinking alcohol to the same level as before		
Option 2: Drinking a reduced amount of alcohol & limiting your intake		
Option 3: Drinking no alcohol		

32   What would you choose to do? Why? Would this affect anyone else? What do your family/friends think of your decision?

Decision

Can the person:

1	Understand the relevant information in relation to his/her own circumstances?	YES/NO
2	Retain the relevant information?	YES/NO
3	Use and weigh up the relevant information to arrive at an informed choice?	YES/NO
4	Communicate that choice?	YES/NO

Does the person have the capacity to make a decision about drinking alcohol at this point in time?   YES/NO

Signed:
Designation:

Note

1 Adapted from semi-structured interview published in: JA Mackenzie, NB Lincoln & GJ Newby. Capacity to make a decision about discharge destination after stroke: a pilot study. *Clin Rehabil* 2008 22: 1116–1126

Recording best interests

A balance sheet example

Best interests balance sheet

Person's name: Freda Smith

Key to weighting: normal typeface – equal weight, *italics* – less than equal weight, **bold** – significant weight.

Key to likelihood of risk occurring: *Rare* – the risk is not expected to occur; *Unlikely* – the risk is unlikely to occur; *Possible* – the risk may occur occasionally; *Likely* – it is likely that the risk will occur; *Certain* – the risk is almost certain to occur

Option 1: For Freda to stay living in her current home – a supported tenancy with 2 other people supported by social care staff – and to receive the same level of support. Freda has lived here with the same provider and co-tenants for 10 years.	
Benefits	Problems/risks
Freda has a positive relationship with her current co-tenants (e.g., she seeks them out to spend time with them).	**Freda's current staff team is struggling to recognise when her mental health is deteriorating and follow the relapse prevention plan.**
Freda has positive relationships with her current staff team (e.g., she seeks staff out to spend time with them).	**Freda's current staff team is struggling to help her manage her diabetes through diet and medication and are contacting her GP practice almost every week.**
Freda can travel easily by bus to see her family with minimal staff support (i.e., to and from the bus stop, assistance to identify the correct bus).	Freda's staff team is struggling to give consistent messages about Freda's diabetes and mental illness to her.

Freda has most of her favourite places and activities nearby (e.g., a fish and chip shop, a park, her college).	**Freda has had 2 hospital admissions in the last 2 months with conditions relating to poorly managed diabetes.**
Freda chose her own single room and has decorated it to her liking.	**Freda is obese and has not lost weight in her current home – she is on a weight loss diet.**
Freda has access without restrictions to her kitchen.	**Freda is unhappy about her weight gain (e.g., telling staff she is fat and ugly).**
Freda has access to her own garden and she likes to potter there (e.g., weeding, planting).	**Freda's staff team and co-tenants struggle to relate to her when her mental health deteriorates.**
Freda prefers to spend time in small groups and often takes herself away from larger groups of people (e.g., at parties).	
Freda knows her local area and her neighbours and goes to her local shop and post office without staff support.	
Freda gets on with her current health staff (e.g., GP and practice nurse).	
This is the least restrictive option.	

Option 2: For Freda to move to another home – a residential home with 4 other people with a learning disability and a nurse on shift during the day.

Benefits	Problems/risks
Freda's mental health will be more closely monitored by the learning disability nurse and strategies to help her stay well implemented more speedily. Likelihood: likely to certain.	**Freda will miss her friends. Likelihood: likely to certain.**
	Freda will miss her current staff team. Likelihood: likely to certain.
Freda's diabetes will be better managed with less reliance on the GP practice. Likelihood: likely to certain.	*Freda will be in an unfamiliar neighbourhood. She will need staff support initially to access local facilities. Likelihood: certain.*
	Freda will be geographically further from her family. Likelihood: certain.

Freda will lose weight and have a BMI in the healthy range. Likelihood: likely to certain.	Freda will have less local facilities as the new property is in the middle of an estate. Likelihood: certain.
Freda will have more consistent health education around her mental health and her diabetes. Likelihood: certain.	Freda will be living with more people and may want to spend more time on her own. Likelihood: likely to certain.
	Due to restrictions in place for other people Freda will have access to the kitchen via a fob. Likelihood: certain.
	Due to restrictions in place for other people Freda will only have access to a paved garden. Likelihood: certain.
	Freda will have a new GP practice, CLDT, dentist, Psychiatrist. Likelihood: certain.
	If Freda is admitted she will go to a new hospital. Likelihood: certain.
	This is the most restrictive option. Likelihood: certain

Option 3: Freda stays in her current home with intensive support for her and her staff from the local CLDT, her practice nurse and dietetic service focusing on health education. Her staff team's managers will be involved in all training sessions. Adult social care will fund step up and step down staffing whilst a Personal Health Budget is applied for.

Benefits	Problems/risks
Freda maintains her relationships with her co-tenants. Likelihood: certain.	Freda's staff team may change (e.g., through ill health, resignation, burn out). Likelihood: likely to certain.
Freda maintains her relationship with current staff. Likelihood: likely.	Freda's staff's manager may change reducing the impact of the input. Likelihood: likely.
Freda remains in a familiar area in a home she loves. Likelihood: certain.	Freda may not engage in the intensive support. Likelihood: possible to unlikely.
Freda retains her current GP Practice, CLDT, dentist, Psychiatrist. Likelihood: certain.	**Extra support for Freda and her staff will be time limited. Likelihood: certain.**

Freda would be admitted to a familiar hospital. Likelihood: certain. **Freda will lose weight. Likelihood: likely.** Freda will receive consistent health education about her health problems. Likelihood: certain. **Freda's diabetes will be better managed. Likelihood: likely.** **Freda's "staying well" plan will be better implemented. Likelihood: likely.** **Freda will get extra support requested before she reaches crisis. Likelihood: likely.** **This is Freda's preferred option. Likelihood: certain**	**Her additional social care funding may be cut when she is well for any period of time if she does not get a PHB. Likelihood: likely.** It will be difficult to coordinate input from services with differing criteria for access and waiting times. Likelihood: likely to certain.

Example of a best interests meeting agenda

Intermediate Neuro-Rehabilitation Unit best interests meeting agenda

(Adapted from the British Psychological Society, 2008)

1 **Before the meeting**

- Decide on the most appropriate decision-maker (see guidance, e.g., social worker for discharge decisions, unless patient is awarded CHC funding; doctors for medical decisions) – ensure you identify any existing Advance Decision to Refuse Treatment (ADRT), Attorney or Court Deputy.
- Is the person eligible for an IMCA? (see guidance)
- Ensure each aspect of the best interests checklist is followed.
- Consider having the person in the meeting – could he/she cope with it cognitively? Would a summary at the end be more appropriate?
- Make sure everyone who has an interest in the person's care is invited.
- Consider any written statement of wishes.
- Decide on the options available.
- Advise the family about capacity assessment outcomes and the reason for the meeting. If the person's capacity is contested, then the meeting cannot go ahead.
- Before meeting, decide who is chairing (usually not the decision-maker) and who is taking minutes/filling in the paperwork (type minutes onto the laptop).
- Liaise with the decision-maker to discuss who will chair the meeting.

2 **Introductions**

- Ground rules, e.g., everyone will be allowed to state their opinion, discussions will be kept polite, turn mobile phones off (except doctors who need to have them switched on).

- Remind those present that the aim is to establish the best interests of the person (dependent on funding) – NOT what attendees think the person would have wanted (this is a consideration but not the deciding factor) or what they themselves would want. "We have to make the decision, but we welcome your views and we'll take into consideration (the person's) past and present wishes."
- Avoid asking attendees their views on the decision that should be made at this point in the meeting.
- "You're welcome to take notes, but we will be taking minutes of the meeting, which you will get a copy of, and so you don't need to if you don't want to. We would appreciate it if you don't record the meeting in any other way."

3   Purpose of the meeting

- Outline the nature of the decision that needs to be made – decision-specific.
- "We have assessed (the person's) capacity to make this decision and found that he/she doesn't have it at this point in time."

4   Giving information
Attendees should share information at this point about:

- The person's past or present wishes, views, beliefs or values
- The options available to the person (ensure you are confident that the same options would be made available to anyone who had capacity to avoid discrimination) – clarify that some of these options may be dependent on funding and that all have to be considered, even if it appears that some are not the best choice or not the person's choice

5   Discussion
Pull together all the information available about the benefits and risks posed to the person in relation to EACH option available – use the balance sheet – pros and cons

- Consider using a flipchart or whiteboard on the wall to set out the pros and cons so that everyone can see them clearly.
- Encourage everyone to participate and don't allow one person to dominate with their views.
- Some attendees may feel that it is their role to persuade other attendees which may limit their ability to listen to, and use, information presented. In these cases, remind attendees that the aim is to make a decision based on evidence and discussion – not solely on previously held views.
- Weight the pros and cons individually, e.g., use stars to indicate the importance of different points – it is not just about the number of points on each side of the balance sheet.
- Add "least restrictive" to the pros of one option and "most restrictive" to the cons of another option.

6   Summary and conclusion

- Summarise the information gathered and the discussion.
- Ask each attendee their opinion about what is in the person's best interests.
- Make the decision (remember that leaving things as they are is also a decision).
- Decide if you wish to review the decision at a later date, e.g., after a funding decision.

Final notes for chair:

- Consider attaching the balance sheet or minutes to your final best interests documentation.
- Send minutes round to each attendee.
- Failure to agree: If there is a disagreement consider the options outlined in the MCA Code of Practice (2007):

  - Involve an advocate.
  - Get a second opinion or attempt some form of mediation.
  - Pursue a complaint through the organisation's formal procedures.
  - Inform the Safeguarding Matron, who may involve legal services.

- Decision-maker to fill in the City-wide Best Interests paperwork, but minute-taker can offer to do so since he/she has the electronic version of the minutes.
- Each decision requires a separate best interests document.

References

Department for Constitutional Affairs (2007). *Mental Capacity Act 2005: Code of Practice.* London: The Stationery Office. Available at: https://assets.publishing.service.gov.uk/government/uploads/system/uploads/attachment_data/file/497253/Mental-capacity-act-code-of-practice.pdf

Joyce, T. (2008). *Best Interests: Guidance on Determining the Best Interests of Adults Who Lack the Capacity to Make a Decision for Themselves.* London: British Psychological Society.

Capacity assessing in practice

Pre- and post-training questionnaire

1   What area of health or social care do you work in?
    (e.g. community general, community LD, hospital, mental health)

2   What area do you cover? (e.g. north, central, citywide)

3   How many times have you undertaken a capacity assessment in the last 12 months? (please highlight/underline)

    None   *1–5*   *6–10*   *more than 11*

4   How many cases do you have at the moment that raise issues relating to capacity? (please highlight/underline)

    None   *1–5*   *6–10*   *11–15*   *More than 16*

5   How confident are you about undertaking capacity assessments?
    (please highlight/underline)

    Very confident   *Confident*   *Fairly confident*   *Not confident*

6   How often do you provide relevant support in order to enhance someone's capacity to make their decision? (please highlight/underline)

    Every assessment   *Most assessments*   *Some assessments*   *Never*

7   What forms of support have you used in order to enhance capacity?
    (please tick or highlight – you may select more than one)

Adapted communication style/materials to suit the needs of the person

Considered psychosocial factors

Repeat visit

Information in different formats

Advice/support from family

Joint assessment with a colleague/specialist

None

Used information from relevant case law e.g. "relevant information" for a specific decision domain

Used a specific template e.g. semi- structured interview/capacity assessment/MDT questionnaire

Professional interpreter

Additional time to consider the decision

Advice/support from specialist e.g. speech therapist

Other (please indicate what you do):

8 How often do you write a summary of the outcome of an assessment in the person's notes? (please highlight/underline)

Always   *Most occasions*   *Sometimes*   *Never*   *Not applicable*

9 What are the main barriers for you in relation to assessing capacity? (please highlight/tick – you may select more than one)

Access to specialists

Opportunity to discuss assessments with a manager

Access to reports or case notes prior to an assessment

Opportunity to discuss assessments with colleagues

Confidence (please expand if possible):

Other (please expand):

10 What development needs do you have in relation to assessing capacity?
(please tick/highlight – you may select more than one)

Knowledge of the legislative framework including recent case law

Knowledge of cognitive problems, how they relate to capacity and how to support improvement

Basic questions to ask in relation to cognitive problems and risk factors

Opportunity to discuss complex cases with colleagues

Knowledge of communication problems and strategies to help overcome them

Knowledge of psychosocial factors that can affect capacity

Information on specialist services and referral criteria

None

Other (Please expand):

Five month follow-up with course participants
Semi-structured interview

1. What did you learn/take away from the course?

2. Have you shared any of this learning with others? If yes, how?

3. Did you have an opportunity to discuss the training and your reflections on it within supervision?

4. Can you give any examples of how the training has impacted on your practice?

5. Did your manager/organisation support you to apply new learning in your practice? If yes, how?

6. Have you encountered any barriers when applying new learning in practice? If yes, what?

7. On reflection, were there any areas of the training that you thought could be improved or done differently?

8. Do you have any other thoughts about the training you'd like to share or discuss?

Do you need to apply to the Court to withdraw (or withhold) clinically assisted nutrition and hydration (CANH) from someone with a prolonged disorder of consciousness (PDOC)?

Although the Mental Capacity Act (MCA, 2005) does not set out specific decisions that require an application to the Court to be resolved, the MCA Code of Practice (2007) does provide some examples (see Chapter 23). One of these examples is the proposal to withdraw (or withhold) artificial nutrition and hydration from a person in a permanent vegetative state (PVS). However, case law (*An NHS Trust and others v Y and another* [2018]) has since clarified that this is not always necessary for various reasons, including:

- There is no legal requirement to do this
- It is not easy to explain why clinically assisted nutrition and hydration (CANH) should be treated differently from other life-sustaining treatment or why people with prolonged disorders of consciousness (PDOC) should be treated differently from other people
- Such decisions are made by determining what is in the person's best interests, taking into account the person's previously stated wishes and beliefs and the opinions of those close to him and those involved in his care.

Therefore, if the family and professionals agree that it is not in the person's best interests to continue, or start, CANH, then the decision can be taken without proceeding to Court. Providing CANH to someone if it is not in his best interests would be unlawful.

The ruling in the case of *NHS Trust and others v Y and another* [2018] stated that a second opinion regarding this decision from an expert external to the organisation caring for the person is vital to protect the person and his family from "errors in diagnosis and evaluation, premature decisions, and local variations in practice" (at paragraph 124). It also stated situations in which an application to the Court should be made:

- When the decision is finely balanced
- When there is a difference of medical opinion
- When there is a lack of agreement between those interested in the person's welfare.

References

Department for Constitutional Affairs. (2007). *Mental Capacity Act 2005: Code of Practice*. London: The Stationery Office. Available at: https://assets.publishing.service.gov.uk/government/uploads/system/uploads/attachment_data/file/497253/Mental-capacity-act-code-of-practice.pdf

Mental Capacity Act 2005. London: HMSO. Available at: http://www.legislation.gov.uk/ukpga/2005/9/contents

Case law

An NHS Trust and others v Y and another [2018] UKSC 46

Index

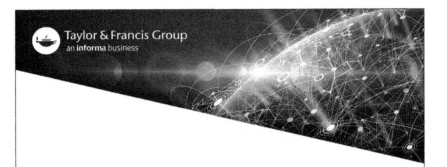